41035515

HIGH TECH and HIGH HEELS

in the GLOBAL ECONOMY

Women, Work, and Pink-Collar Identities

in the Caribbean ✓

Carla Freeman ✓

Duke University Press   Durham & London   2000   ✓

© 2000 Duke University Press
All rights reserved
Printed in the United States
of America on acid-free paper ∞
Typeset in Scala by Keystone
Typesetting, Inc.
Line drawings by Annalee Davis
Library of Congress Cataloging-
in-Publication Data appear on the
last printed page of this book.

To my parents, Elaine and Leo Freeman

Contents

List of Tables, Maps, and Figures

Tables

Maps

Figures

Acknowledgments

This project has incorporated virtually all of the dimensions of my life and has linked many communities of colleagues, friends, and family. I have many people to thank for helping to usher it into its published form. My professors at Temple University fostered its initial rendition as a dissertation. I wish to thank Thomas C. Patterson, my graduate advisor, for pushing me to think broadly theoretically and to both question and assert any argument with a secure backbone. Sherri Grasmuck introduced me to many of the questions about "third world women," movement, and transnationalism that sparked this research in its earliest phases and continue to motivate and fascinate me. Kristin Koptiuch's critical insights and bold approach to ethnography and the global scene made a lasting impression on my approach to anthropology. To the memory of Peter Rigby, I express both gratitude for his probing and often wrenching interrogation of what anthropology is and should be, and sorrow for his untimely death. At Temple, I was fortunate to find teachers and fellow students who became mentors and friends, and their continuous support has nurtured me through all of the hurdles of the past decade.

Two years of my field work in Barbados were funded jointly by grants from Fulbright, the National Science Foundation, the Wenner Gren Foundation, and the Organization of American States. I am grateful to all of these sources for their interest and generosity, enabling me to devote several years to a project that has changed my life in immeasurable ways. I wish to thank the editors of *Cultural Anthropology, Critique of Anthropology,* and *Folk,* as well as Indiana University Press and Ian Randle Publishers for their permission to publish in revised form portions of articles they previously published.

Academic work in general, and the ritual of anthropological fieldwork in particular, are often lonely adventures. Completing this project is hardly imaginable without the support and involvement of my family on both sides of the Caribbean sea. My parents' support and involvement in this undertaking has been long and deep—from making possible my first "reconnaissance" trip to Barbados in 1988 to providing a calm and nurturing "room of my own" when I returned after three years to write. Jan, Nancy, and Rick Freeman have all helped to nurture my work and keep me well fed along the way. Jean and Roger Goddard have provided a home away from home in Barbados. I wish to acknowledge, as well, the memory of my uncle, Joseph Freeman, and my great aunt, Clara Morris, whose union activism in the first half of the century inspired my own concerns about the lives of working people everywhere.

At the University of the West Indies, Cave Hill Campus, I would especially like to thank Christine Barrow, Kathleen Drayton, the Women and Development Studies group, and my Women's Studies students (1991–92), who deepened my understanding of gender in the Caribbean. Christine Barrow, Linden Lewis, Rosemarie Mallett, and Evelyn O'Callaghan provided marvelous intellectual companionship as well as friendship, for which I will always be grateful. I came to know a number of fellow "foreign academics" in Barbados, whose insights about the predicament of "outsidership," and the daunting task of writing a dissertation and book led to close friendships. My deep thanks to Michael and Monya Anyadike-Danes, Kathleen Barnes, Elizabeth Barnum, and Ken Corsbie.

Several extraordinarily generous colleagues tackled the manuscript in its entirety and at lightning speed. My heartfelt thanks to Micaela di Leonardo, Cynthia Enloe, Maria Patricia Fernandez-Kelly, Cory Kratz, Sidney Mintz, Viranjini Munasinghe, Donna Murdock, and Gul Ozyegin for their probing and rigorous reading of these chapters. Their critical insights—from style to theory—have made this a better book. Many others helped to sharpen my thinking and tighten my prose by reading versions of this material at all stages of this project: Peggy Barlett, Lynn Bolles, Don Donham, Rosario Espinal, Margot Finn, Peggy Heide, Dorothy Holland, Ivan Karp, Aisha Khan, Bruce Knauft, Cathy Lutz, Don Nonini, Mary Odem, Karen Fogg Olwig, Helen Safa, Ninna Nyberg Sorensen, Debra Spitulnik, Connie Sutton, and Kevin Yelvington. Thank you to Mark Franklin of the Ministry of Labour, Carol Mills of the Central Bank of Barbados, and Kate Browne for help in revising my tables, and to Erin Finley, indexer extraordinaire.

I have been fortunate to have supportive colleagues at both the University of North Carolina–Chapel Hill and Emory University whose intellectual engagement and friendship have eased the pressures and celebrated the milestones leading up to this book. My deepest thanks to the Department of Anthropology at UNC–Chapel Hill, and to the Department of Anthropology and the Institute of Women's Studies at Emory.

My life in Barbados was enriched by two individuals, Annalee Davis and Robert Goddard, who introduced me to numerous complexities of Barbadian culture and the centrality of family in Barbadian social life. Annalee Davis's bold artistic vision, and warm and embracing extended family, awakened me to many transcendent qualities of Barbadian culture across class and color lines. Through countless holiday celebrations and evening meals spiced with active debate, I began to grasp the depth of creolization and its continuum across class and racial boundaries. Robert Goddard's brave and tenacious spirit, and his deep love of Barbados, taught me more about sugar, politics, and the history of this small island than any graduate course could have done. He has given me courage when my confidence has waivered and has enriched the many years leading up to this book in ways I cannot put into words. He has weathered the moves and displacement with grace and good cheer, and has been my anchor and home.

Although I have agreed not to name them, I would like to thank the managers of the pseudonymous companies, Data Air and Multitext Corporation, who allowed me access to their workplaces and offered hours of their own time to answer my questions and reflect on their operations. Members of the Industrial Development Corporation and the Export Promotion Corporation were generous with both their time and information, especially in helping to set up my initial industry survey. I am profoundly grateful to the data entry operators and supervisors whose ideas and experiences, and dreams as well as difficulties, fill these pages. The stories of their lives go much beyond the short extracts I have chosen, and my appreciation far surpasses what I can express in these few words.

I wish to extend many, many thanks to Ken Wissoker, my editor at Duke University Press, for his enthusiasm and extraordinary patience, as well as his quiet persistence in seeing this project through. To Katie Courtland and Pam Morrison at Duke and to Debbie Stuart, who copyedited the manuscript with enormous care, I thank you.

Finally, I acknowledge with my deepest love and thanks, Isabel Bess, whose birth coincided with my writing the book, teaching me in the most immediate ways much of what I learned from this research—the *pleasures* of work and motherhood amid all of life's difficult demands.

Chapter 1

Introduction

Minivans with open doors are parked tightly in front of the Harbour Industrial Park's newest addition—the Barbados Data Processing Centre. By half past seven vendors are well in place with trays of "rock buns," meat pies, tuna sandwiches, and sweet drinks. Dozens of Bajan women in animated conversation rush to their morning shift, turning the heads of passersby with their colorful and fashionable dress.[1] Within moments the high-heeled workers of Data Air are ensconced in the air conditioned hum of their "open office."[2] These women, dressed proudly in suits and fashions that identify them as "office" workers and performing jobs recently unheard of on this small island in the eastern Caribbean, represent vast changes in labor patterns and technology in the global arena. As offshore data processors, they are linked with service workers in such disparate places as Ireland, the Dominican Republic, Jamaica, Mauritius, and the United States as the information age signals an intensification of transnational production and consumption—of labor, capital, goods, services, and styles.

On the data entry floor of this offshore information processing facility, a hundred women sit in clustered computer stations, entering data from over three hundred thousand ticket stubs for one airline's two thousand daily flights. One floor below, an equal number of women work as "approvers" entering data from medical claims sent for processing by one of the largest insurance companies in the United States. This expanding company alone hires close to one thousand workers, almost all of whom are women. As fingers fly, the frenetic clicking of keys filling the vast and chilly room where Walkman-clad women work eight-hour shifts at video display terminals, constantly monitored for productivity and accuracy, and typing to the latest dub, calypso, or "easy listening" music. The muffled clatter of keys creates a sort of white noise. Against the green glow of a sea of computer screens, it lends an Orwellian aura to this unusual workplace set in a nation better known as an upscale tourist destination.

This scene encapsulates new conditions of the international economy that have implications for multinational capital, national governments, and large numbers of women workers across a wide array of local cultural contexts. Categorized under the general heading of offshore manufacturing, and marking the latest version of high-tech rationalization of the labor process, this rapidly expanding new industry, known as informatics, represents a massive and transnational commodification of information. Its forms include airline tickets and consumer warranty cards, as well as academic texts, literary classics, pornographic novels, and specialized scientific articles. Indeed, apart from the shape of the "product" and the uniquely officelike setting of production, the shift of information-based work offshore looks like a newer version of the export processing model of industrialization embraced through much of Asia, Latin America, and the Caribbean. Yet, despite the industry's highly regimented and disciplined labor process, closely resembling factory assembly work, informatics workers adopt a language and set of behaviors for describing and enacting themselves as "professional" nonfactory workers in ways that effectively demarcate them from traditional industrial laborers.

This study explores the convergences and distinctions between "traditional" industrial settings across the global assembly line and these new informatics operations. I examine the ways in which Barbadian women confront highly regimented labor processes in which every minute of their day is monitored by supervisors and managers, as well as by the hidden gaze of the computers on which they work. In the course of their workday, as these women experience multiple levels of discipline, they also draw pleasure from the "professionalism" informatics demands of them.

I take as my point of departure three broadly interconnected questions. First, how is "transnationalization" experienced, and, in turn, shaped by social actors in the specific context of Barbados? Second, what does "informatics" mean along the continuum of the global assembly line? Are these new transnational workplaces best characterized as "electronic sweatshops," as their critics claim, or, instead, as an expansion of white-collar services and a source of "development" for third world nations? Finally, how are women's identities shaped by their incorporation into this newest form of transnationalized labor, and how are these identities informed by the gender ideologies and practices of their Afro-Caribbean cultural context, as well as by their multinational employers? What resemblance do they bear to their sisters at other ends of the global assembly line?

To begin answering these questions, I have positioned this anthropological study at the intersection of political economy and cultural studies. For contemporary anthropology and cultural studies, this is a reminder, very simply, that labor is integral to the transnational flows we are increasingly attempting to analyze and describe. This ethnography is grounded in the premise that work, in a multitude of settings (e.g., informal, formal, waged, unwaged), plays a central part in shaping people's place in the world and informing their identities. By situating work in the broad context of people's everyday lives—including their families and their daily routines, as well as their desires and aspirations—I am asserting a view of culture and transnationalism that puts workers center stage amid global political economic forces and cultural flows. As such, they are seen as integral not simply to the workings of globalization but as helping to shape its very form.

For labor studies and political economy, I argue that culture and workers' gendered subjectivities must be taken into account in conceptualizing labor markets, labor processes, and the macro-picture of globalization. The movement and impact of multinational corporations around the world does not take a uniform and monolithic form. The case of offshore informatics in Barbados demonstrates the need to look more closely, not only at how global workers and local cultures accommodate the demands of multinational capital, but also how, in small as well as large ways, they force foreign companies to attend to their own cultural practices and desires. This book suggests that the transnationalization of work closely ties production and technology to consumption and image making in the lives of third world women workers. In doing so, it challenges longstanding paradigms based on antinomies: "first world" consumers versus "third world" producers, and "first world" white-collar/mental workers versus "third world" blue-collar/manual workers.

The concept "pink collar" is central to my insistence that the dialectics of globalization/localization, production/consumption, and gender/class be analyzed in a way that keeps them linked.[3] "Pink collar" denotes two major processes within informatics and its workers. The first is the feminization of work such that informatics is itself gendered, not only because it recruits women workers almost exclusively, but also because the work process itself is imbued with notions of appropriate femininity, which includes a quiet, responsible demeanor along with meticulous attention to detail and a quick and accurate keyboard technique. The second process is the linking of work and clothing—production and consumption. The particular appearance of informatics workers—the boldly adorned skirt suits and polished high heels—and the physical space they inhabit as workers—the air-conditioned and officelike setting—are integral to women's experience of these jobs and ultimately to their emergent identities.

"High heels" are important to the industry and to these women workers in several ways. They are a sign with which data processors, their bosses, and the wider public distinguish informatics workers from factory workers in the economic sectors in which Barbadian women of the lower classes have traditionally been employed—agriculture, manufacturing, and domestic services. Dress and appearance not only set informatics workers apart symbolically from other women in the working classes but also blur the boundaries between informatics workers and other sorts of clerical workers who are assumed to be middle class.

The focus on dress and feminine image-making is central in representing dimensions of women's experience in informatics that are simultaneously burdensome and pleasurable, and that tie their engagement in the "formal" informatics sector directly to a range of practices in the "informal" sector of the economy as well. To meet the complex desires and demands of "professional fashion" that are prescribed by company dress codes and, more subtly by peer pressure, women enter into other production/consumption "shifts" beyond their formal workdays. Before and after their work as data processors and on weekends and holidays, they spend their time designing, producing, and purchasing the clothes and accessories that create the "professional feminine" look they and their employers ascribe to informatics. As such, their pink-collar identities are tied not only to their informatics jobs but also to their shopping trips overseas, their clothing design courses, and the variety of other means by which they supplement their formal wages in the informal market. Thus, these multiple dimensions of the "pink collar" call for an analysis that explicitly links practices and identities associated with production/consumption and gender/class across local and transnational terrains.

Pink-Collar Workers in the Caribbean

Globally, the new pink-collar informatics worker represents both a reconfiguration and a cheapening of white-collar service work. What was once considered skilled, "mental" information-based computer work can now be performed "offshore" without compromising the "product" or the speed with which it is produced. Simultaneously, the informatics worker offshore also represents a growing third world market for a wider and wider range of commodity goods, including fashions, housewares, electronics, music, and videos, and the expansion of transnational networks of trade. Locally, in Barbados, the pink-collar informatics operator represents a new category of feminine worker, symbolically empowered by her professional appearance and the computer technology with which she works. Her air-conditioned office appears to be a far cry from the cane fields and kitchens in which her mother and grandmothers toiled, while the work she does represents a significant new emphasis of economic diversification by this sugar- and tourism-based island economy.

These processes have profound implications for our understanding of the gendering of class identity and consciousness. They help to explain, for example, why these particular global workers remain nonunionized in a nation known for its strong tradition of trade unionism. As such, they invite us to rethink the relationships between discipline, agency, and pleasure. By taking seriously the dimensions of these jobs that give women pleasure even in the face of numerous stresses, speed-ups, and monotony, we see that women are agents in ways that simultaneously inscribe patriarchal notions of femininity and create a space of invention and autonomy. Afro-Caribbean culture and history are integral to our understanding of how these processes work.

Two themes within Caribbean culture make the position of these pink-collar workers unique. The first relates to the transnational underpinnings of Caribbean political economy since the 1500s, challenging the premise that "modernity" is a new form of globalization that is only now taking hold in the developing world. The second involves the particular place of women in Afro-Caribbean societies and the complex set of gender roles and ideologies that have not only allowed but often insisted that women be both mothers and workers. This prescription stands in stark contrast to the profile of the third world woman worker as typically articulated by transnational industries in search of "ideal" labor.

The Caribbean is an ideal setting for today's fascination with exploring the juxtapositions of "traditional" and "modern" culture encoded in dichotomies of "local" versus "global" processes, practices, and artifacts. Formed out of colonial conquests and global migrations of the enslaved, the coerced, and the free, the Caribbean emerged by the seventeenth century as a prime locus for resource extraction, forced labor, and accumulation of wealth by competing European empires. Its "natives" were quickly decimated by warfare and disease, and its inhabitants (including African slaves, European colonists, and indentured labor, first from the ranks of the poor, imprisoned, or politically dissident from the British Isles, and later from India, sent to replace the emancipated slaves) came to constitute a new, creolized[4] culture that reflected these diverse origins and the brutal manifestations of tropical plantation life. A place that anthropologists not long ago dismissed for its lack of purity and authenticity now presents a particularly intriguing site of study for precisely these reasons.[5] Indeed, the Caribbean has been described as quintessentially "modern" by many of its preeminent scholars. For example, Eric Williams, Trinidad's father of independence, and one of the region's foremost historians, and Sidney Mintz, whose anthropology of the region spans nearly half a century and criss-crosses the region's colonial/linguistic boundaries, both describe Caribbean sugar plantations as "factories in the fields" representing the origins of industrialization itself. Furthermore, according to Mintz:

> The Caribbean region had begun to figure in European thinking nearly two centuries before North America was even a vague image in the minds of most knowledgeable Europeans. Perhaps we can only begin to assess the changing significance of the Caribbean region in world affairs by remembering that, before the Caribbean had begun to do Europe's bidding, there had not been any "world" affairs. Otherwise said—and with no apologies for this formulation—"the world" (in quotation marks) first became a modern concept in the Caribbean. (1993:4)

If transnational movements of people, goods, capital, and culture define the very essence of the Caribbean's creation and the sugar plantation and factory stood as incipient forms of industrialization before Europe experienced the modern industrial age, clearly the dichotomies of tradition/modernity and local/global cannot be employed here as simple oppositions. This study of informatics in Barbados challenges the premise that late twentieth-century transnationalization has suddenly, and for the first time, brought modernity to the underdeveloped world and explores the dialectics of local and global culture and economy to reveal the specific implications for the Caribbean of today's conditions of late modernity. West Indians across class and racial divides have been moving between and across the region and the metropole for centuries, and they continue to do so according to old and new patterns. The people of the Caribbean have, likewise, produced for the metropole for centuries—from sugar and bananas to

Map 1. Barbados and its parishes

computer chips and animated cartoons. What is less well explored are the continuities and contemporary novelties in the realm of consumption—the extent to
which Caribbean peoples have not just produced for foreign markets but also
have enjoyed foreign goods and culture themselves.

The importance of the Caribbean island of Barbados in the channels of transnational trade belies its small size (14 miles wide and 21 miles long) and contemporary reputation as little more than an upscale tourist destination. The most
easterly of the Caribbean islands, lying only 200 miles northeast of Trinidad and
Tobago and 270 miles northeast of Venezuela, Barbados is a small but densely

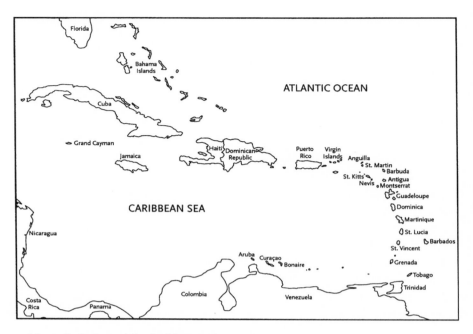

Map 2. Barbados and the Caribbean region

populated country of 260,000 inhabitants. In 1966 the island gained its independence from the British, who had colonized it and operated it as a mono-crop sugar economy for over three hundred years. One of the most politically stable countries in the region, characterized by a quiet conservatism and governed by a parliamentary democracy this small island has long been known as "little England." Some visitors even claim that its landscape more resembles that of the English countryside than that of its West Indian neighbors.

Barbados, one of the cricket-playing former colonies, takes pride in things English, as reflected in numerous place names, its tea-drinking tradition, and the dominance of the Anglican church, though the influence of the United States has begun to usurp the British cultural stronghold. Gordon Lewis's description of Barbados (1968:226–56) as "cautious and complacent," "conservative," "slow moving," "puritan" in spirit, "culturally backward," and unshakably stratified by class and color takes the notion of Bajan conservatism to an unflattering extreme but is a typical rendering of this small island and one not missed by transnational corporations looking for an amiable production site.

The perception of Barbados's conservatism and "properness" that has made this conservative, stable country an attractive site for foreign investment has also made it the butt of jokes and the source of stereotypes by its Caribbean neighbors. Barbados was targeted early as a pilot location for offshore data entry by companies investigating cost-cutting and profit-making ventures in the arena of information services, including airlines, public utilities, insurance companies, and credit card companies that sought many of the same labor conditions and tax concessions as their manufacturing predecessors. The prerequisites of the North American companies scouting offshore sites for informatics are a well-developed infrastructure that includes good roads, an airport, electricity, reasonable telephone rates, and suitably configured telecommunications technologies; as well as political stability, customized factory spaces with low rents, "quiet" or cooperative labor unions, and a cheap and available labor force. For some, sharing the English language and the same time zone as the eastern United States and being available by short daily flights to and from major North American cities provided other key attractions in Barbados's favor. Topping off all of these assets is the long tradition of Barbados as a safe and genteel, upscale tourist destination for British and North American visitors.

While undoubtedly sharing many commonalities, not the least of which include the well-tried experimentation with export-led development strategies, Caribbean nations also reveal extraordinary differences in political and economic structures, pre- and postcolonial histories, language, geography, ethnicities, culture, and ideologies. Most studies of multinational penetration and the implications of offshore industries in the Caribbean region have focused on the Spanish-speaking countries of Mexico, Puerto Rico, and to a lesser extent, the Dominican Republic. At the time I began this research, two brief but notable accounts (Bolles 1983 on Jamaica; Kelly 1987 on St. Lucia) led me to suspect that differences in gender ideologies and the historical roles of women in the English-speaking Caribbean would make the circumstances of foreign industries and their employment of female labor forces there differ in interesting ways.

Early accounts of the global assembly line consider "reserve armies" of female labor unproblematic and essential to an expanding capitalist world economy, and they note similarities in the exploitative modes of incorporation experienced by third world women across the developing world (Fröbel, Heinrichs, and Kreye 1980). Since then, however, it has become more clear that understanding cultural differences along the global assembly line is central to understanding the conditions and responses of women in these new enclaves. Despite the uniform portraits of female factory workers that all foreign industrialists draw when asked to explain their preference for female labor, circumstances of incorporation are strikingly different in distinct cultural contexts. This study of Barbadian women in the new arena of offshore data entry illustrates some of these differences and their implications for understanding globalization.

Women's inherent physical and temperamental qualities that are said to make them ideally suited to sedentary, meticulous, and repetitive work have long been the rationales for the employment of cheap female labor. This explanation was frequently uttered by corporate managers during my research. In general, hard physical labor and sophisticated intellectual work are assumed to be "masculine," and "simple" "fine-fingered" work to be "feminine." These ideal profiles are contradicted and reformulated, however, within the information processing zone in distinct and intriguing ways that relate specifically to the Barbadian cultural milieu.

Women in the Caribbean have always worked outside their homes—in the cane fields, in factories, in kitchens, as well as in other settings in the service and professional sectors—while maintaining their domestic and familial roles. This fact challenges a widely held presumption that third world women make ideal workers for transnational corporations because they are new to the wage labor force and therefore their earnings merely supplement a primary breadwinner's wage. Furthermore, women's long history as workers in the Caribbean has been coupled with gender ideologies that construct femininity in contradictory ways. One of the competing paradigms of Afro–West Indian femininity—that of the powerful black matriarch—equates femininity with strength, resilience, and fortitude. This definition stands in opposition to the natural docility and malleability widely and erroneously attributed to third world women by global industries. Also at odds with the paradigm of the powerful black matriarch is the assumption that Afro-West Indian femininity within the domestic sphere embodies (at least in part) Christian morality as expressed through the conventions of respectability—formal marriage, monogamy, and a "modest" demeanor.

Elements of these two feminine ideals—the physically strong and the morally proper woman—find their roots in colonial discourse. Their coexistence and strategic deployment have been operative to different ends for centuries in the Caribbean. For instance, the paradigm of "woman as strong matriarch" legitimated back-breaking female slave labor on the plantations and explained their self-sufficiency as both mothers and workers in the absence of any organized help with child care. The feminine ideal of domesticity, morality, and respectability provides a counter-rhetoric for explaining women's secondary wage and their economic dependence on men. These competing gender ideologies coexist, not only in the discourse of the state and multinational corporation, but also among the women workers themselves. *High Tech and High Heels* demonstrates that women in the Caribbean enact their lives and configure their identities in ways that draw upon and reinvent these competing ideals, producing both liberating and constraining effects for the new pink-collar workers.

Doing Fieldwork in the "Open Office"

Anthropological studies, like all forms of inquiry, emerge out of specific cultural and historical contexts, invariably blending intellectual and political interests of the time with personal concerns. This work is no exception. Along with thousands of women of varied backgrounds and work agendas, I worked as a temporary word processor through several of my graduate school years. In the offices of banks and private companies, I encountered opera singers, young mothers, recent college graduates, and a host of other women relying on temporary computer-based clerical work as a solution to various financial needs. The settings for these jobs ranged from one noisy open production area where dozens of women typed furiously in concert to plush and quiet cubicles connected to the offices of legal partners or corporate executives where I typed alone.

The relationship of a temporary typist, word processor, or data entry operator to the work she performs and the "boss" or "client" for whom she works is typically fleeting, fragmented, and anonymous. "Temps" occupy the bottom rung of the clerical ladder, and even secretaries adopted the practice of referring to me as "the girl" when signaling my transient and low status in "their" workplace. Whether this form of work is fundamentally alienating or "flexible," as it is frequently hailed, depends greatly on the broader strategy it represents in a given woman's life. For me, as a graduate student, the relatively high hourly wage and ability to accept or turn down a job at will made this ideal part-time work. For a single mother, being a temp may mean weighing flexibility against a more restrictive, lower-wage job with such benefits as health insurance.

My understanding of this sector of work was radically reframed in November 1988 aboard a flight between Philadelphia and Phoenix. Bound for the meetings of the American Anthropological Association, I was flipping through the in-flight airline magazine when my gaze settled on an advertisement that read, "Do your data entry in the Caribbean. We can guarantee high quality data processing at a fraction of your present back-office costs." At the same moment that information-based jobs, including word processing, were being proclaimed by politicians as the panacea to the rapid "de-industrialization" of the U.S. economy, these new service industries had already begun to imitate the flight of their manufacturing predecessors. This advertisement and the questions it spawned ultimately led to the several years of fieldwork on which this study is based.

The research I conducted in Barbados included three interconnected methodologies: open-ended interviews, a semistructured interview survey, and participant observation. These three methodologies represent, to some degree, distinct phases in my research. I began in 1989 by interviewing representatives from Barbadian development agencies, managers from the local and foreign-owned information industries, labor unionists, and educational leaders in the country. My objective in this first phase was to investigate the general shape of the industry; no existing research had described the kinds of companies participating in these ventures, the investments involved, the strategies they employed for recruiting and training labor, and the working conditions they presented. These initial interviews brought to light the agendas and practices of the companies and national planners and helped to inform my questions and observations within the longer period of participant observation and interviews with the women workers. I ultimately selected two of the largest foreign-owned operations for the primary foci of my study. Together, they depict some of the range of work within informatics—airline tickets and insurance claims at Data Air, journal and book publication at Multitext—and similarities in labor process and management techniques between Barbados's most significant foreign powers— England and the United States. The study focuses more extensively on the larger, American-owned enterprise, Data Air, because of its position as a "showcase" of the data entry business. Much of the interviewing and the final survey were conducted at its facility. Multitext, in contrast, allowed no on-site interviewing of the data processors. I was therefore forced to conduct interviews and talk with Multitext operators in the lunchroom and other off-site locations. As a result, several of the women I came to know best were Multitext employees. By conducting our conversations outside the physical context of work during the three years I spent in Barbados, we readily moved to other topics such as family and relationships, travel and entertainment, and I came to spend many a Saturday shopping trip and Sunday lunch with them.

In anthropological research, gaining access to one's community of "subjects" often involves a complex series of hurdles and mishaps. Because of the competitiveness of this new industry and its highly monitored work setting, I anticipated some wariness among company managers when I requested permission to conduct the study. In fact, I was astonished to find the management of both Data Air and Multitext entirely agreeable to my research, framed as a study of women's work in this new industry requiring one full year of observation, interviewing, and informal interaction with the workers. Both companies offered me open access to their operations, and Data Air provided release time for management and workers alike so that I could interview them on the company premises. I assured both companies that their client base, staff, and workers would remain anonymous, and that my interactions would not disrupt workers' concentration on the production floor. They seemed to have no fear that I might expose negative aspects of their enterprises. Indeed, they saw my work as potentially beneficial to them. Because I would listen to the complaints and aspirations of the women workers, I was providing, as one manager put it, "an opportunity to enable the company to improve working conditions and communication." Another intimated on several occasions that if I was ever interested in employment as a "consultant" that my services would be welcomed in the industry. But more important, these firms are so clearly convinced of the benefits they provide to the Barbadian economy and to the individual workers and their families that they believed any exposure they received through my research would constitute free public relations.

In the first month of research, I followed the expected formal protocol by writing letters of introduction to the managers of all the data entry operations, educational institutions, and government offices involved in this new industry. A few companies quickly granted me interviews and offered me tours of their facilities, and I began to sketch out the shape of the industry and to note variations among foreign and local, large and small companies. At Multitext, after interviewing the manager, I quickly learned about the production process and became acquainted with some of the operators and staff. I began to catch on to more of the lunchtime jokes and banter that earlier had baffled me with the unfamiliar Bajan dialect and references.

Having soared fairly effortlessly into the fieldwork and well into daily visits at both Data Air and Multitext, I was shocked one week to find my research brought to a sudden halt with little explanation. At Data Air, I was told that the American multinational parent company required a fuller explanation of my research, and that until permission was granted from the head office I could not proceed with the study. I quickly drafted a letter and waited anxiously for a reply. The following morning I arrived early at Multitext, rattled by the abrupt break in contact at Data Air but pleased with my progress at Multitext and intent on making the most of my time there while I waited for a response from Data Air's Texas management. As I began my usual rounds on the data entry floor and in the lunchroom, however, I learned from the manager at Multitext that an owner from the United States had arrived in Barbados and "did not like the idea of an anthropologist being on the premises." As she put it, he was "disturbed about the idea of anyone seeing the problems going on and the work that was being performed." Furthermore, he "couldn't see what data entry had to do with anthropology anyway." Permission for ongoing fieldwork on the company premises had already been granted by the British multinational owners, and this was the first I had heard of an American partner. This obstacle to what had seemed an ideal fieldwork arrangement left me in a sudden quandary. All of my requests to speak with the man himself were denied, and I began to contemplate giving up on Multitext altogether. Finally, in desperation, I wrote a letter explaining myself and the peculiar nature of sustained ethnographic research and was promptly granted a meeting the next morning before the owner's departure for New York. In the end, my access was restored, and even more than that, this American publishing veteran revealed himself as a "closet anthropologist" himself, "a great fan of Margaret Mead" with enormous interest in all that I was discovering about women's experience and gender roles in Barbados. On numerous subsequent occasions, he expressed interest in hiring me to analyze the problems on the production floor of Multitext, and in knowing more about the family circumstances and lives outside of work of the Barbadian women he employed.

The basis for the brief but abrupt banning of my research, it turned out, was the fear that I was a corporate spy, sent by a new data entry operation and intent on "stealing their trained workforce from under their feet." This sort of worker poaching had apparently happened more than once before when a new company began recruiting typists. One week later the general manager of Data Air said that permission to conduct my research had been approved by the head office, provided that it did not "interfere too much with the production process itself." Much relieved, I began interviewing workers the next day and maintained my involvement in both companies for the next two years.

Participant observation in the data entry facilities (on the production floor, in the lunchroom, in the bathrooms, and at the bus stop and fast-food areas outside the facilities), and open-ended interviews with forty workers formed the second major phase of research. While some excellent labor studies have been done by anthropologists working "under cover" on factory production lines (e.g., Fernandez-Kelly 1983; Westwood 1985), my employment in informatics was precluded by several factors. My being white and American made going "under cover" impossible, and company production demands and limited space made my working on an unpaid temporary basis untenable all around. I chose, therefore, to observe and simply be around the production floors of both Data Air and Multitext often, on all shifts, and over a long period, and to rely on breaks and meetings outside the workplace for other interactions with the women workers.

Roughly a year into the fieldwork, in 1990, I made a short research visit to Santo Domingo, where Data Air had recently set up a sister operation.[6] I had learned that there, in dramatic contrast to the Barbadian operation and offshore multinational enterprises in general, about 40 percent of the operators were young men. The emergence of this operation gave me a unique opportunity to probe the specific permutations cast by local culture in the establishment of a new multinational enterprise, and to cross boundaries within the Caribbean region that are rarely traversed in the academic arena (Trouillot 1992). Two operations sharing the same parent company and performing essentially the same sorts of work in similar physical work settings but with one operation in the Spanish-speaking Caribbean and the other in the English-speaking West Indies presented an intriguing basis for comparing the processes of recruiting, training, and retaining a work force. On this basis I make comparative observations throughout the text, but because my visits to the Dominican Republic were brief, and my research there confined to semistructured interviews with a translator, these comparisons are preliminary, and more hint at distinctions than explore them fully. This area of the research remains to be developed further.

I conducted most of my interviews with the informatics workers on the work premises of Data Air with the cooperation of managers and supervisors. The company gave workers release time for the interviews and therefore did not penalize them for being off the system. The shift manager asked operators whether they would like to participate in the interview and then scheduled them to meet with me. Sampling, therefore, was not conducted in a formally random fashion, although from the interviews themselves, it was clear that the manager selected individuals representing a wide range of work experience, "productivity levels," and general attitudes about their jobs. Many workers expressed reluctance to end the interview, clearly enjoying the break from the monotony of their work and the opportunity to talk about themselves and their work and family lives. Often these exchanges led to social invitations and long-lasting involvements.

Despite the convenience and ease of interviewing on the work premises, and the relief many operators expressed about having a break from production to talk about themselves and their jobs, the negative implications of the location of the interviews cannot be ignored. As a white American woman, I was easily confused for a foreign management representative among those meeting me for the first time. Indeed, during the course of my fieldwork, I witnessed on several occasions other white Americans visiting the premises or conducting training. The Industrial Development Corporation, for example, frequently gained permission from Data Air to offer tours to prospective foreign investors investigating the industry. I was very careful, therefore, to explain my agenda fully, making explicit that their identities would be kept in strict confidence, and that our discussions had nothing whatever to do with company management. Much to my dismay, one young keyer who was on probation for poor productivity quit her job and walked out when she was asked if she would participate in an interview with me. I learned later from another operator that having received several warning letters about her work performance, she was convinced that my interview was actually a meeting to dismiss her, and said she would "rather quit than be fired."

My long-term and sustained involvement within the companies made it possible for me to engage in other kinds of interactions against which these interviews could be read. Only through the familiarity I gained by continued observation and daily interaction, month after month on the production floor, was I able to decipher the subtle expressions of corporate discipline and control, and of accommodation, compliance, and resistance, that became central to my investigation. Participant observation both inside and out of the data entry operations enabled me to link women's experience of their data entry jobs to the context of their families and everyday lives.

Having been cautioned by several academics about the "reserved" nature of Barbadian women, I was amazed at the openness expressed in these initial interviews. Some of our discussions focused almost exclusively on experiences at work, and others focused at length on families, relationships, politics, television shows and videos, comparisons between Barbados and the United States, and the women's aspirations for the future. I conducted these interviews as much as possible as conversations in which I talked about myself and my own life and family rather than trying merely to elicit information.

At Multitext, my on-site interviewing was restricted to management staff because workers were not granted release time from the production floor, and my time there was spent observing on the production floor and talking with operators in the lunchroom or the bathroom during their breaks. These sites and the fast-food restaurant across the street, Chefette, as well as the bus stand, became key locations for my research. I subsequently interviewed a smaller number of women more informally, in their homes. Ultimately, six women became the focus of more intense, long-term interaction and repeated interviews. Again, these women were not selected formally but instead emerged from the participant observation as closer relationships with them evolved. After many Sunday lunches, picnics, church services, birthday celebrations, and family outings, I got to know these few women better, seeing them not only as workers but also as members of families, as partners in complex relationships, as mothers, as daughters, as co-workers, and as friends. We spent time together in my rented flat, and in their wood and "wall house" homes, cooking and eating meals together, sometimes watching videos as we talked. I persuaded them, on rare occasions, to picnic at the beach,[7] and they took me to their churches and fetes and on special outings—to the circus, to the calypso contests, and to national sites enjoyed by tourists and locals alike. Sometimes we went shopping, and sometimes we bought ice cream after work. Several women and their partners and children noted to me, often laughing at the time, that I was the first "white lady" they had had to their home, and I was certainly never an inconspicuous guest. Through their direct and jocular references to our differences (race as well as class, education, and life stage), they eased the tensions that these differences typically embody. I was often chided for being single and not having a child and told I am too "bony" to be attractive to a man and odd for living alone in a flat without a man or family. My whiteness was remarked upon as often as (indeed, it was equated with) my being American, and questions and comments about "how you do things up there" were acknowledgments of the differences my nationality and race implied.

As we came to know each other better and the parameters of my role as anthropologist became increasingly blurred, the complexities of these women's lives became more clear to me, and perhaps to some extent I became more clear to them. The stories and perceptions I collected from these women along with the open-ended interviews among Data Air workers provided me with rich and varied narratives that inform my discussion and analysis. Over the three years I spent in Barbados, my relationships with these women changed, and just as I followed their experiences in and out of jobs, sticking firmly to one, or leaving the data entry business altogether and starting up a small shop, or having a baby and staying home for a while, they came to know me in a number of different capacities as well, from that of interviewer/fieldworker associated with their work lives, unusual guest at their dinner tables, and gradually as more of a friend, with whom shopping trips, weekend afternoons at home cooking and chatting, and outings to special events were ordinary occurrences.[8]

In my third year, when I was primarily teaching women's studies at the University of the West Indies, my fieldwork took on a more informal and sporadic form. My new identity linked me to an esteemed national institution and seemed to evoke a new status for me among some of these women. It removed me somewhat, in that I had less time with them, but it also made me less "foreign" in the sense that I was part of a place they all had some connection to, whether through friends and family or more remotely through the press and other means.

I concluded the research by surveying another forty-four women from Data Air, using the earlier open-ended interviews and fieldwork to structure specific questions about work and family, informal economic activities, and life experiences. This proved to be an important concluding phase of the research because significant economic changes had taken place in Barbados in the three years since I began the study. A period of economic recession and escalating rates of unemployment and inflation were clearly reflected in these final interviews and gave a sharper meaning to the role of the informatics industry and these data processing jobs in women's lives, self-images, and dreams.

Because of the island's small size, there were numerous occasions, after the more formal period of my fieldwork had concluded, when I would bump into women I knew from Multitext or Data Air in the supermarket, at musical events, or on the street in Bridgetown. I often heard remarks like, "Hey, I saw you were at such and such a place Friday last week" or "What were you doing up by so and so." The waves and beeps I received in my rust-eaten car were additional reminders that little stays private or anonymous in Barbados and made me even more inclined to bridge the public and private parts of my own life. In doing so, it became increasingly clear to me that many aspects of my fieldwork represented a new kind of anthropology than that which makes up the major corpus of Caribbean ethnography. The most obvious difference was that I was not living in a wooden chattel house in a rural village, as most anthropologists studying Barbados have done, but instead in a rented apartment just off the busy West Coast Highway 1. My selection of this apartment reflected two realities—my need to get easily to the informatics operations on both morning and evening shifts, and the simple reality that the women workers who were the subjects of the research represented, not a geographically bounded "community" in the traditional sense of a given physical locality, but rather a constituency formed by individuals who commuted to work from every corner of this small and densely populated island.

Living where I did put me along a busy bus route to Bridgetown and therefore, an easy fifteen-minute ride to the Harbour Industrial Park where the data entry operations are located. By living amid suburbanized local residents and tourist hotels, I missed what has constituted the very essence of much ethnographic work—the village-based rhythm of daily life, in which anthropologists have long explored the webs of social relationships as well as weekly and seasonal rituals that bind people within a given community in complex ways. On the other hand, by being mobile and disembedded from any single locale, I was engaging in a form of ethnography that mirrors the ways in which contemporary Barbadians live—beyond village boundaries, and across suburban subdivisions. The days are long gone when one could find people living in the more remote parishes of St. Lucy or St. Joseph (parishes evocatively referred to as "behind God's back") who had never been to Bridgetown. Today, the hustle and bustle of Barbados's capital city is marked by tour buses and taxi cabs shuttling cruise ship passengers on sightseeing trips and to local restaurants and beaches, and by an escalating number of imported cars and recreational vehicles. Local shoppers ride new Mercedes buses and Japanese "maxi-taxis" between town and home and are as likely to carry home breadfruit and local carrots as they are imported apples and mangoes. Broad Street, the major commerce street in town, is dotted with duty free shopping venues with elaborate window displays of perfume and jewelry, while the vendors on Swan Street continue to sell their fabric and notions, stationery and clothes, as they have done for the past half century. The marketplace is still a lively bartering spot for fresh produce sold by weathered-faced old women in colorful aprons and head ties, but it now also houses Rastafarian artisans peddling their red, green, and gold bracelets, hats, and sandals to tourists passing by. For Barbadians of all classes, kin networks remain primary in people's lives, but they are no longer reflected in physical spaces of habitation in the ways they once were. Extended families continue to be important support systems, though grannies and aunties living in other neighborhoods or parishes now must be reached by buses and cars.

These changes and the increased mobility they reflect introduce a new wrinkle to our critique of the traditional ethnographic frame in which the anthropologist's power and unique gaze are embodied in large part through her travel to (and within) far-off places and her ability to depict her subjects in their fixed place in space if not in time. What became powerfully clear to me was that in today's ethnography of the Caribbean, and in particular in contemporary Barbados, movement both within the country—between Bridgetown and everywhere else— and between Barbados and numerous other nations—predominantly, though not exclusively, the old and new colonial metropolitan centers of London, Toronto, New York, and Miami—prevails over a once more village-centered life. Travel and all that it implies about placing oneself in the world and exposure to difference and to experiences once imagined only for the privileged ceases to be associated solely with the authorial voice of the anthropologist. The extent to which the subjects of my research themselves draw on travel and transnationalism as markers of their own identities and experiences (through the work they perform for foreign companies, through their travels to other countries as facilitated by these foreign employers, and through their even more widespread consumption of imported goods and culture) poses new challenges to the performance of ethnography and invites us to venture into a new anthropology.

Chapter 2

Pink-Collar Bajans:

Working Class through

Gender and Culture on

the Global Assembly Line

One hot afternoon at the crowded Lower Green bus stand in Bridgetown, Barbados, schoolchildren in neat uniforms and shoppers laden with heavy parcels hiding from the baking sun found their own hushed conversations punctuated by sudden shouting and defensive retorts. The morning shift at Global Informatics Ltd. had been busy, and most of the data processors had worked overtime the day before, catching up on a heavy batch of credit card receipts from a Canadian client company. Five of the sixty young women workers in the shift emerged from the glass doors of Barbados's newest informatics company, animated as they compared their daily work rates and resultant pay. All were data processors and all but one had achieved the "incentive" bonus earned by fulfilling a ten-thousand-keystroke-per-hour minimum. The bonuses, together with overtime pay, had boosted their wages for the week by roughly 25 percent. At the shift's end, comparing their newly posted production rates, the women had changed from slippers to patent leather or well-polished high heels and now they ambled slowly toward the bus stand. The commotion that erupted there centered on Christine, one of the data processors who was nicely turned out in a bold floral skirt suit and an elaborately braided hair style. Suddenly Paul, her former boyfriend, who had been waiting for her under a shady breadfruit tree, began shouting and motioning wildly for everyone around to look closely. "You see *she*? You *see* she?" he exclaimed. "Don' mind she dress so. When Friday come, she only carryin' home ninety-eight dollar." What his outburst conveyed was, "In case you people might mistake her for a middle-class woman with a good office job, let me tell you, she is really just a village girl with a factory wage." Onlookers shifted their feet. Some showed signs of disdain for the public airing of a domestic dispute; a group of schoolgirls laughed. The taunts so disturbed another group of data processors at the bus stand that some beckoned a manager to come outside and "stop the palava."

The threat posed by mocking the image of prosperity and professionalism of the data processors is conveyed in a Barbadian adage that warns, "Gold teet don' suit hog mout" and implies that even extravagant adornments can't hide one's true station in life. The adage and the story together reveal a deep tradition of propriety and expectations of conformity between class status and appearance. For "Little England," the once-prized sugar isle of the British empire, conformity and respectability lie at the heart of cultural tradition, and "knowing one's place" is an admonition well known to Bajans of all generations. By exposing the reality of Christine's meager wage in contrast to her impressive appearance, the disgruntled former boyfriend threatened to undermine a powerful set of images conscientiously created and enforced by women workers and the informatics industry that employs them. While dress may seem peripheral or "superstructural" to a study of women workers on the global assembly line, here amid the high-tech glow of computer terminals within this new niche of the "office-factory," dress and appearance become vital embodiments of the informatics sector and of new feminine identities for working women as members of the new pink-collar service class.[1]

This brief story elucidates a convergence between realms of tradition and modernity, gender and class—where transnational capital and production, the Barbadian state, and young Afro-Caribbean women together fashion a new "classification" of woman worker who, as gendered producer and consumer is fully enmeshed in global and local, economic and cultural processes. This new classification of pink-collar worker is made possible by the ambiguous place of informatics within the bounded categories of manufacturing and service sectors of the economy, and between blue-collar as opposed to white-collar labor. The story suggests how problematic these polarities are. Informatics is predicated on some of our most potent icons of modernity—sophisticated computer technologies, new satellite communications, and jet transportation—and the power of these images and symbols contributes significantly to the appeal of these jobs to recent secondary school graduates. Indeed, modernity and traditional notions of Barbadianness are bound up together in this new enclave, as they have been in the very formation of the Caribbean as a region. Eric Williams ([1944] 1994) asserted that the scale and global importance of the region's sugar industry placed it firmly in the forefront of the modern industrial world, and he provocatively argued that the Caribbean was modern even before Europe itself (see also Mintz [1974] 1989; Sutton 1987; Trouillot 1992). This view challenges us to think of modernity, not as a singular benchmark set by Britain or by Europe as a whole, but in a plural form (modernities), and to see the Caribbean, not as a "backward" outpost of the "modern" West, but as an early expression of the economic and cultural complexities of modernity.

Starting from the premise that the Caribbean is quintessentially modern, transnational, and creolized, this book explores the ways in which tradition and modernity and local and global culture and economies inflect the experiential and symbolic dimensions of gender and class in Barbados in the new industry of informatics. This chapter sets the scene by describing the ways in which recent changes in the transnational economy and its restructuring of clerical work affect Afro-Barbadian women and gendered identities associated with particular kinds of work in the Caribbean. I begin by exploring the emergence of the "global assembly line" and its recent incorporation of clerical work as a feminized, proletarianized "pink-collar" sector. In the Anglophone Afro-Caribbean, where women's work has long been integral to the island's economy and to its emphasis on "respectability," what emerges from this global/local conjuncture is that women's identities, as feminine members of the working class, become refashioned through a set of gendered practices encoded in the concept of "professionalism" enacted on the production floor, as well as in modes of consumption associated with the new informatics industry. This observation demands that we look simultaneously at their engagement in production (both formal wage-earning jobs and informal "after hours" income-generating labor) and the importance of new practices of consumption in ways that are seldom brought together in analyses of globalization. In the light of the important recent emphasis on the triangulation of race, class, and gender, especially for Caribbean studies, I note at the outset that race is a less central workplace issue at the local industry level of informatics given the relatively homogeneous Afro-Caribbean racial identities of both management and labor force of the companies studied. It operates more dramatically, however, at the macro level of the international division of labor. The movement of multinational industry has tended to go from "whiter" industrialized nations to "darker" third world countries, and as such we witness a racialized international division of labor.[2] In some territories of the Caribbean, most notably Trinidad, Guyana and Suriname, race and ethnicity are the central divisions of social and political life, and in the region at large, color and class stratification are tightly interconnected. In Barbados, while part of this continuum, the racial and ethnic matrix is somewhat distinct. There remains a small local nonblack population (roughly 5 percent), including (but not limited to) a white corporate elite that owns or controls a significant portion of the island's major industrial sectors (Beckles 1989a), though the public sector is entirely under the control of Afro-Barbadians.[3] Within informatics, race enters the scene less in explicit structural hierarchy than in the form of verbal play and rhetorical styles of reference,[4] and ownership of local informatics companies is both "black" and "white."[5] Black Barbadians own two of the three local firms, and a North American company and a local, historically white company jointly own the third.[6] Management and supervisory positions are held almost entirely by black Barbadians, trained by overseas representatives, with no apparent "color" hierarchy in which phenotypically lighter managers appear higher in the organizational structure than darker ones. Similarly, hiring and promotion practices at all levels show none of the pattern of racial hierarchy that is often described in other parts of the region. I therefore focus on the relationships between gender and class with regard to Barbadian history and culture and the island's embeddedness in the global cultural economy. In my emphasis on the relationships between production and consumption, I take up recent theoretical debates about social class and status by probing the ways in which the gendered emergence of off-shore services as a new arena of work challenges previous conceptualizations of class identity and expectations of class consciousness. I begin with the global picture and move to the local.

Globalization and New International Divisions of Labor

"Globalization" and "transnationalism" can be seen as clichés of the 1990s, conveying the idea that the world is getting smaller through expanding telecommunication networks, ease and affordability of air travel, and the rapid movement across national borders of capital, migrants, travelers, media, consumer goods, and even drugs and disease.[7] Among advertisers and politicians, academics and journalists, we find some extolling the "democratization" of expanding markets of goods and information, others bemoaning the loss of "local" culture, distinctiveness and tradition, and still others decrying the so-called demise of the nation-state.[8] The question at stake, as Robert Foster (1991) frames it, is whether homogenization or heterogenization will win out.

Has this emergent order taken a single shape—recognizably American, relentlessly commercial—a shape reflective of transnational corporate control over the flow of media goods and services; and if it hasn't, will it? Or does this order contain (if not generate) possibilities for "creolization" and "indigenization," new syntheses of cultural forms that, however derivative or similar, always remain disjunct and different? In other words, are globalization and localization of cultural production two moments of the same total process, a process conditioned by increasing "flexibility" in the structure of capitalist accumulation? (236)

What most studies of globalization and transnationalism share, regardless of theoretical or disciplinary approach, is the sense that something radically new and dramatic is taking place in this era of late-twentieth-century capitalism and a new millennium. Even among those who acknowledge long historical roots to the transnationalism we now witness (e.g., Eric Wolf, Sidney Mintz, Immanuel Wallerstein), there is general agreement that today's global flows are marked by a decisively new scale.

In the broadest sense, globalization and transnationalization imply an intensification and expansion of capitalism—with all its economic underpinnings and cultural manifestations—across the world. Popular metaphors such as "global village" and "transnational communities" imply that distances and borders shrink and fade as jet travel, mass media and telecommunications technologies, and fast flows of capital and commodities bring even remote areas of the world in contact with metropolitan centers. For David Harvey (1989), the "conditions of postmodernity" of late capitalism are marked by periodic time-space compressions—a speeding up of economic and social processes such that novelty is ever fleeting, whether in arrangements of production or in styles and designs of consumer goods and fashions. Modes of manufacturing and the organization of the global financial landscape manifest these changes most dramatically. Capital's inherent tendency to fluctuate and change is part and parcel of these accelerations.

"Flexibility" lies at the heart of the forces of change embodied in global capitalism. Flexible accumulation derived through flexible production, labor, and specialization, for example, have entailed dramatic reorganizations of work, markets, and finances on both local and global arenas. Scholars have referred to these changes as a new phase of capitalism, "disorganized capitalism," or "post-Fordism" (Lash and Urry 1987; Offe 1985).[9] For Harvey, the regime of "flexible accumulation" emerged out of post–World War II Fordism. Based on Henry Ford's five-dollar, eight-hour day on the automobile assembly line, and grounded in F. W. Taylor's early tract *The Principles of Scientific Management* (1911), Fordism established the basic concept of dividing the labor process into discrete tasks for maximal productivity based on time and motion studies of labor and explicitly tied mass production to mass consumption in its vision for a democratic society. Postwar Fordism, Harvey says, was not merely a system of mass production but a total way of life. "Mass production meant standardization of product as well as mass consumption; and that meant a whole new aesthetic and a commodification of culture" (1989:135). By the 1960s, the postwar recovery and economic rise of Japan and Western European countries, followed by several other newly industrializing countries in Southeast Asia, meant greater competition for the United States. The oil crisis and recession of the early 1970s pushed many corporations to find measures of cost-cutting, rationalization, and control of labor all conceptualized under the rubric of "flexibility."

Flexible specialization and production implies small, decentralized firms oriented toward niche markets in contrast to the large firms under postwar Fordism that were centralized and oriented toward mass production. Flexible accumulation embodies the whole gamut of late-twentieth-century corporate capitalist rationalization strategies, including technological innovation, automation, the creation of new product lines and specialized market niches, the movement of production enclaves to geographical regions with abundant and controllable (cheap and nonunion) labor, and corporate mergers and efforts to accelerate capital turnover (Harvey 1989:145). Some scholars have argued that flexible specialization along with the use of robotics and artificial intelligence have supplanted mass production itself. In this mix, however, mass production has not disappeared; it has been internationalized. Furthermore, the new informatics "open offices" are highly sophisticated realms of work in terms of technology and the organization of labor. Like maquiladoras (the name given to offshore manufacturing plants in Mexico that are subsidiaries of transnational corporations), these operations are the product of corporate restructuring strategies that rely on flexible arrangements of labor and mechanisms of control, as well as changing electronic and telecommunications technologies—both central dimensions of contemporary globalization.

The popular and evocative expression "global assembly line" denotes this fragmented process by which an increasing number of goods and commodities are now produced. When we picture a traditional assembly line, we see workers arranged in a neat row, each performing a distinct piece of the total production of a given commodity. But on the global assembly line, a pair of sneakers or a shirt, for example, may be cut, sewn together, and "finished" in three different countries, possibly three different continents, with the materials originating from a fourth. Even automobiles bearing the logo of American production may similarly be assembled from foreign-made parts. As the new assembly line spans multiple continents, it also hops over language barriers, cultural traditions, and state authorities. Now special terms concerning conditions of employment, environmental restrictions, and rates of taxation and building rentals are set within a given nation but outside of state law in export processing zones, or free trade zones. The new "international division of labor" on which this global assembly line is based represents a shift in the production, distribution, and consumption relationships between countries that began on a mass scale in the 1960s.[10] It has meant a dramatic restructuring of both capital and labor on the world stage (Fröbel, Heinrichs, and Kreye 1980; Sanderson 1985).[11] Whereas colonial and, later, "third world" territories have long been the source of raw materials and the powerful "first world" "mother countries" have represented the privileged realm of industrialization and consumption, the new international division of labor signaled a change in the organization of production and ultimately of consumption as well. Third world countries have increasingly become central producers of commodity goods and parts in labor intensive industries,[12] and management and research, the white-collar strata of industrial interests, have increasingly become the preserve of "core" or industrialized nations. This geographical separation of management from production constitutes one of the essential characteristics of what some have called a new "world order."[13]

The proposal and passage of the North American Free Trade Agreement (NAFTA) raised public awareness of these reconfigurations and generated debate among wide-ranging political constituencies in the United States, Canada, and Mexico, as well as the Caribbean. These discussions introduced to the conundrum of the global assembly line a complex set of issues involving the impetus toward protecting "American jobs" and the pressures on the part of developing nations to diversify their economies and generate foreign capital by wooing foreign industry. David Harvey's "new world capitalist order" (1989) and Fredric Jameson's "post-modern global space" (1991) agree that the intensification of globalization has developed unevenly. Some communities and groups are more deeply enmeshed than others in global networks, and some are virtually left out of them. Some nations and some neighborhoods have greater access than others to the fruits of globalization, and some are differentially affected along the demographic lines of gender, race, and class.

Critiques of the globalization of production, the power of multinational corporations, and anxieties over the changing role of nation-states are increasingly echoed in the realm of culture, where charges of cultural imperialism are employed by many who bemoan not just "globalization" but more specifically the Americanization of global flows of culture, media and commodities. Tied to the strong influence of dependency theory in recent decades, the concept of cultural imperialism has been the predominant framework for evaluating globalization (Tomlinson 1991). As such, a growing body of literature now addresses the ways in which transnational capital, labor, and culture have permeated and transformed local cultures and economies, thereby presenting a threat to indigenous cultural traditions. Some have treated various ways third world cultures resist such penetrations or at least incorporate foreign commodities and culture in specific, localized ways. Accounts of tourism, for example, often depict local cultures as synthetic wholes vulnerably positioned in a losing battle against the invasion of white, western culture. On the other hand, attempts to assert the voices and agency of third world peoples who "talk back" to the metropole have challenged the depiction of a unidirectional flow of culture from core to periphery and the image of the third world as passive and powerless. In an insightful commentary on this tension, Akhil Gupta and James Ferguson (1992) have warned against a naive "celebration" of creative consumption within the periphery at the expense of situating these acts within Western global hegemony.[14]

In this ethnography I locate the simultaneous forces of globalization and localization and women's agency within the malleable context of global capitalist hegemony. I say "malleable" here to emphasize that hegemony, in the Gramscian sense I intend, is a relationship through which consent to power is manufactured, and thus mutable. The forces by which the social order and multinational corporate power maintain legitimacy in the Barbadian context of the informatics industry involve not only capitalist discipline but also the flexibility on the part of the corporations and the state to heed women's interests that are grounded in their particular, gendered, Afro-Caribbean, late-twentieth-century culture. In this region, whose colonial and postcolonial history is entirely permeated by transnational movements, both forced and voluntary, economic, political, and social, there is simply no way around the articulation between these spheres of "local" and "global" economy and culture.[15] Such an articulation is not a matter of unidirectional force, but rather takes place in a number of ways—

through resistance to global pressures and corporate policies, assertions of traditions (recent or centuries old), and demands for access to a wide array of transnational culture and commodities.[16] The purpose here is not to glorify global production or consumption but rather to emphasize their interconnections and to interpret their meanings for women as key actors in a part of the world where "local" culture has always meant a complex creolization of European, African, and Asian derived traditions and where the economy has always been transnational.

Recent treatments of transnationalism and global culture demonstrate a number of difficulties posed by how to conceptualize and study the unwieldy set of processes bound up in "globalization." As many scholars have pointed out, analyses of globalization have tended to come in two basic packages: the subject of global culture has largely been taken up by the humanities, while the global economy has been the preserve of the social sciences (King 1991:ix), with a further division between ungendered studies of world systems and gendered studies of workers (and, to a lesser extent, consumers) in specific "local" places. Anthropology represents a unique realm for rectifying these divides. With its tool of ethnography, and its central concept, culture, its emphasis on history, and, for Caribbean anthropology, its transnational, modern, and creolized subjects, anthropology provides a useful set of theoretical and methodological ingredients for coming to grips with an increasingly complex set of social phenomena.

Several interesting questions remain to be explored more deeply: How do imported images and goods, tied to notions of modernity and progress, come to be desired and imbued with value, localized in their uses and meanings, and expressive of cultural differences and histories? What meanings (gendered and otherwise) do they come to have in people's everyday lives? And, how are they bound up with new capitalist hegemonies and relations of production broadly speaking? To begin to address these questions within transnational and globalization studies we need to take the workings of culture more seriously as both constituted by global processes and constitutive of them. To date, we have few rich examples of ethnographic analyses of these interrelationships.[17] Some have advocated broadening our conceptualizations of "diasporas" and transnational communities, with an emphasis on "travel" as opposed to the village as the locus of cultural inquiry. Along similar lines, notions of hybridity, creolization, and spatial metaphors of place, locality, and a "third time/space" of transnational experience have been proposed as tools for encompassing these new ways of experiencing daily life through the articulation between local and global forces

(Bhabha 1994). For Arjun Appadurai (1990; 1996) the spatial metaphor is expressed in his array of "scapes" (ethnoscapes, finanscapes, technoscapes, ideoscapes), which, in their fluidity, undermine the utility and significance of nation-states as the central arbiters of modernity and transnationalism. Moving beyond those general assertions, I suggest that states, transnational corporations, and local groups of social and economic actors both challenge and support each other as they face new sets of circumstances and contexts for enacting power and identities. Within this dialectic, the specificity of local cultural-political economies is crucial to our understanding of how globalization is configured and how it is experienced by different people across the world.

Barbados and the Caribbean: Situating Export Production and Transnationalism

Export-oriented industrialization in the Caribbean, as in many other regions of the developing world, has become the dominant economic model, following a long history of monocrop agricultural extraction under colonialism and unsuccessful attempts following World War II at "import substitution." As early as the 1960s, investment policies of developing countries began to shift from models of import substitution to "export diversification" because of changes in international trade and tariff regulations (Nash 1983). For Barbados, as chapter 3 explores in detail, this shift involved diversification of a sugar-based economy toward a tripartite structure that includes tourism and manufacturing.

Growth and change in sectors of the Barbadian economy in the postwar years falls into three periods: the period of agricultural dominance, between 1946 and 1962; the period of transition, between 1963 and 1970; and the period of export diversification first to manufactured goods and now into services, from 1970 to the present. The dominant economic role played by sugar for more than three hundred years of Barbadian history declined significantly between 1946 and 1980 (in terms of share in domestic output, employment, and foreign exchange earnings). Successful efforts at economic diversification accompanied the decline in the sugar industry itself.[18] Between 1963 and 1970, tourism and light manufacturing surpassed sugar as the primary source of economic growth, and the hope was that one sector might support another in the face of market swings or downturns. The transformation began in the 1950s with the establishment of the island's first Board of Tourism and continued in the decade after with the enactment of the first incentive legislation for enclave manufacturing.[19] The three sectors, however, represented different sorts of economic security. For example, sugar exports continued to yield greater potential value added while manufacturing exports signified perhaps twice the employment gain achieved by an equal advance in the tourism or agricultural sectors.

For Latin America and the Caribbean nations, the debt crisis of the 1980s, rising interest rates and cost of oil, and weakening terms of trade with the United States led to severe balance of payments problems that were soluble only through increasing exports. The United States responded to the crisis with several economic initiatives aimed at promoting political stability in Central American and the Caribbean (Deere et al. 1990), and alleviating the economic crisis in these developing countries, as well as insuring a source of cheap labor for U.S. industry in the wake of competition from newly industrializing nations in Asia. In 1983 President Ronald Reagan's Caribbean Basin Initiative enabled approved Caribbean nations to attain one-way duty-free access to U.S. markets for particular goods for twelve years. Indeed, while vigorous resistance from U.S. unions successfully banned textiles and garments from these initiatives, some Caribbean countries were granted special production quotas, limiting garment production to items assembled from fabric made and cut in the United States.[20] Several Caribbean countries, including Barbados, Jamaica, and Trinidad, now marginalized by Mexico's preferential trade conditions under NAFTA and undergoing severe contraction of traditional export commodities (e.g., sugar and bananas), have applied to the United States for parity in trade relations. With export production as the linchpin of Caribbean economies, it is clear why informatics investors are attracted to a small island like Barbados. Among Barbados's many assets according to these investors are its English-speaking tradition, high literacy rate (98 percent), and "orderly" society, and its well-entrenched tourism sector and reputation for "polite service."[21] Government officials and state bureaucrats also see these factors as the bases for the success of this new industry and the promise it represents for future growth and development of the nation.

Export production and high consumption of foreign goods are not the only expressions of transnationalism in Caribbean history and culture. The ties between the West Indies and England, Canada, and the United States reach back to the earliest days of colonialism and permeate most dimensions of life there today. Nearly every West Indian has some family member living abroad, creating enormously significant networks of social, economic, political, cultural, and emotional exchange. Transnational kin networks rely on transatlantic travel and communications for economic support, information, and nurturance in numerous forms (Olwig 1999). While labor migrations have led thousands of Caribbean men and women to jobs in transportation, nursing, and domestic service in cities such as London, New York, and Toronto, children of school age are frequently sent back "home" to the Caribbean, where they are believed to receive stronger discipline, and better care and education without the racism and gang influence that they are likely to encounter in North America or the United Kingdom. Many families in the Caribbean rely on the remittances and goods sent by relatives working abroad, and in turn, many transmigrants depend on family "at home" to maintain properties for them, or to provide a home when they return for holidays or need an emotional base. Transnational political networks figure prominently in both "metropolitan" and Caribbean elections. Jean-Bertrand Aristide's reference to New York as the "Dizyem Depatman-an" or Tenth Department of Haiti is one example of the importance of Caribbean transnationalism in "local" political economy and culture (Basch, Glick-Schiller, and Szanton-Blanc 1994:1).

Early transnational migrations from Barbados took place largely within the region; in the late nineteenth and early twentieth centuries, roughly fifty thousand people worked as seasonal laborers in British Guiana and Trinidad, and between forty-five thousand and sixty thousand went to work on the construction of the Panama Canal. Migrations to Britain and to Canada and the United States ebbed and flowed during the twentieth century, the largest waves occurring between 1955 and 1961, when nearly twenty thousand Barbadians sailed for Britain as part of the Sponsored Workers scheme. In the 1960s Canada and the United States eased their immigration policies just as Britain was tightening hers, and cities such as New York and Toronto were "Caribbeanized" (Sutton 1987).

The growth of export production and major flows of labor migrations accompanied other manifestations of Caribbean transnationalism in the past century. Most striking is travel abroad for pleasure and shopping. In 1993 alone, U.S. Emigration issued nonimmigrant (tourist) visas to twenty-five thousand Bajans, or nearly 10 percent of the entire population (George Gmelch and Sharon Gmelch 1997:185). Bajans' penchant for imported goods and foreign travel is counterbalanced, however, by an equally strong pride in local culture, deep ties to family, and a pull toward home, which Gmelch and Gmelch see reflected in the fact that Bajans have "one of the lowest naturalization rates of any foreign-born immigrant group in the United States" (1997:181).

This tension between "home" and "away," or the local and the transnational, permeates the lives and experiences of the women in this study. Women working in the informatics sector are at once deeply conscious of the place of their new industry in the global economy, taking pride in working for a foreign company and loving to travel abroad, and little interested in making anywhere else their home. Their work as data processors looks (and feels to them) like modern, high-tech, sophisticated officelike work. Yet their engagement in a "triple shift" of domestic responsibilities, wage work, and numerous informal income-generating activities such as cake baking, sewing, and trading of goods and services resembles the strategies that women of the Caribbean have employed for hundreds of years to make a living. The complexities of this juggling act are discussed in greater detail in chapter 6. It is important to note here, however, that the confluence of new and old, "modern" and "traditional" practices and identities is heightened in the informatics arena because of its strikingly new, global image and structure. A highly valued "perk" of working for Data Air, for example, is the possibility of winning airline travel vouchers (called "thank-you cards") for trips to destinations across the Caribbean, North America, and Europe. In addition to visiting far flung family members abroad, women use these trips to buy foreign goods, some for their own consumption and some to sell at home to supplement their low wages.

Travel opportunities also contribute to these women's emergent sense of themselves as "modern" working women. But, as the public scene between Paul and Christine at the bus stand suggests, there are ambiguities and even dangers bound up with these new appearances and by informatics workers' pursuit of transnational fashion and display. The threat that a "factory girl" might be confused for a "middle-class office worker" and undermine Barbadian respect for social (class) boundaries and their distinguishing appearances is merged with Paul's sense of marginality from the money, status, and time commitment bound up in Christine's employment in informatics. Another key dimension of the emphasis on dress and appearance is its demonstration of the interconnections between local culture and imported, multinational corporate culture. Some scholars writing about global factories present western dress and appearance among the female workers as superficial compensatory practices that mute women's inclination to resist (in an organized manner) the harsh labor conditions they face in their jobs (Elson and Pearson 1981a, 1981b; Grossman, 1979; Fuentes and Ehrenreich 1985) and provide an excuse to enhance local measures of surveillance and discipline over women. This form of consumption becomes equated with sexual promiscuity and a threat to proper femininity and religious decorum (Ong 1987; Fernandez-Kelly 1983). The Anglophone Afro-Caribbean context of Barbados presents both similarities and some striking contrasts to these earlier accounts. In Barbados, European and other Western styles and cultural practices are not necessarily construed as "threats" to local culture.[22] Furthermore, women's ability to dictate their own work identities and practices without the interference or control by male kin places them in remarkably different circumstances than those of many of their Asian and Latin American sisters. While forms of patriarchy certainly underlie some aspects of women's home and work lives in Barbados (Senior 1991), informatics workers' employment is in no way mediated or controlled by their male kin.[23] Whether married or single, these women control their own labor. Similarly, references to women's "mercenary," "exhibitionist," and acquisitive habits often made in such popular cultural arenas as contemporary calypso and dub music, are not part of any specific campaigns to restrict the movements and sexuality of high-tech workers in Barbados as some have reported elsewhere (Ong 1987). Whereas working in a factory and wearing new kinds of clothes can bring charges of promiscuity and immorality to Malaysian or Mexican women and can threaten their marriageability, Bajan informatics workers have little such concern. They resent these characterizations and at the same time enjoy a sense of prestige from many of their associated practices (e.g. travel abroad). Furthermore, to them and their employers, their special way of dressing is appropriate to their jobs. As such, the meanings pink-collar workers interpret from and ascribe to "femininity" and its associated prescriptions for habits of work act to both challenge and re-formulate both local and transnational conventions.

Global consumption among today's data processors, along with their role as high-tech offshore producers in the information age, are potent examples of the "conditions of postmodernity" to which Harvey refers. Indeed, these women's identities as producers in this new sector are very much bound up in a set of consumption practices that both enable and demand them to look like "professional" office workers. The task for anthropology, as I see it, is to connect the ways in which new modes of consumption together with new modes of production give rise to new meanings of local culture and newly flexible identities.

Consumption across "First" and "Third" Worlds

Extensive debates have emerged in the 1980s and 1990s surrounding the forms and meanings of consumption and consumerism in everyday life (e.g., Appadurai 1986; Breckenridge 1995; C. Campbell 1990; Fine and Leopold 1993; Friedman 1994a; Howes 1996; Miller 1995a; Wilk 1990). On the one hand, many scholars express interest in and concern about the meanings of new forms of consumption for people in the third world. On the other hand, however, global consumption, when discussed in relation to transnational production, is generally seen as the privilege of those in the "West" afforded by the (exploited) labor of third world workers. These formulations raise two important issues.

First, consumption is often presented as a novel phenomenon for people in the "developing" world when technology and media-hyped goods and symbols are involved. Images are conjured of a nearly naked Masaai warrior sporting Ray Ban sunglasses, a dark-robed Bedouin woman drinking a Coke, or, for that matter, a Caribbean native leaving the languor of palm trees and beaches for the air-conditioned office to work at a computer eight hours a day (Lutz and Collins 1993). What we sometimes miss, however, is the long history of transnational movements that have given rise to the high valuation of these goods and their particular meanings and modes of incorporation into specific cultural contexts. Second, the new anthropology of consumption and consumerism, regardless of perspective, includes a gendered dimension. Consumption in one sense has long been the realm of women standing in necessary counterpoint to production—men produce whereas women shop, or consume—where the former constitutes work and the latter pleasure.[24] Where the "new international division of labor" model presents production and consumption as geographically and hierarchically opposed—the poor and powerless of the third world produce for the rich and powerful first world—Maria Mies (1986) introduced a provocative gendered dimension to this framework. For her, the world economy is predicated on a system of capitalist patriarchy that incorporates women in strategic roles on both "sides" of the international divide: third world women as proletarianized producers and first world women as consumer "housewives." What Mies, more than a decade ago, drew our attention to were the complex mechanisms through which women are mobilized around the world to fuel the expansion of capitalist accumulation and the integral relationship between consumption and production in this process. Her work represents an unusual treatment of the global arena in linking the experience of people of the first and third worlds and also in emphasizing the gendered dimensions of the workings of global capitalism.

More characteristic of the globalization literature is a peculiar divide between apparently ungendered macro analyses and gendered micro analyses. Women as gendered subjects often take center stage in studies of factory production along the global assembly line (Peña 1997; Sklair 1993; Ong 1987, Fernandez-Kelly 1983) or of consumption of particular goods and media in global outposts (Abu-Lughod 1993, 1995; and in Breckenridge 1995; Howes 1996; Miller 1995a, 1995b). These studies generally conclude with the implications of global production/consumption for women, households, and gendered ideologies in the given local context. However, in analyses of the wider forces (both cultural and economic) shaping these movements and their implications for nations and local cultures, the role of gender and of women as the central producers and consumers strangely recedes (see works by Appadurai, Featherstone, Hannerz, Harvey, and Robertson). Mies's formulation, limited though it is in its binary portrayal of third/first world women, is a notable exception.

Global assembly lines are as much about the production of people and identities as they are about restructuring labor and capital. In a discussion of third world women workers, Mohanty (1997:5) integrates transnational realms of practice and the ways in which gender and race hierarchies become naturalized by the maneuvers of late capitalism. She argues that "the relation of local to global processes of colonization and exploitation and the specification of a process of cultural and ideological homogenization across national borders, in part through the creation of the consumer as 'the' citizen under advanced capitalism, must be crucial aspects of any comparative feminist project" (1997:5). Her project is to explore the connections between actors on the worker/producer side of the equation, asking, "Who are the workers that make the citizen-consumer possible?" However, while her discussion of the ideologies underlying these constructions of third world women workers is persuasive, she merely hints at her initial provocative connection between "worker-producer" and "citizen-consumer."

What Mies could not anticipate, and what Mohanty underplays in her 1997 analysis, is the significance of women's increasingly simultaneous engagement in both production and consumption on both "sides" of the international division of labor. The informatics workers in Barbados demonstrate through a variety of practices that they are not the passive pawns of multinational capital they have sometimes been depicted to be. Nonetheless, the agency they enact as workers and as new transnational consumers may ultimately have the ironic effect of challenging their sense of class consciousness and of gender-based solidarity. In the following chapters I explore the tensions between hegemony and agency by bridging the realms of production and consumption, economy and culture in this new transnational industry in the Caribbean. In doing so, I address both a new category of work and a newly emergent "class" of worker. By highlighting the culturally specific and locally gendered ways in which new workers in the offshore operations of major multinational corporations experience their incorporation into the global assembly line, this study contributes to a growing body of scholarship on gender, power, and agency in transnational capitalism (Fernandez-Kelly 1983; Kondo 1990; Ong 1987; Peña 1996; Safa 1995; Ward 1990b; Wolf 1992; Yelvington 1995). As such, a brief discussion of this literature is called for to demonstrate where Barbados and informatics fit into the broader picture.

Women and Production on the Global Assembly Line

In the 1970s and early 1980s, studies of "women and development" paved the way for explorations of the ways in which an increasingly global economy, and its vast movements of capital, labor, and changing technology, pose radical implications for third world women (e.g., Boserup 1970; Etienne and Leacock 1980; Nash and Safa 1986; Reiter 1975; Rosaldo and Lamphere 1974). Several notable studies from those decades expand on Folker Fröbel, Jürgen Heinrichs, and Otto Kreye's articulation of the new international division of labor by questioning the fact that the massive labor pools that form the crux of international movements are predominantly female and examining ways in which various and sometimes contradictory notions about gender have constituted third world women as ideal workers on this new global assembly line.[25] Despite competing theories about the inherently exploitative or advantageous nature of the global assembly line for economic development in the third world, it has been made clear that the ever-expanding free trade zones have enormous ramifications for local, regional, and global economies and play major roles in transforming communities, households, families, and the lives of individual women who are selectively incorporated to perform these jobs (Wallerstein and Smith 1992:253–62).

Two aspects of this study of Barbadian informatics workers make it important as a point of comparison with the existing literature, in my general assertion that global capitalism is not monolithic. One relates to the cultural context of the Afro-Caribbean and the long and well-recognized tradition of women's waged work as central to the national economy and the survival of households, as well as to women's self-images and identities. Some have described greater gender equality and historically high labor force participation rates for women within the Afro-Caribbean as a vestige of slavery, where despite some divisions of labor based on gender, women worked shoulder to shoulder with men doing the most arduous jobs in the cane fields, proving their physical strength and tenacity (Mathurin 1975). Rosina Wiltshire-Brodber (1988:143) argues simply, "Slavery had the effect of leveling the sexes. Human worth was measured purely in labour terms and women laboured as hard as men. To speak of Caribbean male dominance in the context of slavery is to parody the concepts of power and dominance. . . . This Caribbean context provided fertile ground for the reordering of gender relations among slaves. The process was to continue into post-slavery Caribbean society."

The other factor relates to the pink-collar aspect of this new industry itself, and its relationship to assembly work in the garment and electronics industries, which have been the predominant employers of women on the global assembly line. Transnational labor and women workers have been relatively well documented in parts of Asia (Heyzer 1989; Ong 1987; Wolf 1992), Mexico (Fernandez-Kelly 1983; Peña 1997; Sklair 1993; Tiano 1990; Wilson 1991), and the Hispanic Caribbean (Casey 1996; Ortiz 1996; Safa 1983, 1995).[26] Relatively little has been written about transnational labor in the Anglophone Afro-Caribbean, with the exception of Bolles 1983 and 1996 and Pearson 1993 on Jamaica and Kelly 1997 on St. Lucia. One aspect to this focus on Asian and Hispanic women has been a presumed dichotomy between "traditional" culture and modern transnational or global capitalism and a generalized sense that women working in multinational factories are largely new to wage labor and are deliberately drawn from patriarchal societies that have not traditionally seen women as breadwinners or as active in the formal capitalist economy. Several accounts make clear that employment in these sectors has relied heavily on migrant labor from agricultural regions, where women's labor was unremunerated or contained within the domestic realm.[27] Maria Patricia Fernandez-Kelly (1983), Vicki Ruiz and Susan Tiano (1987), Gay Young (1987), and Helen Safa (1995) describe ways in which rationales based on local notions about machismo and conventional gender ideologies about women's so-called natural ties to the domestic realm and family, and their prescribed temperaments of self-sacrifice and nurturance, pervade explanations of female labor on both sides of the Mexican border and between multinationals and the state in the Hispanic Caribbean.[28] Aihwa Ong (1987) demonstrates the complex ways in which traditional village patriarchs and religious leaders mediate between foreign (male) corporate employers and women workers in their recruitment into and experience of factory assembly work in Malaysia. Each account explores the complicated maneuvers and convergences between capitalist and noncapitalist, local and foreign patriarchies, and their manipulations of female workers across the global assembly line. While each takes up the question of women's expressions of agency and modes of resistance to conditions of capitalist discipline and exploitation there emerges an image of multinational capital, as a monolithic force, roaming the world and eagerly tapping into convenient pools of available female labor, ideal because of their position within cultures of "traditional" gender roles and ideologies. This general pattern of "footloose" industry has been dramatic. The forms of women's response to these conditions vary, however, according to the culture, and several accounts demonstrate the way in which these often involve the manipulation of "traditional" feminine predispositions.

Ong describes a convergence between tradition and modernity in the responses of Malay women working in foreign electronics factories. They challenge patriarchal Muslim authority and control at home through their new status as wage earners, and at the same time exercise spontaneous and contagious episodes of spirit possession, in which they effectively shut down their rigid and high tech production line by drawing upon cultural resources deeply embedded in Muslim tradition. In Silicon Valley, Karen Hossfeld (1990:173) describes tactics in which Asian and Hispanic women turn managers' racist and sexist stereotypes to their individual advantage by feigning a language barrier to avoid taking instruction, or by complaining of "female problems" to avoid heavy work. In Ong's account, capitalist discipline is exerted through the combined forces of factory surveillance, public scrutiny, and self-regulation, each weighing the feminine morality of the neophyte workers against the threats posed by capitalist incorporation. Spirit possession, then, according to Ong, became the medium of protest among women caught between capitalist modernity and Muslim tradition. Diane Wolf (1992:256) emphasizes even more explicitly the multiple forms of and interconnections between traditional and capitalist patriarchies and, consequently, the simultaneously exploitative and empowering implications of assembly jobs for the Central Javanese factory daughters she studies.[29] Michael John Watts (1992:6) concludes, "The arrival of global capital, and of industrial work discipline, no more imposes the dead hand of subordination or marginalization on women workers than the patriarchal authority of the 'traditional' Javanese family always produces a passive capitulation by household members to its demands. Globality and locality are inextricably linked, but through complex mediations and reconfigurations of 'traditional' society; the nonlocal processes driving capital mobility are always experienced, constituted, and mediated locally. *An industrial and distinctively gendered working class is made; yet, through its own use of cultural and symbolic resources, it makes itself*" (italics mine).

In the Caribbean, as in other regions incorporated into the global assembly line, we see women engaging strategies for accommodating or resisting the pressures of capitalist production involving ironic reformulations of "traditional" gender ideologies for rebellious ends. The same gender ideology may be deployed on different occasions for different, perhaps contradicting, ends. Many data processors take excused absences from work to care for children because corporate employers are flexible in accommodating women's expected feminine roles; alternatively, employers cite the tradition of the extended family and involvement by aunties and mothers in raising children as a reason not to provide day care facilities for the workers' children. Simultaneously, we witness various convergences between "traditional" and global capitalist forms of patriarchy in the incorporation and shaping of a new feminine proletariat. For example, women's suitability for low-skilled and monotonous assembly work is often associated with their naturally docile and patient temperaments as secondary wage earners, and women's low wages are explained as appropriate to their status in households with husbands or fathers as the primary wage earners. While several treatments of women's incorporation into transnational factories, such as those mentioned above, shed light on the varied and simultaneous expressions of power, agency, resistance, and accommodation among the feminized workers in these industries, we have generally seen these processes within an apparently monolithic framework of multinational capital. To go beyond this, a transnational perspective demands that we keep specific local contexts in view. In the context of informatics in Barbados we can examine the accommodations and redefinitions performed by transnational corporations in the face of local demands and conditions (by the state as well as women workers). In recruitment practices, the maintenance of a labor force beyond the course of a decade, and in numerous day-to-day ways, foreign-owned corporations attend to the cultural traditions, gender ideologies, and aesthetic values of the Barbadian workers they employ.

Most accounts of multinational industries describe their search for the ideal female worker: single, childless, young, well educated, and without previous work experience. Indeed this profile is echoed around the world as the most "naturally" suited to the labor-intensive assembly work involved in export production. The extent to which this profile draws on specific cultural or uniform multinational corporate gender ideologies (associating femininity with docility, patience, dexterity, and dependency) needs closer scrutiny. In the informatics industry, we need to ask why the same company, Data Air, with the same capitalist agendas in its two Caribbean operations, employs almost all women for its Barbados facility and roughly half men in the Dominican Republic.[30] More generally, how are invocations of "natural" femininity deployed to similar or different ends?

The Afro-Caribbean context of Barbados presents some important differences in women's circumstances of industrial incorporation. Although the "family" becomes a potent metaphor for the paternalistic role played by corporate employers, there is little expectation that women's actual families have any role in their availability or performance as workers.[31] Unlike cases around the world described by Cynthia Enloe (in Fuentes and Ehrenreich 1983), in Barbados, fathers, husbands, and influential female kin and friends exert little control over women's employment decisions. The only involvement of family or friends in women's recruitment into informatics is typically that of providing information by spreading the word of job openings or putting in a good word to an inside contact. Ethnographic accounts of Barbados demonstrate that industrialization, wage work, and a woman's family responsibilities are not seen as antithetical or in competition with each other. Constance Sutton and Susan Makiesky-Barrow (1977:306) observe, "A job or career for a women is never spoken of as an alternative to marriage or maternity. . . . This reflects not only different expectations and assumptions about a woman's economic and social roles but also the presence of a family and kinship system that acts as a support for women of all ages." Furthermore, and in stark contrast to policies and practices in many parts of Southeast and East Asia, in Barbados not only is there an assumption that women will continue to work after marriage, but also the Barbadian state guarantees (and enforces even within the offshore sector) a three-month maternity leave for all working women.

Women's movement through stages of the life cycle has not precluded their wage earning even within the realm of new and competitive industries like informatics.[32] With regard to fertility patterns and women's work, there is clear evidence that employment in the formal sector corresponds to lower rates of fertility among Caribbean women (Senior 1991:126–27; Yelvington 1995:96).[33] However, the virtual absence (even rejection of) punitive measures imposed by corporate employers on women's desire to work and be mothers[34] and what I show as the increasing longevity of women workers in these industries across stages of the life cycle and well past the short-term employment trends within multinational industries elsewhere in the world together demonstrate important counterpoints to the portraits drawn by both Ong (1987) and Fernandez-Kelly

(1983) in their landmark case studies. To ground these distinctions in their particular local context, I discuss at greater length in chapter 3 the history of women's work and the relationship between matrifocal families and divisions of labor in the Afro-Caribbean. For the moment, it is important to reiterate the point made simply and strongly by Joycelin Massiah (1986:177) that "women in the Caribbean have *always* worked" and to add that, in contrast to many other cultural contexts of global production, motherhood and work have always together been central to defining femininity in the Caribbean. The point to be emphasized here is that local cultural traditions and, in particular, the meanings of gender influence the shape of transnational production in specific ways along the global assembly line. Where others have emphasized the central role played by women in the expansion of transnational production, this work specifically aims to unpack the specific gender ideologies (local and global) that have, in complex and sometimes contradictory ways, conceived women as and in turn made them into "ideal" global workers. This emphasis on gender ideologies is important not just in relation to Barbados and the Afro-Caribbean culture but also in relation to informatics as a new realm of work that occupies an ambiguous place between traditional "white"- and "blue"-collar labor.

The "Pinking" of White-Collar Services

In the past two decades, the "information age" has signaled a dramatic shift in the U.S. economy from manufacturing to service industries. Services now outrank manufacturing in their share of national output (more than 67 percent of GNP in the "developed" economies and 51 percent of GDP in the "developing" world) (Posthuma 1987:7). One out of every five employees in the United States is a clerical worker and over three-fourths of the entire labor force works in a service industry. In the 1980s, while services accounted for 21 million new jobs, more than 2 million in manufacturing disappeared (9 to 5, 1992:8).

The shift to a service-based economy, denoted by the expression "postindustrialism," is integral to the notion of the new world economic order that Harvey (1989) and others describe. This notion implies that, facing the loss of manufacturing industries to the "third world," these advanced or postindustrial nations will retain an expanding service sector, and it includes the broader argument that, the world over, services are increasing in their representative importance in the labor market. Certainly, the Caribbean's emphasis on tourism as the major source of foreign exchange and employment represents a vast expansion in the importance of services compared with the traditional sectors of agriculture and manufacturing. Informatics in Barbados presents an intriguing case for investigating these trends. Its "product" is information, manipulated and produced in electronic form as a service to clients overseas. Its labor process, however, operates on a piece-rate system much like factory-based production, in which systems of monitoring and assuring consistent levels of "quality" more resemble a manufacturing plant than an office.

Before I explore the tensions over these boundaries in the informatics arena it is important to emphasize the extent to which the expansion of services, like the expansion of industrial labor along the global assembly line, is tied to increasing numbers of women workers and to gendered conceptualizations of work itself. The particular form in which white-collar labor is refashioned for a specifically feminine labor force within an unusual "factory" context constitutes the "pink-collar" nature of the setting for this research.

The shift to services, or the so-called second industrial revolution, is in the process of reshaping the industries where women are heavily concentrated, and presents new and complex implications for our analyses of the global economy as well as for the day-to-day lives of thousands of working women and their families. In the United States, several changes are reorganizing the clerical work that has spawned the offshore data entry industry. First, new computer technologies and digital telecommunications systems are capable of generating, handling, and transmitting work that was once labor intensive, highly skilled, and confined to paper transactions. Facsimiles and data communication equipment have drastically cut costs and made possible simultaneous transmission of information regardless of geographical distance. The shift to digitalization, for example, means that whereas a telephone line may transmit 10,000 bits of information per second, satellite transmission can speed the process exponentially, sending 6.3 million bits per second. The current thrust toward privatization and mergers of telecommunications companies is also encouraging increased usage of new services (e.g., electronic voice services, electronic mail, interactive computer networks, high-speed facsimile transmission).

Concomitantly, production in all economic sectors of the United States has become increasingly information intensive, and there has been a proliferation of knowledge-based industries that themselves rely on new labor forces and technologies. Even in 1986 there were roughly three thousand on-line databases, and over 90 percent of these were located in the United States (Posthuma 1987:6). In a competitive marketplace where production and distribution have become increasingly integrated, information technology becomes indispensable in meeting communications demands. And at the same time that more and more data are being generated internally, management requires greater amounts of information for strategic planning and research. On-line information searches by industries are estimated to be growing at over 30 percent a year. The variety and number of new products and services surrounding this proliferation of information is staggering, ranging from data processing operations, software development and evaluation houses, and outfits that update on-line databases to those companies that service and maintain computer equipment and support the telecommunications and technological demands of these changing industries.

The impact of computer automation and the rise of the "paperless office" for clerical work has received increased attention as technological advancements in telecommunications coupled with rapid changes in both local and global economies have presented new labor processes, recruitment patterns, and the reorganization of work itself. Until quite recently, labor studies focused almost exclusively on skilled, heavy industrial work that comprised an essentially male domain. Now, with the expansion of light industries where female labor is typically favored, a new kind of labor study is emerging, with greater exploration of the ways in which gender has historically intersected directly with technological innovations (e.g., typewriters, sewing machines, video display terminals). The feminization of certain job categories is often correlated with lower skills, lower rates of remuneration, lower prestige, and recently, extensive automation, and computer regulation and surveillance.[35] In the sphere of information-based industries, banks, insurance companies, airlines (reservations), and credit card companies are among those arenas of heavily female-centered fields undergoing radical technological restructuring—again, we are witnessing a historical shift in which those arenas undergoing automation, deskilling, and demotion are also feminized.[36] What is at stake is a process by which the concept of skill itself is gendered, and that which is associated with women, devalued.

With the introduction of new office technologies and the accompanying hype by hardware vendors, technical schools, politicians, and the press has been a tendency to raise the expectations of secretaries and clerical workers for new skills, access to better jobs, and, thus, better salaries and greater status (Murphree 1987). The new technology is presented as bringing an end to the traditional boss-secretary relationship, and the paperless office is hailed as a means for paring down the numbers of office workers and transforming those remaining into "all-round communications workers with sophisticated computer skills" (Pringle 1988:97). In theory, the new technology provides the opportunity for secretaries to do a greater variety of tasks that include high-level functions such as planning, managing, developing databases, and preparing financial analyses, but in general the reality is not so rosy. The technology alone does not insure any of the promised rewards, and many studies have noted that the attitudes and agendas of management have played a much more powerful hand in reshaping the conditions of office work than the technology itself. In short, the same technology may have significantly different effects on the labor process in different environments, depending on the context of use, size, and agendas of the workplace managers.[37]

In the realm of information-based services, two major trends have emerged as part of the increased implementation of office automation technologies. First, information-based jobs have become fragmented such that fewer people with lower levels of skills are required to perform the same work. Restructuring most often takes the form of dividing office work into two separate categories, administrative support and typing and data entry. Each category requires limited training and lower levels of skills and subsequently commands a lower rate of remuneration than the original diversified secretarial job. Second, the physical arrangement and geographical location of work are simultaneously being decentralized such that clerical workers are often moved to separate "operations floors" or, even more dramatically, clerical work is housed outside the physical domain of the company, up to thousands of miles away and "offshore." The shift to total operations performing the discrete jobs of data entry, word processing, and claims adjudication, such as those in the Caribbean, has meant that face-to-face relationships between clerical workers and professional and managerial staff is becoming increasingly rare. These offshore workers represent one extreme on a continuum of clerical-work rationalization that also includes part-time, temporary, and home-based clerical workers in the United States.[38]

On a typical shift at Data Air or Multitext, between about fifty and one hundred Barbadian women sit in partitioned computer cubicles of a given production floor from 7:30 in the morning until 3:30 in the afternoon, taking a half-hour break for lunch and sometimes a fifteen-minute stretch in between. Their keystrokes per hour are monitored electronically as they enter data from airline ticket stubs, consumer warranty cards, or the text of a potboiler novel for top U.S. airlines, appliance houses, and publishers. In each case, the surveillance of the computer, the watchful eye of supervisors, and the implementation of double-keying techniques are all aspects of the production process integral to the companies' guarantee of 99 percent accuracy rates.

These trends allow little opportunity for computer operators to learn the more complex capacities of their machines and drastically shorten their career ladders by limiting their tasks and allowing them little or no access to managers and professional associates.[39] Furthermore, the constant monitoring and measuring of productivity and error rates of these operators increases their stress.

Part-time, temporary, home-based, and offshore work are examples of expanding schemes described as "flexible" in the clerical sector. This new pool of workers is characteristically female, and these "flexible" jobs are often presented as ideally suited to women's multiple roles as homemakers, caretakers of dependent children and sick and elderly relatives, and wage earners. Part-time, temporary, and home-based work are often presented as providing a sort of "safety net" for women whose domestic roles make full-time work impossible. Embedded in the corporate rationales are familiar, essentialist notions about women as secondary wage earners whose lower rates of pay and minimal benefits merely supplement those of a primary male breadwinner. As Mohanty (1997) points out, these ideologies about femininity and domesticity situate third world women and women of racial and ethnic minorities in the United States in especially vulnerable and exploited positions in the economy of late capitalism.

The flight of clerical work offshore is explained by multinational managers and company owners with a familiar litany of rationales that are subtly but inextricably bound up in these gendered (racial/national) ideologies of production. They claim that "you simply can't get Americans to do this sort of work anymore" and that attrition levels and wage rates in the United States make back-office costs prohibitive. Some companies have moved step-by-step through alternative labor forces and work arrangements, first trying automation devices in their home offices and cutting back employees from full- to part-time status, then experimenting with other contingent arrangements such as temporary, home-based, or subcontracted clerical work, and finally moving their work out of the United States altogether, either by setting up their own offshore shop or contracting work to an existing vendor. Like corporate investors in other industries, they are drawn to the Caribbean by its proximity and the availability of frequent, inexpensive flights to the United States (this is especially so for East Coast companies) and by its tax incentives, low-waged and well-educated work force, good roads, airport, and custom-designed factory shells, and, as a special lure to traveling executives, its beaches and luxury hotels.

For labor forces in Barbados and other parts of the developing world, offshore clerical work represents new employment opportunities, enhanced by the power and novelty of informatics technology and officelike work setting. Despite the strict disciplinary pressures, other aspects of these jobs make them especially attractive to the hundreds of Barbadian women who apply each year. Considering the exploitative conditions under which thousands of offshore assembly-line operators work across the world, the working environments and benefits offered to offshore pink-collar operators in Barbados may even be better, in some respects, than those provided to their counterparts in the United States. While wages are less than half that of a U.S. worker, strict labor laws established by the Barbadian state ensure that all Barbadian workers are guaranteed certain basic employment benefits, such as maternity and sick leave, severance pay after two consecutive years of employment, and three weeks of paid vacation.[40]

Barbadian, Dominican, and American operators for Data Air, for example, all confront increasing stresses of electronic monitoring devices and measures, such as production quotas and incentive schemes, to further reduce costs and maximize production, as well as the insecurity created by rapidly changing technology. They differ, however, in their specific relationship to these various rationalization measures and in the cultural meanings associated with them. For example, the special meaning of "pink collar" is particularly pronounced for the Barbadian women I interviewed and differs from that of their counterparts in the sister plant of Data Air located in Santo Domingo. There the average length of employment for operators is two years, in marked contrast to the longevity of operators in the Barbadian plant. Male informatics operators in the Dominican Republic describe their jobs as stepping stones toward better, computer-based jobs. Because they are able to work permanent day or night shifts to accommodate class schedules, they see their jobs as means of gaining relevant experience while in school. The Barbadian female operators, however, generally hope for stable, long-term employment and seldom express at the outset the expectation to move up to higher-level computer work. These differences point to some of the ways in which gender ideologies and the structure of the labor market intersect.[41] These differences also demonstrate that even within branches of the same company, local cultural and economic conditions weigh heavily into the recruitment and incorporation of workers, and into the ultimate meanings these jobs have in their lives. Irene Padavic (1992), writing about U.S. workers, asserts that industrial "demand factors" need greater consideration in looking at occupational segregation between the blue- and white-collar realms. She argues that women's preference for clean white-collar jobs, though strong, does not actually determine their occupational choices, and when given the choice between a higher-paying, blue-collar and traditionally masculinized job and a lower-paid but white-collar job, women generally choose the former. In the United States, she concludes, economic reality wins out over comfort and the symbolic status associated with office work.

In Barbados, however, data processors openly acknowledge in their testimonies that they could earn more money in the cane fields but prefer the clean, cool and computer-centered realm of offshore informatics—a powerful illustration of their valuation of this new industry's symbolic capital and physical appeal. This preference is not a matter of false consciousness but a phenomenon grounded in West Indian culture and traditions of "getting by," through which women piece together their livelihoods by engaging in multiple economic activities (in formal and informal sectors) and place great value on cultural as well as economic forms of capital. Before moving ahead to the nuances of this process, however, it is useful to place the discussion of offshore informatics in Barbados within the broader context of labor studies, specifically those that explore the intersections between gender and class.

Labor Studies and the Culture of Production

Class as a concept for understanding the differential positions of groups within the social structure has undergone numerous challenges in recent years. Several converging phenomena—including the transformation of the manufacturing sector in western industrialized nations, the globalization of production, the restructuring of the service economy and its accompanying technological changes, and the increasing emphasis placed on consumption in defining lifestyles and identities—have led some to argue that the concept of class has reached the end of its usefulness, or at least that the traditional bases for categorizing class groups require rethinking.[42] Such challenges have emerged in discussions of the political and economic "conditions of postmodernity" (Harvey 1989). Heeding many of these cautions, I argue that class, nonetheless, is pertinent to this discussion in two ways. First, simply, workplaces, as the centrally recognized realms of production, continue to be powerful loci for structuring socioeconomic status and identity, as informed by cultural, symbolic, and economic capital. As such, this study of informatics and its somewhat ambiguous status as an "industry" or "white-collar" service sector leads us to consider its new producers in relation to class. Simultaneously, we need to rethink the foundations on which class identities are based. Indeed, the exploration of an apparently simple question—Is information processing "factory work" or is it "clerical work"?—underlies much of this book. If we rely on the shape and execution of the labor process itself, we can argue that this is factory work in secretarial clothing. The women workers in informatics are not a bourgeoisie; they own nothing with which they produce; they earn no capital, only wages; they can have no organized effect on the use or organization of either capital or the political order in the society in which they live.[43] Yet, so powerful are the images and appearances (of the computer technology, the officelike setting, and the professional look of the workers), and the desire on the part of workers that these jobs represent, if not in themselves, at least the possibility of future white-collar work, that I argue for a more complex reading of what this new arena represents in the traditional paradigm of "blue"-versus "white"-collar labor. Such a reading demands that we define more broadly our sense of class, in ways that draw from and expand upon the classic theories of Karl Marx and Max Weber.

Classes are broadly understood by both Marx and Weber as groups that emerge in the social structure from their particular relationship to patterns of production, distribution, and exchange. For Marx, the group's relationship to the dominant mode of production was of primary concern, and, as such, the two significant classes bound up with industrialization and the capitalist mode of production in a relationship of dependence and antagonism are the bourgeoisie and the proletariat—capitalists and working classes. The power of Marx's conceptualization of class and capitalism as a mode of production is unmistakable in the emphasis of most labor studies on the occupational structure and people's relationship to the means of production as workers or owners—as the basis for identifying class identity, consciousness, and struggle. For Weber, on the other hand, whose emphasis rests on the workings of the capitalist market and the social differentiation among status groups, the significance of intermediate classes (or what are often called the "new middle classes") situated between the proletariat and the bourgeoisie and fragmentation within and between these class groups are also salient. Weber asserts that status further defines and complicates economic divisions of class, and he acknowledges lifestyles and consumption practices as integral to the demarcation of status groups. This awareness has gained greater analytical appeal as economies are increasingly based on service sectors, and consumption takes on greater importance in people's lives. Following in the tradition of Thorstein Veblen ([1899] 1953), and, in a sense, by marrying Marx and Weber, Pierre Bourdieu's emphasis on status and prestige (1984) in structuring and giving meaning to the lived experiences of class helps us to interpret the multiple factors involved in the creation of informatics as a new category of work lodged between traditional factory production and white-collar services.[44] This exploration attempts to resolve two problems that have been persistent in class analyses and labor studies. The first relates to an older Marxist assumption that labor and capital are generic, that their structural positions are of primary importance, and that culture, therefore, has little bearing on relations of production or on what constitutes class identity. The second problem involves the constraints to understanding women's experience of class when class relations and identity are tied exclusively to production. These two issues, that of culture and gender and their relationship to class, are central to my discussion.

Michael Burawoy's *Manufacturing Consent* (1979) and *The Politics of Production* (1985) contribute to our understanding of workers in the capitalist labor process, moving from economistic structures to the practices of human agency. In particular, he explores the role of games in both legitimating the underpinnings of capital (securing the accumulation of surplus) and in resisting or struggling against these very conditions. Paraphrasing Marx, he says, "We do make history, but not as we please. . . . The game metaphor suggests a 'history' with 'laws' of its own, beyond our control and yet the product of our actions" (1979:93). He draws our attention to the multiple dimensions of the labor process and of worker "adaptations" to this labor process, resisting the separation of superstructure (political/ideological) from the base (economic) dimensions of "objective" class analysis by insisting that we take these as integrally connected and mutually defining. "Day to day adaptations of workers," he points out, "create their own ideological effects that become focal elements in the operation of capitalist control. Not only can one not ignore the 'subjective' dimension, but the very distinction between objective and 'subjective' is arbitrary. Any work context involves an economic dimension (production of things), a political dimension (production of social relations), and an ideological dimension (production of an experience of those relations). These three dimensions are inseparable" (1985:39).

It is not only the inseparability of these dimensions that must be emphasized, but also the mutually defining properties they take on, and their relationship to a wider context than the production process alone. To make this leap, it is essential that culture be brought more squarely into the picture. For Burawoy, culture, like other dimensions of "imported consciousness," lies outside the crux of production. Thus, the lived experience or "behavior" of work is grounded essentially in the capitalist organization of production, and, as such, factors that distinguish workers (e.g., race, age, gender, and rank) and experiences they have had outside the workplace have little bearing on the way in which they will experience their work inside. Human nature, Burawoy argues, leads workers throughout the reaches of capitalism to construct games, follow their "instinct to control," and, in accordance with his Marxist framework, assume the power to create the "possibility of an emancipated society" (1979:157). In short, "the organization of work may vary with the social, political and economic context but the behavior of workers is in accordance with the organization of the labor process and largely independent of any precapitalist consciousness they carry with them" (1979:156). I argue, however, that because production is not generic in either its organization of labor or its recruitment and discipline of laborers, we must incorporate into our reading of the labor process the simultaneous processes of the culture of production and the production of culture. That is, we must do more than simply interpret workers' understandings and experience of production from the point of view of culture. We must look at how culture shapes these living structures themselves. As such, informatics production is incomprehensible outside of its particular cultural context.[45]

In a recent critique of the theoretical divide between class and culture, Edward LiPuma and Sarah Keene Meltzoff (1989) argue that class itself "should be treated as an emergent cultural category." Employing the work of Bourdieu (1977, 1983, 1984) in an ethnography of Galician fishing communities in Spain, they propose that class is constituted by economic capital (e.g., money, wealth, and position in the production process), cultural capital (e.g., lifestyles, tastes, and manners such as speech), and social capital (one's ancestry as well as one's relations with significant social others). Together, these forms of capital constitute class distinction and identity. In contrast to those who base social class on the occupational structure (Goldthorpe 1987; Parkin 1972; Wright 1979) and deny the relevance of status to the essential productive bases of class (Wright 1985:79), Bourdieu in his conceptualization of social class goes beyond the economic base of both Marx and Weber, and he argues that multiple forms of capital are employed in distinguishing between classes. He sees taste and consumption as integral to class identity and steeped in ideologies as well as structures. In turn, these become naturalized and foundational in reproducing broader social inequalities (Miller 1995a). Like gender, then, class, understood to encompass both material and symbolic economies, becomes an expression of social boundaries and cultural limits construed as essences.

LiPuma and Meltzoff use Bourdieu's multiple capitals to demonstrate the intrinsic connections between the so-called objective realm of production and the apparent morass of culture. "Class statuses are the product of the way in which a community objectifies patterns of correspondence between economic, social and cultural capital, . . . [and] what we call class identity is the necessary, mediated, and manifest product of the culture/production unity" (1989:322–23). One of the central implications of this class/culture formulation is that individuals and groups may have ambiguous class identities if their embodiment of forms of capital challenge those objectified patterns of their culture.[46] If we look at production, not as a separate domain from culture and nonmarket activities, but as deeply bound up with them, and if we see that class is constituted by multiple and changing forms of capital, which themselves are deeply gendered, then what is dismissed by some as "another electronic sweatshop" or "factory work in a showcase" will be revealed to mean much more to the women inside.

A Caribbean study that also draws on Bourdieu by adapting LiPuma and Meltzoff's culture/production framework is Kevin Yelvington's analysis (1995) of a locally owned Trinidadian factory. He uses the concept of "embodied social capital" to describe ethnicity and gender, denoting their physicality and relatively fixed character. "Certain configurations of embodied social capital, then, both facilitate and preclude the acquisition of other kinds of capital, including various forms of social capital, embodied or generalized" (32). As Yelvington himself acknowledges, the convertibility of one form of capital to another is not always easy (or even possible). His use of embodiment to describe the complex of given and ascribed nature of gender and ethnicity is useful for interpreting the particular case of Barbadian women workers in informatics. Yelvington asserts that ethnicity and gender are commodified identities, but that class is "constituted by the kinds of labor being sold and the kinds of labor doing the selling and . . . by the ways in which labor and laborers are appropriated" (38). He demonstrates the multiple ways in which economic and noneconomic capital are employed and exploited in the process of enhancing capitalist power. By structuring identities in particular ways, Yelvington says, owners wielding the power to extract profits define identities that in turn insure their accumulation. While their power is not complete, it is strong enough to "symbolize" and construct ethnicity and gender in ways that situate groups of workers in opposition to each other, and thus to preclude their shared class consciousness. Again, we are reminded of Paul, the angry former boyfriend at the start of the chapter. For him, Christine's new "professional" femininity is a powerful symbol of distinction that he is intent on deflating.

My own study begins where studies independently exploring production (e.g., Yelvington 1995) and consumption (e.g., Miller 1994) have left off. I look at the relationship between class and gender and contextualize their mutually defining properties within both local Barbadian culture and among the multiple forces of globalization. In doing so, I show not only that class identity relies on gendered practices and ideologies but also that gender identity draws on configurations of class. Fundamental to this dialectic are complex relationships between production and consumption.

Labor Studies and the Gender of Class

Contemporary analyses of changing labor conditions, the continuum of restructuring that connects blue- and white-collar work, and the role played by technology in these transformations can hardly be initiated without mention of Harry Braverman's *Labor and Monopoly Capitalism* (1974). Braverman posed a major challenge to the dominant approach in studies of work and technological change that focused on the structural organization of occupations as distinct from the social and economic forces that shape particular divisions of labor. He argues that capitalists used technology to fragment, deskill, and generally weaken the working class, which comes increasingly under the scrutiny of management through its use. Braverman's approach to production has been widely applied by the "critical labor process school" to a variety of industrial work settings. Technology in earlier studies was often seen as unilaterally progressive, enhancing skills and upgrading the skill level of the labor force. This is a view often espoused in business and development literature. Braverman asserts, however, that in order to extract the greatest profits from purchased labor power, capitalists try to maximize control over the labor process and that to achieve this control, capital separates mental from manual work, conception from execution, in restructuring production. In removing conceptual work from the manual producer and putting it into the hands of managers, the production worker is supposedly "freed" from the need to know about the work process and is thereby proletarianized.

The proletarianization argument of the Braverman school asserts that by way of Fordist measures—rationalizing and fragmenting skilled work into lower skilled and repetitive tasks—workers (including white-collar office workers) who were once in control of their labor, become de-skilled and marginalized within the labor process. For example, offices that once performed such duties as data entry or word processing within the context of other more highly skilled tasks have become fragmented into independent divisions in which workers perform more limited jobs. As demonstrated by Barbados's informatics sector, these jobs have been physically separated into spaces that blur the boundaries between factory floors and professional offices. These spaces provide increased structure and allow greater control over production but minimize personal contact between workers and managers and among workers themselves. Additionally, a restructuring of the work hierarchy has squeezed its middle level, leaving a small managerial/professional level of staff in the upper strata and a large production level of workers who perform the lower-skilled jobs in the bottom strata. Braverman's inclusion of office work in his proletarianization argument was, from the perspective of labor studies, a provocative step, and though he does note that women constitute the actors in these "reservoirs of mass occupations," he does not take up the ways in which gender plays an integral part of the proletarianization process itself (1974:385).

Braverman's inattention to gender as a central component of production relations has inspired several feminist critiques within the critical labor process school. Michael Apple's analysis (1984) of the feminization of teaching provides a useful point of reference here. Apple extends Braverman's model in noting that the decline in the number of jobs with autonomy is closely related to the change in the sexual division of labor, and that de-skilling has had a profound effect on female labor. He notes that there is a close relation between the entry of women into a sector of work and its subsequent downward transformation in pay and skill levels, and he links these trends in the teaching field to those in the clerical sector. Even in such attempts to describe the patterns of a segmented and gendered labor force, we are often still left wondering why and through what mechanisms particular arenas of work simultaneously become rationalized and feminized.

Women's entry into the paid work force has typically been configured so that it does not threaten men's position of authority in instances of technological change and labor market restructuring. The story of Paul and Christine at the start of this chapter, on the other hand, hints at the tensions that can arise when this gendered class hierarchy is put into question. In instances when women appear to be replacing men, Maureen McNeil (1987:192) says, "you can almost always be sure the job has been redesigned and devalued in some way." By the 1930s, women's entry into the clerical arena in the United States coincided with a juncture in which these jobs simultaneously ceased to be the training grounds for managers (Davies 1982). Both teaching and clerical work shifted from largely male occupations in the nineteenth century to largely female enclaves in the twentieth, and reveal drastic reorganizations in their respective labor processes. The changes, Apple says, relate to patriarchal relations in the wider social and economic spheres. Bourgeois ideologies about domesticity and women as nurturing and empathic, with "natural" qualities that make them ideal teachers, coincided with greater bureaucratization in the field, as positions of principal and superintendent were filled more and more by men. As Ken Prandy (1986:147) adds, even when there appears to be parity in the kinds of work men and women perform, there is "typically a difference in the way in which the occupation fits into an overall career pattern. So, for example, male bank clerks are seen as being on the bottom rung of a promotion ladder which will lead through supervisory positions, perhaps to bank manager. The same ladder may in principle exist for women, but in practice is climbed by them much less frequently."

In the realm of the "new office," clerical work, much like garment assembly, "became sex-typed as appropriate for women due to their supposedly greater manual dexterity, patience for repetitive work and attention to detail. The fact that women could be paid less than men was also an obvious advantage" (Carter 1987:206). In these studies, new office arrangements, including word processing and data entry pools, are treated as dressed-up factories, differing predominantly in their clean and professional-looking ambience. The " 'sexy secretary' with her 'bourgeois' pretensions is here overtaken by the proletarian figure; (and in Marxist critiques) her gender is subordinated to her changing class position" (Pringle 1988:97). This view of the informatics sector in Barbados has led some critics to describe it as an "electronic sweatshop" and to perceive the officelike environs as an insidious veneer on top of a familiar assembly-line workplace. What emerges, however, from this study of informatics is not strictly a proletarian figure, and certainly not a bourgeois one, but instead a blurry category of feminine worker who is created by corporate prescriptions and who chooses this realm of work much because of possibilities generated by its ambiguous position in the industrial/services hierarchy. Central to my discussion, then, is the question, How are gendered notions of work connected to these "reclassifications" of labor? That is, how do they become naturalized and incorporated such that they become explanatory justifications for situating women in particular realms of labor with particular prescriptions for demeanor, mindset, and social value? In short, how is work transformed from white- to pink-collar sectors, and how is this transformation experienced? In what ways does the emergence of the pink collar encompass new modes of consumption that are tied to new arenas of production? These questions and perspectives transcend some of the limitations of Braverman's critical labor process school, which tended to suspend the notion of the secretary as a feminine subject in favor of identifying her solely within the category of the proletarianized working class. For Braverman, as for Burawoy, it is the labor process that defines the worker and her/his experience. As Micaela di Leonardo (1985), Cynthia Costello (1985), Louise Lamphere (1985) and Patricia Zavella (1985) have demonstrated, women's particular forms of work culture— embodied in processes of organization, modes of resistance and consent, the formation of networks, and the "double consciousness" of their family and workplace responsibilities—challenge such a generic formulation of work and of people's relationship to it (di Leonardo 1985:494).

Where Braverman privileged the class dimension of proletarianization, Pringle (1988) leans in the opposite direction, asserting that the decline in status among clerical workers is due not simply to their proletarianization but to "shifts in the structure of femininity" whereby secretaries "lost some of their status as 'ladies' and were thrown into the mass category of 'girls.' This happened via a process of sexualization rather than through loss of control over the means of production" (193). Taking this observation further to explore the relative absence of class consciousness among clerical workers, Margery Davies (1982) argues that the emphasis on femininity and the view of office workers in the early twentieth century as women first and workers second obscured their proletarianization and declining status relative to male office workers of the nineteenth century. "The nineteenth-century clerk had not turned into a proletarian; he had merely turned into a woman" (175).

Despite a voluminous literature on work, economic restructuring, and the implications of new technologies for labor, the experience of clerical workers in increasingly automated environments have fallen between a number of cracks in labor studies. As women workers who are seldom unionized and frequently (if erroneously) viewed as middle-class, pink-collar workers have been the focus of study much less than hard-hatted, blue-collar men in heavy industries, or women on assembly lines in light manufacturing plants (Freeman 1993). What this trend reveals is a perpetuation of the image of office work (and even merely officelike work) as somehow exempt from the critical concerns of industrial labor because of its pleasant surroundings and perhaps its personalized nature. In short, labor studies seem to have accepted the very ideology that perpetuates this mythical but powerful perception. Furthermore, when there have been discussions about the process of proletarianization that include women, they tend to avoid altogether the gender permutations involved in their process of incorporation.

The concepts of gender and class are receiving increasing attention in discussions of power and human experience, from fields as wide ranging as sports and fashion to politics and factory work. Here I define "gender" as the socially imputed meanings associated with maleness and femaleness, or the "social magic" by which females are cast as a certain kind of feminine subject and males as masculine ones (Moi 1991). "Social magic," according to Toril Moi, "is a socially sanctioned act which attributes an essence to individual agents, who then struggle to become what in fact they are already declared to be. In other words: to cast women as women is precisely to *produce* them as women. . . . Like all other social categories, the category of woman therefore at once *masquerades* as and *is* an essence" (1036). By unearthing the processes through which sexual difference is socially constructed, we may critically assess the creation and effects of such institutions as the sexual division of labor and traits asserted as "naturally" predisposing women or men to possess particular temperaments or to perform particular jobs. Imprecision over the usage of "gender" in recent years has been reflected in murky conflation of "gender" and "women's" studies within studies of labor in Latin America and the Caribbean. While studies of women have inspired a new focus on gender relations and identities, they are certainly not a privileged realm for such analysis, as demonstrated by several studies of masculinities in the region (e.g., Gutman 1996; Lancaster 1992). Nor do studies of women necessarily portray gender as a fluid and contested category. In short, a discussion of gender, like class, is one about power and both the practice and representation of social identities.

Flexible labor along the global assembly line has routinely been equated with female labor despite a long tradition of masculinized factory work, but the reasons behind the feminine face of global production are far from obvious and indisputably not "natural."[47] Following Simone de Beauvoir's assertion that one is not born a woman but made one, recent literature about women workers in global capitalism makes clear that ideal pools of flexible labor are actively created and not simply found; their creation relies heavily on both local and transnational forces that employ strategies of "gendering" (feminizing) embedded within capitalist production.[48] In fact, what makes the equation of "docile girls," "feminine third world women," and "ideal worker" so insidious is its very taken-for-grantedness. Even explanations that seem to cut to the quick of women's incorporation into the global labor force (e.g., that women are preferred because they can be paid less than men) still fail to probe deeply enough the question "why?" How is women's labor cheapened so that both men and women come to believe that women can be paid less than men? To answer this question, and to explore its specificity in a cultural context that in many ways challenges the presumption that femininity equals docility and domesticity, we must turn to the gender ideologies this presumption reflects and the contexts in which it is articulated—the "pink-collaring" of offshore office work in Barbados.

A recent increase in the literature on gender in the Afro-Caribbean is connected in part to the emergence of Caribbean-based gender studies programs and to a growing number of scholars interested in mapping historical and contemporary expressions of gender ideology and practice as they relate to colonial pasts and transnational futures.[49] These are novel and important discussions building on and often critiquing earlier paradigms in which gender was treated solely in the context of kinship or within the bi-polar framework of "reputation" and "respectability" (Wilson 1969). Locally, Barbadians speak about gender in terms of what behaviors are deemed appropriate for women and for men, and they do so in ways that often naturalize culture through discourses about sexuality and human nature.[50] Childbearing in Barbados is considered an essential element of femininity (superseding and often preceding marriage, for example), and women's bodies are said to be better suited to sedentary factory and office work than are men's bodies, which, as one woman put it, "need to be moving around all the time." Often these values reflect cultural "ideals" that fly in the face of actual practice, as we will see with regard to notions of "respectability" and "reputation." In interpreting these disjunctures, my aim is to read "emic" or locally derived expressions and understandings about gender (and, in particular, women's roles, identities, and experiences and their imagined pasts and futures) against "etic" analyses—those derived through observation and interpretation of the contemporary Barbadian context and its social history.

In particular, changing gender ideologies surrounding women's work and the relationship between women's income earning and their consumption practices are crucial to understanding the meanings of informatics and its status in the hierarchy of occupations. For Afro-Barbadian women, a number of double standards have pervaded social and economic life and power relations. On one hand, female heads of households and women generally have been hailed as the backbone of this matrifocal society. Their strength, creativity, and sheer tenacity in supporting their children and maintaining the social fabric are alluded to across the realms of literary production and popular culture, as well as on political platforms and in historical and sociological treatises. On the other hand, their still limited representation in positions of political and economic power is striking, and it bears repeating that female-headed households remain the poorest of the poor. Women in Barbados are simultaneously revered, as mothers and providers, and ridiculed, as mercenary, manipulative sexual partners. The tension between these two stereotypes lies at the core of the informatics workers' emergent identities and perception within the wider arena of Barbadian social life. An analysis of gender ideologies as they are tied to those of class will help us better understand the contradictions here.

Class analyses and gender analyses have endured a somewhat fraught relationship, and even of late, as the interrelationship of race, class, and gender is increasingly acknowledged as integral to most human experience and expression, the tension persists. In part this residual tension is the legacy of competing approaches of Marxism and socialist feminism. This tension must be mediated in order to adequately analyze women's relationship to the means of production—the base from which they experience gender oppression with regard to the subjugation of women in patriarchy—including male control over women's sexuality. Attempts to bring these dimensions of oppression together have ranged from a "dual systems" approach, according to which capitalism produces the "places for a hierarchy of workers" and "gender and racial hierarchies determine who fills the empty places" (Hartmann 1976:18), to more integrated approaches that view "capitalist-patriarchy," for example, as a mutually reinforcing system of oppression reliant on specific strategies of gendering workers and "class-ifying" women.[51] A number of studies have demonstrated the dynamic interconnections between women's household-based, informal sector, and formal waged work in ways that challenge us to engage the multiple dimensions of women's lives in our attempts to study the impact of the international economy. Furthermore, women's stage in the life cycle, as daughters, mothers, partners, and wives, together with their relationships to the means of production and household distribution play a significant role in shaping and reworking their class identities.[52] In Caribbean studies, as Sonia Cuales (1988:120) aptly notes, analyses of gender and class have engaged less in a "marriage" than, at best, a "visiting relationship."[53]

Building on these earlier approaches, I demonstrate here, through the experience of women working in the new transnational arena of informatics in Barbados, how class, gender, and culture are integrally connected in shaping individual women's sources of identity and in framing the transnational economic systems in which they live and move.

Feminist critiques have been crucial in reframing class analysis by asking where women fit into the picture of class structure: Are women's class identities defined necessarily by their relationships to husbands and fathers and within households? Can production be understood without consideration of the multiple dimensions of reproductive labor? They ask also how the "life-chances" associated with the same occupation vary according to whether the worker is a man or a woman. These two sets of questions, one from a neo-Marxist position identifying the bases for defining women's class identities and the other, a more neo-Weberian approach, focusing on the gendering of labor itself, resonate strongly within the context of pink-collar workers in Barbados.

As many have already pointed out, if women's class identity is subsumed under the rubric of the household, and if it depends on the occupational position of their husbands as breadwinners, then women present clear contradictions to the presumed configuration of nuclear and patriarchal family/household structure. This is especially true for the majority of the women in this study, whose work is essential to the survival of their households, whether they are heads of households or not. Also, if we rely on women's own relationship to the means of production, or their structural economic position as workers, without examining the particular ways in which their incorporation into the labor force is itself predicated on gendered realities, and relates to their simultaneous positions within a household, we fail to realize that women's entry into wage labor typically weakens and strengthens patriarchal relations—at home and at work (Sokoloff 1980:143). Furthermore, as Christine Delphy and Diana Leonard (1992) demonstrate, the distribution and consumption of resources within a family cannot be assumed to be equal; thus we must question the extent to which individual members, young and old, male and female, share an identical "class situation." Consumption is as an increasingly central arena of not simply survival but also creativity, pleasure, and self-definition among the Caribbean women workers. As such, a consideration of consumption demands that we look closely at these patterns within households and their respective meanings for individual women. Finally, within the sphere of production, the call to question the gendering of labor has particular significance within clerical work, where men and women have faced different manifestations of technological and structural transformations of labor processes.

The feminine identities that become central to the formation of the informatics sector clearly reflect (and serve) corporate prescriptions and agendas in many of the ways that others have asserted, especially in regard to the desire for cheap labor and its translation into natural properties of women workers (see Fernandez-Kelly 1983; Ong 1987; Wolf 1992; Yelvington 1995). Indeed, given the peculiar nature of informatics as somehow (symbolically if not structurally) in between blue-collar industry and white-collar services, class becomes an embodied identity, through particular notions of femininity (proper, respectable, maternal, fashionable, modern, and professional). Cultural orientations not only set the terms through which workers experience their identities but also create the medium for their very definition (and counter-definitions). This places a somewhat different emphasis on the relationship between production and culture. What lies at the crux of this relationship for the Bajan informatics workers is the way in which gender permeates labor and laborers in every market and nonmarket field. Bajan pink-collar identities come to reflect and to refashion those designed by multinational capital, and they do so through local cultural practices. The ways in which these definitions are drawn and reworked rely on dimensions of cultural capital (themselves both "local" and "global" in form). The pursuit and exchange of cultural capital together with economic capital ultimately reconfigure women's class consciousness and its modes of expression. Even though informatics does not present these women with a clear vehicle for actual class mobility, their work status gives them the sense that new identities are nonetheless possible. This sense of possibility is bound up with a host of symbolic elements (appearances of the workplace and the workers, computer technology, new management practices, and so on). These elements, in turn, are integral to refashioning women's class consciousness and in their pointed disinclination to unionize.

Global industrialization and the incorporation of women workers into this process brings our attention back to a basic premise of Marx and Engels, as well as that of Esther Boserup (1970), the mother of "women and development" studies: that the material basis of women's subordination would be challenged through their integration into social as opposed to domestic production (Crompton and Mann 1986:4). For Boserup, women's entry into wage work is a necessary step to their incorporation into the economic development process and is therefore liberating insofar as capital confers power. Although her work has been critiqued for its modernization premise (Beneria and Sen 1986), she paved the way for a significant body of research that has taken up the gendered (and now) international division of labor, and the relationships between women's domestic or "reproductive" labor and their social or "productive" labor. Class figures into this picture in the growing recognition that even when women are incorporated into the formal sector of the economy as wage earners, their position and experience is distinct. Use-value as well as exchange-value production is integral to defining active labor. That this has not historically been emphasized (by colonial administrators or development officials alike) has significantly affected the extent to which women and men have shared a class consciousness. In Barbados, like much of the rest of the Caribbean, despite a strong tradition of trade unionism, in which agricultural and manufacturing workers have won powerful political representation, women are marginal participants in organized labor. Their recruitment into export processing industries has been said to exacerbate this trend, by virtue of the nonunion status of most foreign-owned off-shore plants. Additionally, the patriarchal tradition of the trade union movement and the spirit of competitive individualism inculcated in the high-tech workplace accentuate this situation. Thus, on one hand we witness increasingly proletarianized populations of women and on the other, limited traditional possibilities for their expression of class consciousness.

Producing and Consuming Feminine Identities and Class Consciousness

Without taking into account the status-based associations that both workers and the general public ascribe to particular occupations, we cannot begin to predict or interpret the emergence (or rejection) of class identification, consciousness, solidarity, and action. In one of few discussions of the relationship between class and gender in the Caribbean, Cuales (1988:119) argues that women located in the expanding and rationalized "grey" areas of white-collar and commercial services (e.g., clerical workers, nurses, and social workers) are increasingly occupying class situations that resemble the working class but not necessarily adopting working class positions (political side-taking). As Christine and Paul's bus stand episode reveals, images are powerfully linked to notions of appropriateness, status, and, ultimately, class consciousness. Within the broad sweep of capitalist globalization, and the expansion of the global assembly line into new realms of work, local culture and notions of identity enact themselves in significant ways, reshaping the very contours of multinational industries and therefore, even in a small way, of global capitalism itself. The medium through which this "localization" of the global takes place is an array of gendered practices that demand simultaneous consideration of class and status, economy and culture, production and consumption. Though Bourdieu neglects to consider the gendered dimensions of class, he articulates this general aim well:

> The movement from probability to reality, from theoretical class to practical class, is never given: even though they are supported by the "sense of one's place" and by the affinity of habitus, the principles of vision and division of the social world at work in the construction of theoretical classes have to compete, *in reality,* with other principles, ethnic, racial, or national and more concretely still, with principles imposed by the ordinary experience of occupational, communal and local divisions and rivalries. (1987:7, quoted in Crompton 1993:174)

In the offshore informatics sector, we will see that structural and economic underpinnings of class are uneasily bound up with and challenged by elements of status that blur distinctions between wage and salaried workers in the realm of clerical services, in part through the new practices of consumption made possible and encouraged by the operators' status as informatics workers. But keeping up with the styles, as prescribed by corporate dress codes and worker self-fashioning, costs money and takes time, and the emphasis on professional looks merges with expectations of professional work habits, availability, and commitment. For these women the pride of distinction associated with defining themselves in contrast to their factory counterparts in the garment and electronics operations next door is subtly supported by the industry and the state (itself invested in the image of modernity and progress tied to informatics).

This is not to say that by simply wearing imported suits and jewelry, workers are duped into thinking they have the high-level secretarial or white-collar jobs that, indeed, many aim for or that they are blinded to the factorylike nature of both their labor process and their paychecks. A host of "professional" images and practices within the industry have an unmistakably powerful effect on their perceptions of themselves and their work. Their pride in their association with informatics and their link to modernity through their computer-based work are expressed in part by the fact that they are inclined to keep these jobs long beyond the average tenure of offshore production jobs elsewhere in the world.[54]

C. Wright Mills in his classic work *White Collar* (1956) says, "When white-collar people get jobs, they sell not only their time and energy but their personalities as well. They sell by the week or month their smiles and their kindly gestures, and they must practice the prompt repression of resentment and aggression. . . . Here are the new little Machiavellians, practicing their personable crafts for hire and for the profit of others, according to rules laid down by those above them" (xvii). The "emotional labor" Mills associates with the white-collar workers has oddly permeated the pink-collar realm of offshore informatics, despite the fact that the employees are located thousands of miles away from their customers, linked only through voiceless, faceless computer technology.[55] A particularly intriguing element of this added labor of gentility and "professionalism" is the emphasis on gendered identity and workplace appearance. Bourdieu's modes of "distinction" (1984), which are widely expressed in the medium of clothing, recall the white-collar workers' "claims to prestige" described by Mills. Of the new middle classes he discusses in *White Collar,* Mills says, "Their occupations enable and require them to wear street clothes at work. Although they may be expected to dress somewhat somberly, still, their working attire is not a uniform, or distinct from clothing generally suitable for street wear. . . . The wage worker may wear standardized street clothes off the job, but the white collar worker wears them on the job as well" (241).[56] Remarkably, neither Mills nor Bourdieu pursues the gendered dimension of these acts and meanings of distinction, though the relevance of their formulations for the informatics enclave and its specific emphasis on a particular brand of femininity is striking. The lengths to which data processors go to set themselves apart, in their own minds and in the eye of the public, from traditional factory workers in neighboring garment and assembly plants is revealing of the importance of what Mills calls "white collar prestige" (1956:240) and of Weber's concept of closure explored by Parkin (1979) and Yelvington (1995) in which groups exert their power to create exclusionary boundaries around resources and opportunities. Again, by broadening our sense of capital to include cultural, social, and symbolic dimensions, we can better interpret the sense of affront and shock expressed by a group of data processors when their fellow worker quit her job to work in the cigar assembly plant next door, and their multiple efforts to distinguish themselves from their "traditional factory worker" peers. While their wages may not be much better, the cache of informatics and its superior image in the industrial hierarchy make it feel like a "higher class" operation, and not one to leave for the fumes and dust of a factory.

The question of women's class consciousness and its relation to other dimensions of women's identities as workers, members of families, and feminine subjects raises important issues about the extent to which culture and class interact. Helen Safa (1990:95, 1995:88) concludes her discussions about women and industrialization in the Hispanic Caribbean by saying that "women's increasing importance as wage earners should enable them to achieve greater recognition and higher levels of class consciousness as workers in their struggle with unions, management and the state." She says, however, that while in the context of their families women have been remarkably successful in challenging traditional patriarchal gender ideologies, these other institutions have been far more resistant to change. No wonder, then, that women continue to identify themselves proudly as wives and mothers—it is in the arena of the family that they feel themselves most powerful. An outcome of this emphasis on women's domestic identity, Safa argues (along with Gallin 1990:190), is that it simultaneously precludes a woman's identification as a worker and therefore her class consciousness. The Afro-Barbadian women workers of the informatics industry stand in contrast to many of their sisters in the Hispanic Caribbean, and even farther reaches of the global assembly line, in that they do identify themselves proudly as workers, even if their femininity is also a significant locus for corporate control and discipline. The implication here is that women's engagement in "femininity plays"—fashion statements that blur the imagery of class—serves to reconfigure their class consciousness at the same time that it situates these women workers in a complex of transnational and local relations from which they derive pleasure and pride.

If we agree that the working class is not homogeneous, and that data entry operators in Barbados experience class as gendered Afro-Caribbean subjects within a distinctly feminized arena, we might argue that despite the similarities of family background (the vast majority cited the occupational and educational base of their parents as solidly working class), education, and economic means between themselves and traditional factory workers, they occupy a new class fraction whose identity is shaped around a complex of cultural-economic and production/consumption relations.

Chapter 3

Localizing Informatics:

Situating Women and

Work in Barbados

"Prosperity through increased productivity" is the motto of the 1993–2000 Barbados Development Plan, articulated by former prime minister L. Erskine Sandiford. The plan is the sixth since Barbados attained its independence from England in 1966, and, according to its authors, represents a significant departure from the direction of previous plans for the island's development. The new strategy advocated in this national development initiative is to adopt a direction that is "more export-oriented and relies more in increasing the productivity of the Barbadian people" (Government of Barbados n.d. :40). Growth in productivity and technological advancement are emphasized as key to managing the increased global competition brought about by new trading blocs such as the North American Free-Trade Agreement (NAFTA) and the European Union, a process that is expected to intensify in the 21st century. The emphasis on "export orientation" and productivity, however, is not new. Within a generation of its first settlement in 1627, Barbados had already made a name for itself as a highly successful producer of sugar for export to Europe. Eric Williams (1970) emphasizes the extraordinary importance Barbados held for the whole of Britain by recounting the well-told story of an enthusiastic cable sent from Barbados to England on the eve of the First World War that read, "Go ahead, England, Barbados is behind you!"[1] Although today the story is no more than a humorous example of a small island's inflated sense of its own importance, Williams (1970:142) points out, "Two and a half centuries ago this was no joke. It was sound politics, based on sound economics. . . . Barbados was the most important single colony of the British empire, worth almost as much, in its total trade, as the two tobacco colonies of Virginia and Maryland combined, and nearly three times as valuable to Britain than Carolina, New England, New York and Pennsylvania together."[2]

Two factors are fundamental to understanding the historical underpinnings of offshore informatics on this small island. The first is that Barbados's economy has, from its very inception, been grounded fundamentally on exports. Indeed, the phenomenal rate at which the colony both produced sugar exports for its motherland and consumed the imports her ships bestowed embedded Barbados early in the webs of transnational trade that lie at the core of its "new" development agenda.[3] The second is that women have consistently been integral to this export production, as the slave laborers in the cane fields, as mothers reproducing and socializing generations of labor forces, and ultimately as wageworkers incorporated in large numbers in newer export manufacturing industries.[4] As I explore these two fundamental themes within Barbadian history, it becomes clear, as well, that the modernity associated with the new informatics industry is rooted, as Sidney Mintz (1996b:295) points out, in the very formation of this plantation island:

> The processes set in motion by the creation of the New World plantations have never stopped. . . . It was what these reborn enterprises achieved in mobilizing resources, adapting to stolen labour, producing capitalism's first real commodities, feeding the first proletarians, and changing the outlooks of so many people on both sides of the Atlantic, that embodied a dawning modernity. . . . [This modernity has historically entailed the "twinning" of] field and factory, colony and metropolis, producer and consumer, European and Other, slave and proletarian, field hand and factory worker, colonial subject and citizen.

In short, this small and seemingly "simple" tropical island has been steeped within transnational geopolitics and economics that long predate the "globalization" we talk of today. Indeed, the first signs of Barbados's intensive orientation toward export production, and of women's role as export producers, are visible as early as the seventeenth century.

Caribbean Modernity through Export Production: Slavery, the Plantation Economy, and Beyond

The establishment of a sugar economy is the single most important phenomenon of Barbadian history. Little in the island's history over more than three hundred years is unrelated to this fact. Producing sugar, however, was not the preconceived plan of the early British settlers. Sugar rose to prominence only after the failure of several agricultural experiments that included tobacco and cotton. Tobacco lost out to Virginia's more successful cultivation, and the cotton market in London was soon glutted by producers from the other British West Indian settlements, bringing prices down and making Barbadian production less profitable. It was the Dutch who are credited with introducing sugar to Barbados in the 1640s, after growing it successfully in Brazil and developing its manufacturing technology as well. In these first decades of Barbadian settlement the Dutch West Indies Company orchestrated the slave trade and provided vital capital and trade outlets to Caribbean territories even as they lost control over Brazil. The influence of the Dutch was timely, in Barbados coming as it did while England was mired in civil war (Beckles 1990:21; Campbell 1973:5). Within a decade a sugar revolution had transformed the island, as small land holdings were amalgamated and large numbers of African slaves were imported, roughly 134,000 between 1640 and 1700.[5]

If sugar has defined the contours of Barbadian society and political economy, labor has been at the nexus of this process. Unlike many of the other Caribbean territories, this island had no Amerindians when it was first settled by the English in 1627, and so from its earliest days the colony's labor supply had to be specially recruited and transported.[6] The early settlers relied largely on the labor of indentured servants from England, Scotland, and Ireland.[7] These were men and women who saw little opportunity in their homelands and, in return for passage to the colony, contracted for up to seven years of labor. Some were drawn by fanciful tales of the riches that lay in store at the end of their passage; others were kidnapped and "Barbadosed," or forcibly sent out to the colony in servitude. The harsh conditions under which the indentured servants worked have led historians to compare their treatment with that of the African slaves who replaced them. (Beckles 1989a; Williams 1970). "Barbados, a word of terror to the white servant, became to the Negro, as a slave trader wrote in 1693, 'a more dreadful apprehension . . . than we can have of hell' " (Williams 1970:104).

From early in the island's settlement through the time of the primacy of the sugar plantation, four groups comprised its population: white freeholders who owned at least ten acres of land and were thereby entitled to vote and stand for election in the House of Assembly; white indentured servants; free men, who were freed slaves or indentured servants who had served out their terms but owned less than the requisite ten acres to entitle them full franchise, and black slaves. The population of the island rose dramatically from about 6,000 (almost all of whom were white, with a negligible number of African slaves) in the mid-1640s to about 150,000 by the century's close (Williams 1970). As the importation of slaves escalated, the numbers of white indentured servants arriving on the island slowed to a trickle, and 30,000 whites left the island, unable to secure employment or farmland. "Barbados changed from being over 90 percent free and white before the sugar revolution to being over 70 percent slave and black within a century" (Williams 1970). High mortality rates kept the importation of slaves at a consistently high rate.[8] By the 1660s, Peter Campbell (1973:7) says, "Barbados reached its apogee of prosperity . . . [and] had an importance entirely out of proportion to her size; she was possibly still the most important of England's overseas possessions, and in the Caribbean she certainly had no rival." In 1673, the island's governor "submitted a list of the seventy-four 'most eminent' planters to the Colonial Office. The acreage of these planters ranged from 200 acres to 1,000 acres. In all, they held 29,050 acres out of a total of 92,000 acres of farm land. . . . According to the 1680 census, the 175 biggest planters, who constituted 7 percent of the island's property holders, controlled 54 percent of all landed property and 60 percent of all the slaves" (Beckles 1990:24). Within the next thirty years, however, with Britain's capture and development of Jamaica, and with the rise of the French territories of Martinique and Guadeloupe, Barbadian planters were faced with competition on the sugar market that eroded their place as England's prime sugar producers.

By this time, however, the basic contours of Barbadian society and political economy were well in place—a class- and color-stratified society structured around the central institution of sugar estates. These were agro-industrial enterprises, both growing a primary agricultural crop and processing it in factories into marketable products for export: sugar, molasses, and rum. The modern nature of these agro-industrial enterprises had dramatic significance for every stratum of Caribbean socioeconomic life and, as Mintz (1985) so provocatively demonstrates, for the very emergence of the European industrial working class.[9] In short, the growing and processing of sugar requires aspects of efficiency, discipline, and supervision that are reminiscent of the qualities sought by contemporary industrialists investing in developing economies. As Mintz explains:

> Plantation labour was mostly organized on a crew or gang basis, and not much by individual talent. Workers were disciplined to work interchangeably, and by the clock. Caribbean industry was thought of as simple, since most of

its labour over time was enslaved, and it was typified by few skilled categories, meagre artisanry, and seemingly uncomplicated industrial processes. Yet it was complex in so far as the unity of field and factory was an unvarying essential of labor efficiency. The system required overarching supervision to ensure that time schedules were met—and in the case of sugar-cane, the most important crop, those were dictated by the characteristics of the plant itself. Sugar-cane must be cut quickly when its sucrose content is highest; it must be ground as soon as it is cut, so that it does not lose that sugar; its juice must be heated quickly, prepared for crystallization and "struck"—emptied into the coolers—at exactly the right moment. The water- and wind-powered factories were enormous mechanical devices for their times. . . . These technical features, many tied to careful timing, introduced more than just an aura of industrial modernity into what were operations which predated, in many cases by whole centuries, the Industrial Revolution (1996b:295).

Along with these structurally modern qualities of sugar plantations are equally strong social effects on the labor forces and management of these institutions.

Sugar shaped the structural demands of labor and production on the plantation and created a highly stratified racial/class hierarchy on the slave plantation that resonated long after emancipation. With the exception of the poor white segment of the population, some of whom became wage proletariats while others scratched out meagre existences on poor "rab" or "scrub" lands unsuitable for plantation cultivation, Barbadian plantation society resembled that of other sugar-producing colonies in the Caribbean—a pyramidal structure with small numbers of white planters at the top, free-blacks and "free-coloureds" in the middle, and large numbers of black slaves on the bottom. What was particularly remarkable about the Barbadian slave population by the eighteenth century was its female majority and the growing predominance of creoles—or island-born slaves. After Emancipation, Barbados differed somewhat from other sugar-based plantation societies, such as Jamaica, in having no peasantry and in having most of its planters resident on the island rather than absentee. This structure, according to Stuart Hall (1977:167), created stable systems "of stratification where race, colour, status, occupation, power and wealth overlap and are ideologically mutually reinforcing. . . . Though the free coloureds form a distinct, intermediary group, the barriers between them and 'white settler society' remain high. One consequence is that this intermediary coloured stratum tries even harder to assimilate and to distinguish itself from those poor blacks beneath."

Social control was maintained in Barbados by a well-developed internal militia system and a series of "slave codes" passed by the Barbados legislature granting planters the right to discipline their slaves (as their property) with free license.[10] Characteristics of the system unique to Barbados further insured order. The few absentee landlords, for example, granted certain concessions to slaves, such as a home, land for their own use, relatively free travel, access to stable sexual partners, and some control over their children. In addition, the increasing proportion of creole slaves, who were noted to be "conservative, with a dislike for change and an attachment to places or persons with whom they had identified themselves" (Beckles 1990:57), had a stabilizing effect. Some have argued, too, that the presence of significant numbers of women—both white and black— contributed, along with the intensive creolization process in Barbados, to the island's particular history as a conservative, stable, and segregated society. Writing in the late eighteenth century, William Dickson argued that "the white female majority tempered the brutish frontier mentality of planters and integrated white men into developed family structures"—which, he believed, tended toward the gradual amelioration of the slaves' condition (cited in Beckles 1990:42). For example, the noticeably smaller and slower emergence of a mulatto group in eighteenth-century Barbados, and the limited opportunities for "free-coloured" women to climb the ranks of respectability through association and marriage with white planters was curtailed, Beckles argues, by the presence of large numbers of white women. By the early eighteenth century, generations of slaves were born and raised on plantations, and the emergence of grandmothers and great grandmothers as strong female figures of morality and familial support was a striking quality of social life in slave yards (Watson 1979:91). If the presence of white women had the effect of discouraging a great degree of recognized mixture between black slave women and white men, and subsequently curtailing the upward mobility of "coloured" women and men, so too did the establishment of black women as workers and mothers—as producers and reproducers—become vital to the maintenance of the island cultural economy.

Historical Perspectives on Women's Work and Gender Identities in Barbados

For Afro-Caribbean women work and motherhood have *always* gone hand in hand. From the earliest days of plantation slavery, their labor has not only been integral to the formation and growth of Caribbean export economies, but also to the survival and nurturance of children and families, and to the very conceptualization of womanhood itself. Indeed, as Richard Ligon observed as early as 1657, work and motherhood are not only vital dimensions of what it means to be a woman in the English-speaking Caribbean, but their double burden is also imbued with a sense of extraordinary pride:

> A child is born, (which she calls her Pickaninny) . . . and in a fortnight, this woman is at work with her Pickaninny at her back, as merry as a foal as any is there. If the Overseer be discreet, she is suffer'd to rest her self a little more than ordinary; but if not, she is compelled to do as others do. . . . Times they have of suckling their Children in the fields, and refreshing themselves; and good reason, for they carry burthens on their backs; and yet work too. Some women whose Pickaninnies are three years old, will, as they work at weeding which is a stooping and painful work, suffer the Pickaninny to sit astride upon their backs, like St. George a Horse-back . . . spur a mother with his heels, and sings and crows on her back clapping his hands. . . . The mother is so pleased . . . she continues her stooping posture, longer than she would do, rather than discompose her Jovial Pickaninny of his pleasure, so glad to see him merry. (Ligon [1657] 1976:48)

For Afro-Caribbean women, the concept of work itself is connected to their responsibilities as mothers, biological or not.[11] And, likewise, having a child is fundamental to the very meaning of womanhood. The maroon women, honored by legend, who played leadership roles among escaped slaves and their more numerous but less visible sisters who performed back-breaking labor in the cane fields set the stage for more than three hundred years of Caribbean women's strength, vitality, and fortitude.[12] The simple fact that motherhood and work have, together, been expected of Afro-Barbadian women of the lower classes, and the implications of this reality for contemporary explorations of gender and identity, lie at the heart of this study.

This long history of women's labor is central to understanding the significance of the phenomenon of contemporary Barbadian women working on the "global assembly line." In order to interpret the relationship between local and global and the implications of new configurations of labor and capital, we must begin by exploring the local context and, in particular, the ways in which Barbadian colonial and postcolonial cultural political-economies created a longstanding expectation that work is fundamental to a woman's life. From the earliest days of slavery, women were an important part of the organization of production on sugar plantations. Barbados was unusual in this respect, and historically women have consistently slightly outnumbered men.[13] Ligon noted in 1657, only thirty years after settlement, that there was a remarkably balanced sex ratio in Barbados. He described this phenomenon as an attempt to avoid male revolt by providing wives for comfort and consolation, as well as to take advantage of African women's well-known agricultural experience and expertise.[14] Historians of slavery have noted that rates of fertility fluctuated dramatically according to the demands and conditions of plantation labor. In the eighteenth century, when access to new adult slaves was easier and cheaper than the cost of reproduction within the plantation, fertility rates tended to be low. Disease, strenuous work, and what some have cited as women's practice of infanticide and other efforts to control their fertility in the midst of the horrors of slavery, kept the birth rate low (Patterson 1967; Beckles 1989a; Bush 1990). Native-born slaves were more highly valued because their rates of mortality were lower, and they were perceived to be less rebellious. As such, island-born slaves were valued at twice the price of African-born slaves. In Barbados, by the 1700s, in fact, the labor supply was insured more by natural reproduction than the importation of new slaves, and female slaves typically outnumbered males by that time.

Gendered ideologies and divisions of labor on plantation Barbados were imbued with double standards that reflected the island's racialized calculus of power. White-planter women's femininity was defined as vulnerable, weak, and in need of vigilant protection, in contrast to that of black women, who were simultaneously depicted as (and expected to be) strong, self-sufficient (by growing provision crops for their families' consumption in their "off" time), and knowledgeable (about herbal medicine and midwifery).[15]

The belief that women would endure measures of "superexploitation" with less likelihood of revolt than men, and that intimate contact between female house slaves and their planter families would forge ties of dependency and affection, ran counter to the sexual "egalitarianism" of the fields where strength not sex was said to be key.[16] Little distinction was made between male and female labor in the assignment of the most arduous field work, and the ratio of women to men in estate labor increased gradually. It is said that planters were proud of this "egalitarian" approach, where weak and strong, male and female worked side by side (Beckles 1989a:24). As Senior describes Jamaican plantation labor, "not only were the majority of Jamaican black women labourers in the field, but the majority of Jamaica's labourers in the field were black women" (1991:106–7). Slave women in Barbados dominated field cultivation on the sugar plantation; in their advanced years, or in the face of waning productivity, fortunate ones might look forward to promotion to the position of driver. "For these women, it was a welcome elevation into the supervisory elite, the top echelon of which was dominated by men. It was the one avenue for mature field women to achieve status in production" (Beckles 1989a:32). Beckles adds, however, that masters' rationales for promoting women were not so much a way of honoring the hard labor of their female slaves as it was a way of insuring the continuity of the slave system among the young. By acknowledging women's power not only as laborers but also as socializers of children, the planters confirmed the important place of these women in maintaining order and compliance within the slave system.

The association often drawn between Afro-Caribbean women as hard working and as powerful has rested, in part, on this tradition of women's engagement in heavy physical labor and their ingenuity in the market. As "hucksters" or "higglers" growing and marketing provisions from lands allocated by the plantation, women under slavery were able not only to improve only their diets but also to own property and to travel about freely in a system that otherwise defined them as property and constrained their movements (Beckles 1989a:73). Some, in noting the so-called equality under the whip of male and female slaves, have argued that the historical legacy of slavery acted to "level the sexes," to minimize patriarchal relations, and in effect to create the ground for a more sexually egalitarian society (Mathurin 1975; Wiltshire-Brodber 1988:143). However, the apparent disregard for sex in some domains of plantation slavery was not extended to all realms. Male and female slaves did not, for example, have equal access to training and upward mobility within the slave hierarchy. In fact, while men were able to become skilled craftsmen, women tended to be relegated to field or domestic tasks (Mathurin 1975; Sutton and Makiesky-Barrow 1977). Equating the sheer drudgery and onerousness of Afro-Caribbean women's work to that of field animals, Zora Neale Hurston ([1938] 1990:58) wrote, "It is just considered down there that God made two kinds of donkeys, one kind that can talk."

Men were heavily represented in the skilled factory jobs of pan boilers and distillers, and in the fields as drivers and watchmen, setting the stage for a sexually stratified labor force that continues to exist today. During the early post-Emancipation period, when opportunities beyond waged plantation labor were limited, women became increasingly visible as hawkers or "higglers" who quickly expanded and ultimately dominated the internal marketing system (Mintz 1955, 1971; Beckles 1989a).[17] Their importance was great, both economically and symbolically, in reinforcing a sense of women's acumen for trade and business, as well as their independence (Katzin 1959; Beckles 1989a). Historically, however, women's range of occupational possibilities has been narrow compared with that of men. The majority of women in post-Emancipation Barbados, like their men folk, continued to struggle amid lives of hard work and sacrifice as they performed agricultural labor and fought to support their children and families. Contrary to the "leveling" hypothesis in which plantation field work is said to have set the precedent for egalitarian relations, wage differentials became established in 1834 dictating that women receive less pay for the same work, a pattern that operates unofficially still.[18]

Emancipation in Barbados in 1838 brought nominal freedom to seventy thousand slaves but living conditions for the majority did not improve. Opportunities for work and landownership were scarce, and most were tied to their work on the plantation, now as wage earners rather than slaves. Former slave women sought work either as wage workers or as "self-employed" entrepreneurs of sorts, using the experience they had gained in the marketplace under slavery (Mintz 1955; Massiah 1986). Black women thus moved into the public marketplaces and small retail shops, dominating the internal marketing system. Just as black women's work positions changed in the half century after emancipation, so too did those of mulatto women, progressing upward or diversifying into new sectors. They took control of the island's existing hotel industry and began to make inroads into teaching and nursing. Meanwhile, poor white women were incorporated into clerical services and retail sales positions, and more well-to-do white women pioneered voluntary assistance organizations for poor women on the island (Massiah 1984a:43, 1986:179). Despite these shifts, in the early decades of the twentieth century, labor conditions were noted to be abysmal within the agricultural sector and beyond, and possibilities for upward mobility were limited. The Orde-Browne Report on labor conditions "noted how, in the nonagricultural sector of the economy, the imbalance between a high-density population pressing upon limited resources produced a system of sweated labour for shop assistants, low wages for schoolteachers, and unduly long hours of work for waitresses, laundresses, bakery employees, bus drivers and conductors" (Lewis 1968:228).

In the Barbados of the 1920s, 80 percent of adult women worked in agriculture and domestic service and as seamstresses or milliners. An additional 15 percent worked as laundresses and hawkers or informal peddlers. Only 1 percent worked as clerks and even fewer as teachers (Massiah 1986). It was not until the emergence of manufacturing and the expansion of the public sector and the educational system a generation ago that opportunities for women began to

broaden. Women have benefited, in particular, from the expansion of free education—those gaining secondary education increased from 15 percent to 71 percent
in the 1960s—and the increased demand for better-educated workers coincided
with their greater access to schooling (Barrow 1986a; Senior 1991:123).[19]

With a narrowly defined economic base and an increasingly dense population, Barbados's options for economic development were seen in the early twentieth century, very simply, as a matter of balancing industry, which meant sugar,
and emigration. As George Lamming's character Old Man laments, "Twus a
high burnin' shame to put on a piece o'land no more than a hundred an' something square miles . . . two hundred thousand people. . . . When you put us all
together from top to bottom [it] was . . . a record population for the size o' the
piece of land anywhere in this God's World" (Lamming 1953:83). These two
options, sugar and migration, were also historically gendered. From the late
nineteenth century until the depression of the 1930s, Panama, Cuba, and the
United States drew large numbers of laborers from the West Indies. In Barbados, 70 percent of all emigration in these years was by males and again in the
postwar years through the 1970s large numbers migrated to Britain, Canada,
and the United States. The large numbers of Barbadian males who emigrated in
search of work was an important factor as well in establishing the independence
Barbadian women have long been known for. Both periods are associated with
increased numbers of women joining the formal work force (table 1). In 1921, the
sex ratio fell to 679 males to 1,000 females and women were "fully employed"
(Barrow 1998b:xv). Women gained greater autonomy as they joined the wage-
earning ranks and at the same time took on the full responsibility for their
households. The tasks of generating an income, managing the household, and
having responsibility for child care all fell on women's shoulders in the absence
of their men.[20] These processes, together with women's longer history as a vital
source of physical labor on the plantation, helped to establish what would become coexisting, and to some degree, contradictory, gender ideologies valuing
domesticity and housewifery and the expectation of women's labor. As I show in
the following chapters, these two expectations cannot be looked at separately in
examining changes in women's status.

Interestingly, in the years between 1921 and 1946, the number of women
labeled "housewives" in the census jumped fourfold, from 6,186 to 27,032, representing roughly one-third of the female population. These figures reflect two
processes persisting well into the decades of the 1950s and 1960s. As Christine
Barrow has observed (1986a:16), women were voluntarily withdrawing from

Table 1. Male and Female Labor-Force Participation Rates in the Commonwealth Caribbean, 1891–1995

Territory	1891		1921		1946		1960		1980		1995	
	M	F	M	F	M	F	M	F	M	F	M	F
Barbados	79.1	78.3	79.5	76.9	78.1	49.2	80.7	42.2	74.4	47.7	74.5	62.7
Trinidad and Tobago	87.4	73.9	85.4	62.7	78.6	26.1	68.9	28.3	69.3	26.6	75.5	44.9
Jamaica	22.7	81.3	75.4	78.4	64.7	72.5	33.9	86.3	43.3	42.0	76.8	61.8

Sources: Senior (1991:111); Barbados Ministry of Labour 1999.
Note: Data derived from census data for the years 1891–1946 refer to number of males and females in the work force aged 10 and over as a percentage of the total number of males and females aged 15 and over; for the years 1960–80, data are for those aged 15 and over.

the labor force after they married, choosing "to leave menial jobs, thereby raising their status and prestige." At the same time, "other factors suggest that the decline in female labor was not strictly voluntary." From 1946 to 1970 agriculture declined as an area of employment for both men and women. There was a drop from 31 percent of the male working population to 18 percent, and among women from 26 percent to 16 percent of the employed female labor force. Both men and women displaced from agriculture found work in manufacturing. In 1946, women represented 14.4 percent of the total manufacturing labor force, a proportion that jumped dramatically to 53.0 percent by 1979. As noted above, enclave manufacturing industries were overwhelmingly a female preserve, particularly after 1970. Women accounted for over 85 percent of clothing and textile manufacturing jobs, and over 75 percent in miscellaneous manufacturing (Cox 1982:64). It is important to emphasize, however, that this increase in employment did not reflect overall higher levels of labor-force participation of women, since the boom in manufacturing went hand-in-hand with a withdrawal of female labor from the traditional arenas of services and agricultural work. In fact, the female labor-force participation rate gradually declined at the same time that the number of women in the manufacturing sector increased, a point often noted in other countries pursuing export industrial models with the hopes of curtailing unemployment (Cox 1982; Fernandez-Kelly 1983). Additionally, one must reiterate that increased labor-force participation among women did not automatically bring with it wage equity or equal upward mobility. Richard Stoffle, writing about industrialization and its impact on the family in Barbados in the 1970s, notes "frankly, almost any job occupied by a male in Barbados will pay him more than an equally skilled job in industry will pay his spouse. It is no wonder then, that the family authority of these males is not greatly challenged by their spouse's employment in industry" (1977:265).

Challenging the premise that wage work necessarily improves women's status (within realms of family and public life), Stoffle argues that one must attend as well to existing household and gender structures. Not only are these fundamental to shaping the conditions for women's work but they can also be transformed in the process. He noted in the 1970s that in Barbados, women's industrial wage work typically accelerated their movement through family/union stages (single, visiting, consensual/cohabitation, and finally, conjugal union) and ultimately reinforced "traditional [by which he means nuclear, legally married] patterns of family formation" (1977:264). Indeed, Helen Safa, writing about women and industrialization in Puerto Rico and the Dominican Republic, echoes this observation when noting the numerous factors associated with the effects of industrialization on women's lives: "wages, working conditions and other job-related factors; the structure of the household economy and in particular, the nature of male employment patterns; the life cycle of the women employed, which partly determines the degree of dependence on their wages; alternative income sources for women including not only jobs, but transfer payments and the possibility of migration; and the role of the state and unions in supporting women's demands and workers' rights generally" (1990:92). As in Barbados, when women make significant contributions to their household economies, they increasingly bargain for more egalitarian relationships and effectively challenge traditions of patriarchal authority. "The key to understanding the impact of paid wage labor on women's status," Safa says, "is the importance of their contribution to the household economy" (1995:172). In short, greater egalitarianism cannot be fostered simply by increasing the numbers of women in wage work (women continue to view their wages as secondary to the primary earnings of their husbands and fathers), or even by reversing the male/female breadwinner roles.[21] The sheer difficulties faced by women who head their own households in both the Hispanic and Anglophone Caribbean seem to imply that they "prefer to bargain for more authority and respect in the household rather than to live alone with their children" (Safa 1990:93). The movement toward more egalitarian relations within a household, according to Safa's comparative study

Figure 1. Women mending roads in Barbados. Courtesy of the Barbados Museum and Historical Society.

(1995), is dramatically enhanced when both partners contribute to the household economy, when levels of education are higher, fertility levels are lower, and marital unions are legalized. Even in the most egalitarian households, she adds, women continue to see their domestic roles as central, and, citing Stolke (1984), she claims that the social identity provided by a woman's family is not diminished by the proletarianization process (Safa 1995:182).

These arguments lead us to two important observations. First, there are clear contradictions between what are deeply embedded gender "ideals" in the realms of households and workplaces and the practices that emerge in those same locales. And second, the tendency to romanticize the power and autonomy of female heads of households must be weighed against the often cruel reality of their economic condition and the fact that these configurations are not necessarily life choices but may be matters of resourceful survival. Female heads of households, after all, are typically situated in the lowest-paid and lowest-status jobs (see figures 1 and 2), and their households represent the poorest households across the Caribbean region (Senior 1991:102).

The historical processes and changing political economy underlying the gen-

Figure 2. "Hawking Flying Fish in the Streets" by A. Gascoigne Wildey. Courtesy of the Barbados Museum and Historical Society.

dering of labor in Barbados are fundamental to understanding why and how Barbados became one of the earliest sites for offshore high-tech services. In particular, the persistent and powerful coexistence of feminine ideologies valuing motherhood and work, family and independence are vital to our discussion of this new pink-collar sector. But first we must consider the history of government policies for economic development that have helped to woo informatics to Barbados's shores.

Caribbean Models of Development and the Political-Economic Context

Postindependence Caribbean states have generally followed two alternative development paths, one reliant on a free market and foreign export industrialization and the other emphasizing statist development through nationalizing industry with the aim of socializing the means of production (Howard 1989). The free-market approach owes much to the work of St. Lucian economist W. Arthur Lewis, who emphasized the limited capacity of the agricultural sector to absorb the labor supply from an ever-increasing population. This factor, together with the limited sources of domestic capital available for economic investment, led Lewis to advocate externally financed industrial development—in short, a modern sector to coexist with a traditional agriculturally based one. Thus, during the 1950s and early 1960s, on the eve of political independence, West Indian nations began to establish industrial development corporations (IDC) and pass laws giving generous tax incentives to industrial investors, thereby putting in place the infrastructure for manufacturing enclaves. According to Denis Benn (1989:88), "so self-evident had these propositions become, that even New World economists, at first, tended to be influenced by their assumptions" of the limited capacity for "self-propelled development" and of the necessity of export-led industrialization.

The formation of a social sciences faculty at the Jamaica campus of the University of the West Indies gave rise to a new and critical focus on development within the region, and, along with a strong influence from the Marxist-oriented party of Cheddi Jagan in Guyana, a group who called themselves New World placed pan-Caribbean scholarship and social change on the academic and political agendas. The core premise of the New World group stood in direct response to the "Puerto Rico model" of political economy espoused by Lewis (Benn 1987:87). They spoke on behalf of an indigenous view of economic development and saw the West Indies as a region of nations linked by certain overriding similarities (e.g., small size, similar colonial histories, and plantation economies) that allowed for a generalizable dependency paradigm to encompass them all. Lloyd Best's formulation (1971) of nationalization and regional integration, as well as Norman Girvan's study (1967) of the role of multinationals in the Caribbean bauxite industry, exemplified the group's position on economic development in the region. Advancing a structuralist version of dependency theory, the New World group emphasized the need to reduce local dependence on overseas capital and viewed the multinational corporation as the primary locus of the dependency problem.

In addition to the notion of foreign multinationals, the notion of the "plantation economy" and "plantation society" was central to the New World group's version of dependency theory and development in the Caribbean. Echoing the well-known core/periphery dependency paradigm, Kari Levitt and Lloyd Best (1975) describe the structural relationship of dependency between the "hinterland" (the supplier of raw material) and the "metropole" (the center for decision making) that characterized the plantation-centered economy and led in turn to a system of extensive import orientation and a declining local agricultural sector. George Beckford's comparison (1972) between the plantation economies and export-led development with multinational corporations at its core is even more specific. He argues that the predominant dependence on an overseas economy not only subverted the autonomy of a nation in the immediate sense but also put into place a system that would continue this relationship long into the future.

Beyond economic underdevelopment, Beckford argues that the plantation further entrenched a social underdevelopment in separating the majority of the populace from the ownership of resources and producing in turn a labor force with little motivation to promote growth and development; by this he meant the wider and more encompassing plantation society. In this sense, according to Beckford, the plantation constituted a total social and economic context that circumscribed subsequent historical social formations and both their internal (hinterland) and external (hinterland and metropole) relations. This extension of the economic analysis of the plantation to a generalized means for describing social relations was widely adopted within the New World group. As Benn (1989) points out, however, Beckford's all-encompassing plantation society model is flawed in precisely its totalizing form. He attempts to relate the dynamics of social life in the Caribbean to the socioeconomic parameters set by plantation slavery, extending Best's early economic focus to incorporate the entirety of social life.[22]

If, however, we pursue the historical and structural links between the original plantation, based on slavery and mono-crop agriculture, and multinational corporate enterprise, steeped in mining and export manufacturing, insofar as both are based on "dependency" relationships with the "metropole," we must also acknowledge that new social relations within this vastly internationalized arena have emerged, and that the plantation alone cannot explain contemporary Caribbean social and economic life. The New World dependency school, in its core/periphery view of estate production, fails as well to address the dynamics of local or native industrialists and middle classes in shaping the relations between Barbados and the international economic arena. Increasingly significant today is the solicitation/penetration of multinational capital for joint venture investments within the promotion of new forms of service and export industries. In turn, these transformations and interventions place every imaginable aspect of Caribbean nations solidly within a global economy, and within relations that complicate the earlier dualisms.

The New World group ultimately moved from theorizing about dependency and underdevelopment in the region to a more participatory and in some instances the original leadership position. As Best puts it, "thought is the action for us" (Benn 1987:102). The group reached the acme of its influence in the 1970s when many members, most notably Norman Girvan, played key roles in advising the socialist government of Jamaican prime minister Michael Manley. In Barbados, however, the New World program of nationalizing important industries was never adopted, and while Barbados did establish some minor state-controlled institutions in its early independent years, its predominant development thrust took a decidedly more conservative direction.[23]

Perhaps nothing summed up the paradox more than the attitude taken by political leaders from both the Barbados Labour Party (BLP) and the Democratic Labour Party (DLP) toward the sugar industry, symbol for most of the island's black population of slavery and post-Emancipation political oligarchy. Grantley Adams, leader of the BLP, swore in the 1940s that he would one day nationalize the industry, while his successor and the nation's first prime minister and DLP leader Errol Barrow promised a generation later to eliminate the industry entirely. Yet neither ever made a move to appropriate either land or property from the industry. What they did instead reflects the different temper of Barbadian politics compared with that of her sister territories of the Anglophone Caribbean. Rather than implementing a complete or partial government takeover, as occurred in Guyana, Trinidad and Tobago, St. Kitts, and Jamaica, the governments of Barbados that followed the enactment of adult suffrage in 1951 levied many and various taxes against the sugar industry. The funds thus realized provided the capital for such major projects to improve the infrastructure as the Deep Water Harbour, the Queen Elizabeth Hospital, the National Housing Corporation, and the Agricultural Development Corporation. Money from the sugar levies even went to construct a labor college for the Barbados Workers Union. The sugar industry, together with the Bridgetown Port, became bastions of union power. To some extent, therefore, the sugar industry paid to bring about its own obsolescence by providing seed capital for tourism, agricultural diversification, and union organization.

The strategy followed by political leaders in Barbados with regard to the symbolically charged issue of the sugar industry was, therefore, distinct from the strategies of neighboring sugar producers. Rather than take the path of state ownership, the Barbadian authorities adopted the solution of permitting ownership of the industry to remain in private, mostly white hands and instead used its political leverage to extract financial resources from it as they saw fit.[24]

The pragmatic impulse toward public policy shared by both political parties in Barbados reflects the often-sited "conservatism" of the country. It has been reported as a feature of Barbadian society for generations (Trollope 1860, Froude 1888) and has attracted the attention of contemporary observers as well (Beckles 1990; Greenfield 1966; Lewis 1968; Puckrein 1985). Where Mintz says that Caribbean individualization and depersonalization are characterized by "a learned openness to cultural variety, . . . an openness which includes the expectation of cultural differences" (1977; 1996:295), Barbadian society is known as well for its cultural insularity and conservatism. The combination of these two cultural traditions and their expression in shaping the Barbadian political economy may help to explain the island's particular attractiveness to foreign investment.

The governor of the Central Bank during my fieldwork encapsulates this stereotype of conservatism in a speech about the Barbadian cultural personality as it relates to its work ethic and the economy in general.

> A nation's culture is the foundation of its economy, and [ours is] a peaceful, passive nature. Bajans . . . must have been spirited away from a region of Africa that was much less war-like than the part from which Jamaicans were hustled into bondage. . . . Barbados can boast of quality education because the best missionaries had opted to come to this peaceful place when asked to choose. . . . [We are] a civil people, . . . a plodding, dogged people. We are reticent, and would prefer to say nothing for fear of being wrong. . . . There are many many Barbadians who absolutely prefer autocratic styles of management. They like to be told what to do and when you try to give them more freedom, more flexibility and more participation, it makes many Barbadians quite uncomfortable. . . . We are a basically conservative nation. (Barbados, *Sunday Sun*, February 17, 1991)

Again, it is helpful to examine the sugar industry for clues to this so-called conservative temper. For one thing, the Barbados sugar industry at the time of independence from Britain was still in the hands of local whites, as opposed to British companies, which dominated export agriculture in other territories.

(Guyana was referred to jokingly as "Bookers Guyana" after the powerful Bookers group of companies during the last decades of colonialism.) Local control of the Barbadian industry was the result of a decision taken by Barbadian sugar planters during the sugar crisis of the late nineteenth century. Rather than distributing financial aid offered by the British government among the planters as did their counterparts in the rest of the Caribbean, the Barbadian planters used the aid as seed capital for an agricultural bank. This had the effect of stabilizing the ownership patterns of the industry while creating the framework for local financial institutions.

Thus the sugar industry in Barbados had continued to be in predominately local hands until 1992, when Booker Tate, a British agricultural management company, assumed control. And although the majority of estate land is in white hands, there have been black owners, as well, for generations. Indeed, there was a point in the mid-1980s when both the prime minister and the leader of the opposition came from long-time plantation-owning families. In this small society, the extensive intertwining of politics (and political families) and sugar cannot be understated. This nexus of family connections within the sugar industry was reproduced throughout the private sector as a whole, making private capital markedly less vulnerable to the political pressures for nationalization that prevailed elsewhere, particularly in Guyana and Jamaica. Policies that at first protected local owners and economic interests meant that during the period of decolonization and after, Barbados was able to credibly project an image of itself as a safe haven for foreign investment, a process that sparked the diversification of the economy away from sugar into tourism, manufacturing, and, latterly, offshore services. In all three sectors, foreign direct investment has been the major engine of growth as well as the source of new approaches to management.

Economic Diversification and Postwar Development in Barbados

Understanding external economic circumstances is key to understanding the course of development strategies in Barbados. A favorable international sugar market in the 1940s and 1950s, for example, helped to create the conditions for Barbados's economic fortunes during those years, just as its fluctuations during the 1960s, 1970s, and 1980s mirrored those of its North American trading partners (Worrell 1982:44).[25] When the United States reduced its sugar import quotas for all Caribbean Basin countries between 1979 and 1981, the Barbadian industry suffered badly. Today, plagued simultaneously by its symbolic connection to a history of slavery, low outputs, and the immediate threat of dissolving foreign-guaranteed markets, the sugar industry faces a precarious future.[26] Tourism, also subject to the whims of foreign markets, experienced lean years in the 1980s and early 1990s. Furthermore, tourism is criticized as a contemporary plantation-style playground for foreign whites and charged with creating a society of barmaids, domestics, and busboys and generally perpetuating a history of servitude. The emphasis on (nonagricultural) manufacturing increased in the mid-1950s, and manufacturing quickly became the centerpiece of economic development planning.

In the years just preceding independence, along with the move in 1966 to provide free secondary education in government-assisted schools, came a growing commitment to industrialization. One might say that the two agendas were connected. With universal education and shortly thereafter the establishment of a local campus of the University of the West Indies, the Barbados government gained prestige at home and abroad. Along with these signs of modernization came developments in industrial relations, and in these pre- and early independence years, labor legislation was enacted that insured workers' severance pay and compensation for occupational illness or injury. In this regard, development and industrialization were seen as synonymous. Partnership between government and the private sector characterized both the waning years of the BLP under Grantly Adams and DLP administration of Errol Barrow, which took Barbados into independence in 1966. Social security for the working public was touted as the core of the DLP platform and industrialization as the answer to diversifying away from plantation agriculture. Despite his own family's position as plantation owners, Barrow was long known as "sociopolitically opposed to planter interests" (Beckles 1990:200), a sentiment reflected in the much-quoted speech in which he pledged to hasten the day when not a single blade of cane could be traced on the Barbadian landscape.[27]

Manufacturing within the Caribbean community was long considered the answer to economic self-sufficiency and a sort of spiritual independence. Behind Arthur Lewis's framework (1954) that drove industrialization in the region was the assertion that it would provide the means for transforming the structure of production in primary exporting countries with high rates of unemployment. A combination of import substitution and export orientation therefore became the economic development models of choice. Labor-intensive import-substitution industries were of particular interest in the early industrialization period and later gave way to a stronger export orientation with the implementation of attrac-

Table 2. IDC-Assisted Enterprises: Companies and Employment by Ownership, 1992

Ownership	Companies		Employees	
	No.	% of Total	No.	% of Total
Barbados 100%	149	69.0	2,611	36.1
CARICOM[a] 100%	5	2.3	81	1.1
U.S.A. 100%	17	7.9	2,493	34.4
Canada 100%	8	3.7	194	2.7
Europe 100%	5	2.3	671	9.3
Other foreign	2	0.9	56	0.8
Joint ventures	30	13.9	1,136	15.7
Total	216	100.0	7,242	100.1

Source: Government of Barbados.

Note: Percentages may not total 100 because of rounding.

[a] Caribbean Community.

tive tax holidays and incentives for foreign investors. Through the Pioneer Industries (Encouragement) Act (1951–54) and its revised Pioneer Industries Act (1958), the Industrial Incentives Act (1963), and the Industrial Development Act (1969) for export industries, provisions were made to entice foreign investment into Barbados. Though the industrial acts varied in the length of guaranteed tax-free operation, the last one ensured a ten-year tax holiday, duty-free concessions on raw materials and production equipment imported from outside the region, and provision of subsidized factory shells. Incentives were designed to reduce the cost and to insure the return on investments made by foreign companies. The most recent legislation of this sort is the International Business Companies Act, which offers tax exemption to foreign-financed companies registered or incorporated in Barbados.[28] As of 1992, the IDC-assisted enterprises, that is, all companies (local and foreign) that use IDC facilities, accounted for 72 percent of all jobs in the manufacturing sector (see table 2). Altogether, today, foreign-owned enclave enterprises and IBCS represent roughly 10 percent of all IDC-assisted enterprises, and 50 percent of the total employment in this sector.

As for the governments of other countries following this path, the expectations of the Barbados government in soliciting the investment of foreign corpo-

Table 3. Sectoral Contributions to GDP, 1946–94 (in percent)

	1946	1950	1960	1970	1980	1990	1994
Manufacturing	8.8	7.3	8.0	9.3	12.3	8.0	7.1
Sugar	37.8	41.5	20.3	9.3	6.2	1.9	1.6
Tourism	n.a.	n.a.	n.a.	9.3	12.0	11.4	14.0

Sources: Haynes 1982:82–83; Barbados Statistical Service 1998: Gross Domestic Products by Sector of Origin, 1978–1997.

rations have been essentially three-fold: the creation of jobs, the earning of foreign exchange, and the transfer of technological expertise. While growth in employment through manufacturing did not entirely meet the employment hopes of development planners, this sector did expand during the 1970s, largely because of the expansion beyond food, beverages, tobacco, and soap production for the local market, into clothing and electronics for the export market. Despite noticeable growth in manufactured exports within the Caribbean Community market in the 1960s, by the 1980s an overriding proportion of Barbadian exports went to the North American and European markets.

Barbados focused largely on light manufactures, where wages present the most significant domestic costs. Between 1970 and 1980 the value of export manufactures grew from a mere US$12.5 million to in excess of US$100 million, surpassing sugar in representing the most significant portion of domestic exports (Long 1989:120). While a wise emphasis in terms of start-up, Barbados's needs for jobs, and labor resources, this emphasis also created vulnerability later to competition over labor costs with other countries. Interestingly, Delisle Worrell (1982:14) charted a comparative wage index between Barbados and Mexico in 1982, foreshadowing the current anxieties in the Eastern Caribbean associated with the North American Free Trade Agreement (NAFTA), which formally brought Mexico further into the competitive trading fold. He shows that while recession had slowed the growth of wages in Barbados relative to those in Mexico after 1973, Mexican rates still undercut the Barbados wages by at least two to one. Manufacturing, therefore, lasted as the keystone of the development plan a mere twenty years, from its beginnings in the mid-1960s to the mid-1980s. During that time, Barbados's relative advantage in wage costs was eroded in the face of Asian and Latin American competition. Even within the region. Barbados's sta-

Table 4. Foreign Exchange Contribution of Leading Sectors, 1946–90 (in percent)

	1946	1950	1960	1970	1980	1990
Manufacturing	7.1	5.8	8.5	9.0	18.4	9.9
Sugar	55.0	65.7	53.1	17.1	8.4	3.3
Tourism	19.6	15.2	24.4	31.3	41.0	53.1

Sources: Central Bank of Barbados: Balance of Payments, 1996 and 1998; Economic and Financial Statistics, April 1999.

ble currency in effect priced labor out of the export market as the currencies of Jamaica, Trinidad and Tobago, and Guyana became devalued. Today, manufacturing exists largely with the help of tariff walls, which are becoming harder to defend in the free-trade orthodoxy that now dominates policy at lending agencies and among trading partners such as the United States, Canada, and to a lesser extent, the European Economic Community.

During this same period, tourism was launched as an expanding industry and became an important contributor to a rapidly increasing gross domestic product (GDP). Representing only 2 percent of the real GDP in 1956, tourism grew exponentially to become the leading economic sector in the 1960s and 1970s (see table 3). Expanding trends in the international tourist market in the 1960s reflected the increased availability of jet transport, rising incomes in the industrial countries, and increased marketing. Similarly, increased air transportation costs and high inflation rates slowed the growth of tourism in the early to mid-1970s (Worrell 1982:10). In the 1980s tourism stabilized at just over 28 percent of GDP (Howard 1989:68). As a direct creator of employment, tourism has not been as fruitful as manufacturing, though its informal employment is estimated to be larger and more difficult to measure (Levy and Lerch 1991). Estimates of direct employment in the tourism sector have hovered between 3.7 and 4.7 percent of the labor force between 1970 and 1985, and for indirect employment, between 7 and 10 percent (Howard 1989:73–74). Although tourism generates huge inflows of foreign exchange (see table 4), at least 70 percent of gross foreign exchange earnings are leaked back out of the domestic economy to pay for tourism inputs such as hotel supplies, fuel oil, food.[29]

Since the mid-1970s, member countries of the Caribbean Community (with the exception of Trinidad and Tobago during the oil boom years) have experienced deepening economic recession (Bennett 1987:22). Declining foreign exchange earned from exports as a result of the global economic recession led to increased borrowing, and Jamaica and Guyana continue to reel from their levels of indebtedness. The Caribbean Basin Initiative (CBI) was originally presented by the Reagan administration in 1983 to promote trade and capital flows between the Caribbean and the United States.[30] "Security through development" was its explicit strategy, and development was conceived as the promotion of export industrialization within the region. The CBI represented the economic dimension of U.S. policy toward the region more generally elaborated in the Caribbean Basin Economic Recovery Act. At the core of the program were provisions for duty-free access to the U.S. market for a range of Caribbean exports along with tax concessions for U.S. investors in the region. Because of the strength of particular lobbying groups in the United States, certain Caribbean exports were barred from these concessions, (e.g., textiles and apparels, leather products, tuna, and petroleum and petroleum by-products). In 1983, leather goods, garments, and petroleum had constituted over half of Caribbean Basin exports to the United States. While manufacturing exports indeed increased between 1983 and 1989, the fastest-growing export was garments, which were excluded from the duty-free concession. Indeed, the export products that seemed to pose the greatest potential for growth (textiles and apparel) were precisely those that were excluded under the legislation (Deere and Melendez n.d.; Deere et al. 1990; Klak 1993). In recognition of this conundrum, Reagan introduced a special addendum in the form of program 807-A, which allowed higher quotas for garments assembled in the region but cut in the United States from U.S. fabrics. The most substantial outcome of the CBI was the extent to which Caribbean economies were integrated into the U.S. economy. Barbados, for example, which had directed only 7 percent of its exports to the U.S. in the early 1960s, was channeling 53 percent of its exports by the 1980s. The integration was mirrored in imports as well, as Barbados found itself importing greater proportions of foreign goods from the United States (Deere et al. 1990:164).

The Barbados government articulates its projected development plan for 1993 and beyond as a collaboration between public and private sectors and in keeping with a "mixed economic model." Moving away from manufacturing, the service sector is envisioned with the dominant role. Export-led development lies at the core of the economic plan, resembling that of many developing countries at the turn of the century faced with mounting demands for imported goods and a shift away from agricultural economies. Manufacturing and sugar, the cornerstones of the export economy since independence, experienced contraction during the recession of the early 1980s and again in the latter part of the decade. The exports revealing growth trends have tended to be those previously titled 806.3 and 807 of the U.S. Tariff Code, which imposed duties only on the foreign value added in the offshore production process, and thus made foreign export subsidiaries attractive to U.S. multinationals. Other exports from the region, however, demonstrated declines following the CBI. Most notably, petroleum and mining exports, which had accounted for 70 percent of all Caribbean Basin exports by 1989, dropped to 34 percent of the value of total exports. Agriculture, which had represented 22 percent, saw its proportion drop to 8 percent, while manufacturing, which began at 8 percent, jumped to 31 percent of all exports (Deere and Melendez n.d.:3).

However, the significant question for export industries is the amount of value added, or what the Central Bank captures in foreign exchange as a result of the export production. Net foreign exchange proceeds from sugar are estimated to be 90 percent, for example, while garments assembly generally averages at most 25 percent. The typical export assembly operation in Barbados and elsewhere in the developing world has hired young women at low wages to perform low-skilled jobs, requiring little investment in training and minimal capital investment. In other words, these have generally been low value-added industries, and considering the investments in infrastructure to house such operations, and the low tax concessions allotted them, it is not surprising that little in the way of fiscal gains were reported from the CBI's promotion of light manufacturing exports (Deere et al. 1990).

As in most export processing arenas of developing countries, textiles and electronics assembly have represented the most significant areas of employment, particularly for women. In Barbados since the 1960s, increases in female employment corresponded directly to the growth in precisely these industries. Between 1986 and 1991, however, textiles lost 572 jobs and electronics 824 jobs, whereas data processing grew by 1,054 jobs. The most recent figure for the female labor force participation rate in Barbados stands at 56.6 percent—very high when compared with figures of 15 percent for Latin America, 24 percent for Africa, and 29 percent for Asia.[31] Unemployment during the period of fieldwork was also high, 25.9 percent among women and 19.3 percent for men (with an overall percentage of 22.4), and women's employment overall continues to be concentrated in low-wage, low-skilled service jobs.

The most recent statistics for employment distribution in the industrial sec-

Table 5. Female Employment in Manufacturing, 1946–94

	1946	1960	1966	1970	1979	1991	1994
As a percentage of							
Total employment in manufacturing	14.4	19.0	27.1	39.2	53.0	54.1	53.0
Total female employment	1.2	2.3	5.6	13.4	12.5	12.0	12.0
Female participation rate (%)[a]							
Overall	55.7	42.4	40.2	39.1	42.5	57.4	61.5
In manufacturing	0.6	1.1	2.3	5.2	5.3	5.4	5.7

Sources: Cox 1982:63; Barbados Statistical Service 1996: Continuous Labour Force Sample Survey Report, 1987–1995.

[a] Ratio of females employed to total females aged 15 and over.

tor (industries assisted by the IDC) reflect similar patterns of heavy representation of women (see table 5), though now data processing employs a greater number of women than any other single subsector (roughly 2,500, or 2 percent of the total labor force). In services, which have always been a stronghold of female employment, there has been little evidence, until recently, of occupational diversification. The vast majority of women in services are still performing domestic work. Furthermore, the increase in importance of services with the expansion of the tourist industry, as in manufacturing, has been accompanied by a reduction in the numerical predominance of women as well as a sexually stratified job hierarchy (Gill and Massiah 1984; Levy and Lerch 1991). Men occupy the majority of managerial and white-collar service jobs, while women are concentrated within jobs seen to be tied to their so-called natural feminine domestic domain, such as housekeeping, waitressing, and sewing. Despite their high labor-force participation rates generally, women continue to be concentrated in a few sectors that have become traditional female preserves, and despite the optimism associated with some women's recent entrance into politics and other traditionally male professions, as many as 85 percent of women in professional areas are teachers and nurses. Political power and decision making in both the public and private sectors of the economy continue to rest predominantly in men's hands (Barrow 1986a:19).

The heavy export emphasis of development planning has long been criticized by dependency theorists. As Michael Howard (1989:19) puts it, despite the employment created and foreign exchange generated, ownership stays largely in foreign hands and the control of industry is increasingly handed over to non-nationals. Confirming the sense of vulnerability associated with foreign owned industry, INTEL, the large electronics assembly operation employing over one thousand Barbadian workers (largely women), closed its doors in 1985 after it reached the end of its ten-year tax holiday. In the face of relaxing trade barriers, however, and increasing fluidity across the international economy, even some of the staunchest critics of "free-market" growth (e.g., Jamaica's People's National Party, Cuba's communist government) are now in the process of opening themselves up to foreign markets. In view of the consolidation of the European Community and (NAFTA), small island economies in the Caribbean are anxiously proposing strategies to better secure their economic futures and can see little way around the export oriented free market model. As Harvey notes, the intensification of transnationalism has put nation-states in an increasingly uncomfortable position, squeezed between promoting themselves to foreign capital investors and keeping local capitalists happy. "The state is now in a much more problematic position. It is called upon to regulate the activities of corporate capital in the national interest at the same time as it is forced, also in the national interest, to create a 'good business climate' to act as an inducement to trans-national and global finance capital, and to deter [by means other than exchange controls] capital flight to greener and more profitable pastures" (Harvey 1989:170).

Given this recent economic and political climate, the importance of the off-shore information sector has become even more central to the island's development plan. But the wheels were set in motion for establishing an enclave of high-tech information services almost two decades ago. The labor and infrastructural context for high-tech industrial development in Barbados are touted as ideally suited, and despite higher labor rates than some of her regional neighbors, Barbados was targeted early in the emergence of offshore information services as an ideal location for fledgling operations.

Particularly relevant for the information industry are the modern (though expensive) telecommunications facilities, including leased circuits for continual and exclusive use by a company (for transmission of voice, facsimile, and data communications), a satellite earth station, and low-cost custom-designed office/factory spaces. In terms of human resources, Barbados boasts a 98 percent literacy rate and, thanks to state-funded universal education, a well-educated, English-speaking labor force. Additionally, the simple geographical proximity and ease of travel as well as time zone concordance with the east coast of the United States have been significant drawing cards for companies contemplating the offshore movement of labor-intensive back office work.[32] The comfortable climate, political stability, and unblemished reputation as a safe and hospitable tourist destination have also been factors in managers' consideration of Barbados over other Caribbean territories.[33]

As part of its foreign investment development scheme, Barbados offers several incentives to investors that qualify for international business company status: duty free import/export of all raw materials and equipment required (e.g., computer hardware and software, office furniture, and other equipment for the data entry facilities); assistance in recruitment of workers and start-up grants to offset the cost of training them (US$35 a week per employee for eight weeks); subsidized rental of factory and office shells equipped with all the necessary specifications (telephone phone lines, electricity, space dividers, carpeting, etc.); no income tax required of nonresidents; and most important, a specially reduced tax rate of only 2.5 percent on profits.

The general manager of one of the newest offshore insurance claims processing operations listed among the many advantages Barbados offers over several other potential sites wage rates roughly half of those in Toronto, where his company is based. Wages in Ireland, he said, were lower than in Barbados, but the volatility of the Irish pound was cause for concern. At the time the company was investigating new sites, for example, the exchange between the Canadian dollar and the pound was Can$ 1.50 to I£ 1.00 It went quickly to Can$ 1.90 to I£ 1.00 and now stands at Can$ 2.00 to I£ 1.00. The Dominican Republic was considered as another possible site, but the political climate was deemed "too unstable," and the unreliability of electricity, problematic. Other Caribbean countries such as St. Lucia and Grenada, he said, were simply lacking in the necessary technological infrastructure and guaranteed power supply to make them serious contenders.

During the 1990s eleven offshore data processing firms were reported to be located in Barbados, employing 2,306 workers—representing 23.9 percent of those employed in all manufacturing industries and leading the way above textiles, garments, and leather and electronics (see table 6). Anticipating further growth in this area, the IDC has expanded its investment in infrastructure for the newly built information processing "zone," and has vastly increased spending for building and renovating suitable spaces for these "open offices." Now exceeding traditional manufacturing in employment, the capital investment demanded

Table 6. IDC-Assisted Enterprises: Employment by Subsector and Gender, 1990

Subsector	Companies		Employees			
	Number	% of All Companies	Male	Female	Total	% of All Employees
Food, beverages, and tobacco	30	13.9	531	252	783	10.8
Textiles, garments, and leather	37	17.1	234	1,268	1,502	20.7
Wooden products	24	11.1	208	86	294	4.1
Paper products and printing	16	7.4	259	193	452	6.2
Chemicals and toiletries	15	6.9	221	111	332	4.6
Plastic products	9	4.2	108	59	167	2.3
Nonmetallic mineral products	6	2.8	138	22	160	2.2
Fabricated metal products	24	11.1	451	154	605	8.4
Precision instruments and electrical equipment	2	.9	29	52	81	1.1
Electronics	12	5.6	101	798	899	12.4
Handicraft	21	9.7	25	67	92	1.3
Other manufacturing	9	4.2	53	92	145	2.0
Data processing	11	5.1	154	1,576	1,730	23.9

Source: Barbados Statistical Service 1991.

by data entry in terms of "factory" space and training also outweigh those of a manufacturing plant.

Given all the attractions of Barbados as a site, the IDC sees tremendous potential for generating employment through informatics and has mounted an aggressive promotional campaign. Further, its importance as a symbol of future growth and change in terms of computer technology and the information revolution cannot be underestimated in a society for which education has been given high priority. Ralph Henry, generally critical of the overriding export-led development scheme of Arthur Lewis, ends a recent essay in much the same vein as the Barbados government development plan. "Knowledge based industries and services" he says, are the key both to Caribbean development and to the incorporation of women into its mainstream in the context of our new internationalized economy. The "dynamic human resource model," as he calls it, will transform the Caribbean out of neocolonial dependency and into a horizontal relationship of external trade (Henry 1988:21). And similarly, Michael Howard's final words in *Dependence and Development in Barbados, 1945–1985* (1989), note that the future demands greater collaboration between public and private sectors and that data processing and other offshore financial services offer new hope in the waning moments of a failing manufacturing-based development strategy.

Labor Force, Trade Unions, and Women's Work in Offshore Informatics

Despite a long history of trade unionism in Barbados and the well-known strength of the Barbados Workers Union, the largest industrial workers union representing a number of public and private sector trades and occupations, foreign-owned data entry companies are uniformly nonunionized. The Industrial Development Corporation claims that within the industrial relations context of the island, "collective bargaining is the accepted practice for the agreement of employment terms and conditions, but union membership is not compulsory" (IDC n.d.:14). However, as one labor unionist from the Barbados Workers Union described labor and the offshore sector, "there is a sort of unwritten understanding that [the unions] are not to go in there." While several union representatives expressed both annoyance at being kept out of these offshore industries and keen interest in recruiting within this expanding new sector, during the DLP-led years of the fieldwork (1989–92) they avoided any strong efforts to unionize. They stated matter-of-factly that in the face of rising unemployment, and the government's strong push to recruit foreign investment, there was little point in making waves within established offshore operations. And not surprisingly, from the management standpoint, the consensus was quietly but clearly against unionization. As one foreign general manager put it, "I'm not against unions; I used to be a union man. Unions have a role to play, but obviously as a manager of a company I would prefer to work without them. I can respond to problems without the interference of a middleman who is motivated by political ends." His comment reflected a current and widely held sentiment toward the Barbados Workers Union, whose leader was a central member of the DLP around whom frequent charges of "conflict of interest" revolved.

The quiet agreement by the unions to keep out of the offshore enterprises reflects, to a large degree, their compliance with the export-led economic development plan as articulated by the state and clearly espoused by the then-ruling DLP. Though no official free trade zone exists in Barbados as such, the industrial parks that house the offshore industrial enterprises and data entry operations effectively constitute free zones in providing the same sorts of fiscal incentives and effectively preventing union organization. On the other hand, foreign investors have found that Barbadian labor legislation in some instances imposes even more stringent conditions than those under which they operated in North America (e.g., maternity benefits, vacation, sick leave, overtime, and severance pay requirements are closely enforced). For companies that run sweatshoplike operations with recent immigrant and sometimes illegal workers in their home countries, the benefits and conditions demanded by the Barbadian state far outweigh those provided in their northern shops.[34] Barbados's labor legislation dictates no established minimum wage, though suggested wage rates set out by the IDC for foreign investors tend to represent roughly 50 percent of wages for comparable work in the United States and Canada (see table 7).[35] Along the lines of the International Labor Organization Protection of Wages Convention of 1949, Barbadian law also establishes a number of additional provisions.[36]

One of the goals of this work is to explore the directions being taken in Barbados's attempt to pursue information services as an economic development path and to evaluate the implications of this strategy for the national economy as well as for the informatics workers themselves. While no single grand theoretical movement has supplanted the dependency/plantation economy paradigm in the Caribbean, some recent treatments of the specific nature of the region's place within the global economy have shed new light on these issues and challenged their parameters. Especially provocative has been a growing concern with gender and the specific implications of industrialization and the restructuring of capital and labor within the lives of women workers and their families. Recent works have contested conventional gender-neutral labor market theories and class analyses and made significant contributions to analyses of economic development (Acevedo 1995; Beneria and Roldan 1987; Mies 1986; Nash and Fernandez-Kelly 1983; Nash and Safa 1986; Ong 1988; Wolkowitz and Mc-Cullagh 1981). Originally an outgrowth of the women in development school (Boserup 1970; Chaney and Schmink 1980), these themes are being addressed in varying ways in the Caribbean context, responding both to general development theories and the historical specificity of Caribbean social formations (Antrobus 1988; Henry 1988; Bolles 1983, 1996; Massiah 1986, 1989; Safa 1986a, 1995). The general theoretical premise of many of these works continues to be that of dependency, though most make clear that the Caribbean as "periphery" is not merely a pawn manipulated by the whims of metropolitan capital. These approaches not only emphasize the central role played by women in these

Table 7. Average Wage Rates by Pay Period, 1990

Job Title	Wage Range (US$)
	Hourly
Data entry trainees	1.44 – 1.55
Data entry operators	2.00 – 2.55
Preprocessors	1.60 – 2.23
Data entry supervisors	3.75 – 6.00
Typesetter (trainee)	1.75
Proofreader (trainee)	1.75
	Weekly
Sewing machine (trainee)	44
Sewing machine operator	58 – 70
Quality control	75 – 93
Sewing machine mechanics	102 – 176
Production supervisor	85 – 125
Electronics assembly (trainee)	50
Electronics assembly (skilled)	63 – 80
Electronic technicians	150 – 170
Artisan / woodworker	91 – 150
Agricultural worker	77 – 100
Equipment technician	95 – 175
Production coordinator	175 – 250
	Monthly
Accounts clerk	450 – 750
Clerk typist	400 – 700
Secretary	750 – 1,000
Accountant (trained)	1,500 – 3,000
Plant manager	1,500 – 3,500
Programmer	1,000 – 1,750

Source: IDC n.d.:15.

economic transformations but begin to elucidate the fundamentally gendered global practices and ideologies on which they are based.

State as well as local corporate interests, what Leslie Sklair (1991) refers to as the "transnational capitalist class" together shape the particular economic development strategies and diversification initiatives across the Caribbean region, like that of the developing world in general, and Barbados's informatics sector is an important example of such innovation. In this instance, foreign-led developments have spawned significant growth of local involvement (as joint venture partners or owners and managers) in a new "postindustrial" service area well suited to this small, densely populated, well-educated, English-speaking island. Again, as with the modernization and dependency theorists before them, the majority of today's analysts of these global transformations fail to emphasize, however, the central role played by local women workers in facilitating these new expressions of economic flexibility (e.g., Appadurai 1991; Gunder Frank and Gills 1993; Harvey 1989; Sklair 1991; Wallerstein 1974, 1993; Waters 1995). Feminist critics and postcolonial scholars such as Cynthia Enloe and Chandra Talpade Mohanty emphasize both the central role played by women in nationalist and development initiatives, as well as the confluence of gender and race in shaping their local position as social actors in this global arena. They remind us of the importance of history and of local specificity in coming to grips with what globalization means for everyday people "on the ground." Such approaches are now finding expression within the Caribbean, particularly among postcolonial scholars who themselves live transnational lives.[37] It has become more and more clear that when looking at the changing configurations of labor, capital, and industry in today's global economy, one cannot grasp these fundamental and radical transformations without attending to the changing shape of women's work, family lives, and gender ideologies. For Caribbean women, who have always been defined as workers, their challenges to what have seemed to be ubiquitous transnational prescriptions for particular kinds of feminine labor represent a crucial starting place for rethinking the relationships between local and global cultural economies, especially because transnational production and consumption are the tradition of Caribbean societies and are not radical departures from their histories. The new permutations of this globalized economy and culture as they take shape in and are transformed by the Afro-Barbadian women workers in this study form the crux of the following chapters.

The incorporation of women into industry is not a new phenomenon. In fact, many parallels may be drawn between nineteenth-century Europe and New England, and twentieth-century Asia, Latin America, and the Caribbean. A century ago, mills and factories in towns and growing urban areas drew girls and young women away from rural areas and out of their homes. Women's work became defined no longer in terms of household labor needs but in terms of the household's need for capital (Lin 1987). In both periods, employers have justified hiring young women on the basis of the secondary nature of their wage supplementary to that of a male breadwinner. Social taboos and stigmas surrounding factory work reveal similarities in both periods; while families welcomed contributions to the household income, concern for women as the bearers of moral value and the backbone of the family was expressed as widely in the nineteenth century as it is in Asia and Central and Latin America today (Lin 1987). Drawing parallels of this kind is both useful and problematic. They are useful in that many of the similarities that link Barbadian women in this new offshore industry with women in New England mill towns of the turn of the century or Mexican maquiladora workers on the border are striking dimensions of industrialization and proletarianization. But the feminization of labor is not a singular or simple phenomenon in which "global womanhood" can be tapped as a limitless reservoir of well-mannered and willing workers.[38]

It is crucial, then, to analyze the convergences of women's experiences in geographical and historical contexts as they are incorporated into new arenas of work, as well as to highlight the ways in which the specificity of postindustrial, late-twentieth-century capitalism, the peculiar nature of informatics as an industry situated between blue- and white-collar labor, and the particular context of Barbadian culture have created different meanings and experiences for this particular group of working women. While there are historical and cultural continuities, there are also historical and cultural specificities marking the distinct ways in which women become pink-collar workers on this small island in the Caribbean sea.

Within the informatics industry itself, the extent to which the Barbadian workers are conscious of their place within this global economy and their counterparts in North America, other Caribbean countries, and Central and South America, Europe, and Asia is difficult to ascertain. The relationship between local conditions and experiences and the transnational nature of their companies is seldom explicitly raised. While industry critics bemoan the easy and unexpected flight of offshore companies in general, the informatics workers rarely express these worries. Those with experience in other industries or with mothers or sisters who were laid off with previous plant closures are most aware of that possibility within the data entry industry. As one data processor said:

> I think there is always the fear that Data Air could leave like INTEL did, because everyone knows that if the work doesn't get done, they'll find somebody else to do it. If the quality of the work is good and they can see further use for us, then it's good for the business. [For] what we're doing . . . the cost is cheaper than having it done in the States. . . . It's something that more and more people would be getting into, and I think it could be very big, but it all depends on if the market is out there for things like this. Everything is being computerized and there is a lot of room for growth in the industry. . . . What these big corporations want is usually what the world wants so [the direction of informatics] would mostly depend on them.

An incident in which a check receipt from an American keyer for Data Air accidentally appeared in a Barbadian keyer's envelope as a result of centralized payrolls made the production workers painfully conscious of the relative wage scale across the industry. "Well, you can imagine what people said when they saw what the people up there were working for—doing the same thing as us. [Can] you imagine seeing somebody's stub—somebody doing actually the same thing as us, and they are working for much much much much more money?" Data processors intent on publicizing information about comparative conditions (wages) quietly and widely distributed this U.S. pay stub across the production floor at Data Air. In a small way, their indignation also registered their consciousness of the international division of labor that marks their lives. What they are even less likely to realize, however, is that Dominican operators working for the same company and doing roughly the same jobs are getting paid about half the wage they earn in Barbados.

Chapter 4

Myths of Docile Girls

and Matriarchs:

Local Profiles

of Global Workers

Across the production floors of Data Air and Multitext, amid colorful poulazzo skirt suits and the latest styles of hair weaves and fashion jewelry, scarcely a male voice is heard, or shirt and tie in view.[1] Why are the offshore data entry operations in Barbados, like a variety of multinational industries the world over, filled with women workers? Do these data processors match the international profile of the "ideal" offshore factory workers across the developing world? Simple though these questions appear, and consistent though the replies they prompt tend to be (among local and foreign corporate managers, development officers, and workers themselves), the answers are not self-evident. I begin this chapter by challenging the assumption that women around the world constitute a cheap, available, and therefore "ideal" and ready-made source of labor for multinational corporations aiming to cut costs by relocating production facilities abroad. By drawing on the historical realities of women's work in Barbados from the previous chapter and describing the current (and divergent) profiles of Barbadian informatics workers, I show that rather than "tapping reserves" of local women, multinational industries engage in complex and active processes of incorporation—actually creating ideal workers for particular sorts of offshore production.

This process of incorporation relies heavily on particular formulations of gender, and in particular, of femininity. The "young and malleable" "docile girl" is, without a doubt, the most idealized caricature of the global assembly line worker. Multinational industrialists and representatives from third world governments have for more than two decades recited a litany of rationales for why young, single, childless, and well-educated women represent the ideal labor force for their corner of global production. Indeed, they take for granted the abundant existence of precisely this type of female worker in nearly every part of the world.[2] The following comments are typical explanations, from both ends of the spectrum in the informatics industry in Barbados for why export industries hire predominantly women workers.

> I suppose the men would get frustrated just sitting there keying all the time; most men like to know they're moving around or delivering something. (Angela, an informatics worker, 1990)

> Women tend to do light assembly work which involves sitting and manipulating fine objects. Some persons claim that men don't have that good coordination. . . . I think it might more be a matter of aptitude, and aptitude is probably cultivated by your society and so on. A man is seen in movies and in real life doing things, moving and so on. A man is never seen sitting . . . especially on a line manipulating fine things. And he may not have the practice. . . . Women have had practice manipulating needles and doing fine intricate things, embroidery or cake icing, or being more delicate. And also they have smaller hands, so if you're going to manipulate fine things their physical structure may have some impact. . . . Whatever the reason is, it so happens that women tend to do data entry, garments, electronics assembly, and men tend to do heavier work. (Representative of the Barbados Industrial Development Corporation, 1990)

Such sentiments are echoed virtually everywhere across the global assembly line—from Mexico to the Philippines, even in contexts in which the patterns of recruitment have shown signs of change. The fact that these gendered rationales are given voice in Barbados presents a number of ironies, in the light of both historical and contemporary realities of women's work on this small Afro-Caribbean island.

This chapter explores the international corporate prescriptions and the Barbadian realities in which the profile of the ideal worker for this new high-tech service sector is negotiated. It reveals some intriguing contradictions in both managers' and workers' conceptualizations, presenting twists in the long-held portrayal of young and docile female workers that relate to both historical and contemporary aspects of Barbadian social life, family and household formations, patterns of industrialization, and the competing gender ideologies that underlie them. In turn, they demonstrate the prescriptive and adaptive capacities of international corporate capital and particular cultural localities as they reshape themselves in relation to each other.

Why Do Women Make "Ideal" Global Factory Workers?

Several excellent studies of the new international division of labor have shed light on the sorts of prerequisites sought by foreign companies establishing offshore industries in developing countries (e.g., Fröbel, Heinrichs, and Kreye 1980; Harvey 1989; Henderson and Castells 1987; Sklair 1991). Among these are generous tax holidays, a peaceful political climate, the absence of trade union organization, low rent on production facilities, and well-appointed factory shells. In addition to these incentives multinationals have generally been drawn to regions where industrial, community, and family life are strongly influenced by patriarchal relations. Mention is often made by government development officers and corporate representatives of large and available pools of untapped female labor, with the promise that these women make up an ideal and previously ignored reservoir of malleable workers. In fact, cheap labor in the form of young women workers has been described as the single most important factor in the international movements of labor intensive industries, such as garments and electronics, and gender has played a fundamental role in constituting vast labor forces around the world.[3]

Women's youthful and strong bodies are advertised by industrialists and national government representatives around the world as ideally suited for meticulous work and long hours of tedious labor. Their fingers are described as nimble and dexterous and used to fine-detail work from traditional feminine arts of embroidery, sewing, and other needlecrafts. Women are presumed to possess a natural innocence, inexperience, and eagerness to learn that insure a temperament that is ideally suited, as well. Their positions within their families and within third world economies are also integral to many foreign companies' notions of their suitability. They are assumed to be socialized within "traditional," often rural households where patriarchal relations dictate obedient behavior on the part of daughters, and their employment may even have been arranged by a male member of the family. Their status as daughter, furthermore, is said to imply that while their wage will contribute to the household economy, it is not the primary source of support. Their single and childless status insures their availability and undivided sense of responsibility to work. Their youth and recent completion of secondary school (a requirement for many offshore industries at the upper tier of export production sectors, including informatics) implies that they are literate, disciplined to the rhythm of a regimented day, and first-time wage earners. In brief, these young women in terms both of "body" and "mentality," as individuals or as members of households, families, communities, and the international marketplace, have come to represent the quintessential offshore assembly worker across the globe.

There is a long historical precedent for conceiving women workers as "reserve armies of labor." Following Karl Marx's lead, Harry Braverman (1974:383) used this notion to describe the process of capital accumulation, whereby an industrial pool of labor can be incorporated or discarded as wage workers as required by capital. Braverman argues that with increased rationalization of a wide range of work (in both industrial and service areas) as well as increased geographical mobility of these jobs, larger numbers of workers are recruited into employed and then reserve armies of labor. The reserve army functions as a flexible reservoir of labor that responds to the demands of capital and now serves as a cheap labor source for expanding service industries. Recent work has turned attention to the fact that women have systematically been drawn into these footloose industries. Braverman (1974:385) notes that "women form the ideal reservoir of labor for the new mass occupations. The barrier confining women to much lower pay scales is reinforced by the vast numbers in which they are available to capital." Women are presented as constituting massive pools of labor, patiently waiting for the tides of capital to pull them into wage work for the first time. And, by definition, women as low wage workers are logically concentrated in those industrial sectors of the economy undergoing rationalization.

This argument has formed the core of several works by anthropologists and sociologists specifically addressing the expansion of export production and multinational factories around the world and the incorporation of women workers into these new industries (Fernandez-Kelly 1983; Nash and Fernandez-Kelly 1983; Ong 1987; Safa 1983, 1990, 1995; Wolf 1992). Without problematizing the logic behind the equation of women and cheap labor, however, we risk repeating the tautology that women make up a natural source of low-wage workers because women are paid less than men. Luz del Alba Acevedo (1995:90, citing Redclift 1985) expresses the relationship as follows: "female labor is advantageous because women are economically dependent, and they are dependent because they are low paid!" Why and how women's labor comes to be defined as "cheap" is, in fact, a complex process in which gender is created, contested, and refashioned in particular, culturally specific ways. Women are no more "naturally" cheap labor than they are "naturally" docile or nimble fingered relative to men. And even when, as a group, they are defined in these terms across cultural locales, the ways in which women's work is defined as cheaper than or different from men's bear their own cultural and historically grounded marks. Understanding this process requires that we look not only at sexual divisions of labor and the structures of labor markets but also at the ideologies that underlie their "logic."

Historical analyses of labor and households have demonstrated that the incorporation of women workers into low-wage labor-intensive jobs is not a new phenomenon. Textile mills and factories of the early nineteenth century revealed similar patterns and rationales for hiring large numbers of women workers, as young "mill girls" formed the image of prototypic wage-earning women in expanding industrial enclaves (Tilly and Scott 1978:63). The relationships, however, between international, local, and household economies, as well as between the state and individual, family, cultural, and corporate conceptions of female labor are historically, culturally, and industry specific (Hartmann 1976; Westwood 1988; Beechey 1987).

The informatics sector in Barbados raises two issues that prompted my persistent questioning of the portrait of the "docile girl" as the universal "ideal" worker in global industries. The first relates to recruitment. Given the clerical white-collar association with computer-based work, I wondered whether even higher educational levels and skills would be demanded than are required in traditional offshore industries and whether the emphasis on youth and first-time work status would continue to be preferred or assumed. Early reports of some other countries entering the offshore informatics business (e.g., Ireland and India) observed that data entry was not a strictly female domain.[4] When offshore data entry work first began in the Republic of Ireland in the late 1970s, a large proportion of men were hired as operators. Indeed, it is particularly noteworthy that in Data Air's sister plant in the Dominican Republic, roughly 40 percent of the operators are men performing virtually the same data entry jobs as their Bajan counterparts.[5] Informatics' predominantly feminine profile in the Barbadian context, therefore, needed explanation.[6] Would the introduction of this impressive computer-centered industry invite greater numbers of men to enter what have been largely female enclaves of offshore production? Related to this point, there has also been some suspicion that clerical workers represent a different (higher) class of workers than factory workers, and the distinction poses important questions in the light of the official placement of the data entry sector under the same umbrella as traditional export industries. In short, I wondered whether the informatics workers represent a group of women workers distinct from their counterparts in the garment and electronics assembly plants that surround them.

A second set of questions relates to the realm of gender ideology and practice in Barbados and the contradiction between the history of Afro-Caribbean women as workers and mothers whose dual roles have been important to Barbadian society and economy (as well as to defining womanhood itself) and the depiction by multinational corporations of third world workers' femininity as "docile and submissive." The portrait of West Indian femininity that emerges from a wide range of sources related to Afro-Caribbean culture—including ethnographic literature on kinship, social structure, and women's work, and fiction, poetry, and music by and about Caribbean women—is not that of the "docile and submissive" woman worker. More common, especially in the realm of labor, are portraits of strong, resilient, resourceful, and hardworking matriarchs, such as those honored by calypsonian Adonijah.

Woman helped to build this nation
She helped it advance,
So when you sing, please give her a chance.[7]
She cut the cane to make the sugar,
Make parts for computer,
Is doctor, teacher, lawyer.
She can do more than dance.
It takes two, if we must go on,
Without woman, the human race is gone.
Jah, Jah, know what I sing is true.
Is time to give the woman her due.

(Chorus)
She is mother of our children, bearer of life,
My queen, my friend, my woman, my wife.
Come with me, hand in hand,
We will guide you to the promised land.

Ideal and Real Ideologies of Femininity and the Legacy
of Reputation and Respectability

Virtually all accounts of gender ideologies in the Caribbean identify a gap between socially prescribed and ideal notions of masculinity and femininity and what goes on in the "real" lives of the majority of Afro-Caribbean people. The models are internalized, as Erna Brodber says (1982:55), as "right" if not as "possible." For the majority of lower-class Afro-West Indians, the gap between "real" and "ideal" is wide and, some would say, insurmountable.[8] Despite this distance, the power of the ideal, according to much of Caribbean studies, poses a particular problem for women, especially poor, hardworking Afro-Caribbean women who find themselves held to this ideal (Brodber 1982:21; Hodge 1982:ix; Senior 1991:41).[9] Invariably, the ideal/real dualism is configured around traditions linked to the cultural roots of West Indian society itself—Europe and Africa and the implications of the ideals for the realities of both men and women are profound.[10]

The combination of slavery's brutality (culturally and in every other sense) and the fact that for Caribbean societies like Barbados there existed no indigenous or "native" culture prior to colonization has led many cultural analysts to argue that women and men in this part of the world have faced an unparalleled struggle to counter the Western metropolitan culture of their masters—and for Barbadian women this has been the Victorian cult of femininity (Hodge 1982). According to Senior (1991:41), "historically, the model for 'right behavior' for women in the Caribbean was an imported one—the model which emerged elsewhere in Western society: that of woman as a being whose purpose is derived from the existence of another, whether husband, father, or extended family, and whose locus is the home or household."

No iteration of this dualism could be better known (and better critiqued) than that by Peter Wilson, through the gendered paradigm of reputation and respectability.[11] The reputation/respectability model polarizes masculine/feminine traits, physical spheres, and cultural traditions such that Afro-Caribbean masculinity is said to draw its forms of expression (verbal wit and displays of male prowess and virility) and primary loci of activity (public spaces, such as rum shops and street corners) from African roots, and Afro-Caribbean femininity is depicted as mirroring the conventions of European womanhood.[12] If reputation is best demonstrated through informal, face-to-face, noninstitutional exchanges, respectability is best embodied in the interior domains and associated values of the church and home—Christian morality, propriety, and decorum.[13] Legal marriage is perhaps the penultimate demonstration of respectability and, as such, is described as desirable and achievable for men as well, though typically at a later life stage. Where Wilson makes much of the separate spheres and separate "value systems" of men and women along these African/European derived lines, others have emphasized greater fluidity across these divisions.[14] The mapping of femininity onto respectability and masculinity onto reputation, however, continues to be a salient theme in analyses of Caribbean gender. The commentary and revision of the reputation/respectability model tends largely to dismiss the relevance of respectability and the portrayal of Afro-Caribbean women as striving mimics of their white European masters and mistresses (Barrow 1998). Meanwhile, the realm of reputation, that set of values and practices grounded in African tradition and embodying a sense of "comunitas" across those of a low social status, is subtly held to represent what is "real" and true to Caribbean culture (see Miller 1994).

In this study I see reputation and respectability, not as isolated, ideal types purely derived from their African/European origins, but rather as a persistent and fluid dialectic within contemporary creolized Caribbean culture. The tensions that emerge within and across these ideologies and associated practices of reputation and respectability continue to surface in Barbadian social life, and they manifest themselves in multiple and contradictory ways. The fact that throughout West Indian women's history the desire for and sheer necessity of economic independence has been an important dimension of identity and self-image has meant that even idealized prescriptions for femininity are imbued with the notion that independence and work are integral to womanhood. For some, this reveals an inherent tension between the dominant historical traditions of an African-derived culture of independence and autonomy for women (Barrow 1986a) and a European culture of respectability and domesticity (Bolles and D'Amico-Samuels 1984).[15] Janette, a twenty-year-old claims approver at Data Air, expresses a common feeling about formal marriage compared with a visiting relationship of girlfriend and boyfriend in her comments: "To me, no, it doesn't matter [if a woman gets married or not] but religiously, they say that people should get married. People mostly agree with one another when they are single. Men tend to think that they are boss when they are married. They want to rule everything; the women don't have any say. [When they're just boyfriend and girlfriend] everything go'long fine. To tell you the truth, I would like to get married although I'm still yet young." She recognizes marriage as a church-sanctioned institution and a status that confers "respectability," and she desires this status. On the other hand, she expresses a widely held belief in Barbados that, once married, "men tend to think that they are boss," and for this reason she is disinclined toward formal marriage. I am arguing here that respectability as it is understood today in Barbados reflects, not a superimposition of nineteenth-century European values of feminine domesticity, but rather a femininity imbued with the ideals of marriage, nuclear family, propriety, as well as those of wage/professional work and independence. The tension between or simultaneity of these ideals is itself a creation of creolization, and a particular Caribbean reality.[16] Two points require emphasis here. The first is the relational dimension of these concepts. Like W. E. B. DuBois's notion of "double consciousness" (1961), the dialectic of reputation and respectability implies precisely this tension within and against which people conceive, define, and enact themselves.[17] The second is the creolized nature of the tension as a whole, and not merely of the realm of reputation. Wilson's model of reputation and respectability tends to idealize the former as creative and even, in a sense, liberating, and to condemn the latter as a direct expression of "mental colonialism" in which Caribbean people strive to imitate their white masters and mistresses in their conservative conventions. Ironically, perhaps, by adopting the paradigm in a bipolar and historically flattened manner, we lose any sense of the dynamic, creolized expression of Caribbean culture and, in particular, of Caribbean notions of gender, as they have emerged over the past three hundred years. In particular, we miss the fact that there are competing ideals as well as multiple realities across the gendered terrain inhabited by Afro-Barbadian women, and that both the ideals and the real life circumstances they attempt to represent and shape are always themselves in flux.

A study of male images of women in Barbados reveals this fact, and though not presented as such, demonstrates the creolized nature of reputation, as well as of notions of respectability. Barrow (1986c:60) says that male stereotypes of women present us with what she calls an "ought/is" dichotomy—a polarity similar to reputation/respectability, or what she renamed Afro-Real/Euro-Ideal. In her study, however, some subtle differences emerge from the model as Wilson originally defined it. For example, while fidelity and submissiveness were emphasized as valued feminine traits, the "delicate frame" associated with white European respectability was not. Poignantly and strongly portrayed, the subjects of her study demonstrate a pattern in which Barbadian men hold in their heads a romanticized sense of a past in which women were "more respectable." Likewise, they find themselves affronted by contemporary young women whom they describe as ambitious, aggressive, "flashy," and generally unrespectable.[18] Notably, women too express a romanticized view of the past in which men were breadwinners, and women could be housewives. Women's "independence" then, is presented by men as a threat to their rightful power and responsibility as patriarchs, and by women as a necessary manifestation of economic need and increased opportunity. Kathleen, a young lead operator at Data Air, reflects on the changes:

> My mother's mother was a maid at a lady's house not far from us. The other [grandmother] did the same line of work. My life is much better. In those days there were a lot of hardships compared with now. Things [now] are much easier. . . . Women are more independent now than then. . . . you find women driving cars a lot more. . . . they live by themselves with their kids without a man in the house. You find women working in industries and other different work places. . . . Before, I guess, the men used to provide for the women while they stayed at home but now the women are getting out and finding themselves jobs to support themselves without the help of a man. I guess it's okay to have a man around, but if push come to shove, I could handle it on my own, too.

The participation of women in the realm of reputation (through expressions of independence and distinction) is increasingly represented in portrayals of women in popular calypso and dub songs, in street talk, and in the realm of informatics. The image of the strong black matriarch is frequently invoked in what seems to be a way of combating the unflattering portrayals of women's independence. Women workers in the informatics industry may be likened to generations of Afro-West Indian women who, through self-sacrifice, ingenuity, and sheer hard work, have pieced together a living in order that they may nurture their families. This has taken shape in the creation of a competing ideal to that of the domesticated and frail white housewife. The idea of a strong black matriarch draws on the history of women in the Caribbean who shouldered much of the burden of slavery, incipient nationhood, and a modern political economy through their tenacity as mothers and workers.[19] On other occasions, praise for the "responsible high-tech worker" is rooted in what Wilson construed as a European formulation of femininity—that of the dependent daughter who diligently preserves the moral fabric of society, here, through hard work, a sense of propriety, a naturally patient disposition, and acute manual dexterity. This version of womanhood resonates with Wilson's description of respectability, with the notable exception of the workplace (rather than the home) in which it is enacted.[20] For this version of femininity, as for that of the matriarch, family and home are the motivating force behind the women's responsible performance as workers, and, thus, wage work is interpreted solely as an expression of familial obligation, in which wages constitute a vital contribution to household survival.[21] Both of these ideals present limitations and distortion, as well as apertures for creative expression and the possibility of redefinitions of "worker" and "woman" in the context of the informatics industry. To explore these implications, it is important to begin by establishing a worker profile, identifying more precisely which women have been incorporated into this pink-collar industry. This process, in turn, demands that we look more closely at the interrelationships between women's household and family lives and their work in the information industry and the ways in which these challenge and reshape both local and global ideals.

Who Are the Informatics Workers?

CHARLENE

When I met Charlene, she was working at Data Air in the "lifts prep" department, sorting airline coupons for different destinations. She was twenty-five and had been employed at Data Air since the firm opened in 1983. During the first two years of work, she had developed a skin condition related to the carbon on the backs of the airline tickets and stopped working for eighteen months. During that time, she took a full-time correspondence course from the United States to learn BASIC and COBOL computer languages. "I wanted to find another job, but I think now that my navel string is buried in Data Air," she explained with a laugh. Charlene and her seven-year-old daughter lived with her grandparents, both retired now. Her grandfather had been an accountant and her grandmother a seamstress. When Charlene's mother emigrated to the United States to work as a baby-sitter, Charlene came to live with her grandparents, and "then when she came back I didn't want to go with her as such. I was so attached to my grandparents, so I stayed with them." Her mother works as an "executive housekeeper" at one of the expensive West Coast hotels, and her father works for the Barbados Transport Board. Charlene's relationship with her daughter's father ended a year ago, after a six-year visiting relationship. Her daughter's father helps to support her with monthly payments, and Charlene contributes to maintaining the household with her grandparents. "They own the house, so for the bills, they would put half and I put the other half." "I got my daughter the year before I came here and my grandparents took care of her and [her father's mother] took care of her. I worked part-time at the reservations desk at Sandy Lane [one of the island's top hotels] but I was always interested in computers from going to school at Queens College [one of Barbados's top schools]. So this was the first real opportunity for me to go into this. I went and did a little course with computers after I finished school. I had seven O-levels and two As.[22] At first my family thought this was a good thing until they heard about the pay, and they said, 'What?' Why am I doing this job when I'm so qualified? But, it's what I like doing, so I think that's best. I want something in the computer field . . . computers are the money."

SANDRA

Sandra is new to Data Air. She is eighteen years old and finished school less than a year ago. After a few weeks of temporary work at a local branch of Woolworth's, she applied for the job here and was successful. She works as a claims approver in the new insurance division of Data Air. She lives with her mother, a brother, three sisters, twin nieces, and a nephew. Two other brothers live on their own, and her father lives close by with his wife and children. Her mother works as a maid for a Trinidadian woman who works for an international bank and travels a great deal. Sandra's mother cares for her employer's baby, cooks, and cleans her house. "I learnt a lot from her. [. . .] she been in that business for long, cleaning and such. She is happy. I always say to myself, you should make for yourself your opportunities, because they will not pass your way again. Right now I am happy here. I have no plans for another job at the moment, but I am always looking for a higher post here—to be a lead—collecting and sharing out the work—or QR— quality reviewing the work—and supervisor or anything like that. One of my grandmothers [. . .] she worked on a plantation in St. John, and she would come down sometimes to visit on weekends or sometimes we would go and spend weekends up by her. To me, the sun out there real hot, and I can't take it on [working in the cane fields]. Where here, it be cold [. . . she shivers]." Sandra's brother works for the government-run National Conservation Corps, cleaning the parks and public facilities; one sister works in an electronics assembly plant, another baby-sits two little boys, and the last sister works as a domestic in a private home, like their mother. At home, Sandra says, "I do the cleaning and my biggest sister usually do the cooking, but if I get home first, I will start the cooking. My last sister, she washes, another helps clean the house. My brother do all the men's stuff around the house. . . . Every two weeks I give my mother [BDS] $40, put some in the bank [BDS $50] and then I buy any toiletries I need, clothes. I'll keep money to last me the other two weeks. Maybe I'll buy foodstuffs, snacks, maybe tinned foods to use to bring to work, underwear or shirts for my nephew or nieces."

ROSEMARIE

Rosemarie is a woman wise and responsible beyond her years. At twenty-seven she has become the head of her household, following the death of both of her parents in a span of three years. She lives with her seven-year-old son, two older brothers, a sister, and niece. The day I met her was Rosemarie's sixth "anniversary" at Data Air as a data processor. Describing her household, she says with resignation and in a somewhat weary tone, "I'm the backbone of it, so I must make sure that it's on par at all times. I'm probably making the least [money of all the siblings] but I contribute the most. That's the way my parents left it, so, after my mother died it was my father, and it was, you know, almost unwritten, but everyone assumed that since she was ill, I would run the household, and I've been doing it ever since. It's a lot on my shoulders. I do most of the cooking, most of the cleaning, most of everything [she laughs]! Everybody else do their own laundry and on the weekend, my sister take over the house. She has the weekends and bank holidays. We take meals together only on the weekends because during the week I am at home when they are at work. [. . .] I always work second shift. I find it's good because I find during the mornings I can get things done[. . .] and I get home normally at a quarter to 12. [. . .] We decided that we're all going to give BDS$200 each month and if there's extras then we divide it by four. I put $100 to the credit union each bi-weekly pay period to save. The house was owned by our parents. Our neighbors give us vegetables from their garden, and we have a few fruit trees. We're, each one of us, hoping to own our own homes as we get more economically able. My sister's twenty-three now [a clerical worker for the National Insurance office], I'm twenty-seven, my brother's twenty-nine [an auto repairman], and the other is thirty-one [a carpenter]. We all have dreams of moving on."

In Barbados's pink-collar enclave, competing portraits of women as ideal workers are increasingly evident. Charlene, Sandra, and Rosemarie demonstrate some of the variation in household configuration, age, life stage, and economic circumstance of the total labor force in this new arena. The new pink-collar workers are simultaneously and paradoxically described by their employers (and themselves) as strong, selfless, and hardworking, frequently the main breadwinners for their children, indeed, as the backbone of society; and they are depicted as materialistic consumers obsessed with fashion and appearances, clever and even mercenary in their strategies for deriving support and piecing together a living. This latter characterization of women frequently asserts that these "girls" are young, dependent on the support of their families, and drawn to these jobs for the "extra" pocket money they provide. As such, these competing profiles of femininity draw on the presumption of an apparently universal "docile girl" but also dramatically contradict this portrait with that of the "strong black matriarch." They echo the familiar notions that women are well suited to low-wage industrial work because they are structurally dependent and temperamentally malleable and simultaneously express equally well-entrenched West Indian gender stereotypes of female strength, fortitude, and guile.

The competing gender ideologies of the powerful matriarch and the docile girl underlie numerous rationalizations for changing divisions of labor and patterns of labor recruitment and are invoked at will to explain why women make ideal workers in one or another domain, or why women are not eligible for particular enclaves of work. For example, within the sugar industry, the belief that women do not have the technical skills and cannot handle the responsibility as well as the night work demanded by factory jobs has kept them out of the higher-paying and skilled areas of the industry (e.g., pan boiling) while in field work women are paid at a lower rate. The call for a middle-class femininity reminiscent of the nineteenth-century European cult of domesticity has at some moments led to the expulsion of Barbadian women from the waged labor force, and at other times the assertion of women's legendary tradition of hard work and physical strength has been the prevailing rationale for their incorporation into new realms of wage work.

These contradictory images of womanhood and femininity emerge in a particularly heightened manner within the offshore information industry, as they are marked by constant allusion to the impressive high-tech, white-collar appearance of these enterprises. When adopted into company rhetoric, these opposing profiles of women workers take on particular importance. On one hand, as implied above, and contrary to accounts of traditional offshore industries in other countries where the idealized profile of the multinational assembly worker has been a young, single, first-time worker, managers in informatics are now known to assert that hiring women who have children (married or single heads of households or not) creates a more reliable and hardworking labor force.[23]

Mothers are believed to work harder and generally take their jobs more seriously because regardless of the assistance of their extended families and "child fathers," they are the primary breadwinners for their children. One manager of a data entry operation contemplated hiring women for four-hour shifts to encourage those with children to take the jobs. He thought that the shorter workday would ease their child care burden, and at the same time enable the employment of these superior, more responsible workers. In contrast to the traditional argument for a family wage, where a male head of household is paid at a higher rate on the basis of his breadwinning role, these female heads of household, however, are paid low wages despite their higher levels of responsibility and job commitment.[24] On the other hand, like their counterparts in other countries, local managers were also frequently heard describing the work force as consisting of young girls in their first job who are working essentially for pocket money.[25] In short, this is the familiar "pin-money" argument so often used to described women's work and to rationalize the low wages they receive. These rationales and explanations are invoked as needed to maximize continuity and reliability of the labor force and to minimize wages and overall labor costs. Women, too, echo these competing rationales, even when their own life circumstances directly counter them.

A Barbadian manager of a small data entry company gave the following comment to explain the predominance of women workers:

> One of the factors is that there are about three or four women to every man in Barbados. [He hesitates . . .] maybe you should check that out with the statistical department, but I think that's true. Many of the people out there are females that are unemployed, fairly intelligent people, and typing is a skill that somehow seemed to fit into a female society.

In fact, women have historically outnumbered men in Barbados (the 1990 census figures cite a male population of 123,000 and a female population of 135,000). However, this manager's gross exaggeration reflects his sense of the "cheap reservoir" of female labor created more by women's economic vulnerability than their numerical disproportion.[26] As in many other developing countries, women between the ages of 19 and 25 represent the highest proportion of the unemployed labor force.[27]

The rationales I heard for the unmistakably feminine profile of informatics were grounded in such phenomena as the nature of the production process (typing; performing sedentary and meticulous work), the economic circumstances of both the nation and the family (disproportionate numbers of women out of work and needing employment), and the physical and emotional qualities of femininity that make women well suited to this work over other kinds. These rationales for hiring young "school leavers" (those who have just finished secondary school) bear resemblances to the international characterization but also point to specific dimensions of Afro-Caribbean lower-class culture—in particular, that of its "matrifocal" kinship and household structure. In the Barbadian informatics sector, employers say, on one hand, that they hire young women because their subsistence needs are insured by the safety net of their families and they are "secondary" earners with little financial responsibility. Employers characterize the young women as energetic youth who are eager to work hard both to help their families and to satisfy their own materialistic desires. They do not assume that the women come from patriarchal or nuclear families but instead acknowledge the multiple and extended form Afro-West Indian families have historically taken. Nonetheless, the expectation that youth implies minimal economic responsibility even in the absence of a male breadwinner links these rationales to those commonly articulated across the global assembly line and reinscribes the assumption that low wages are acceptable in the light of young women's structurally dependent position. Departing further from the typical international rationale is the explanation these companies now assert for retaining older women. Mature women are assumed not only to be experienced in the work world and therefore well socialized within the corporate work ethic but also, as Afro-Caribbean women, to be mothers and therefore particularly responsible, dependable employees.

The "Old Guard" and the "Young Girls": "Generations" of Workers and Competing Ideologies of Femininity

When Data Air opened its doors in 1983, its initial batch of operators fit what has become the international stereotype of multinational factory workers; they were predominantly young, single, childless women largely between the ages of nineteen and twenty-two. Although recruitment was not organized around some of the extreme measures used in other countries (e.g., mandatory pregnancy tests), the general demographic profile for the initial informatics labor force strongly resembled what had become an international norm. Six years later, when I began this study, a majority (67 percent) of women workers in my sample of eighty-five were single and lived at home with their families; 24 percent were married or living with a partner; 7 percent were in visiting relationships, and 2 percent were separated or divorced. Of the same group, 12 percent recognized themselves as head of their household, generally made up of other siblings and their children.[28] Mothers constituted one-third of the group, 75 percent of whom had one child and 25 percent of whom had two or three children.[29]

Barbadian workers and managers alike concur that these enterprises are filled with women because women know how to type and, since typing is a prerequisite for the job, it is logical that the companies hire women workers. This "supply side" rationale was frequently bolstered with arguments about the gross overrepresentation of women in the Barbadian population, as well as women's greater tenacity in looking for work in order to support their children.[30] Many of these discussions were also permeated by gender stereotypes about women's natural predisposition toward fine and meticulous, sedentary work and corollary notions about men's natural inclination toward heavier physical work and the need to "move around."

More often than not, women workers themselves offer the "labor supply side" rationales by saying simply that "women are the ones who learn to type and since these jobs require typing, men don't bother to apply." The logic seems self-evident; in Barbados, like most places, typing is considered a feminine activity (higher-level computer work, incidentally, is not). Therefore, according to management and workers alike, the industry is not really selecting women because they are women; they select themselves insofar as they fall into a "naturally" or "traditionally" female domain of work. As one keyer said, the industry is filled with women "because one of the stipulations for applying [. . .] was knowing how to type. I know, in my time, I don't think a guy would be caught dead typing." Another offered, with a grin, "Sometimes I think guys think if they work among so many women, they'll become feminine—it will rub off on them!" Grantley, one of the few men employed, has been working in one of the ticket "prep" areas at Data Air. He began there as a temporary maintenance worker, then interviewed for a job in the prep department, and was successful.

> What I had in mind was to be a police officer [. . .] but to be a police officer you got to be between the age of nineteen and thirty and when I left school I wasn't that age yet, so I was looking to hold onto something until I reached that age and then move from there. I never really thought about one of the keying jobs. [. . .] Probably my fingers are too big for the keyboard. To me, a lady would handle that a lot better than a gentleman [. . .] 'cause [. . .] the touch a lady has,

it would be much more comfortable to her. Personally, I am the type of guy that like to be moving around [. . .] active [. . .] I mean, lifting things and that kind of thing. After working here, it open my eyes to a lot more things that I would like to do [. . .] I'm not only thinking about being a police, but being an accountant or anything like that.

Interestingly, Grantley's gendered notion of appropriate work for men and women is somewhat contradictory. Like many others, he cites the "natural" predisposition for men to be active, physically mobile, and unconstrained by close, focused, sedentary work but then admits his new aspiration to be an accountant (shared, incidentally, by a striking number of other data processors, male and female).[31]

These gender stereotypes, and others relating to women's roles within the family/domestic arena, permeate the process by which they are incorporated as the predominant labor force in informatics. The general manager of Data Air presented the following worker profile as representing the core of his operation.

I would guess off hand that they are largely still living at home with parents [. . . and] that at least 50 percent or more have at least one kid. I know that, largely speaking, they do not *need* [. . .] this job [. . .] this whole question of clothes and jewelry and entertainment and that type of thing, they seem to work a lot for that. We watch their savings patterns and we encourage membership in the credit union. We practically sponsored a credit union in-house, and one of the complaints we get from the credit union is that as soon as the savings hit [. . .] they go back for it. They're taking it and you can see very conspicuously how they are spending it. [. . .] I think the wages *are* crucial *to them,* and the more the merrier [. . .] but very frequently, you'll almost get threatened "I'll stay home, then" and I think really it has to do with the feeling that "I can be no worse off if I stayed home"—that "I will get all of the basic things that I need"—and that largely therefore, "I can give up that job."

These remarks are revealing on several fronts, both in terms of the basic demographic portrait of his employees and in terms of his sense of the importance of these jobs in their lives. Living "at home" (i.e., with one or both parents or guardian) is viewed as insuring a certain basic level of support, and this manager implies quite clearly that regardless of the presence of a woman's own child, or the particular circumstances of her family, if she lives at home her wage is supplemental to the household budget. Again, he reiterates the old "pin money" rationale for why women's wages are lower than men's. The misconception, however, lies in the assumption that living "at home" insures basic subsistence and therefore places one's earnings in the category of supplemental or extra income. Of the eighty-five informatics workers I interviewed, 38 percent cite themselves as the primary breadwinners of their households; 53 percent cite others as making the largest contribution to the household budget, and another 9 percent say they contribute equally with other members of their households.[32] The manager who assumes that the women he employs can depend upon the primary support of their families fairly characterizes roughly half of them. This does not imply, however, that the operator's wage is superfluous to the household budget among those who enjoy the predominant support of another household member. And certainly the 47 percent who describe their own contribution as essential to the household's survival cannot simply be ignored.

The extent to which motherhood figures into this picture is also crucial. Among those who recognize their own wages as representing the most important economic contribution to the household economy, 41 percent have children and are either in visiting relationships or separated from their partners. The others represent households in which few if any other members are wage-earning contributors. Together, these are the women who comprise the other popular stereotype within industry circles and the nation at large; the strong black matriarch. As primary breadwinners and mothers, these women workers embody and represent a modern rendition of the historically hard-working, self-sacrificing, maternal, plantation laborer. In fact, they comprise the most economically vulnerable sector of both the informatics workers and the region as a whole (Massiah 1982).[33] While a minority in numbers, this last category of data processors signifies as well the emergence of a powerful alternative image to the young, carefree, self-indulgent school leaver. Their age and job experience confer on them an air of authority within the "office-factory" context.

Quite distinct from the global trend in which workers are hired and then quickly let go (Safa 1990:80), the low attrition rates (2 percent at Data Air; slightly higher at Multitext) imply that the vast majority of Barbadian data operators have tended to keep their jobs well beyond the international average of two to three years in other offshore industries. This phenomenon is all the more remarkable considering the position of informatics at the very apex of the offshore industries. In other industrial arenas across the world (e.g., garments, textiles, and food production), the maintenance of women workers beyond their twenties is believed to be a reflection of an industry's inability to compete with the more attractive export industries (e.g., electronics). Despite state requirements for maternity leave and the guarantee of a worker's job when she returns, as well as the relatively higher wage scale in Barbados compared with that of other islands in the region, Barbadian women are keeping their data processing jobs for what seem in the global market to be unprecedented lengths of time. In fact, according to Data Air's general manager, of the original workers hired in 1983 a majority are still with the company.[34] Those workers hired from the start and still with the company have average ages of between twenty-seven and thirty-five. Within the newer parts of the company, which began in 1990 and continue to hire new recruits, the average age continues to hover around the original bracket of late teens and early twenties. It remains to be seen whether these divisions will also retain workers over similar time spans.

In essence, there has emerged a two-tiered work force of young school leavers and an "old guard." They can be seen as generations, in two senses.[35] They are generational by age or motherhood status and household responsibility, and they are generational by their seniority within the informatics industry. Both notions of generation are bound up in the contradictory portraits drawn between the hardworking and mature single mother and the frivolous school leaver. Graphic stereotypes, offered by management and workers alike, about work ethics, demeanor, and dress distinguish between the two groups as well. The young school leavers, for example, are considered by their "older" compatriots to be less committed to the "mission of the company" and more intent simply on making money. The implication is that they spend their money exclusively on their own frivolous whims, and contribute nothing to household support.[36] Social interaction and cliques of friends who regularly meet for lunch, dinner, or shift breaks tend to parallel these generational differences, in part because work areas become age stratified based on hiring waves and length of job tenure. For example, when the new insurance claims division opened at Data Air, new recruits were young school leavers. Entire shifts in this new division, therefore, are made up of the "younger" generation of workers, giving rise, as well, to new social networks of friends.

Because these school leavers are grouped together both within the workplace and outside it, then, their style and overall look becomes especially pronounced. Upstairs, in the airline ticket processing area the presence of the old guard is more pronounced. Reflecting on the difficulty in pinning down one worker profile or even an average age, the general manager told me, "We have two companies, really; the claims operation, where the average age is probably twenty or even younger, and our airline division where it is probably twenty-five or even higher, twenty-seven or twenty-eight." Barbara, a member of the "old guard" who began working for the company when it opened in 1983 and was thirty at the time I interviewed her, illustrates the divide in describing the "young" workers as follows:

> They don't think like the people of before. That's the basic bottom line. They don't have the same serious-minded approach to a job. Like, say, what I had when I started. They treat it like school, like they think they can come and go as they please and you really have to railroad them to get them to think straight.

Julianna, another operator, age twenty-eight, remarked:

> You will find that an old person like me will concentrate on the errors [maintaining higher accuracy] 'cause we are working for Data Air, right? But they're not. They are strictly thinking about money. So if you lose it in incentive [earned through high accuracy], make it up in overtime.

Marcia, twenty-five, and promoted to trainer in the newer insurance division of Data Air, noted that among the women who came into the company with her, most are still working as keyers.

> I find that in here when you are doing a job, you don't really want to leave and look for something else [. . .] it's sort of comfortable. But in this section [the insurance area], we have a higher turnover, I think because in here they're younger people. They just come out of school, mostly teenagers [. . .] and they wouldn't have the dedication and commitment that the older people upstairs who came in and saw this company grow would have. When we first came here it was nothing like this [. . .] it was just an empty shell. All the wires and everything [. . .] so we really saw the company transformed. But they came in and I don't think they have any commitment as such [. . .] or the same interest that we may have. I think the generation now are different. [. . .] They don't take the same hassles that we have in our day. They're less tolerant. Most of these people in here was born in the seventies and I was born in the sixties. I think if you want, you could call it a generation gap. In my day, we didn't have any dub [she laughs]! Now I'm twenty-five. When I came here I was eighteen,

one of the youngest people. I was the youngest in my department. Now I'm one of the oldest down here, and although the age difference is only about five to seven years apart, I think it is very noticeable. When I came here I was working for [BDS$187.50, bi-weekly]. That is one figure I will never forget. How many of these people do you think are going to work for that? What they are making now is considerably more than what I was making then, but they don't think it is enough. I know people that even resign from here and just went home and sat down because they didn't think that coming in here and working for that salary made it worthwhile. They say that when they go home they get more money. [. . .] I don't know!

In defense of themselves as the "younger" generation, some of the workers in the newer insurance division of Data Air resent the standards to which they are held—in terms of both productivity and appearances. Rachel, eighteen, said, "I think it's [the dressing up] not really necessary. They all do it, the older ones, but it's not worth it. People just overdo it. There are people out there who look at the people from Data Air and say, 'Why do they dress like that?' I mean, it's just Data Air, nothing else, so I don't know why they do it!" Others aspire to the level of proficiency and "professionalism" of their more senior counterparts, and hope to advance within the company or outside it. Noelle, a new claims approver said, "I'm not proficient as yet. There are only three persons who came in October with me who are proficient. I have to work on my quality. The work is there but not my quality. It's not hard [. . .] I think that we ourselves should try to do it on our own. [. . .] It's not the supervisors that are keying, it's us and we have to watch out for our mistakes. [. . .] I feel I could improve over time and maybe become a supervisor." Still others fit the image that managers and the "old guard" have of them, in which "living for today" and dressing well are their major concerns. The younger, newer workers describe their annoyance with the strict rules regulating each minute of the workday and all the procedures related to the job itself, as well as going to the bathroom or using the telephone. Indeed, they complain that "it's just like being back in school," and having just left school, with its uniforms, bells, and regulations, they find the similarities confining. Sondra, age nineteen, said one day with exasperation:

I could as well be at school, the whole thing is really a school atmosphere. For instance, the headmaster—if he walks into the form you got to keep quiet and shut your mouth [. . .] and here if [the general manager] walks in, everyone is supposed to shut up. Our lead goes like, "Okay people, Mr. R. is here, you're going to have to stop talking." I mean, why is that? Sometimes I just want to go up to him and say, "Excuse me, Mr. R., why do we have to shut up every time you enter?" I don't think he expects us to, because he talks with us [. . .] so I don't think he expects us to sit and shut up every time he comes into the room. But the supervisor, she says you can't talk. You can't talk too loud [. . .] you can't laugh too loud, I mean, you can't sit down all day at the terminal and key! You need to breathe!

From the management point of view, coming directly from school, young girls are accustomed to following directions and are considered well suited for the discipline of the "open office." A Barbadian manager of one of the smaller, locally run data facilities said that young school leavers with no prior data entry experience are ideal because they are eager to work on a computer but learn only his program and are not faced with relearning or "unlearning" another. From this perspective, prior work experience in other data entry facilities makes an applicant less attractive, and youth becomes associated with eagerness to learn and receptivity to the acculturation of the company.[37] He said:

> We have sort of pointed ourselves in the direction of hiring school leavers. I have found that we have had some problems with people who have worked— specifically with those who have worked in other data entry establishments! It's mainly an attitude problem [. . .] and also, in actual fact, there is very little difference between the training required between someone right out of school and someone from another institution, used to their software. I mean, typing is typing whether you typed on a computer or on a typewriter, it doesn't really matter. But you come to my system and you can type but you don't know my software, so you have to learn all over again, so basically you need the same training as an individual just out of school who can type. *So it was easier for us to mold people just out of school.* (Emphasis mine.)

His was a widely held belief, and despite the fact that some shuffling of employees between operations is a regular occurrence, several top managers confessed that in the long run they preferred hiring bright young people with a good basic education, and perhaps no typing experience at all, over keyers from one of the other informatics firms. One operation began its training program with basic typing on a special keyboard that meant even proficient typists had to go through rudimentary keyboard training. At Data Air, a majority (53 percent) of the women I surveyed had no prior full-time wage work experience before their data entry employment. Of those who had held a previous job, roughly one quarter (24 percent) had worked in other factory or export industries (data entry 4 percent; electronics 9 percent; garments 4 percent; other factories 7 percent).

First-time working status is, as well, an important element in the international profile of the export worker and feeds into the pervasive rationale for the young female labor force in that youth and lack of work experience go together. Inexperienced workers are easier to train and less likely to have encountered or participated in labor unions, as one manager explained to me.

On the other hand, the personnel department of Data Air undertook an experiment, indicating their awareness of these two distinct "generations" of workers and revealing the company's preference for those values and work ethics that have become associated with their "older," more mature work force. Ten women were hired who fell into the age bracket of the "old guard" (between twenty-four and thirty) in the belief that they would be "more mature and reliable" workers than the young "girls" generally hired directly out of school. But the personnel manager was deeply disappointed when she learned that most did not survive the three-month probationary period. Their low productivity was accounted for by a lack of familiarity and general anxiety about computers, which have only recently been introduced to some of the secondary schools. Another reason cited for their failure was a reluctance to take direction from supervisors who were often younger than themselves. Only one member of the experimental group remained employed after the three-month trial period.

What this experiment seemed to imply, therefore, was that age alone was not the key ingredient to a "mature" and "ideal" worker.[38] Rather, age (and motherhood) associated with a woman's longevity within the company became the preferred characteristics. Preference for the "mature" worker reflects a shifting priority associated with the company's identity, which along with its work force, has evolved over its fifteen years of operation. The informatics companies, therefore, are not recruiting a qualitatively different work force, since young school leavers continue to be the favored candidates when new divisions or positions open up; but because workers are being retained longer, a competing profile of the "ideal" mature operator has evolved. These women's active determination to remain in the jobs through different stages in their life cycles, and the companies' acknowledgment of their own benefits derived from this new pattern have challenged a widespread characteristic of multinational industries around the world to hire and fire at will. In turn, this phenomenon has given new expression to the companies' own life cycles, and to their rhetoric. Multinationals have adopted what appear to be contradictory rationales to describe their labor force, in the light of its distinct "generations." These rationales point to women's position within their households and family constellations, and in turn, draw on both ideal models (nuclear patriarchal families) and real (multiple forms, such as matrifocal, extended, and nuclear) expressions of Afro-Caribbean kinship and household structure.

Interestingly, in other parts of the world, motherhood is interpreted as such a threat to maintaining smooth production operations that regular pregnancy tests are required, and positive tests warrant immediate dismissal. In Mexico, for example, Tiano (1987:84) cites managers who argue that "lack of concentration, absenteeism, and frequent resignations . . . are common among wives and mothers who put their family's welfare above their job-related responsibilities." In Barbados, by contrast, these same domestic responsibilities are believed to make workers more committed to their jobs, and sometimes better producers (depending on the age and previous employment experience of the women when they entered their jobs).[39] Different cultural ideologies about women's productive and reproductive roles underlie these two very different perspectives—one in which marriage and motherhood are seen to draw a natural conclusion to a young woman's wage earning work, and another in which these activities are understood to go hand in hand.[40]

Families, Households, and Divisions of Labor

Managers' descriptions of and rationales regarding their workers demonstrate some sense of the different household and family structures of their Barbadian employees, even if they rely on simplified or stereotypic portrayals. To understand how these different "generations" encompass a range of specific domestic situations in Barbados, we must account for the multiple and complex forms of Barbadian domestic life in which women act both as individuals and as members of households, and where they derive and offer essential economic and emotional support. This is also central in addressing the interplay between macroeconomic demands and the local cultural context, and their respective competing ideologies of femininity.

Households, when addressed at all, have often been presented as undifferentiated conglomerations of individuals, with the implication that income is pooled for the interest of the household as a whole and that all have equal access to power and resources (Dwyer and Bruce 1988; Wolf 1990). In effect, women and households have been treated virtually synonymously. Joycelin Massiah (1982, 1983, 1986) and others writing about women in the Caribbean have made important contributions to distinguishing between households and families, noting both that family members do not all reside together in the same domestic residence, and that within the same household, there may be nonfamily members as well. Hermione McKenzie (1982:xi) points out that in Caribbean households certain family members are often permanently nonresident, the most important being the nonresident father, as well as "outside" children (step-siblings), and that other members of a household would not be considered "family" if not for their residence within the domestic group. Her own analytical preference in this often confusing set of competing definitions is that of the "family network" that includes those kin not necessarily residing within a single household but who constitute an important group from whom women draw support and identification. Both the family network and the household are central to women's experience, however, and it is the often fluid interaction between the two that, she argues, needs further study.

The rural and patriarchally structured households often described in other parts of the developing world where multinational industries have located (e.g., Colombia, Mexico, South Korea, Philippines, Malaysia) stand in striking contrast to Barbados, where a substantial proportion of household forms often do not include a male authority figure at all. The predominance of matrifocal family organization, coupled with the fact that Afro-Barbadian women have long combined income-earning work with rearing children and caring for families has meant that going to work in export processing industries, per se, does not pose a threat or challenge to the status quo of family life.[41] The argument that the long historical pattern of women's work obviated an otherwise pervasive international precedent for privileging male over female labor (Mathurin 1975) is given a contemporary twist by Helen Safa (1986:66), who asserts that the particular history of gender relations and women's work in the Afro-Caribbean have meant that the incorporation of women into export production has been less disruptive to the sexual division of labor and family life than it has in more patriarchal societies of Latin America and the Hispanic Caribbean.

Responsibilities to family members and to the "general upkeep" of the household certainly constitute an important dimension of women's desire for and commitment to employment in informatics. Central to describing the household context of women workers, therefore, are questions of economic contribution and support, as well as divisions of labor in the home. To what extent are women's wages integral to the household economy, and what are the relationships between wage earning, household composition, and domestic responsibilities? Susan Tiano, Diane Wolf, and others have noted that focusing on the household as composed of undifferentiated individuals, assumed to pool their income for the maintenance of the whole, has distorted our sense of women's particular position within intrahousehold power relationships along the lines of gender and generation (as daughters, wives, etc.) (Wolf 1990:47). For example, compare a woman whose wage is the only consistent income within a household in which others work informally for small and variable amounts of income with a woman whose father and mother are both employed in stable public sector jobs and provide the basic livelihood for the household. The two are likely to impute different meanings to their work and their wages within the household.

It is important to emphasize, however, that women's simultaneous engagement in domestic and wage-earning work (or private/public spheres, as some continue to argue), if anything, further complicates our original question, Why are (Barbadian) women ideal global workers? If the rationale behind women as "ideal workers" in offshore industries (even occasionally) centers on their role as mothers and as heads of households, then we are left to wonder how their low wages are explained away, other than by the invocation of different models of "ideal" workers to suit different occasions. Only by identifying all the ingredients of the "ideal worker" concept can we fully appreciate the power of this "flexible" "ideal." Some of the aspects involved thus far have been women's "natural" physical abilities ("nimble fingers"); their reliability and commitment (older, mature matriarchs); their trainability (youthful school leavers); low wage requirements (again, by virtue of youth and supplemental nature of their wage). By now adding assumptions about the specificity of the Afro-Caribbean family, and in particular, its matrifocal, extended form, corporate managers (local and foreign) and women workers alike add another ingredient in the "ideal" mix. Among the variables to consider within this rationale, are motherhood status, child care responsibilities, household makeup, and overall household economy.

Still, across racial and class groups, women are believed to be the natural and necessary minders of children and the domestic arena in general. In the lives of Caribbean women children are of primary importance. As many have pointed out (e.g., Hodge 1982; Senior 1991), women often put the importance of having a child well above that of getting married or being in a relationship with a man. At the same time, marriage continues to constitute a social ideal, and together with a nuclear family and homeownership, it figures prominently in the life dreams described by a majority of the informatics workers. Acknowledging the gap between common practices and idealized models of family, Sondra, a nineteen-year-old claims approver, said wistfully, "Very few get married—it's always been so. They live together and get children, but they don't usually get married. I want to have a home of my own and if I ever get married, just two kids, no more [. . .] a boy and a girl, and if it's not a boy, I don't mind [. . .] and just live a comfortable life. I'm not going to get children unless I get married because it's really costly to be a single parent in Barbados."[42]

The extended family, and in particular, shared child rearing, have traditionally made women's wage work possible, as grandmothers and other female kin have assumed responsibility for child care and domestic chores while those formally employed have gone out to work. Recently, however, the pattern of reliance on extended kin networks as a safety net of support has shown signs of contraction, in particular with regard to child care. At the same time, day care facilities are still scarce and represent an expense that women in factory jobs can ill afford. The popular press in Barbados has run letters recently, for example, decrying the new phenomenon of "latchkey children." Some of these changes appear to result from a dispersal of family members away from village enclaves and into new housing developments across the island, as well as the involvement of women's mothers and other female kin in wage work, precluding their availability as caretakers. "The breakdown of the extended family" has been described as a great concern in the popular media and by government officials who recognize the increasing need for state-supported child care facilities. Most notable in these public statements is a general lament over the "demise of the family" as the primary locus of social life, economic resourcefulness, and Christian morality. More generally there is a sense of conflict over changing perceptions about what constitutes a "good mother." Contradictory arguments and accusations are made in letters to the local newspapers and radio call-in programs, in a scramble to explain and come to terms with these social changes. On one hand, working women are blamed for neglecting their maternal obligations; on the other, there is the acknowledgment that grandmothers and other female kin who once bore great responsibility for socialization are playing a diminishing role. While it is still widely presumed that the extended family network persists, my data from the informatics sector indicates that this institution that has for so long characterized the basis for family and social life may now be contracting.[43]

In my survey sample, of the 38 percent of women who have a child, 18 percent rely on family members or neighbors for child care, 24 percent use preschools or day care facilities, and 6 percent use paid baby-sitters. A full 53 percent have children of school age, and are thus spared the need for daytime child care. This means that 63 percent of those mothers whose children are not of school age must pay for the care of their children while they are at work, either to organized day care programs or individual baby-sitters. Interestingly, despite the small number of women whose families provide regular care for their children, when women without children were asked who would care for their child if they had one and returned to work, 44 percent said their mothers, and 34 percent said other family members. In other words, 78 percent assumed, like the manager cited above, that family would help them retain their job and care for their child at the same time. I point this out to emphasize a disjuncture between the "ideal" and the "real." Despite the changes in the historical pattern that places the extended family at the core of Barbadian social life, as noted frequently in the academic literature, everyday conversation, and the popular press, the young women in my survey continue to believe in the extended family. Nonetheless, only half of these women are predominantly supported by others, and only a small proportion of these by husbands or partners. These "matriarchs" may be symbols of pride and strength and they may challenge international prescriptions for "ideal" global-worker femininity, but at the same time they must endure the most difficult struggle to manage their employment and domestic responsibilities.

Joycelin, one the shift managers of Data Air, expressed the contemporary contradictions and conflicts surrounding child care and work. She said matter-of-factly that mothers "simply have to find some family member to take their child," but, she also sympathetically described the frequent difficulties women face juggling child care with their work shifts. Her own story reveals some of the conflict and sacrifice experienced by many women with small children.

My mother is working, my husband is working, my sisters are all working with the exception of one and she's all the way in the country, so I had to find a way to get her there and also get work. So for six months [my daughter] slept at my mother—my sister used to keep her there and my mother would take care of her in the night. I would only see her on the weekends. It was quite difficult for me until I got adjusted. [. . .] Now my husband would collect her on evenings after work and then he would bring her home. When I get home, she would obviously be sleeping, so I would see her, well, between seven and two and then she would go back into the country. Some persons would try to get switched to first shift because they don't want no other person to keep their child—this is my child and I don't want my mother to keep her cause my mother is going to spoil her [. . .] but what do you do? Either you stop working and mind your own child or [. . .] have your parent keep the child.

Suzanne, a data operator at Data Air, made similar comments about her friends' difficulties juggling a job with being a mother. For one, the benefits of "child fostering" in which her friend's mother took primary care of her young daughter were offset by the sense of lost attachment. For the other, even with extended family support, the costs were apparent.

A girl upstairs was telling me that when she was on evening shift, her mother used to keep her little girl and when she go to pick up the little girl on the weekends, the little girl used to cry. She said that her little girl was growing up to think that her grandmother was her mother. And she said that she was really getting annoyed, cause the girl cries and don't want to go with her, she's so accustomed to her grandmother. So, she said right now she is working the morning shift and so she is there, and if she has to go back on the evening shift, she'll have to look for another job, because she is finding that her child is not knowing her. My other friend on second shift says that when it's time for her to leave, her child is always saying, "Mummy, can't you stay at home with me? You're always going to work and leaving me here by myself." The only time she gets to see him is on weekends. Sometimes he has homework and she has to say, "I can't help you with that now, I have to go to work." So you see there's nobody to help. They aren't married. At least she is a little better off because she lives with her extended family so I guess there is someone there to help [. . .] her problem really is talking to him and seeing him, because when it's time for her to go to work, he's not home yet from school and when she comes home at night, he's sleeping. On mornings she's sleeping still when he go [. . .] so she don't see him. [. . .] Lots of them on the evening shift have children, and on evening shift it's a problem. *But, like I say, you have to comply. There are some who would prefer to stay home and keep the children, but you can't do it [. . .] you can't afford to.* (Emphasis mine)

"Child sharing" as a solution to the dual demands of work and child care has long historical roots and continues to be one strategy that single and married women use when possible (Senior 1991), though as the figures above show, few of those in my sample are able to fully depend on these extended family resources.

Marlene, a twenty-six-year-old data processor working at Data Air for her eighth year, speculated about the predominance of young women employed in this industry: "I assume that the company would really like people that don't really have much responsibilities with children and because the hours that you have to keep. You know if you had a family, with the different shifts, you would not be able to work as much. [. . .] So I think they want young people that can endure the hours." She comments that being young and without the responsibility of children would imply greater flexibility to work long hours, along the lines of the standard multinational industry rationale. However, Marlene, and the managers she refers to, know very well that many women do indeed play a significant role in the maintenance of their households whether or not they themselves have a child, and that particularly during a period of economic recession, such as the one during the time of these interviews, in fact, women really do need these jobs.[44] Interestingly, Marlene herself says that she would like to have children but not until she is married and owns a home. On the other hand, she says, "If you plan your life well and have someone there who can keep the children, and if the husband or whoever the father is, is helpful, then it should be easy" to work and be a mother too.

Many scholars writing about women in the Caribbean have noted the great extent to which women's days are stretched between reproductive and productive responsibilities. Despite women's increased participation in the formal work force, and some indication that men are beginning to play a greater role in domestic activity, women continue to perform most household duties and child care, and are frequently involved, as I make clear in chapter 6, in income-generating activities in the informal sector as well. Elsewhere, this hectic combination is referred to as women's "triple shift" (Ward 1990b; Freeman 1997), extending the well-known concept of the "double day" to incorporate these three arenas of women's work—formal wage work, informal economic activity, and domestic labor. As for the juggle between home-based and "office-factory"-based labor, women's strategies vary according to the composition of their households and the extent to which others contribute to the family economy.

In contexts such as the Afro-Caribbean, in which extended families have predominated, women's "double day" may be mitigated by unemployed or underemployed female kin who are able to maintain the home while other members go out to work. Isis Duarte (1989), writing about the Dominican Republic, challenges the relevance of the "double day" thesis for contexts other than the industrialized West. She asserts that the middle class is saved from the double day largely because they are able to buy the services of working-class women to perform their domestic chores. Furthermore, working-class women, like their Afro-Caribbean counterparts, are also spared the double day because other female kin are available to assume most of the domestic responsibilities. Duarte argues that women in export-processing industries and domestic workers who are generally single and live at home tend to fall into the latter category and be exempt from household chores. Factory exploitation, according to this argument, in effect "liberates" women from domestic work. Living at home with families, often including unemployed female kin, guarantees a variety of services and support that precludes the wage worker from engaging in the "double" responsibilities of domestic and wage-earning labor. The Barbadian case reveals two fundamental contradictions to this portrayal of third world women workers. First, women in informatics are not uniformly single and childless; second, they are not necessarily able to count on their extended kin to care for children or provide basic household services, as both they and social scientists writing about them might have imagined. In short, the "single girl" and the extended family may both be more "ideal" than "real" for many of these women workers.

Of the Barbadian data entry operators I surveyed, 22 percent perform most of the household duties, including cooking, cleaning, shopping, and washing. Again, divisions of labor vary widely, depending on the household makeup— with married women or those in stable residential unions tending to do the most housework and single women in large households, the least. The majority (69 percent) say that they share these responsibilities with other household members, 13 percent with their partner, and 56 percent with other women in the family. Women in offshore industries, then, tend to be spared the "double day" only when they are single and have other women at home to perform the domestic tasks. In effect, as Duarte (1989) argues, their unemployed or underemployed kin subsidize their demanding jobs and insufficient wages. In the event, however, that all other household members are also employed in wage-earning jobs outside the home, no such support is guaranteed, and two or three shifts is not uncommon.

Moreover, for those women in conjugal residential unions (either married or common law), the responsibilities of household work falls increasingly on their shoulders, and like their North American counterparts, they indeed are often confronted with a double day. In a context in which the traditional networks of extended kin are eroding, it appears, ironically, that women in married or co-habiting unions who have achieved the nuclear family ideal suffer the greatest in terms of competing demands of time and labor. In many ways they are beginning to resemble the isolated families that have long characterized the white western middle class.

Family networks are more likely to provide Barbadian women workers with economic and social support that enables them to manage income earning and domestic responsibility, or to place them in positions that demand their wage-earning role, than they are to restrict these women to a purely domestic realm. Indeed, women without children stated unanimously that if they were to become pregnant they would return to their job following the birth of their child. The fact that women do not routinely leave their export processing jobs (both in data entry and in other industries) upon marriage or the birth of a child and the fact that the data entry operations have come to prefer to maintain a steady and secure work force despite its "advanced" age sharply distinguishes the work lifespan of these women, and thus the overall profile of the Barbadian operator, from the tenure and profile of many of their international counterparts.[45]

The level, duration, and timing of women's wage work within their life cycles are all very much influenced by the nature of their household economy, its sexual division of labor, and, in general, the cultural mores surrounding women's productive and reproductive roles. Thus, while companies around the world generally prefer young, unmarried, childless, female workers, it is also clear that women's own preferences as well as household reproductive demands are integral to the way in which a particular work force "formula" is defined. Age, then, not in and of itself, but as it relates to particular life cycles, becomes a significant variable within the workings of the data entry industry and, as well, on the ways in which women's varied family roles and responsibilities are perceived by employers. In addition to "traditional" feminine attributes of passivity and malleability associated with women workers, corporate managers within the international marketplace also have notions about feminine roles—women's social and familial responsibilities as daughters, wives, and mothers. Women's responsibilities, from household organizer, cook, and child minder to sexual partner and moral and cultural educator, also affect how they are defined as workers within the international economic arena.

The distinct "generations" of workers and varied profiles according to age, union status, children, and household makeup and economy, as well as seniority within the company, add new dimensions to what has seemed to be a uniform stereotype of the young, single, offshore "factory girl." In the realms of both ideology and practice, women are challenging singular, prescriptive notions of femininity and what has been assumed to be a uniform and ideal profile of multinational workers. Instead of representing the relational opposite of a presumed male worker (aggressive, unionized, etc.), the comparison here is between two kinds of femininity, and two stages of womanhood. The varied configurations of women's households and their longevity within the industry together create structural challenges to the conventional "young, single, childless, docile girl" ideal, and women's changing self-images together with those they project on the public simultaneously challenge both local and global, ideal and real gender ideologies. The new pink-collar workers are not merely the mercenary shoppers and hungry consumers or the selfless matriarchs or the dutiful daughters they are often caricatured to be. However, two images, of the "dependent girl" imagining and counting on a family wage from a male breadwinner and of the "autonomous and hardworking matriarch" who valiantly manages both income earning and childrearing, are invoked as dominant tropes of femininity—by the state, the transnational corporations, and the women themselves. These tropes point powerfully to the ways in which reputation and respectability are simultaneously at work in defining and reconfiguring who the "pink-collar" workers are. The very concept of informatics workers' "professional" looks, the focus of chapter 6, is predicated on the coexisting values of decorum (respectability) and distinction (reputation). For these women, the consumer image is not negative but part of the new identities they claim and at the same time use to challenge feminine ideologies of constraint.

In reality, most women over the course of their lifetimes engage in multiple forms of labor (reproductive, productive, formal, and informal), and a variety of unions (visiting, cohabitation, marriage) and household configurations. In short, women may at different moments in their lives live out any or all of these "ideal" expressions of femininity and womanhood. Joyce, eighteen years old and working as a claims approver at Data Air, expressed precisely and honestly the shift in profile from "young girl" to "mature and responsible woman" within informatics and, generally, in Barbadian society, in her reflections on her current life and her dreams for the future. Her reflections demonstrate the importance of life-cycle stage for women's gender ideologies and the simultaneous valuation of reputation and respectability.

I can't wait to have a family [she laughs with some embarrassment]. But having a family is a big responsibility. First I have to be married [. . .] have my own house and make sure I have everything there, cause you need savings before the child come [. . .] with expenses, you got to be able to stand up on your own two feet [. . .] "Hold up my head" [. . .] "Don't let no one fool you and push you around," that's what my mother always tell me. She want me to get a good basic education and save some money, settle down. But [. . .] I don't really go to church anymore. I stopped last year, 'cause I feel that you can't really have a boyfriend and stuff like that and still go to church [. . .] praising God, and outside still, you know, partying and doing this and that [. . .] I can't go to church knowing I do that, so I decide to stop altogether. You be leading like two lives [. . .] you be sweet in church and next minute you know you like this party and thing [. . .] so it don't make no sense. When you get settled, then you probably think about going back [to church].

Joyce's description of her own "wild" youth and her expectation of "settling down" are echoed in Diane Wolf's discussion (1992:260) of Javanese factory workers. When Javanese women move through the life course and shift from "single daughter" to married woman and mother, "suddenly the rebellious and testy daughters become tame and 'responsible.' Parents are finally pleased with their daughters' economic behavior and go on to complain about the next generation of adolescent, unmarried factory daughters who are following the same path their predecessors did—retaining their income and spending it on themselves."

As the following chapters will reveal, Barbadian women of varied ages work in these jobs and value them both for the money they provide to fulfill economic needs and for the pleasure they bring, and in turn, their work comes to take on both repressive and empowering meanings. In the span of only a few years, an individual woman, like Joyce, may well embody different patterns of femininity, particularly if she moves through significant life stages. The tensions between competing "ideals" and between a multiplicity of "real" expressions of femininity are manifested at all points along the continuum.[46]

With regard to the global patterns of export production and multinational labor, the implications of these tensions and contradictions are no less significant. Certainly, as many scholars are quick to point out, foreign corporations' receptivity to local cultural differences (e.g., the centrality of motherhood and coexistence of wage work and motherhood in Afro-Caribbean history), their flexibility in maintaining two "generations" of informatics workers, and likewise, espousing two apparently competing sets of rationales all serve the interest of their own capital accumulation. Indeed, Fordism itself was predicated on a flexible approach to defining labor. Fordism, as Devon Peña (1997:38) aptly points out, "is a system that manipulates the demographic composition of the work force in order to impose multiple divisions of power based on skill, wages, age, seniority, race, ethnicity or nationality, gender and many other factors. This manipulation is necessary in order to make adjustments in response to fluctuations in the organized resistance of workers and in the *supply and quality of available labor*" (italics mine). For Stuart Hall (1991:29) the anxious focus on the homogenizing thrust of globalization has obscured the fact that contradiction and difference are fundamental to capitalism itself. "One of the most profound insights in Marx's *Capital* . . . is that capitalism only advances, as it were, on contradictory terrain. It is the contradictions which it has to overcome that produce its own forms of expansion. And . . . until one can see the nature of that contradictory terrain and precisely how particularity is engaged and how it is woven in, and how it presents its resistances, and how it is partly overcome, and how those overcomings then appear again, we will not understand it. That is much closer to how we ought to think about the so-called 'logic of capital' in the advance of globalization itself." In essence, by working in and through difference (gendered, "ethnically and racially inflected labor forces") and not through homogeneous and totalizing modes of incorporation, capital has advanced itself. We might take Hall's insights one step further by emphasizing that "difference" itself takes on unpredictable forms. The strategic "difference" therefore, in informatics' move to Barbados is expressed not merely in its sexual division of labor (i.e., the recruitment of women) but also in its ultimate revision of the "idealized" women it originally held sacrosanct. Difference, expressed in a sexual division of labor, is recreated, refashioned and given specific, local inflections.

Across the global assembly line, multinational corporations have recruited not just women workers but women workers whose femininity is defined, created, and asserted in particular, different ways. Barbadian women predominantly are recruited for and drawn to informatics as the "ideal" offshore workers for reasons that involve both ideological and economic realities surrounding work and gender. The relationship between these ideologies and realities is complex, and sometimes even contradictory. For example, Charlene, who was raised by her grandparents and now supports her young daughter with her wages from Data Air and some help from her daughter's father, also hopes that she will marry, raise two children, work, and eventually open her own business. Thus, she readily articulates the "ideal" rationale that women are the logical informatics workers because they are better suited physically to the work and do not need to earn a family wage, and at the same time she recounts the economic insecurity of raising a child and piecing together a living and a future for herself and her daughter. The fact that her wage is necessary to the maintenance of her household contradicts the male breadwinner myth that she also carries in her mind. Examples of such contradictions between women's own experiences and histories and the gendered ideologies and rationales they frequently expressed were numerous. They are testaments to the multiple models of womanhood and femininity that coexist not merely between local and global corporate managers or between managers and workers or between the "old guard" and the "new recruits" but in the minds of individual women themselves.

Bajan women are recruited into offshore informatics, not because they are naturally more docile, dexterous, and nimble fingered than men or because they are dependent daughters who need little money because they work merely for "extras" or, on the other extreme, because their status as mothers guarantees their superior work ethic and reliability. These women are incorporated into the informatics sector through the powerful deployment of gender ideologies—local and global—in which the work of processing data is conceived as feminine by virtually all of the actors involved. And, women are drawn to informatics because it is one of few expanding arenas within the nation's economy. For these women, informatics offers an appealing entree into the world of high tech and modernity, as well as the promise of a steady wage. In the process of their incorporation, the ideologies of femininity (both local and global) that construe them as docile, patient, responsible, and even mercenary are invoked and reinscribed in order to make them ideal workers for this new industry. Fundamental to the process is the very fact that femininity is not embodied within a single profile. And, just as the "docile girl" stereotype has simultaneously misrepresented and disciplined women, the idealization of the "matriarch" runs similar essentializing risks that distort the realities of Barbadian women's changing experiences.

While Hall and Peña both draw our attention to the strategic power of difference, they see this difference as merely part of capitalism's strategy and design.[47] What I am arguing here, however, is that women workers have been important actors in the process of defining and making use of difference. History, culture, and women's collective and individual will have all conspired to challenge informatics companies' prescription for "ideal" pink-collar workers. Their insistence, for example, that motherhood and wage work are both integral to womanhood, and the state's support of this reality through laws guaranteeing maternity leave, has lead companies not only to abandon their insistence that workers be childless but also to embrace a new "ideal" profile of the "strong matriarch." In doing so, informatics firms find they can profit from this culturally induced flexibility, just as Hall and Peña imply. What their arguments miss, however, is the active participation played by women workers in this drama, in both defining and reconfiguring "difference" amid the advance of global capitalism.

The effects of introducing a counter "ideal" in the form of the powerful matriarch are themselves contradictory. On one hand, women have been able to keep jobs that may otherwise have been turned over to younger school leavers and thus may move into new life stages (as partners, mothers, and wives), retain their jobs, and experience simultaneously the autonomy of a working woman and the affirmation that comes from being a mother. In the context of their informatics jobs, their motherhood confers added esteem and flexibility, as well as economic burden. Their responsibility to their children makes them serious, committed workers who are reliable and loyal to their employer; the employer's recognition of this benefit also makes him or her sympathetic in the event of a child's illness or familial obligations that require flexibility in an otherwise highly regimented work environment. On the other hand, these "matriarchs" increasingly forgo the guarantee of support from their extended kin networks that they might have expected, as well as facilities such as day care and related affordable domestic services that a modern market might otherwise provide. As such, their pink-collar work and their domestic responsibilities place them not as truly independent, powerful matriarchs or "leaders with men as their lieutenants" (Errol Miller 1991:283) but as Afro-Barbadian women who continue to bear the burden of a double (if not triple) day.

The adaptations and juggling acts women perform in order to maintain their wage work through changing stages of their own life cycles, often in conjunction with informal economic activities as well as domestic responsibilities, make it impossible to perceive them merely as pawns, or as cookie-cutter versions of a global worker in the multinational labor game. Simultaneously, the foreign corporations make strategic use of the variations in family constellation and range of cultural ideologies of femininity and womanhood, as they incorporate them (and maintain them) within their labor force. With their own ends in mind, women and corporations exercise strategies of adaptation and of creative flexibility in redefining the profiles of offshore pink-collar workers in the Barbadian context.

Chapter 5

Inside Multitext and

Data Air: Discipline

and Agency in the

"Open Office"

Multitext and Data Air are two of Barbados's largest foreign-owned data entry operations. Their modern, mirrored facades and well-appointed interiors are markers of Barbados's recent thrust toward the creation of an offshore information processing sector. They mark not only a new subcategory of work within the "enclave industries" but also a new look and management style of Barbadian workplaces in general. These two companies are neighbors in the newly renovated Harbour Industrial Park, and together they employ roughly thirteen hundred people, most of whom are women. The information processing companies operating in this new information arena range in size from two with fewer than twenty-five employees to one with more than one thousand, and to some extent their size defines the overall ambience of the work environment. In most companies, the simple hierarchy of managers, supervisors, and production workers is reflected spatially in the following way: managers' offices are located in their own wing or hall of the building, separate from the production areas; supervisors and shift managers' offices either line or encircle the production floor, giving them a constant view of the workers through large picture windows, and data entry operators, claims adjudicators, and quality assurance operators are positioned within their own individual work cubbies, either lined in rows or clustered in groups of four across the "open office."

This chapter describes the inner workings of informatics—how these new offshore workplaces function, and to what end. By describing these two companies, their recruitment of workers, and the labor processes they establish, I intend to show that informatics represents not only a new phase of industialization but also a significant new arena for the creation of women's identities as workers. It becomes a site of both creative agency and of constant and multi-layered surveillance and discipline.

Multitext, a subsidiary of a British telecommunications giant, is a text entry operation, providing offshore keyboarding services to numerous publishers from the United States, the United Kingdom, and Europe. Data Air is owned by a U.S. multinational, which is also the parent company of a major U.S. airline, and it began as simply an offshore location to perform its own ticket data entry at a lower cost. Multitext, therefore, acts as a vendor of data processing services for varied clients, and though Data Air now sells its services to other companies as well, it began as an offshore site of its multinational parent company, with the basic aim of reducing in-house costs. Together they demonstrate a set of labor processes and management strategies that resemble other more traditional manufacturing industries in the Barbadian offshore sector and at the same time distinguish the information industry as something new.

As the largest facility on the island, Data Air occupies eighty thousand square feet of Industrial Development Corporation (IDC) factory building space referred to in the industry as an "open office." A great deal of effort has gone into the design of this space, in the partitioning of different work areas and the building of custom-designed computer work stations, as well as in the decorations of pleasing floral prints on the walls, plants in offices, subdued colors of carpeting and paint well suited for fluorescent lighting. Electronically locked doors and the white noise of the computers lend a distinctive aura to these new work settings. Unlike the traditional Barbadian architecture with its high-pitched roofs and louver windows allowing for maximum ventilation, these high-tech buildings are air-conditioned and relatively windowless. After a particularly long stretch of overtime, Grace, a data processor at Data Air, said she could "scarcely tell whether it was day or night" when she was at work. Resounding corrugated metal roofs often signal a heavy downpour, but the brilliant light and heat of the Caribbean sun is almost unimaginable inside these chilly and fluorescent-lit spaces. Dust free and air conditioned (as demanded by the computer technology itself), the informatics environment is constructed carefully to create a distinctly nonmanufacturing-like atmosphere. "Cool" is a term that crops up regularly in many women's narratives about their work in informatics, referring to both the comfortable and inviting respite from the humid heat outside, and the high-tech, modern quality of the "open office." Renaming the production floor an "open office" is part of a new informatics language, tied to the ambiance that management have carefully crafted and representing a significant source of symbolic capital within this zone.

Company Histories

Multitext began as a New York–based company with a work force of fifteen typists who entered the text and typesetting codes of edited manuscripts onto computer disks prior to the final printing process. The company's president, a forty-year veteran of the printing industry, experimented in offshore business in St. Vincent as early as 1975, and in 1983 shifted his New York operation to Barbados, starting with ten typists and five computers. Management was essentially a one-man show. In these early days of the company, jobs were done by trial and error, using different instruction manuals and coding specifications, and in some instances special software sent by publishers with each new job. The workers entered text and publishing codes for a wide variety of books and journals, from popular fiction to scientific manuscripts, and this small operation set the stage for what ultimately became Multitext Corporation. The same brinksman behind this fledgling offshore operation runs and occupies his New York office alone, and with a fax machine and telephone, contracts work from North American and European clients to be sent by courier service to and from Barbados. By the time I began this study in 1989, Multitext had been taken over by a large British telecommunications corporation and had increased its size tenfold, employing roughly 150 Barbadian workers.

Each morning by courier services, original (edited) manuscripts arrive in Barbados for processing that will later be sent back to the customer along with computer disks of the typesetting-ready version. Manuscripts range from short journal articles to six-hundred-page textbooks and encyclopedias. Operating on two shifts, keyers are trained to enter, verify, and quality check manuscripts, guaranteeing clients an accuracy rate of 99.96 percent. Average turnaround time for jobs is forty-eight hours, and in that time the manuscript is "marked up" with the typesetting specifications written in pencil as marginal notes, photocopied, and then distributed in batches of pages to the production floor, where it is keyed and "deferred" or checked and then checked again. According to one manager, a text of six hundred pages given to forty people to type on an average shift can be entered in half a day.

During the course of my research at Multitext, there was a change in management from a Barbadian woman, Rita Brathwaite, whose entrée into the industry was as a keyer in Multitext's infancy, to a white Englishman, Mark Roark, who had been previously employed by the British multinational parent company. When this new English general manager was brought in, Rita Brathwaite was sent to manage a new "off-offshore" branch of Multitext opened on the island of Dominica. The American who originally started Multitext remains a minor partner and continues to be involved throughout the changes in ownership, management, and expansions into other Caribbean sites. A vital component of his role has been that of marketing and management link with the international client base. His role has been to secure contracts and to deal directly with clients from his New York base, as the Barbados and more recent Dominican operation produce the work.

According to Mr. Roark, as well as the American shareholder, Multitext had been run at a loss for the three years of its operation, since it was taken over in 1989. Its majority shareholder, a British telecommunications giant, simultaneously holds a monopoly of the telecommunications services in Barbados and throughout the Eastern Caribbean and has viewed Multitext as a valuable public relations enterprise to boost its image across the region. The expense of sponsoring cricket matches and other cultural events and employing 150 workers in this new and high-profile high-tech industry is considered a small price to pay for maintaining control over the lucrative telephone companies in the region.[1] The recent expansion of Multitext into Dominica and similar proposals for St. Lucia and St. Vincent undoubtedly reflect the same reasoning, and reminders of its primarily symbolic importance shed an ironic light on the many new management initiatives employed and attempts to ameliorate internal company problems.

Data Air also began its operation in Barbados in 1983. At that time, roughly 150 data entry operators were hired to key vital revenue and accounting data from airline ticket stubs, processing over 450,000 documents from close to 3,000 flights a day, and 8 million flight coupons a month. In 1983, Data Air processed 38 million documents and in 1991 the numbers nearly quadrupled to over 145 million, representing two tons of paper each day. Within twenty-four hours of every airline flight, passengers' ticket receipts from every one of the airline's destinations are sent in large yellow mail sacks to Barbados's Grantley Adams International Airport. Trucked to Data Air's facility in the Harbour Industrial Park, they are sorted and distributed to data entry operators, who are seated in clustered computer stations arranged in groups of four on the open office floor. Revenue-accounting information is fed by operators into the computer terminals and promptly transmitted by satellite back to the company's main computer center in Tulsa, Oklahoma. Data Air's parent company has saved roughly 50 percent on operating costs by moving offshore to Barbados, and according to its U.S. office, Bajan operators are meeting and in some cases surpassing the productivity levels achieved in the United States.

In 1989, a new division was added to the company's airline ticket operation, virtually doubling the work force and expanding its scope beyond back office work for its parent company into new profit-making service areas of information processing. Data Air was contracted by one of North America's largest insurance companies to evaluate and approve medical claims, guaranteeing a turnaround time of under seventy-two hours for its clients. Combining airmail, satellite technology, and fiber optic telephone lines, medical claims forms are sent to Barbados, batched according to home office in the United States, evaluated and keyed by the operator using a specially designed software program, and entered into the main North American computers. The complete adjudication process is achieved within 104 hours, ultimately generating for the claimant either a reimbursement check or a letter of denial from the insurance company. One hundred ninety terminals are hooked directly into the company's data base, "as if we are sitting in the client's office," the general manager said. In a single day, Data Air processes between twenty-five thousand and thirty-five thousand medical claims for one client alone.

In the past couple of years, the company's expansion has required an addition of over 75 percent more floor space in the Harbour Industrial Park to accommodate a new research library division for the storage and retrieval of airline ticket information. This addition reflects the company's aim to move more and more back office work from the U.S. headquarters to the Data Air facility in Barbados and fulfills local development plans for the expansion of higher-skilled and higher value-added high-tech services. While providing fewer jobs (sixty) than the more routine end of data processing, this new area signals precisely the move beyond basic data entry into more advanced computer-based areas that many in the IDC, the corporate arena, educational institutions, and academic circles have been promoting for several years. In turn, the BDS$22 million (US$11) generated by Data Air in 1992 alone is a significant foreign exchange boost to the Barbadian economy.[2]

Working Conditions

Much of my discussion of informatics in Barbados centers on its intriguingly ambiguous nature. Officially part of the offshore industrial sector but symboli-

cally imbued with links to the white-collar arena of computing, it is labor intensive, and yet nonunion. The officelike appearance of the workplace seems to
counter the factorylike labor process. It is vital, therefore, to examine in detail
such elements of the working conditions as the recruitment of workers, the
wages they are paid, the training they receive, and the opportunities for upward
mobility.

RECRUITMENT

In a small country like Barbados, news of all kinds travels quickly, from political
and social gossip to news of the opening of a new company creating the possibility of new jobs. Historically, newspapers in Barbados have had extraordinary
circulation rates, and with the opening of each of the data entry facilities on the
island, one advertisement in the two major papers has led to a flood of job applications.[3] In 1983 Data Air received over two thousand applications for barely
two hundred positions and the newest data entry operation opening ten years
later received over three thousand applications for sixty positions.[4] When Data
Air and Multitext opened, hardly a day passed when one or two young women
did not come unsolicited to fill out applications. Additionally, networks of family,
neighbors, and friends are important sources of information about work, and
many of the current data entry operators applied for their jobs on the advice of
personal contacts in the industry.

Each time a new advertisement appears and word travels about jobs in a new
company, the management of existing operations worries about losing trained
workers. In fact, there is frequent movement among operators from one company to another, as well as among supervisory staff. In the course of my research,
I witnessed many individuals cycle through two or three different companies. In
four years, one young man moved from Data Air, where he worked as a supervisor, to Multitext, where he was employed as a shift manager, to a Canadian
company, where he received a similar management-level job. Another Data Air
supervisor, Serena, made similar moves, from Data Air, where she worked as a
supervisor, to Multitext, where she became a trainer, and then to the newest joint
venture operation where she is, again, a supervisor. Slight increases in salary and
sometimes boredom and frustration with their current jobs inspire this kind of
shuffling between companies.

New firms express contradictory strategies toward recruitment of experienced
workers. Managers continue to prefer young women directly out of school, even
though they increasingly retain them for long periods of time. Some companies

are attracted to applicants with experience in a similar operation (data entry or another offshore industry), with the hope that even if retraining is necessary, the more general work ethic is already ingrained. In this vein, Data Air employed several former electronics assembly workers when it opened in 1983, and now newer companies approach Data Air supervisors or lead operators when hiring their own supervisory staff. On the other hand, the owner of a small local firm expressed a preference for just the opposite strategy. Hiring workers away from Data Air, for example, had not worked for him. He found that these operators are so familiar with the labor process of ticket entry or claims processing that they prove more difficult to train on his computer system for coupon entry. As such, he recruited only first-time workers, just out of secondary school, those who "don't have to unlearn another system." In effect, new employers are faced with what is presented as a trade-off between hiring workers who have absorbed the required work ethic (discipline, "sensitivity" to time, and individualized work) but may have difficulty making the transition from one computer system to another, or training from scratch women for whom the general work demands and the specific labor process are unfamiliar.

Across the industry, prerequisites for a job in data processing almost uniformly include three O-level (or equivalent) certificates, including English and Math, as well as typing skills.[5] Most operations have implemented their own screening devices, including a typing test and standardized aptitude tests of basic English usage, math, word or symbol recognition, and memory. One local company manager administered what he called an IQ test, which included geography questions and current affairs.

> The geography part was necessary because the majority of our work comes from the U.S. and we thought that it was good to see how the girls rated in terms of the capitals of the states. [. . .] We found that with our first batch of girls—like if you have Jamaica, New York, and you know our girls know Jamaica, West Indies, and they might get confused. One girl religiously keyed the country code for Jamaica, so this helped us to see how the student rated.

Beyond the application and testing, the interview is the final and often most crucial step in the recruitment process. Although the highly individualized electronic basis for calculating skill levels and productivity implies that personal rapport and favoritism are less evident in informatics than in traditional Barbadian sectors of work, the "plantation model" of social relations is more likely to emerge in the context of the interview. Appeals by applicants are often made on the basis of familial or other ties, such as village or parish origin. The questions posed to prospective employees cover such areas as personal and family background (e.g., whether they have any children, where they live and with whom) and previous work experience. Specific questions about applicants' household composition are intended to uncover potential problems with shift work, and in particular evening schedules. For example, women with children are probed about child care arrangements both during the day and at night. Having a child is not, in and of itself, a cause for rejection, but a woman without acknowledged plans for child care would be less likely to "get through" (be hired).

Applicants are also asked general questions about why they want this job and what "their goals are" (e.g., earning money to support the family or learning computer skills). Indeed, computer skills are cited by most applicants as a significant draw of these jobs. Ultimately, for some, this becomes the basis for disappointment as well. On several occasions I heard a personnel interviewer cautioning the interviewee that she would "not really be learning computer skills" but instead would be "using the computer as one would a typewriter." At Multitext, two trainers argued about whether a young man who applied for a data entry job and expressed his goal as "learning computer programming" was suitable for the job. One said, "Computer programming! He's not going to do that here," implying that his expectations were out of step with the parameters of the job, and that his inevitable dissatisfaction would make him an unsuitable selection. The other trainer argued that any expressed interest in computer-related work was relevant and acceptable and should not disqualify him. Another similar case involved the hiring of a hearing-impaired operator at Multitext. Millicent was twenty-eight years old and, despite having graduated from one of the better secondary schools with six O-level certificates and completing an additional two years of courses at the community college, she had been unable to gain employment. In an interview, she explained, "I wanted to become a computer programmer and doing the [IDC training] course and working here has afforded me that long-awaited opportunity."[6]

Few keyers on the job (including Millicent) would confuse computer programming with operating a computer terminal; nonetheless, the draw of the technology alone continues to attract young first-time workers. Despite attempts by managers and personnel officers to explain how computers are used in these jobs (as a tool like a typewriter, rather than as a device over which the worker has control to manipulate and program) the draw of this symbol of the "information age" continues to be strong. As Cynthia put it:

I know that even though I don't know a whole lot about computers, I've learnt something [. . .] [though] there's a lot more that you can do [. . .] The computer is programmed to do certain things, and at present we're only doing one thing with it, and that's entering and checking the work. I would like to learn more because I think in today's world if you can use a computer you can do 'most anything.

Her comment hints at a widely held view of computers as the very embodiment of modernity and development. Even the frank acknowledgment that data processing does not itself allow one to "learn computers" does not diminish the sense of promise these jobs hold. For a few who are more pragmatic, like Suzanne, on the other hand, there is little ambiguity about the applicability of data processing for securing other, more skilled work. She asserted:

I always say, if I had to go and look for another job, what you learn here when you use the computer . . . it isn't anything that you could use later in your life. [. . .] What we have is to keypunch—you can enter fast [. . .] but to me it really don't give you anything for your future that you could use.

According to Suzanne, simply working at a computer terminal offers no more in the way of knowledge or new transferable skills than working with any other piece of equipment. The contradiction between this reality and the aura surrounding the computer as the symbol of the information industry is echoed in women's feelings about the very nature of their work—highly individualized, quiet, and pleasantly officelike but also strictly disciplined, depersonalized, and alienating. It is not unusual for women, in the same breath, to extol the virtues of Data Air, or informatics as an industry and complain about being "chained to the computer" and reprimanded "like schoolgirls" while making "too little money for all the work." The contradictions surrounding the use of computers derives less from misapprehension than from an optimistic belief on the part of the women that by simply working on computers they will absorb useful experience for the future. For these women, the very elements of their jobs that give them pleasure and pride may simultaneously cause them stress and hardship. But at some level, for most of these informatics workers, the computer as an embodiment of possibility, for them personally and for the country as a whole, supersedes that of the computer as a tool of bondage. Fiona's comment encapsulates this contradiction.

I don't want to stay [. . .] I don't even want to think about it. I just come. [. . .] Not that I look forward to it or anything. I think you should be going to something that you enjoy [. . .] but I don't find that here and that's what I don't like about [Data Air]. I'm hoping with my experience with computers, maybe I will get a new job. Everyone needs someone who knows about the computer, so I think it's a move in the right direction for me.

As a claims approver in the insurance side of Data Air, Fiona expresses both frustration and boredom with data processing, the early shift hours, and the monotony of her work, but she sees the experience as a ticket to better work through the exposure it has given her to computers. She is planning to enroll in a correspondence course on database management and, like some of her co-workers, to enhance her possibilities for another job through further education. This is a pattern that was even more prominently marked among the data processors in Data Air's sister plant in the Dominican Republic. In Santo Domingo, where nearly half of the operators are men, and where the "life span" of a worker averages two years, the jobs are envisioned by many as useful stepping stones toward other computer-related work.[7]

TRAINING

Managers from all of the data entry operations, both local and foreign, noted that it was easy enough to find the bodies to fill these jobs but the difficulty was in finding good typists. All of them commented that despite expectations that competent typists would be hired and subsequently trained on the computer program and individual job specifications, in fact, more rudimentary training and drilling was required to achieve the desired typing speed and accuracy levels. Responding to the need for a labor supply of skilled data entry operators, the Barbados Industrial Development Corporation (BIDC) attempted to implement a training program for recent school leavers who would ultimately be hired by any one of the data processing operations. The government-run National Training Board screened applicants and arranged for their preliminary training in the hope that after a six-month course they would meet the recognized proficiency expectations and be hired by a local company. The Barbados government paid a nominal grant to each trainee (US$25 a week) to subsidize the program. Anne Marie, a keyer who went through this course, commented:

now this money is not to buy anything like clothes, this is just for bus fare to get to work and back home. [. . .] It really isn't anything; but to me, I had never worked for anything, and to me it was a lot because I could still buy my personal things, soaps and what not, and be independent of my father and my sisters.

Upon completion of the program, she and most of the other women who trained with her were hired by Data Air.

Early in 1989, the Samuel Jackman Prescod Polytechnic was approached by the IDC about introducing keyboarding skills to train large numbers of workers for the information processing industry. The Polytechnic, an administrator explained, provides skills training in such areas as welding, carpentry, and design and dressmaking. Keyboarding, he argued, "is an isolated task; you're not preparing someone with a lifetime skill as you are by training a welder or a woodworker or a secretary." Furthermore, as he explained it, the IDC introduced the idea in January and wanted three hundred trained keyboard operators four months later. No computer lab existed at the time, and no instructors or curriculum had been identified that would satisfy a range of different employers. The tension expressed by this administrator reflects ambiguity over the concept of skill within data processing and the applicability of training to a range of employment possibilities. His concept of a "lifetime of employment" as insured by a traditional craft is itself challenged in many areas of work by the speed with which technology is changing. Others have argued, however, that the work ethic appropriate to informatics and flexibility in adapting to new applications and programs (as has been demanded for a variety of reasons in both Data Air and Multitext) are in themselves a valuable skill (Pearson 1993).

All of the data processing facilities have been involved to some degree with the government education system in the attempt to establish a consistent and reliable training program. As a manager at Multitext imagined the logical division of labor, the Polytechnic would provide training for the lower-skilled work, and the more academic community college would provide training for work requiring higher levels of skill and education (e.g., computer mapping, graphics, software development). What has happened, however, is that each of the companies now provides training independently to meet the specific needs of its clients. Foreign companies typically make use of training personnel they bring in from North American headquarters, and smaller local operations tend to borrow American-designed tests and software to conduct their training and evaluation. The pattern has been to use the IDC training funds to offset company start-up costs but to provide their own training courses using in-house software and equipment. One of the operations performing insurance claims work, for example, hired keyers with proficient typing skills and trained them on the specific terms and codes demanded by their program. Others have less stringent typing requirements and count on women to learn or perfect their typing while being trained on the system.

Over the three-year period of my research, however, training operators to the desired production levels continued to be a problem at Multitext. When I first arrived there, no formal training program existed. One or another supervisor performed training activities with each new group of typists in the back of the production floor. These sessions were generally introduced by a lecture about the general expectations of the company (punctuality, reliability, accuracy, etc.) as well as rules of thumb for good typing (e.g., maintaining proper posture and hand position, keying character by character for optimum accuracy, keeping fingers limber and achieving speed and accuracy with finger gymnastics). Facing great dissatisfaction with the proficiency rates and speed of their typists, Multitext introduced several new training strategies, including an entirely new keyboard program. They shifted from recruiting those with typing skills to searching for "better-educated girls" without typing skills and training them on the specially designed Dvorak keyboard. This keyboard arranges the letters in its own unique order distinct from that of the standard typewriter keyboard, according to the theory that its layout maximizes the use of the strongest fingers on the most prevalent letter combinations. Multitext's manager at the time admitted that an added benefit of training workers on the Dvorak system was that typists would not easily be able to leave for other clerical jobs, since their typing skills would not be transferable.[8] The training period was increased from eight to twelve weeks, and new office space in Bridgetown was rented and set up specifically for training purposes.

Typists at Multitext are ranked according to ability, from grade one to grade four. The grade one typists (new trainees) are hired on a probationary basis for six months. During this period, their supervisor calculates and monitors their speed and error rates. At group meetings, each person's scores are read aloud, and keyers are reprimanded or congratulated according to their scores. Strict disciplinary measures are imposed during the probation period. For example, trainees are allowed up to three absences during the six months and each absence must be covered by a doctor's note. Lateness is also cause for admonishment. In the middle of my research period a consultant was hired to evaluate the effectiveness of company policies and to compile a manual for production workers, spelling out every aspect of the labor process and every company rule. Somewhat indicative of other attempts at company reorganization, the manual and evaluation were never completed, and, though many rules and codes of conduct were enforced, no official documents existed spelling out job descriptions or other elements of workplace etiquette.

This greater investment in training is one aspect of the information processing industry that has notably set it apart from traditional manufacturing industries and raised the hopes of development planners and educators. In contrast to the brief on-the-job training common to garment and electronics factories (Lim 1985:57), the combination of computer technology and special courses lasting up to three months have given at least the illusion of introducing workers to new and broadly applicable skills. Now, however, two trends seem to be emerging. One, exemplified by Data Air's recent expansion into less labor-intensive but higher-skilled back office activities, and even more so by the emergence of a new offshore computer software testing operation that hires few but highly skilled university-educated computer science graduates, marks the industry's strides in the direction of higher-level, higher value-added work. The other trend is exemplified by another data entry operation in Barbados that uses satellite transmission to process credit card applications and utility company forms. This company trains its operators only one week on the system, rejecting full use of the IDC's subsidized program providing a low level of training much like that of traditional assembly industries. What emerges, then, is a two-tiered industry with smaller but highly skilled computer-based service firms on one tier and large and low-skilled data entry operations on the other. Already, such factors as wage rates and literacy rates that are higher than those of other Caribbean countries that promote offshore data processing make Barbados more competitive in attracting the former, and this is clearly the direction encouraged by the IDC, local investors, and public officials alike.

MONEY, HIERARCHY, AND MOBILITY

Wages across the data entry industry are kept relatively standard from one company to another, in general slightly above the average for the manufacturing sector, and ranging from US$80 a week for the smaller local firms to US$100 a week for the larger, foreign-owned companies. Firms tend to match the going rate, established both by IDC recommendations and by informal guidelines from Data Air as the largest and longest-operating company. Like large foreign-owned companies elsewhere on the global assembly line, those in Barbados tend to pay slightly higher wages and offer better working conditions than do small local concerns (Lim 1985; Peña 1997), and the variability in wages across the data entry industry reflects this pattern. Smaller local operations tend to be under-capitalized, as well as less secure in their client base, and therefore offer lower wages and often "flexible" or intermittent employment depending on the contracts they have at a given time.

All of the data entry operations in Barbados pay their workers a provisional training salary for the first two to three months of their employment. After meeting a specified target production rate, operators' pay is increased to a "trained" or "proficient" level. For example, at Multitext, the training wage is US$1.62 an hour or about US$260 a month, and once an operator achieves ten thousand characters an hour, the rate is increased to US$1.75 (US$280 a month). At the highest end, a newer foreign-owned operation pays US$2.40 an hour for a three-month training period and then US$2.75 an hour (US$440 a month) for proficient keyers.

Wages cannot be evaluated, however, without taking into consideration the variety of incentive systems built into the pay scale of the informatics industry. Incentive bonuses are determined by productivity (speed and accuracy) rates on top of the minimum proficiency rate. As in the piece-rate systems of garment and electronics factories, these pink-collar "office" workers are paid by the volume and quality of work they produce. Here, instead of blue jeans or computer chips, the commodity is information, and the higher the volume of insurance claims or airline tickets operators can decipher and accurately key, the higher their pay packet will be. As one Data Air Shift Manager told me:

> Without incentive, an average pay would be [BDS$5.35 or US$2.68 an hour] for a person who would have been here [. . .] well, someone who has been promoted to A1 level [proficient status]. Of course there's a raise of pay every April, ranging from 3 to 6 percent. And then there's incentive. You work for eighty hours in a bi-weekly period and there are persons who are able to work for an additional eighty hours of incentive. So the pay can double—that's for a person who is keying at 200 percent. We have one or two of those. Then you have the average person who makes roughly thirty hours incentive a bi-weekly period. So they would get an eighty-hour check which would be about [BDS$448] gross [US$224] and then on top of that you can get an additional thirty hours at [BDS$5.35], so that's basically between [BDS$600 and $700; US$300–350].

At Multitext, manuscripts are graded on a scale from one to four, corresponding to levels of coding difficulty. Incentive wages are graded accordingly, so that a grade-four typist can make a comparable amount of incentive wage as a grade-one typist given the fact that she types fewer, more difficult pages. The incentive system, widely used in production operations, is based on the premise that the worker takes responsibility for her own output and thereby determines her rate of remuneration. An emphasis on individualism runs heavily through the industry and is evident in one manager's enthusiastic proclamation that "the possibilities [for earning] are limited only by one's own drive and determination."

The general manager at Data Air describes the incentive system as the company's "key to success." It allows workers to earn a substantial addition to their base salary, and some keyers have on occasion more than doubled their wages. A labor unionist from the Barbados Workers Union, however, criticizes the incentive system because it makes it difficult to determine workers' actual wages and places the burden of wage rates on the workers. "Their performance is what's stressed, and women think they get little because of themselves, because of their productivity, that they are lazy, weak, that they lack that zip and drive to do better. [The companies] make them think it's them, their fault."

Competitions and intergroup contests are staged to raise the level of individual motivation and to maximize productivity. Serena, a new claims approver, described her early experience with this system.

> I never thought I could make it [. . .] it was hard at first, learning everything. They expect you to learn so much at first and it's so new and [. . .] besides, the stress on the quality of the work you produce, they expect you to do a certain amount of work in a certain amount of time, and I thought, jeez, I'll probably never be able to do this. But I think it has a lot to do with how people look at you and what they think your capabilities are and how you show them what you can do. If people have faith in you, you don't want to disappoint them, and every day you try to do a little more.

Incentive schemes vary from one company to the next, most beginning after a ten-thousand or twelve-thousand keystroke minimum. Again, the range between local and foreign companies is marked. At Computrans, a small, locally run data entry operation, for example, the rate of pay is $.50 to $.70 per one thousand keystrokes. People who are very fast and accurate keyers make about $.80 per one thousand keystrokes. Incentive pay is about $.20 per one thousand keystrokes on average and generally amounts to between US$25 to US$30 in a week, or 30 percent on top of the base wage. An average weekly pay was said to be roughly US$75 plus US$30 for incentive for a proficient keyer, bringing the standard rate across the industry to US$105 a week, and reaching US$150 a week for the newer foreign companies.

Some workers expressed resentment about the incentive system coupled with a low basic wage and said that they would prefer simply making "a fair flat wage." As one might expect, this was a common sentiment among those who had difficulty achieving the production quotas and rarely earned incentive bonuses. One such woman said, "Some people who get like sixty hours [incentive] every two weeks, they would take home six hundred and something dollars [US$300] or more. But if you make errors, then you lose your incentive and you just get your flat pay and overtime if you work any." Because wage rates themselves are based on individual productivity, workers are making a range of hourly wages, in addition to their different rates of incentive pay. Most workers do not know how much incentive or at what rate their fellow operators earn, and there is a strong degree of secrecy when paychecks are distributed.

Workers' comments about their pay provide insight into the meaning of these jobs. The symbolic overtones linking money to sexuality are striking in Lorraine's reflections on the gendered dimensions of privacy and exhibitionism surrounding paychecks.

> Most people are secretive when it comes to their paycheck [. . .] except the fellas; they like to compare. But you know, women are secretive when it comes to money. I don't know why, I guess it's tradition. [. . .] Women like to hide money. I'm not one of those. I compare it with my friend, but usually the women hide their paychecks. It's funny, you know, women are envious. Like if I make $300 this pay period and you make $210, although I might say you are my friend, when I show you my check, I'll see that sudden change on your face [. . .] you know? The fellas would joke about it, if one fella lose his incentive another might joke about it, but a woman, she might want to cry or sulk or something.

Lorraine's comment alludes to several important themes that underlie gender and money in the contemporary informatics zone. Her remarks invite reference, for example, to the familiar paradigm of respectability and reputation according to which secrecy, interiority, and decorum are central tenets of respectability/ femininity and public display and joking are central tenets of reputation/masculinity that level tensions surrounding differential status or wealth. However, the extent to which these expressions of femininity are reflective of Euro-colonial gender ideals (as Peter Wilson [1969] asserts) is easily brought into question.

Afro-Caribbean women's tradition of economic independence and management of their own economic resources, like that of West African women, has been linked to a pattern of secrecy even between husbands and wives (Sutton and Makiesky-Barrow 1981). What Lorraine's comment denotes, is the role that economic realities play in these gendered responses and the extent to which a woman "cries or sulks" because her children's school uniforms must be bought or because the rent payment is due. What seems undeniable, as Victoria Durant-Gonzalez (1982) puts it, is that women in the Caribbean are largely "in charge of producing, providing, controlling or managing those resources essential to meeting daily needs" and secrecy, or "manipulation" often go together in their efforts to "make do." As such, the epithet "working brain" and charges of acting with "cunning" or employing "manipulation" or "Anancyism," the familiar expressions for trickery or "putting something over on somebody," figure prominently in popular discourse on women and run parallel to the visions of women as selfless providers and matriarchs (Senior 1991:139).

Most of those who oppose the incentive system express a sense of anxiety and resentment over the unpredictability of pay. When asked what would represent a fair flat salary for the job of data processor, Joycelin, who has worked in data entry for six years, unequivocally replied, between US$550 and US$600 a month. She currently earns between US$360 and US$500 a month, depending on her incentive rates. Other operators frequently quote exactly those figures when asked to put a fair value on their work. These responses were interesting in what they revealed of women's sense of the status of the job. Joycelin's recommendation for an appropriate data entry wage represents roughly the pay of a secretary in Barbados, and twice that of a domestic worker. In informatics, only those with consistently high productivity are able to achieve these desired rates.

Other operators, however, prefer the incentive system to making a flat wage, saying that it motivates them to work harder and that they like knowing that their salary is not fixed. They are invariably workers who consistently achieve the target production levels and therefore increase their base wage with the incentive program as well as with overtime hours. Top keyers at both Multitext and Data Air are known to make as much as US$600 or US$700 a month with US$150 to US$200 in incentive wages, placing their earnings on a par with or even exceeding those of their supervisors.

Supervisors in the data entry operations, as staff, are paid salaries, and some may earn an incentive bonus based on the productivity rates of the keyers they supervise (.5 percent of the incentive earned by their operators). At Multitext, supervisors' salaries were raised from US$440 to US$575 a month in early 1991, though additional responsibilities for assisting in training efforts were being demanded of them along with the wage increase. At Data Air, supervisors' salaries range between US$600 and US$700 a month. With overtime and incentive, some are able to increase these amounts to between US$800 and US$900. Several supervisors, however, noted that a good keyer can make more than they earn in salary, and, given the amount of responsibility and the emotional labor that comes with managing other operators, they wondered whether it was worth making the change to a salaried job. The pressure they feel from both above and below leads some to reconsider the benefits of their "upward" mobility. Sandra, a shift manager at Data Air, had worked herself up the ranks at INTEL, before its sudden departure, and now she has done the same in informatics. At INTEL she began bonding on an assembly line, and was promoted first to "lead operator" and then to supervisor. When INTEL's tax holiday expired, and the company closed its doors, she applied to the fledgling Data Air, and in 1983, was hired as one of the first supervisors:

> I was at INTEL for five years, and the money I was getting was far less than what Data Air was offering. Here it was [BDS$1,100] a month and at INTEL it was seven hundred and something. When I came here I got the supervisor job. [. . .] I came in with the company, and the motivation was great. It was a new company and you had to be involved in making sure things go right and you had a motivational tool to work towards. Sometime in '88 there was an opportunity to move up to shift manager [. . .] and at first I was hesitant [. . .] I wasn't sure I could get the job done. But, because I had experience as a supervisor, I knew some of the things a manager had to do [. . .] so I kept learning and learned from my mistakes.

Like the supervisor who finds herself earning less than she did as a data entry operator, Sandra sometimes has second thoughts about her move to a managerial position, weighing the benefits of incentive against those of a guaranteed salary.

> When you consider being a supervisor, and making incentive and then overtime, if I was still a supervisor, I would be earning more than I do now [just over US$1,000 a month]. As a supervisor, after two hours overtime, I start to make time and a half and then I have an opportunity to earn incentive on my

group, which can very well push me up, as well. With overtime, a meal allowance [$5 after ten hours of work], and .5 percent of whatever your group earns [. . .] But as a manager you wouldn't get that. I look at my paycheck now and I realize sometimes that I used to get more as a supervisor. Then again, you would have to earn incentive—and it's not necessarily so that you would— so this is better—you are guaranteed.

Reservations about being a salaried rather than an hourly wage worker and about assuming the personal dynamics of power and authority were the reasons that few of the data entry operators I interviewed expressed interest in being promoted to supervisory positions. The disinclination toward promotion included keyers who had been working on the system for more than seven years and echoes Greta Foff Paules's account of waitresses who resist opportunities for upward mobility in becoming restaurant managers (1991:125). Like the manager of a restaurant, the data entry supervisor is squeezed between top-level management and rank-and-file worker. Having been a data entry operator herself, and thus, allied with a core group of other production workers, the supervisor is all too familiar with the tensions that can develop between keyers and those above them. As Pauline, a data entry operator said:

> I am not really interested in moving up. Although it may be boring, I just prefer to sit there [in data entry]. I really don't know much about the upper work, but you have to be able to control the group, bring them together, understand their problems, and then the supervisor gets pressure from management, [. . .] to comply by management and still [. . .] satisfy the employees [. . .] so he's between, struggling. I don't like that. You can't go up to satisfy management and satisfy him, then come down here where the employees be poking at you. So, he's right in between and struggling left and right. [. . .] I think it's tough.

The gendered referent of Pauline's imaginary supervisor is striking, in the light of the fact that the supervisors at Data Air and Multitext were, like the operators, almost entirely women. Despite this reality, the idea of a supervisor generally evoked a masculine image. All of the supervisors either have moved up from the ranks of data entry operator or were hired as supervisors with the inception of the company. Unlike the trend in the Mexican maquiladoras or the foreign-owned factories in Malaysia described by Aihwa Ong (1987), where a gendered division of labor separates women on the production line from men in supervisory and management positions, most supervisors and shift managers in informatics are also women. The "struggle" that Pauline alludes to between management and the rank and file is heightened by the fact that women develop friendships and a sense of shared interest with their fellow production workers. The movement into positions of authority, therefore, involves what some describe as an expression of betrayal—the idea that "she was one of us, but now she has gone to the other side" as Noella, a keyer at Data Air put it. The discomfort felt by many women at the idea of having to negotiate problems, and in effect be caught between production workers and management, in addition to the simple fact that for a good keyer the wages with incentive bonuses may indeed be better than the salary of a supervisor, create strong disincentives to "moving up." Noella described the plight of her friend Cecelia, who was promoted to Shift Manager from the data entry ranks.

> She has to be pushing them to do the work, and now the system they are using is very difficult. [. . .] The response time is very slow, so they are now keying below 100 percent and it is very difficult to be putting your all into your keying and no matter what you do, you put your energy in and even so it's below 100 percent. [. . .] You know, she wanted to resign, she can't take it anymore. She confides in me, and I can tell when she calls me and something happened at work [. . .] she usually go home late with things on her mind about what she going to do tomorrow. [. . .] It is stressful. There are other girls up there with her [on her shift] who came in with her and they are just keyers and some of them don't want to accept the fact that she can tell them what to do, so their attitude would change [toward her]. [. . .] If they're doing something wrong then it's in her authority to tell them they are doing something wrong, but they don't want her to do that. They want her to just lie back and let them do as they like.

Among the waitresses in Paules's study (1991:187) it was widely believed that they earn more money than their managers, and the headaches of responsibility and negotiating conflicts between customers, waitresses, and the kitchen adds to their conviction that they are better off waiting tables. She relates the predicament of the worker/waitress to that of the foreman/manager, echoing the plight of Noella's friend Cecelia.

> Though the possibility is rarely given serious consideration, it is conceivable that the worker's disinterest in advancement is motivated by an accurate ap-

praisal of what foremanship has to offer. This is not to argue that opportunity flourishes in the automobile factory, or that life on the assembly line is gratifying. The point is, rather, that entry-level managerial positions, in the factory as in the restaurant, may no longer represent a clear improvement over wage-level work. It is not that waiting on tables or tending an assembly line is pleasant and fulfilling, but that acting as fill-in men and middlemen is no better, and in some cases worse. (Paules 1991:119)

Margaret, another data entry operator at Data Air, sums up this position by saying, "I prefer keying; with the overtime and the incentive we make a good set [of money]. I don't like to get involved; I prefer to be neutral." The fact that this sentiment is widely held has implications for our understanding of the industry at large, and for interpreting women's opportunities and position in it generally.

Ruth Pearson (1993) points out in a discussion of the data processing industry in Jamaica that women there frequently leave the industry for secretarial or other clerical jobs rather than applying their experience with computer technologies to other related fields and moving up in the skill ladder within information services. She sees their movement into traditional clerical jobs as a regressive trend, further entrenching women in the ranks of low-wage, low-skilled, and easily manipulated labor.

> Instead of being the new "high tech" skilled workers of the future, the women employed in this sector are merely playing out a variation of an old theme. . . . It is a damning reflection on the evaluation of women's skills that workers who have been able to adapt to considerable pressures at work, who have shown flexibility of response to frequently changing programmes on an ad hoc basis and have organized speedy through-put of data entry at a guaranteed level of accuracy and quality should be considered no more qualified than school leavers with basic typing skills. Instead of being channeled towards managerial or information technology training courses and employment, both the women themselves and their past and potential employers are content to allow them to proceed to secretarial training and employment where their skills and talents will remain unrecognized, unrewarded and underutilized. (294)

Placed in the context of an industry that is predominantly *locally* owned and managed, in contrast to informatics in Barbados and in the Dominican Republic, her observation is additionally striking.

By failing to recognize the skills these women are learning in these jobs, critics and industry managers together are, unwittingly perhaps, reinscribing data processors into the old model of female factory workers in tedious, low-paid, dead-end, and short-lived jobs. Challenging the ways in which we define skill, Pearson urges us to look closely at the potential for applying aspects of these jobs to a sector that is growing not just among the foreign transnationals but also among local Jamaican entrepreneurial classes, a phenomenon that is expanding in Barbados as well. In short, she argues that the logic of these information-based industries for small economies of the Caribbean is clear and that the demand for local expertise is great. These new entrepreneurs, as Pearson notes, come not from the traditional landowning or capitalist elite of Jamaican society or from foreign-owned multinationals but rather from an expanding professional black middle class, educated locally at the University of the West Indies. Their fledgling companies (twenty-eight in all) are located in the capital city of Kingston outside the free trade zone enclave of their foreign counterparts. All of these factors contribute to her alarm that women in the data entry facilities are not moving up through the company ranks. The threat, as she sees it, is that an equation of female labor with unskilled low-paid work will be perpetuated and that a new sector of information services that presents vital growth and development for both Jamaica and the region at large will be deprived of essential, talented (female) resources.

What is missing from this formulation is the voice of the data processor herself and what appear often to be ambivalent (if not outright negative) views toward entering the ranks of supervisory or managerial "staff." Labor demand factors and gendered recruitment strategies are powerful forces but they are not the only ones dictating women's movements into and within these industries. The construction of women workers as categorically unskilled and low paid is one dimension of the problem. But it is important also to analyze the forces that lead women to "prefer an ordinary clerical job" or choose to stay within the production ranks rather than move up to become a supervisor in a data entry operation. In other words, the problem is not simply that the new local companies exclude women from the ranks of supervisory, managerial, and research/design positions but that women are only minimally represented in degree programs in computer-related areas from which these new businesses are spawned; the gendering of education in much of the West Indies continues to find girls concentrated in typing rather than programming or design classes and with less access to new applications of computer technologies.

Devon Peña's book (1997) on the Mexican maquiladoras describes a similar phenomenon whereby a majority of women workers reject the opportunity for promotion on the basis of interpersonal networks and friendship, and the frank undesirability of the job. In the cases he explores, the gendered division of labor dictates that a majority of supervisors are male, and in order to enter these ranks, women must become "imitation males." In the Barbadian informatics arena, where supervisors and managers (except the very top level of management) are more often women, this masculinization of authority is not as prominent a theme as we see in other parts of the world. Considering the differences between the Mexican maquiladoras and informatics operations in Barbados and in Jamaica and the Dominican Republic, it is clear that the specific "labor demand" and "labor supply" factors in each context must be taken into account. In so doing, we cannot assume that "promotion" to the position of supervisor necessarily implies advantageous conditions and remuneration for all of these workers. "Upward mobility" is not a neutral concept that we can assume to be uniformly desired by operators and denied by management.

The women in the informatics sector represent a wide range of experiences of movement within the workplace. The success stories of upward mobility include cases in which women were hired as "rank-and-file" data processors and steadily moved up the hierarchy to "lead operator," supervisor, and ultimately shift manager. In the most dramatic case of all, the woman who was "manageress" of the entire Multitext operation when I first began this research had herself begun as a data processor working among a small team of typists to interpret instructions from individual publishers and ultimately to standardize the procedures for the company. But there are other kinds of "success stories," such as that of Kathleen, who worked over four hundred hours in overtime one year (averaging twelve hour days), saved her earnings for the seven years that she has worked as a keyer at Data Air, and eventually realized her dream of building her own house. Her story demonstrates that women's goals of upward mobility are not always manifested in promotion within the workplace itself but may involve that of status through earning to build a house.

> I wanted my own home [. . .] from the very beginning [. . .] from the time I was sixteen, I always imagined having my own home, and *that* I have achieved this year. It's not a very big house, but it's what I can afford, and it's mine and I love it. You find, I don't know if it's because persons are comfortable living at home that they don't want to own their own homes, or move out or whatever,

you get people here that even though they have kids, they're still living at home, but not me. [. . .] At one point in time, I felt I would not achieve it because things were not looking the way they should then especially that the banks were not lending single people money and then you have to think of, hey, where do I get those thousands of dollars from. [. . .] But from the first I began working here, I wanted to save $5,000. I would save and save [. . .] and when I saw my bankbook and it had $5,000 on it I could not believe it. I said wow! [. . . It took] about two years in the beginning. And then I thought if I can save five thousand, I could save ten, and I went ahead and I try to save as much as possible till I reach that 10,000 goal. Then I reach it and then I decided I want to reach 20,000. I save most of my money due to overtime and incentive [. . . in all,] 30,000 and then I was also saving on the credit union. When I first started working here I said, well, I'm not accustomed to working for money as such, when I was baby-sitting, I found that was enough, that would carry me through to the next week [. . .] so why can't I live on that same salary. So I would basically budget for my bus fare and lunch money and what I contribute towards the home and stuff and then I would save the rest. When I started traveling, I started buying most of my clothes overseas and try to save as much as possible because I knew what I wanted. And when I first started building, you get a lot of gossip, a lot of negative thoughts and you get people saying oh, she's building, she's this and that.

Kathleen's drive and energy are truly remarkable, and the resentful comments she refers to among other data entry operators were both real and forcefully expressed by her co-workers. They ranged from accusations of being greedy and selfish to apparent concern about her health and well-being because of her working such long hours every day. Interestingly, though she was among the top keyers in her group and had been with the company for seven years, she had no desire to be promoted or moved to another area of work.

I've been in the same area since I came to Data Air. I guess it's comfortable. I prefer a job where I know what I have to do and just come in and do it and that is it. I don't prefer a job where I have to come in and report to the boss every morning and then you get to do this or that. I prefer to know what I have to do, have the work day set and that's it [. . .] and go home. I guess in another line of work, even though your time is up at 3:30, there's still other little minor things to be done in the office so you probably won't get out of the office until four or after. But here, as soon as it's 3:30, we all out and gone.

The ability to know her job and have no "bother" about personalities, as Kathleen expressed it, are aspects of work as a data entry operator that she most values, in short, a sense of predictability and control. Her comment is ironic in the light of the extraordinary overtime she actually worked and the very long days she typically put in, as well as in the tenuousness typically associated with the offshore industries.

At Data Air, the movement from data entry operator to lead operator to supervisor and eventually to shift manager had been achieved by every shift manager but one—the only man who filled this position. Above the shift managers in the company hierarchy were two women in personnel and human resources and two men, the financial controller and the general manager himself. In general, again, informatics is largely a women's preserve, and that fact holds true across the work hierarchy. When there are men employed, they tend to be located in specific niches that require physical strength (e.g., the prep area in which they need to lift heavy batches of tickets) or higher skills (e.g., the mark-up area of Multitext, or the programming end of the computer room at Data Air). The small number of men who work on the data entry floor are likely to be moved into other areas of work more quickly than are women operators, and the reasons and rationales for this are many. On one hand, the "givenness" of femininity on the production floor leads management to be inclined to see men as anomalies in need of reassignment, and, relatedly, the men tend to make known to their supervisors or managers their desires to move (laterally, into the prep room, or vertically, into more skilled computer work). A combination, then, of the perception that men on the production floor "don't belong" and the tendency for those individuals to voice their desire to be reassigned creates what appears to be a "natural" segregation of work areas and job categories along gender lines.

The sense of mismatch or gender incongruity with a male worker on the production floor is not equally balanced with that of a female worker in one of the more male domains. While certain few domains can be read as masculinized territories of labor (e.g., Data Air's prep area) where joking as well as physical jostling are known to happen, women are not precluded from these areas, or from such behavior. Indeed, the extent to which women are able and ready to participate in many of these acts of "reputation" concurs with Jean Besson's critique (1993) of the dualistic gendered reading of the respectability/reputation paradigm itself. On the other hand, the strength with which femininity is associated with the data entry floor in both Multitext and Data Air weighs heavily on the few men who work in these spaces. Attempting to counteract this sense of stigma, one or two of the young men I interviewed joked about the sexual advantage of having "plenty women" to choose from by working in data processing. Another dimension of the greater maneuverability of the young men in informatics relates to the issue of networks and worker alliances. Whereas many women emphasized the importance of cliques and friendships as part of their work experience (these were all friendships among women, none included men from the companies) and revealed a disinclination to jeopardize these by becoming a supervisor, for example, the fact that men on the data entry floor tended to befriend other men in other divisions and be less integrally connected to their fellow women operators also means that they are freer to ascend the work hierarchy. They are not "stepping on friends' toes" to do so.

SHIFTS AND SCHEDULES

Like many other manufacturing operations, both Data Air and Multitext run on shifts, from 7:30 A.M. to 3:30 P.M., and from 3:30 to 11:00 P.M. In most divisions workers rotate between morning and evening shifts every two weeks. Data Air, during periods of heavy production demands, has operated a graveyard shift as well, from 11 P.M. until 7 A.M., though this practice is strongly resisted by workers. Opposition to the graveyard shift was so strong that one manager said it was worth doing just about any alternative arrangement for getting the work done than to demand such late night hours. He said, "Bajans are homebodies. You find most just want to be back home with their family, and not out at work at night." Again, the quiet conservatism of the Barbadian cultural milieu was contrasted with that of the Dominican Republic, where a graveyard shift operates more steadily amid a lively culture of the street. Meal and rest breaks constitute a total of one hour of the working day on the morning shift. Workers are given a half-hour lunch break and two fifteen-minute rests. On the night shift, which runs seven and a half hours rather than the standard eight hours, only one half-hour break is allotted. Break time finds many workers congregated around an array of food vendors parked outside. During lunch breaks the employee lunch-room quickly fills to capacity, and, outside, workers stand in long lines at a nearby fast-food restaurant, drawn by the shade of the bright umbrella tables.

Data Air provides a ping-pong table for added diversion during breaks, and among the few men employed in the industry, I witnessed animated games of draughts being played as well. Most workers develop a break-time routine that they follow regularly. The routine may include the same small group of friends getting together for lunch, some solitary time with a book, or even a short nap. For others, breaks provide a vital opportunity to "make up time" on the system and not a true rest at all. Operators who arrive late to work or who must leave early for some reason approved by a supervisor may be permitted to work through their break or start early or end late in the day to avoid being penalized for lost production time. Others, simply anxious to bolster their production to increase their wage, forgo their break and remain at their terminals.

Like most other industries, the data entry business has seasonal rush and slow periods. In publishing, the summer months tend to be the busiest, sometimes requiring overtime of Multitext keyers every day. For an airline, as well, summer is a time of heavy travel, and for Data Air, every month-end presents a slight rush in order to make accounting deadlines. In the North American insurance industry, the heavy work period is more likely to fall during the winter months, when illness increases and people submit more medical claims. As required by Barbados law, overtime work and Saturday work is paid time-and-a-half, while Sundays and bank holidays may command double-time pay. At Data Air, Sunday work is rare, and when it is necessary, workers are paid time-and-a-half for the first four hours and double-time for the second four. The company often provides small treats, such as cookies and coffee, and encourages workers to dress more comfortably, in jeans and other casual clothes, as a concession to offset their request for weekend work. One shift manager even noted that child care had been provided during a period when weekend work was more frequent. In contrast, during the slow months I observed many days at Multitext and in the insurance claims area of Data Air during which there was no work at all. On such days operators are encouraged to practice their typing on "dead" work or to play typing games designed to improve speed and accuracy. Hence, on these days, typists are paid their basic hourly wage without incentive increases, and many complain that they would prefer to go home than to sit with no work and no incentive salary. At Data Air, claims approvers are sometimes sent home after half a day or put on a temporary "flex" schedule when there is a slack in the workload.

The Labor Process of Informatics

If aspects of the recruitment and training of workers in informatics and their associated wages and shifts appear to position informatics on one or the other side of the blue- or white-collar divide, the labor process contains even more ambiguous dimensions. Before examining the relationship between data processors and the "products" they produce, the expressions of corporate discipline that underlie their work, and the patterns of compliance or resistance encoded in their experience, it is useful to examine the general labor process entailed in this industry. Additionally, it must be emphasized that informatics represents a combination of new technologies and new management arrangements. While the charges of "electronic sweatshop" often leveled at informatics would seem to imply archaic factory technologies and labor organization, these companies actually resemble those in the highest echelons of Mexican maquiladoras, which are subsidiaries of transnational corporations. They stand in stark contrast with the grim turn-of-the-century-like conditions and infrastructure of many other industrial settings, including some local manufacturing plants. They operate with the latest in microelectronics and telecommunications technologies, and, in combination with their large work forces, they are constantly evaluating and changing methods of production and recruitment and regulation of labor. Their very existence reflects flexible restructuring measures of the new international division of labor, and their striking longevity (since 1983) is enhanced by the "flexible management strategies" they adeptly employ.

PHYSICS AND PORN, TICKETS AND CLAIMS: PROCESSING
DATA IN THE OPEN OFFICE

At Multitext, there are four main job categories, referring to distinct steps of the labor process: mark-up, typing, deferring, and quality assessment. The first, mark-up, involves a small number of people (six to eight) who pencil in typesetting codes on the original manuscript pages, according to specifications sent by individual publishers. In straightforward texts, such as novels and encyclopedias, coding is generally light, indicating, for example, where paragraphs begin and end, how titles and subheads should appear, and where illustrations should be inserted in the text. For scientific journals and textbooks, however, coding can be heavy and complex, involving special marks for scientific symbols, equations, and format specifications. These codes are ultimately typed along with the text and then applied in the typesetting process back in the United States. Although base wages are slightly higher in mark-up, there is no incentive scheme for this division. The rationale for this is that the accuracy of all subsequent steps of the labor process depends on the precision of this first phase, and the markers' accuracy might falter if they rush through their work to earn incentive pay.[9]

When one enters the production floor of Multitext, it is impossible not to notice the tone and ambience of the mark-up area that set it apart from the active hum of the typing clusters. Six "markers," two men and four women, sit at tables poring over code sheets, sometimes working together, sometimes working independently. The supervisor, along with the workers in this area, describe it as "the coolest" job because "you aren't tied to the machine and forced to work non-stop." Some of the markers had worked before as keyers, and none regretted the change. While demanding great care and accuracy, the mark-up area is noticeably more relaxed. Collaborative work is allowed, and a freeness and sense of collegiality is expressed in the chatting and quiet exchange of jokes that goes on in the course of the workday. Unlike the next stage of data processing, in which the computer is relied upon to flag discrepancies or mistakes, mark-up is entirely dependent on human accuracy. Ironically, then, mark-up, like the prep areas of Data Air, allowed perhaps the greatest freedom for informal talk. One afternoon, Stella, working in mark-up, received a delivery of carnations with a card that read, "May you always be as radiant as a carnation in all its bloom." Teasing her, Ann, the supervisor, copied down the poetic message, saying that she might want to use it herself one day. The others laughed and joked when Mary, another supervisor, told Ann to "get control over her area" and to stop "all the noise and commotion from the front of the floor." The open plan of the production floor is such that only a narrow strip of space separates the clusters of computer stations from the mark-up tables, but the space is symbolically charged by the difference in tone between these two work areas. Jokes and playful banter were common among the mark-up crew, creating an atmosphere that stood in stark contrast with the hushed intensity of the other production areas.[10]

When the manuscript leaves the mark-up area, it is divided by a supervisor into batches of two to three pages (or more or less, depending on the level of difficulty of the work) and then distributed to typists for keying. Individual typists notify an assistant supervisor that they need new work by placing red wooden blocks on top of their computer terminals. Meanwhile, they indicate on their own worksheets the batches they have typed and the time it has taken them. "Down time" or the time they spend waiting for work is also noted on their sheet, as is the time taken for breaks, trips to the bathroom, and lunch. These sheets are then turned in to the group supervisor at the end of the shift and form the basis for productivity monitoring. Assistant supervisors act as runners, keeping track of who has what segment of the text and who needs more work. They give each completed portion of text to a second typist, because double typing every page is the first level of quality assurance.

The rationale behind double keying is, very simply, that two typists are unlikely to make the same mistakes. According to an Office of Technology Assessment (1985) report on the data processing industry, while the cost of duplicating work in this manner would be prohibitive in the United States at US$28.50 an hour, in Barbados it is estimated at US$6.30 an hour. On some occasions, however, when questions arise over typesetting codes and formatting, or if poor reproduction makes the original difficult to read, one typist may confer with the other who typed the same page. Strict rules are made against this practice because it defeats the purpose of double keying. The computer will not pick up a mistake in the deferring and quality assessment phase if both original and comparison versions appear the same. Typists, therefore, are encouraged to request help from their supervisor rather than from fellow typists, again emphasizing the individual nature of this work. As one can imagine, however, many keyers, particularly those who are new and therefore on probation or are just insecure about meeting the work quotas consistently, are reluctant to seek help from a supervisor and are more comfortable covertly relying on their fellow keyers. With an aim to perform well and not appear slow to learn the typesetting codes, keyers frequently and secretly confer with one another over questionable markings on a given page. The implications of this practice for lowering the ultimate quality of the final product is significant. What the women are doing, in effect, is leveraging their own individual production against that of the company and hoping not to get caught.

Deferring, sometimes called "compiling," is the round of quality checking that follows the double typing of the text. Each typed version is brought up on the computer and compared with the original manuscript. The deferrer holds a straight edge (usually a ruler) against the original page to keep her place, scans the computer screen to identify any discrepancies, and corrects mistakes as she finds them. The final check is quality assessment. In this round, the computer is loaded with the two versions of the deferred job and in comparing the two documents on a split computer screen picks up any discrepancies. The quality assessment operator then corrects any mistakes the computer has flagged. As the manager of the operation noted, the heavily labor-intensive nature of this system, consisting of double keying and then double checking all entered text, is required to guarantee a near perfect product, and in turn, makes clear the rationale for conducting the work in lower waged offshore sites.

Prior to the actual keying of information at Data Air, airline tickets and insurance claims are batched, sorted, and in some instances labeled in various "prep"

Figure 3. Men working in the "prep" area at Data Air.

areas, according to such categories flight designation, insurance office location, or means of payment. As noted above, one of the most striking aspects of the prep areas, particularly where the sacks of airline tickets are delivered, lifted, and sorted, is the disproportional number of male workers (figure 3). The widely expressed rationales for this striking gender division of labor center on the physical demands of their jobs and the fact that prep work does not involve sitting down in one place all day.

Despite the different nature of the information produced and manipulated, and the simultaneous transmission of the claims data into North American computers, the basic labor process for keyers and approvers at Data Air is similar to that of typists at Multitext. Work is distributed, or "shared out," by an assistant supervisor, and operators sit and type batches of work at computer stations clustered in groups of four or in rows of terminals (figures 4–5). At both Multitext and Data Air, typists are monitored for their productivity (i.e., quality and accuracy). This monitoring determines their incentive pay but also may result in probationary status, or even firing, if their productivity consistently falls below the proficiency target. While operators are being monitored by supervisors for computer "down time," lateness, willingness to work overtime, and other aspects of workplace behavior, they are under the constant electronic surveillance of their computer terminal. The implications of this level of monitoring as a hidden but central aspect of the labor process are explored later in the chapter.

READING AND KEYING THE PRODUCT

The work of entering data from consumer coupons, airline tickets, and insurance claims is frequently and understandably described by many of its processors as tedious and boring. Despite the repetition and narrow dimension of their jobs, some operators note particular aspects of the production process they find to be engaging, and even occasionally riveting. Regardless of the level of interest, all data entry operators become fluent in a short period of time in the "language" of their industry, rattling off long lists of airport codes, insurance regions, or billing codes and diagnoses. Janice, a keyer at Multitext, for example, mentioned that she loves keying Sidney Sheldon and Agatha Christie novels because she gets involved in the story and that makes the work go easier and faster. Another keyer remembered entering the text of a "soft porn" novel called *Hungry Women*, in which she sometimes got so engrossed that she "forgot what she was doing entirely, and made all sorts of mistakes." Susan, a new approver in the claims division of Data Air, joked that she and her friends now know as many diagnoses as any doctor.

The relationship between these workers and their "product" is ambiguous at best, and the link between their production performance and their engagement with this product is also variable. There are debates in the industry, from data entry operators all the way to the general manager, about how to achieve the highest levels of speed and accuracy in entering data. Some say that the "key what you see" technique of simple character recognition (rather than reading for comprehension as one types) guarantees the best results. Using this strategy keyers in China and the Dominican Republic have achieved extraordinary productivity, at a rate of at least 98 percent accuracy despite the obvious language barriers. Yet, a woman working in the deferring department at Multitext commented that a large project that came to them for the final phases of quality assessment, having been keyed by that method in China, was riddled with errors based on the same principle. Because the work was typed without comprehension, the operators had keyed marginal notes and instructions that were not part of the text itself. But as the above keyers noted, reading for content as opposed to keying merely by recognition can also lead to errors. One quality assessment operator said, "Sometimes when they read the text, they type what is in their

mind, like 'the man *jumped* over the wall' instead of 'the man *hopped* over the wall' and those mistakes really keep me back."

Workers at Multitext, and to a lesser degree in Data Air's insurance claims division, frequently comment about the content of the work they produce. In some instances the materials they key prompt self-reflection and associations with their own lives and experiences. On one occasion, after talking at length with June about her marital problems, her difficulties managing the care of her daughter, and her dilemma about seeking professional psychological help, I noted the self-help text she was typing on the screen, from a pop psychology manuscript. It read: "Don't over-commit yourself and feel as though you have to be superwoman, but don't totally give up activities you enjoy. Adjustment to motherhood is more difficult if you feel your life has been completely disrupted. . . . Do not hesitate to get professional support if you are having problems." She laughed at the aptness of the advice for her own life. Stella recalled working on a book about Burmese women "where men thought women were unclean and had all sorts of strange ideas about them. The men there did what women here do, and the women have to carry heavy bags and do the heavy work in the fields while the men stay home." These "very strange" and "interesting" practices made keying this book enjoyable and conveyed a dimension of the job in which she feels she breaks the tedium of keying by learning new things.

Figures 4 and 5. Data processors on the morning shift at Data Air. Photos by Michael Rowe.

The texts that cross the typists' desks range from such highly technical works as physics journals and books on psychoanalytic theory and medical studies to classical literature and romance novels and mysteries. The level of engagement with the actual content of the material varies accordingly. For example, one day a teen novel called *There's a Boy in the Girls' Bathroom* was being keyed, and several typists eagerly brought it to my attention that the story's protagonist was named Carla. In hurried synopses they recounted the plot line to me as they typed from their manuscript pages. On another occasion, I experienced what felt like a postmodern twist on the ethnographic experience when I noticed an article on criminology, authored by a sociologist on the faculty of my own university, flashing across the green and black screens. I could not help contemplating the strange possibility that my own manuscript might one day find itself parsed into bits and distributed across this very data processing floor and that these same women would find *themselves* in the text they so diligently enter. Indeed, I was struck by some of the implications posed by doing fieldwork in an age and context in which not only can one's subjects read the text one produces but their very labor as "readers" may be integral to the production and dissemination of the text in the public arena.

As the variety of titles suggests, the actual content of these manuscripts raises some important issues with regard to the keyers' relationship to the work they perform and the company's litany of proposed benefits of these jobs. A manager of the operation remarked on several occasions that "these girls could really get a good education if they paid attention to what they were typing." He added that "if only they showed an interest in their work, they have before them the makings of a solid liberal arts education; they've got science, literature, history, the bible." It bothered him, he said, that instead, "they only seem interested in the porn." Early on, he offered to make copies of the full texts and make them available to anyone interested in reading them, since the typists are generally exposed only to discrete portions of a manuscript and not necessarily in sequential order. Apparently, the only manuscript that anyone requested to borrow was one of pornography, which was ultimately secretly photocopied and distributed widely across the production floor. The typists and those involved in the training process were more likely to emphasize that reading the text while typing dramatically reduces speed and accuracy.

In the insurance division of Data Air, numerous claims approvers commented about what they had absorbed about various illnesses and treatments as well as about the insurance industry in general. As one said, "I learned a lot of codes for different illnesses and whatnot [. . .] I heard a program on the radio and I heard a doctor call this illness that was on my diagnosis code [. . .] and I said, wait [. . .] he knew about that too!" The training of claims approvers includes a discussion about the sensitive and confidential nature of the work they perform. According to the operations manager:

> Hey, this is somebody here who has been to a doctor, who has a problem and who is either waiting for the money that they have spent or they are waiting for the money to be sent to the doctor so that they can honor their commitments. [. . .] They're personal problems communicated on paper and although we don't know the persons, you shouldn't be communicating with others, saying, "Hey, look what happened to this person."

This sense of confidentiality was taken seriously and mentioned often as one aspect of the importance of the job. An approver named Joyce said:

> What I'm doing is confidential, between me and the person I'm doing it for. [. . .] If it was mine, I wouldn't like the person who was processing my claim to take my business to anyone else. So I think that you got to be very careful not to tell anyone, well this person has this or this person has this.

Another response by approvers to the content of the work they produced was much like that of first-year medical students. Several women commented that they would read about various illnesses and diagnosis codes from the claim forms and begin to think they were coming down with the same condition. Like the keyer at Multitext who construes her work as that of the clerical end of the publishing business, approvers in the claims division of Data Air who deal with medical data and thus gain familiarity with hospital terminology see their jobs as more closely linked with the clerical side of the medical professions, than, say, with factory production. The abstract quality of the creation of information as a commodity makes the relationship between the worker and product somewhat ambiguous. Again, these women would not claim, in any manner, to be health care or publishing professionals, though they do come to identify with these industries that they see themselves serving, and to the extent that publishing, insurance, airlines, and credit card companies are distinct from traditional industrial work, they see themselves as distinct as well. The labor process of data processing, however, also involves routinized, high-speed production work, and as such presents very real health constraints largely absent in truly professional, white-collar jobs.[11] It is important, therefore, to turn briefly to some of the health implications of these dimensions of pink-collar labor.

HEALTH AND SAFETY ISSUES

Reports and speculations by unionists and occupational health and safety experts concerning these new and burgeoning computer-based industries have been numerous. Their conclusions are mixed (see, for example, Billette and Piche 1987; Borrell 1990; Brodeur 1990; Council on Scientific Affairs 1987; Schnorr et al. 1991). A survey of the literature on health-related issues of video display terminal (VDT) use, boils down to four main areas of concern: visual difficulties, musculoskeletal problems, reproductive disorders, and "stress" as it is variously defined. The most often cited visual difficulties among computer terminal operators include eye fatigue, irritation, blurring, and headaches. Many of these problems are the result of performing close work and can be remedied by simply insuring that the VDT is at a comfortable viewing distance, that the lighting allows an optimal contrast with minimal screen glare, and that the source document is clear and legible. Additionally, fatigue and eye strain are minimized when the operator takes frequent breaks from looking directly at the monitor. Among the data entry operators I surveyed, the single biggest problem area they identified with their job was health. (Other problems they listed include boredom, fatigue, co-worker and staff conflicts, difficulties meeting work quotas, and difficulties juggling work and family schedules.) Sixty-seven percent mentioned eye problems as the most significant health-related problem they experienced on the job and nearly one-third had needed glasses since starting their job.

Concerns about the link between low-level radiation (produced by electromagnetic fields) and reproductive disorders (birth defects and spontaneous abortions) have generated numerous studies in the past several years but have produced a great deal of inconclusive evidence. According to a report made in Barbados in 1990 by a Canadian doctor specializing in occupational health, the amounts of radiation generated by the VDT are minimal and harmless. He reported that a color television presents health hazards up to thirty times greater than what one would experience in front of a VDT and that the number of miscarriages reported by VDT users has not lent statistically conclusive evidence. A recent study on the topic published in the *New England Journal of Medicine* (Schnorr et al. 1991) essentially supports these claims, arguing against any clear association between radiation emissions from VDTS and spontaneous abortions, birth defects, cataracts, or other physical injuries. All forms of electromagnetic and other emissions have been reviewed and levels are said to be far below accepted standards of exposure. Among the women I surveyed, none reported having had a miscarriage since they were employed in data entry. However, in the context of an interview, this sensitive information simply may not have been elicited. I did learn informally of three cases of miscarriages from women I came to know more personally, and others said that they had heard of cases, but my data do not permit more definitive commentary.

Perhaps the best known work-related illness among VDT operators, including journalists and other keyboard operators, is carpal tunnel syndrome.[12] Repetitive stress injury (RSI) refers to a complex of ailments in the hands and wrist, including cysts, nerve damage, and inflammation of the tendons, that can lead to numbness in the fingers, as well as pain in the arm and shoulder. These problems first revealed themselves in traditional factories and now appear in increasing numbers in the VDT-based clerical sector. Occupational health and safety advisors now familiar with these conditions advocate job sharing and the alternation of tasks such that no worker is performing a repetitive task for an entire day. In large data entry operations, however, job sharing has yet to be considered a feasible option, and in Barbados there is little movement from one job to another even within years of employment. As one keyer at Multitext pointed out, "One girl came back from Dominica and she'd been having real trouble with her eyes; they'd really gone bad, but the only job they said she could do was Q/A [quality assessment] which means staring at the screen all day. The lady said, you can either do that or we'll be happy to pay you out. So they paid her out and she left."

Taking a short break every hour and alternating tasks helps to reduce boredom, fatigue, and the risk of RSI. In Barbados, and many other countries as well, a fifteen-minute break after two hours of work has become fairly standard policy in the industry, although the International Labour Office (ILO) and other medical reports have recommended that for intensive VDT work (such as that performed in data entry operations) breaks after every hour of continuous work are preferable. While attempts in the Barbadian operations (more often in the foreign-owned than in local ones) have been made to introduce stretching exercises before shifts and during breaks for precisely these reasons, breaks are not mandatory, and at any given time of the workday there are always operators working at their stations. Because workers are paid for only half of their one-hour total break time, and because there is often incentive to make up time on the system for lateness or other "down time," many choose not to take all of their allotted time away from the terminals, and therefore they become more susceptible to RSI. Of the women I surveyed, 38 percent complained of stiffness and pain in their hands and wrists.

Musculoskeletal pain is often reported by VDT workers as a result of the extreme postural demands of viewing the screen and typing. Of the women in my survey 51 percent noted back and neck problems. Lack of movement creates stiffness and discomfort referred to as "static load," a condition of fatigue and muscle strain. Frequent complaints include neck and back pain, and pain and numbness in arms, hands, and fingers. The musculoskeletal difficulties result from inadequate equipment and ergonomics, as well as poor job design. The general manager of Data Air himself acknowledged that workers have had a lot of problems because of bad posture. He said he tried to encourage a mandatory exercise program to ease neck, back, and wrist strain but lamented that the data processors thought it was "too regimented—too Japanese." He has seen several cases of carpal tunnel syndrome and worries that the numbers may increase. Two workers had surgery to treat their conditions and others have been moved temporarily to other departments. No preventative action in the form of job variation and mandatory breaks has been introduced, however, and there is no indication that such measures are being considered.

A great deal of money has been spent on the "office" design to create a pleasant and comfortable working environment. Data Air, for example, spent

US$500 per chair to furnish their operation, and a majority of the workers I interviewed commented positively about these "benefits" and "amenities" of the job. Noting his concerns about ergonomics, Data Air's general manager said, "You can buy another chair for $150. I know the $150 chair; I have seen it. But that doesn't help—you're going to lose those people very quickly." A number of the women who began working with this company when it opened had come from electronics plants and other manufacturing industries and they are quick to point out the advantages of sitting down to a "clean" job in an air-conditioned environment. However, given the low attrition rates and the intense nature of the production work, it is likely that more and more workers will begin to suffer from the ailments mentioned, and even the "cool" look of the place will not mask the psychologically and physically taxing nature of the labor process.

The musculoskeletal tension described is often exacerbated by the less easy to define, but often cited, stress of the workplace. Often overlooked in the medical analyses of VDT work are several of these more amorphous problems bound up in the very nature of computer-based work. By definition, the piece-rate and incentive system fosters high levels of stress, as keyers intently aim for high production quotas and often work long hours of overtime in order to boost their weekly wage. Studies note that many VDT operators have reported psychosomatic illness and nervous disorders, as well as sleep disturbances, gastrointestinal upset, coronary disease, and endocrine imbalances. Especially at risk for work-related stress are those who must sit for long hours doing repetitive input operations while being closely monitored, precisely the conditions of work of the data entry operator (Billette and Piche 1987). Computer-based work is isolating and depersonalized: operators sit in individual cubbies; their work requires focused attention on a screen; and social interaction, which has traditionally been one of the major benefits of clerical work, is minimized. For these reasons, as well as the obvious physical demands, frequent breaks and the establishment of maximum working hours become essential.

In the information processing industry in Barbados at large, all of the facilities are air-conditioned and most are carpeted, but only at Data Air and some of the newer foreign-owned companies are work stations systematically fitted with adjustable chairs, the most basic ingredient in a well-designed work setting. Desks that are too high, chairs that cannot be adjusted, work areas that are not fitted with document holders, and screens that are poorly positioned are all factors that can add to fatigue and eye strain, as well as neck, shoulder, and back pains. Furthermore, an ILO (Dy 1985:54) report notes, "Even if the furniture and work station are ergonomically well designed, this is no guarantee against fatigue and discomfort if the job itself requires the operator to maintain a static position."

"Flexible" Management Strategies

The equation of informatics with "modernity" is often cited by observers who note its computer-centered labor process, the satellite technology it requires, and its "professional"-looking workers. Workers are also likely to cite those qualities of their workplace and jobs as marking a new and distinctive niche in the Barbadian employment arena. They often note, as well, aspects of their jobs and their relations with management that the outside observer is less likely to see. These include corporate strategies for raising and maintaining high levels of production that are wholly new to Barbados and that pose new concerns for the country's long-powerful trade union movement. Employee bonuses and new "Japanese" and "American" styles of management are featured dimensions of both Data Air and Multitext.

Despite the foreign ownership of more than half the data entry operations in Barbados, the on-site managers were all Barbadians when I began this research in 1989. At Multitext and Data Air, the employment of local management appeared to be a deliberate decision by the foreign owners of these companies. Data Air's manager is a slight and soft-spoken man in his forties. Despite complex expressions of resistance to management practices and general workplace discipline that emerged in explicit and more hidden ways on the production floor at Data Air, this general manager was both well liked and respected. On some occasions he was viewed as a paternal ally, and disciplinary aspects of the labor process were not perceived as related to him. Instead, they were viewed as the embodiments of the American work ethic and corporate ownership. Several women I interviewed described having gone to the general manager for advice about further education (some were interested in computer-related night classes in Barbados and others in university degree courses abroad) and noted that "he always found the time" and "took genuine interest" in their lives. Alice, a data entry operator at Data Air for five years who started her job at the age of seventeen, said, "I went to him about colleges in New York and he said it's okay if I do get through, I could take the two years for an associate degree and could come back here to work when I'm finished. He even called me and discussed it with me, and he said when I get more information I should come and discuss it with him again. [. . .] He really help[ed] me a lot." Many of the operators and supervisors mentioned the policy implemented by the general manager of using first names across all ranks of the company as an example of the general company ethic that "we're all on one level," even though there is no doubt about his authority and leadership. Not only does the general manager encourage the workers to use his first name, but also he knows many of his employees by name and is adept at enacting a sense of personal relationship in the midst of one of Barbados's largest production operations. Interestingly, though perhaps not surprising given the nature of the work structure with few managers and hundreds of production workers, Data Air operators are more likely to voice their dissatisfaction and register their complaints about their supervisors or about their anonymous corporate owners than about their own general manager.

After the first six months of my research at Multitext, the top management was reshuffled, and with the introduction of a new general manager came a distinctly new management style. As I mentioned earlier, when I began the fieldwork, a Barbadian woman who had been with the original company since its inception managed the production floor. Rita was hired as a keyer in the days of the fledgling keyboard operation when the codes and programs for each manuscript were figured out by "hit or miss," and keyers took the machines home on weekends to decipher and practice the new software. She described her relationship to the company with fondness and a sense of commitment, and her hopes for the future of information processing and the expansion of Multitext with great enthusiasm. When the British manager arrived, he moved into her office and within a short time, Rita was moved to Dominica, where plans to develop a new sister operation were taking shape. A great deal of gossip had surrounded Rita in her days as manager, criticizing her appearance, her weight, her rumored relationships, and her enactment of favoritism on the floor. As an Afro-Barbadian woman, and single mother not much older than the supervisors and operators beneath her, she was, as one of her friends and co-workers said "one o' we." That implied both that she was more open to criticism from her staff and production workers and was expected to exhibit greater sympathy and understanding. She had begun in the industry as a data entry operator herself, and her life circumstances were little different from those of the women she managed. Her replacement, Mark Roark, was a white Englishman with a master's degree in business administration who had been a middle manager of the multinational parent company and had no direct experience in the data entry business or in the Caribbean.

Roark was the first foreign manager I observed in the data entry industry (others arrived subsequently in newer foreign-owned companies), and a number of subtle transitions were marked by his arrival. He came armed with flow charts and models and textbook management strategies to transform the low morale of the production floor and ultimately, he hoped, raise productivity such that Multitext would become a profit-making company. He organized small-group meetings and displayed overhead projections and slide presentations that compared Multitext with the West Indies cricket team, perhaps the most potent cultural icon in the region and one to which many analogies are drawn in literature, the popular press, and business. Despite his obvious attempt to make the illustration culturally relevant, his use of cricket, a predominantly masculine passion, seemed peculiar in this largely feminine terrain. He announced as the company's mission "to be number one in the world in high quality data capture" and eventually employed British management consultants to deliver week-long seminars on total quality management (TQM) in attempts to rescue the company from a mire of staff problems, attrition, and low productivity.[13]

The response among the data entry workers and staff at Multitext to their new foreign boss was mixed. Some found him "nice" and "pleasant" and "trying hard," though inexperienced and maladroit in scheduling work and running the operation. Others, however, were openly hostile to his management of Multitext. There were persistent rumors about his "carrying on" (having an affair) with one of the supervisors. With each new outfit this supervisor wore to work, bitterness escalated on the floor and was exacerbated by a business trip she made to the new Dominica site. Workers referred to the supervisor and manager by their initials when discussing the matter, though the affair was clearly no secret and everyone seemed to have a different story about where the two were seen together and what improprieties they performed. Graphic details about their sex life, apparently reported by the supervisor to a friend, spread through the company, and even the American part-owner, in the comfort of his New York office, had heard some of the tales.

Rumors surrounding this affair encoded women's more general ideas about the calculus of power across gender and racial lines, sexual stereotypes and double standards, and the relationship between sex and the operations of a workplace. Some reported to me that the supervisor wore the manager's wife's clothes while she was on holiday in England, and I heard a host of accusations about her "wutless" (worthless) and mercenary behavior. She was said to have performed sexual acts for money before, and to be complying with the manager's "disgusting" preference for "rough and dirty" sex, purely for monetary gain. Her supposed mercenary and promiscuous character came under the scrutiny and condemnation of the other women (her fellow supervisors as well as her operators), who by implication defended their own more "respectable" ways. Disdain was heaped on the manager as well, for his taste in unwholesome (anal) sex, and for choosing a woman who "isn't even [considered] attractive." He was criticized for his indiscretion ("he jus appear all meek and mild and such, but he do what he like; he ain't no sweetbread") and he was mocked for being impotent ("she say it don' really work well"). The other workers' comments focused relentlessly on the supervisor's "bad looks" and demeanor, and despite the coincidental timing of this incident with the television coverage of the Anita Hill/Clarence Thomas hearings, no mention was ever made of "sexual harassment" at work. Just as most of the data processors criticized Anita Hill and had little to say about Clarence Thomas, so too they gossiped about the supervisor and held back their criticism of Roark. As one woman said, with resignation and echoing a familiar cultural belief, "Men jus' can't help themself."[14] A male supervisor, however, who had been promoted to shift manager at Data Air and later moved to another informatics company was the source of more explicit accusation and condemnation for "pressuring girls under him" and using his rank to achieve sexual ends.

One of the few top female trade unionists from the Barbados Workers Union said of sexual harassment, "Women don't know exactly how to define it, most think of it only in a physical sense, not the subtle effects and mechanisms, the stress that is caused and the psychological effects of it. The women are afraid to acknowledge their personal experiences outright—that the authority figure makes certain gestures at you—out of a sense that it would be seen as boasting [and the sense that] their co-workers would say, 'He's never done that to me. What makes you think you are so sexually attractive that he would do that to you?' They would start to doubt themselves. You know it is sexual harassment, though. Younger women who are more educated are able to stand up and say I'm not going to put up with that, but there is a lot of sexual harassment especially in areas where there are a lot of women, like here in data entry." Although the woman's attempts to get inside the data entry industry as a trade unionist had not been successful, her reading of this female-centered enclave as an obvious site of sexual harassment reflects a reality for women workers across a wide spectrum of employment in the Caribbean. Trinidadian calypsonian Singing Sandra's 1987 hit "Die with My Dignity," which powerfully expresses women's confrontation with sexual harassment as a routine part of job hunting, is applicable in the

Barbadian context and was widely played and appreciated. The song entreats women to resist these unwanted advances even in the face of economic need.

> You want to help to mind your family
> You want to help your man financially
> But nowadays it really very hard to get a job as a girl in Trinidad
> You looking now to find something to do
> You meet a boss-man who promise to help you
> But when the man let on the conditions
> It's nothing else but humiliation
>
> They want to see you' whole anatomy
> They want to see what you' doctor never see
> They want to do what your husband never do
> Still don't know if the scamps will hire you
> Well, if you know this humiliation [. . .] to get a job these days as a woman
>
> (Chorus)
> Well brother, they could keep they money, I will keep my honey,
> and die with my dignity.

Another level of the management problems at Multitext related directly to the production process itself and thwarted Roark's struggles to restructure the ailing company. As another supervisor explained to me, he apparently used his relationship with the supervisor to get information about what actually took place on the production floor. "The supervisors lie to him all the time," she said. Apparently, as she explained it, keyers had been conferring over text and in extreme cases copying the original keyer's text file directly into the second keyer's disk so that fewer errors, or in the extreme case no errors, would show up when the text was deferred and sent through quality assurance. When customer satisfaction did not mesh with the statistics that showed 100 percent quality, Roark never confronted the supervisors who apparently had claimed not to know what was going on. The supervisor he was rumored to be having a relationship with was widely believed to be "an informer." Tensions mounted when the annual awards ceremony was approaching and the manager made no attempt to hide his intention to nominate her for the supervisor-of-the-year award. The owner who was based in New York strongly advised that regardless of the truth or fiction of the rumors, "the message would be bad if she were to win the award." His words framed the relationship in terms of "favoritism." As it turned out, the supervisor in question did in fact receive the award, and that "got the girls blue vex," as one reported to me.

The management and staff seminars on "total quality culture" and TQM presented quite another, idealized picture of the dynamics of Multitext. At the end of the seminar, held at the Hilton Hotel, the British consultant said earnestly to me that Roark was one of the best managers he had ever met. While a number of managers in the region, he said, "are still colonial officers," Roark was an exception in his willingness to learn and implement new management practices. Although the Multitext participants (supervisors and managers) obediently recited the company mission statement aloud, followed along through thick manuals of "total quality" guidelines, and entered in (reluctantly) to the role playing and small-group episodes organized by the consultants, the sessions were rife with contradictions. Participants nodded when asked whether communication channels were open across levels of the hierarchy and whether, as supervisors and managers, they rewarded production workers for their good work more than they criticized them for mistakes. The seminar was an exercise in idealization and false affirmation that made no progress toward confronting deeply rooted management problems, because there, as in the production process itself, those lower on the ladder adeptly affirmed exactly what their superiors said or would want said, regardless of their true beliefs, resentments, and experiences.

With some sense of defeat, Roark described the difficulties he faced in actually realizing his goals of TQM and revealed a number of ways in which understanding the local work force had eluded him. In the first six months, he said, he was utterly bemused. "I didn't understand West Indian culture at all. I'd be telling people to do things and they'd say 'okay, yes, yes,' and nod in agreement and then simply not do them. They'd rather say yes and then figure I'd forgot, than say no and have to explain." To counter this problem, he adopted the policy of carrying around a little book in which he would write down, at the end of a meeting with someone, what was said and the agreement that was reached. "The other party does the same, and each initials the other's book to acknowledge mutual understanding. That way it's on paper—no confusion." Ironically, as he described this new procedure to me, he was interrupted by a supervisor who came to clarify the agreed dismissal time for that afternoon. It was just before Christmas, and there had been a staff decision about giving workers and supervisors time off before the end of their shift for last-minute shopping. The manager asked for the minutes from the meeting, but none could be found. The seminars with the TQM group yielded few results. Ultimately, Roark's reiteration that the parent company's "pockets are deep" was a reminder of the basic agenda at hand and an acknowledgment that regardless of its productivity and profitability, Multitext would be kept afloat for its public relations utility to the parent company.

REWARDS AND "THANK-YOU CARDS"

Another dimension of management relations involves the array of production inducements and "perks" that, again, set informatics apart from its industrial counterparts elsewhere on the island, and to some extent around the world. Offshore industries across the global assembly line are known perhaps as much for their exploits as for their tactics of rewards. The fashion shows and cosmetic sales that are carried out on factory premises are well-known compensatory gestures in feminized global industries. Not surprisingly, informatics firms, too, engage in a wide range of non-work-related activities and community programs extending beyond the realm of the production floor. One informatics manager described these as explicit efforts to "pay back" the Barbadian society and publicly reward individual workers for their hard work. On one extreme, as noted above, the entire operation was described as a "public relations" gesture by the multinational parent company to "do good" in the countries in which it holds monopoly control over telecommunications. But such gestures achieve many other ends as well, both internal to the production process and outside it. Some companies absorb the expense for events or activities unrelated to work ranging from running secondary school computer courses to organizing fund-raisers for community projects. The newspaper proved to be a useful device for keeping abreast of these outside activities. Announcements of a performance by a company choral group and articles about employment of four hearing-impaired operators appeared in the press, praising Multitext and Data Air for their good works. Another article describes the participation of Multitext employees in a seminar in Psychocybernetics "to gain greater self-confidence and master the stress demanded by their jobs." Operators were taught self-hypnosis exercises meant to alleviate "psychological scars and replace them by positive elements," and in doing so, to help them "adopt a professional approach to the demands of their job." Interestingly, the instructor of this seminar on stress reduction was the past personnel director at INTEL, the electronics assembly operation that left Barbados at the conclusion of its tax holiday in 1985.

Data Air's recognition programs include "Employee of the Month" awards and prizes for the most improved worker. The most highly valued reward comes in the form of "thank-you cards," which are distributed each month by supervisors for superior production rates or attendance records and for exceptional dependability and cooperation. These can be redeemed as travel vouchers for trips to other Caribbean islands, Canada, or the United States. For example, two "thank-you cards" are redeemable for a trip to San Juan, and three for a trip to New York. Arlette explained her experiences with the award process.

> I've never been at home sick [i.e., absent from work] since I've been here—three years. I find whenever I get sick it always falls on a weekend. [. . .] I got my first two thank-you cards for perfect attendance, and the company held a dinner for those persons who worked a straight year, and at the end of that dinner we got a trip to Puerto Rico! There were between twenty and twenty-five of us who had worked the straight year. My supervisor gave me another thank-you card for my outstanding work and performance [. . .] for coming in overtime whenever they needed [. . .] so I joined my card with the two from before and got a trip to New York.

Suzanne, another data entry operator, said:

> What I really like about here is, when they see that you're doing your work well, they give you a trip. And so far I have gained two trips from them and I appreciate that a lot. By attending work often [. . .] my proficiency was good and my error rate was good, so I went to Philadelphia. I have friends over there. Then the second one I went to New York and Boston. That was last year. The first time I took my sister with me. [. . .] They allow you to take a relative, like your parent or son or daughter or your sister or a husband. You can't take your boyfriend or a girlfriend or anything, the person has to be your immediate family.

These "bonuses" are integral to the incentive-driven system of management of Data Air, and workers at all levels cited "thank-you cards" as an important reward for hard work and dedication to the company. This award system is a central dimension of their increasingly transnational experience. The perk of airline travel is provided with little direct cost to Data Air because it is a sister company to one of the largest U.S. airlines with a busy hub in the Caribbean region. Because these trips instill a sense of pride in association between the women and Data Air, their employer, their value for the women cannot be measured against the cost to the company. Furthermore, they become integral to an expanding array of transnational economic and leisure activities in which these women are engaged. On trips to San Juan, Miami, New York, and other destinations across the Caribbean, North America, and England, they become transnational consumers of goods and styles that in turn define their image as informatics workers, as well as affect their household economies. At another level, the very name of these production bonus "thank-you cards" embodies a subtle dimension of the rhetoric of a corporate familial ethos and of conformity to feminine mores.[15] In essence, these tokens engender both material and symbolic significance in women's lives.

Describing other ways in which the company aims to supplement employee benefits, Data Air's general manager noted that all revenues from snack machines and pay telephones on the work premises are used to fund the employee health insurance program. He noted that through his pressure alone, he has convinced his parent company to budget US$100,000 annually to support employee benefits and perks and added with pride that these are not offered to the work forces "up north."

> We do these things because there's a feeling in Barbados that that's part of coming to work. In the United States you pay for that kind of stuff yourself—you pay for your own Christmas party generally. Again, we know the whole question of the sense of pride—and this is where I think we are different from the other companies here—we try to get people to see that management is employees too. This has to do with all of us being in the same boat, from a sociological perspective. You're working for a large company; a U.S.-based company. But we are largely managing ourselves and therefore we are all in this thing together. So we have evoked that sense of ownership, I would say, which gives them a real feeling that we have localized our company to the extent that we can [. . .] the first names and everything else, is meant to do that. [. . .] And to the extent that we do it, well, there is less interference, and we continue to be masters of our own destiny to the extent that we can be. In fact it is my operating style, that from day one when I came here, that I recognized that I would have to [implement] as soon as the folks [from the United States] got out of the way and we developed it carefully. We are now even trying to finesse some other things. But we are trying to democratize to the extent that it is possible in this type of environment.

One of the important perks that Data Air's general manager alludes to here is an employee shuttle bus to carry workers to the main bus terminal after six o'clock in the evening. His initiation of this policy set a precedent for other offshore companies in the industrial park. Workers who have been employed in locally owned businesses and industries and now work for Data Air often comment about this as one aspect of working for a foreign company that makes it preferable to working for a Barbadian firm. In the cultural arena, Data Air enters a band every year in the Kadooment celebration and sponsors athletes in national sports events.[16] In-house, consultants offer "self-improvement" programs and health and beauty lectures on such topics as diabetes, nutrition, prenatal care, personal grooming, and make-up. Between the lines of the general manager's remarks one can read his commitment to "localize" Data Air by attending to specifically Barbadian needs, interests, and traditions but along with it his acknowledgment of the limits to his power and directorship as the local manager of an offshore and wholly foreign-owned company. For a small island still smarting from the loss of hundreds of electronics assembly jobs when INTEL left in the early 1980s, the more than one thousand jobs represented by Data Air are unquestionably, if anxiously, significant. There are, therefore, real limits to the general manager's power. In effect, he is squeezed, somewhat like the supervisors, between the interests of his overseas parent company and the interests of his work force and the nation at large. He describes with pride the gains he has won for his workers with respect to what is offered to their counterparts in North America or elsewhere in the Caribbean and at the same time makes clear his adoption of "American style" work ethics and the specific mechanisms for insuring high levels of productivity and quality.

One example of the many new management practices introduced by the informatics sector, and Data Air in particular, is the institution of "participatory action circles" or PACS. Inspired by the Japanese "quality circle," PACS have been implemented by Data Air largely as "morale-building and problem-solving" groups, according to one of the supervisors at Data Air, to promote greater communication within and across levels of the work hierarchy.[17] Beyond airing work-related problems, members of these groups also involve themselves in community projects and fund-raising activities. "We raffled food hampers and organized picnics and even took a trip to St. Lucia," one keyer remarked. Eventually, however, especially because of periodic high workloads and increased overtime, participation in the PACS, particularly the "extracurricular" activities, tended to dwindle. In an attempt to invigorate and reconstitute the agendas of the PACS, Data Air's general manager became a "consultant member" of all groups, bringing their focus more directly to work-related issues. He said, "in some, there have been roaring arguments, and in one the group came up with eighteen ways in which the supervisor wasn't doing his job. They try to get consensus and of course it's not always possible. In the end someone has to have the final say, but we try to negotiate." The tension between a rhetoric of equal participation and voice in the management process and the reality of hierarchy and power is palpable in some of these gatherings. But the general manager did relate an experience that had convinced him of the effectiveness of these groups, noting that he once made a suggestion to a PAC for reorganizing some aspect of the job, and "they all jumped down my throat and said that it would mean hiring more people and getting more machines—that it wasn't cost effective!" He was amazed at the operators' concern for cost and added that since they are the ones doing the job, they know best how it ought to be done. This participatory thrust of the management style of Data Air is persuasive at least at the level of company rhetoric and, together with the distinctive look of the work environment, was remarked upon by numerous production workers and supervisors. Anne Marie, a data entry operator, said:

> We have chairs where we can relax; we have plants. They recognize employees with employee of the month [awards]. And [. . .] one thing I like [. . .] is that you call everybody by their [first] name and to me that shows [. . .] that although he is our supervisor, it doesn't mean that he is above us. [. . .] He's in charge of you, yes, but still you can go and speak to the person and address them by their first name. I think when you call a person by their name you get along much better.

Data Air's experimentation with "Japanese-style management practices," as one manager called them, has taken other forms as well. One involved a lunch and snack concession planned and run by interested employees, who sell food and own shares in the business. "The philosophy of the company," said the general manager, "is all about giving workers the opportunity to participate in its management." Another idea he presented, was to connect "total quality" groups in the U.S. insurance offices with the claims approvers in Barbados, "to give the approvers actual contact with the customer." They could engage in conference calls, he suggested, and thus communicate directly with their counterparts in North America. Although he did not say what they would talk about, the initiative was spawned from his acknowledgment of the anonymous quality of offshore work and the difficulty of impressing upon the operators the importance of meeting a client's needs when they had no contact whatsoever. "People in the

West Indies," the general manager said, "have always wanted to participate more in managing themselves, but the unions and political parties have had a singular power structure that fails to allow it to happen. People may say I'm antiunion, but I'm not. I am against that kind of power structure though. Unions are not participatory organizations."

Another gesture of management relations, meant to combat the anonymous quality of the open office at Data Air, is the practice of honoring employees' birthdays with cards and sometimes holding small parties or baby showers at work. These events are planned by friends and workmates rather than by the company itself, though managers do not discourage the celebrations, and on some occasions group meetings become the site for showers or surprise parties. While it is tempting to assert that women's enactment of traditional feminine rituals such as showers and beauty or talent contests, as well as their investments in fashions for work, are expressions of hegemonic patriarchal forces, this approach misses other complex meanings embedded in these practices. These sorts of "woman-centered" events held to mark traditional milestones (particularly marriage and the birth of a child) have been described by others (e.g., Fernandez-Kelly 1983; Westwood 1985) as reinscribing traditional femininity within the boundaries of the workplace and at the same time posing opposition and resistance by using these rituals, for example, to squeeze free time out of the workday or to alleviate some of the stressful routine of the labor process. Thus, these gatherings are pleasurable and express subtle opposition to the anonymous drudgery of highly rationalized work. As Karen Hossfeld (1990) argues, though women use these forms of manipulation or co-optation of feminine stereotypes to gain flexibility in an otherwise highly regimented day, they seldom see them as resistance. Nonetheless, she adds, these acts do provide short-term gains that cannot be underestimated.[18]

The data processors in the new informatics sector use these events to excuse lateness or to win concessions from their supervisors and managers, such as time off the system. But these events also help to incorporate supervisors and managers into the data processors' nonwork lives and to humanize (as well as feminize) the otherwise antiseptic open offices. They also invite a personal (if paternalistic) relationship between workers and their supervisors and managers that has benefits as well as costs. On the positive side, women receive greater sympathy, for example, in the event of a personal problem, such as a child's illness, that prevents them from achieving optimal production standards. Sympathy translates into dispensation in the form of excused lapses and simultaneously melds the relationship between operator and supervisor or manager in a way that directly challenges the corporate design of labor relations. In a context in which productivity and pay are evaluated and calculated according to computer-generated assessment reports, paternalism as it existed on the sugar plantation is notably absent. While these celebrations establish personal sympathies by supervisors for their workers, they also generate a new layer of responsibility and obligation by the operator to her superior, who might expect more cooperation in response to requests for overtime and, in general, high quality work, as well as small favors, such as picking up take-out lunch during the break.

Unlike Data Air, Multitext offers few employee activities and nonwork schemes that might operate as "morale boosters" and encourage the creation of a "family" identification with the company (Grossman 1979; Ong 1987). And, conscious of such practices at other offshore firms, workers at Multitext complain about the "cheapness" and "meanness" of their general manager, whom they see as the impediment to their receiving such perks. Interestingly, several small groups of women, on their own, initiated some of these "extracurricular" activities in an effort to extend work relations into the realms of leisure and community service. Their doing so implies that these activities evolve not solely as an expression of corporate manipulation but as occasions that serve women in several ways. Insofar as they bring workers together outside the context of the production floor, these gatherings and outings facilitate open talk (criticism and gossip) among women about their jobs, the conditions of work, and their supervisors and manager while forging deeper friendships among women who meet at work and enhancing the social benefits of their employment experience. One consistent trend across even the most exploitative industries on the global assembly line has been that women workers experience the sociability and contact with one another as a benefit of their employment. In some offshore industrial contexts, such as the maquiladoras in Mexico, we have seen that nonwork gatherings often form the context for incipient labor organization. Sharing their feelings of injustice, women come to trust one another and mobilize a range of resistance activities from subtle forms of protest to full-fledged strikes (Fernandez-Kelly 1983; Peña 1997). Among the data processors at Multitext, these gatherings are occasions to air frustrations about work and the "unfairnesses" of certain supervisors or managers, as well as to provide diversions from the work. Conversation revolves as much around general concerns of family, travel, vacations, and food as it does around the cast of characters or work experience at Multitext.

The annual Christmas party and awards ceremony is the only special, nonwork event formally sponsored by Multitext, and even this tradition emerged out of agitation and explicit requests by the keyers. I attended this party in the two consecutive years of my fieldwork, the first at a large and popular dinner theater on the south coast, and the second on a chartered evening dinner cruise on a boat called the *Bajan Queen*.[19] These events are planned long in advance, and women prepare for them in the weeks leading up to the holidays by purchasing, making, or commissioning a seamstress to sew a special dress for the occasion. These are often kept a surprise among groups of friends, and on the night of the party, individual women delight in their display of elaborate styles, many in gold, black, and silver with matching high heels and evening bags.

Each employee is permitted to invite a companion to the evening of festivities, and I was intrigued to find that few invite their husbands or boyfriends as their guests. More often, sisters, female friends, and sometimes even male friends (not partners) accompany them. When I asked one woman whether she planned to bring her husband, she replied matter-of-factly, "Men [meaning husbands and boyfriends]? They're just too miserable." These recreational gatherings, therefore, like the data entry floors themselves, are predominantly women-centered events, where adornment and display play a central role. Women dance and joke with each other, enjoying inside remarks referring to personalities and incidents from work along with the music and bountiful spread of traditional Christmas food and drink. They comment to one another about their outfits, asking where they were purchased or who made them and, sometimes, how much they cost. The emphasis is on newness, the purchase of a special outfit for this one event and attention to the matching of shoes, handbag, and dress or pants suit. In many ways, these gatherings with their emphasis on display, flirtation (with waiters and the few men attending the social event), dancing, drinking, and fun resemble the "reputation" acts of men described by Sidney Greenfield (1966:104) and many others writing about other Caribbean contexts (e.g., Brana-Shute 1979; Wilson 1973). Greenfield says, "it is normal for a man to take most of his entertainment in the company of male friends. No activities are ever planned to which the husband and wife go as a couple. . . . A wide range of behavior may take place at such times, but a man is not guilty of improper conduct as long as his escapades are not committed within his wife's presence" (104). Among the data processors of the 1990s, similarly, social life is also often sex-segregated. The informal outings, picnics, and Sunday lunches that women regularly organized and certainly the work-related forms of entertainment (company sponsored events, bands for Cropover, and the annual Christmas party) are primarily women-centered gatherings, where as one processor laughingly put it, "We jus' talk all kinda stupidness."

TRADE UNIONS

One of the most striking aspects of the offshore informatics sector in Barbados is its nonunion status. Again, while this may be the norm in other developing countries' policies toward foreign investment and free trade zones, no such explicit tradition has been formally established in Barbados. Through an implicit agreement between the Barbados government, however, the Barbados Workers Union (BWU), and foreign investors, companies operating within the offshore sector have been promised the "noninterference" of trade unions, barring flagrant misconduct. Recommended wages are generally surpassed by the foreign companies, and national labor laws (including maternity leave and vacation) are protected. Considering the strength of the BWU in both agriculture and industry, this concession cannot have been made without some reservation. One incentive, however, for the BWU's maintaining this practice of "noninterference" was the strong tie between the union and the Democratic Labour Party (DLP), which was in power during the period of the fieldwork and under pressure to develop new employment areas in the face of economic recession and structural adjustment measures.[20]

In the early days of Data Air, a group of employees were reported to have attempted to unionize, but management was effective in preventing a full-fledged strike and unionization (Posthuma 1987). A leader of the BWU mentioned this attempt at unionization but added that "quickly enough they were pacified with nice working conditions and since you must have 51 percent employee support to be in BWU, that didn't happen." According to Data Air's general manager, with the rare exception of ventilation problems and forced evacuation from the workplace, there has been nothing he would characterize as "industrial action." One afternoon when I was conducting interviews, the fire alarms sounded and over six hundred employees were evacuated from the building in all of five minutes. Within moments the fire department and police arrived, responding to a call about a bomb scare on the premises. When I discussed the incident with one of the managers, he implied that the "fiasco" was a sabotage gesture by a disgruntled worker and apparently the third incident of its kind.

No formal attempts to organize were made during the years of my research (1989–92). Monica described the situation in terms of differences between the working conditions of foreign companies, which exceed the standards of local

Barbadian ones. "From the time I come here I never heard of nobody talking about no union. I guess it's for places where you get unfaired [. . .] like Bajan firms, they could do with a union. But the American firm, you don't really get involved with that. I ain't saying that we need one or we don't. But it's not like the garment factories where the girls get dismissed wrongfully. I guess it's them that need the union." Rochelle, a claims approver said, "We have like a built-in union. [. . .] they say if you have a problem to take it to your supervisors and she will try to solve it. If she can't solve it, go to personnel or manager. [. . .] If you have anything you feel not right, just come to them and tell them, they will try to solve it."

A change in opinion about the benefits of unionization was apparent between the time of my initial interviews in 1989 and 1990 and the final survey I conducted in 1992. Initially, a significant minority of women in informatics described wanting some form of representation in the event of a conflict at work. As Pearl, a Data Air worker, said:

> I understand that the majority of the American companies in Barbados don't like the idea of the union stepping in, they feel that they can handle everything. [. . .] But I feel that some of the actual things that people go through, they don't know, and I feel they should have some sort of representative. [. . .] Like I can remember a time when we were working and the stub from somebody's check came through in our mail. Well, you can imagine what people said when they saw what the people up there were working for—doing the same thing as us. Somebody photocopied it—I can't remember how much it was but [. . .] they are working for much, much, much, more money. But there's no sense in me joining the union when I'm one out of thousands. You have to have a certain amount of people. The majority of women in here have a child or children, and you know the rumors of being victimized [for talking about a union] so I guess that's why a lot of people wouldn't join. Like if you go and join the union, the slightest thing you do they would fire you or they might pick on you.

Some other data processors felt that they might get help from the union in the form of wage increases or a longer lunch break. By 1992, however, not a single woman I interviewed thought that a union would be of any benefit to her, and, in fact, several believed that the poor performance of the unions in recent times revealed greed and self-interest on the part of its leaders and that they were better off working without union affiliation.[21]

During this period as well, three senior officers of the BWU served simultaneously as members of Parliament for the governing DLP administration, provoking criticism that they were "serving two masters." One of these senior BWU members accepted an appointment as a member of the cabinet, making it difficult for him to project an image of singular commitment to union interests. This apparent conflict of interest intensified during the DLP government's negotiations with the International Monetary Fund over a stabilization program. When the government decided to unilaterally impose an 8 percent wage cut for civil service employees, two of the three members of Parliament who were also BWU officers voted with the government to ensure passage of the measure in Parliament. There were macroeconomic forces at play as well, and many of the respondents were likely reacting to the general state of the Barbados economy at the time, when unemployment had risen above 30 percent and the nation faced the worst recession in its history (Editorial, *Barbados Advocate,* October 14, 1997).

Interestingly, by 1997, with the economy expanding and unemployment at 16.2 percent, there again appeared to be some interest in unionization within the industry (*Barbados Advocate,* October 14, 1997) and efforts were made by the BWU to increase the participation of women, who have traditionally been underrepresented in the otherwise large and active organization.[22] Echoing the concern and efforts of unionists more widely, regarding women's representation, a BWU spokeswoman said, "Barbadian women are afraid of losing their jobs; if they think they won't get anything else, they would work no matter what the conditions are in order to feed their children. They don't want to be victimized, but they must make money for their children." The ebb and flow in discussion about unionization in informatics mirrors these broader realities—the general state of the economy, the rate of unemployment, and the relationship between the trade unions and the government in power. Notably, the unions must contend with new management strategies that undercut them within the offshore sector, as well as within some old union strongholds. Indeed, the use of TQM and the employment of foreign management consultants have penetrated large, unionized, public companies and have generated the expected tensions. A strike at the local electric company in December 1996 produced placards denouncing TQM and demanding "fair wages."

The management approaches within informatics are striking in the ways in which they acknowledge and ostensibly attempt to mitigate the anonymous quality of the large open office production floors. The work hierarchy is such that data processors have little direct contact with managers. The gestures toward "total quality management" and "participatory action circles" are experiments that aim to foster greater communication between workers, supervisors, and managers. While they have not achieved noticeably widespread gains for the workers, they have achieved another kind of "gain" for the company. As rhetorical devices, they have been somewhat successful in instilling the idea that the company is open to suggestion, that managers are accessible, and that overall rules and conditions are more flexible than they might seem. Where these notions become even more complicated and contradicted is amid the many forms in which surveillance and corporate discipline are enacted.

Corporate Discipline and the Panopticon of the Open Office

The emergence of competing profiles of the "ideal" informatics worker led me, in the last chapter, to identify two "generations" of women workers—young, single girls just out of secondary school and without prior paid work experience and "older," "mature" women, often with prior work experience and children to support. One contradictory dimension of these two ideals is the "natural" degree of discipline and serious work ethic associated with each one. Whereas young school leavers are believed to be ideal because their recent school experience implies that good discipline, punctuality, and amenability to instruction are all fresh in their minds and experience, Data Air's general manager bemoans the trend to recruit young school leavers because they "still need to learn the terms of business." That is, they need to learn "a general work ethic" and develop the "seriousness that comes from age and prior employment. They need to understand how to get their personal goals to be congruent with what the business is trying to achieve," and this means "more work on our part."[23]

The introduction of a new work ethic is widely considered by informatics companies to be a fundamental part of the training process. Codes of professional workplace demeanor, dress, and responsibility (e.g., being on time, calling in the event of unforeseen absence or lateness, being available to work overtime when necessary, and being helpful toward co-workers) have become part of the trainee socialization process. Regarding the inculcation of a new, foreign work ethic, one data entry supervisor at Data Air mentioned, "Time is so important here, you get up and you got to write it down [. . .] and, you know, we Bajans are used to being late, so it's a problem." When a new group comes through training at Multitext, they are lectured about the rules of the company and the basic operation of the computer, not how a computer works, but how one should work a computer (logging on, exiting, etc.) and work at a computer (i.e., quietly, with no drinks or food or extraneous items on the computer table). Infringement of these basic rules meant, first, warnings, then a suspension, and finally dismissal.

It is seldom recognized that these new high-tech industries demand the acquisition of particular work habits and attitudes in addition to specific skills for assembly work or data entry. As Carl Stone, a Jamaican political scientist and journalist, points out, this demand for specific habits and attitudes is of particular relevance when new labor processes are introduced to countries with different work ethics and practices (cited in Senior 1991:112). Contrary to popular belief, these aspects of the labor process are not inherent in any particular labor force; they are deeply ingrained, socially constructed elements of cultural life. Work ethics as cultural practices are inculcated and reproduced in specific social, political, and economic contexts, and those bound up in the internationalized capitalist relations of the offshore information industry entail a complex of mental, physical, and emotional labor. Stone notes that in Jamaica, the working conditions and expectations of free zone industries differ significantly from those of local enterprises. In demanding high output, they are known to create conditions of intense pressure and strict discipline and to fire workers who fail to conform to the rigors of the line. As Stone puts it, "these are indeed high stress and very exacting work environments that contrast sharply with the casual, easy going, low work norms and low stress environments to be found in most Jamaican-run factories or other work situations" (cited in Senior 1991:112).

When we consider the incorporation experience of women in this high-tech service sector, the importance of the work environment cannot be emphasized too strongly. Work environment encompasses the labor process in its most immediate production sense, as well as the more subtle elements of expected behavior and appearance. In these subtle expressions and expectations of what I will call corporate discipline the intricacies of women's experience as offshore information processors are most strongly felt, and the complexities of internationalization are manifested.[24] As I have noted in chapter 4, the recruitment emphasis on young Barbadian women as ideal workers is much like that of garment and electronics assembly operations in Barbados and throughout much of Asia and Latin America. Similar, too, is the fact that offshore data entry facilities demand high production quotas and present high-pressure working environments. Therefore, the pleasant, air-conditioned, and quiet appearance of the open office seems a vast improvement over the dusty, fume-filled manufacturing plants next door. In fact, to reiterate, this is perhaps the most salient selling point of the industry—it is "clean." But far beyond the stressful quotas and strict decorum described by Stone are the hidden measures of control and surveillance fostered by the computer technology itself. Every operator can be electronically observed without pause or error, her productivity measured for specific amounts of work or increments of time, all without face-to-face contact.[25] If the quotas and discipline of the traditional plants were alien to the Caribbean labor climate as Stone suggested, then this level of hidden surveillance is even more foreign. In effect, the computer becomes a tool not only for the performance of the job task itself (processing data) but also for the evaluation of the worker. These new kinds of surveillance and their implications for particular strategies of discipline involve a complex convergence between technological and human forms of monitoring. In turn, these give rise to relations that vascillate between anonymity and paternalism and between resistance and pleasure.

Early industrialists devised numerous mechanisms for regulating and directing bodies and bodily energies for productive labor. Michel Foucault describes these processes of industrial management as "laying the groundwork for a new kind of society, a 'disciplinary society,' one in which bodily discipline, regulation and surveillance are taken for granted" (Foucault cited in Zuboff 1988: 319). His analysis of these mechanisms has been applied to new contexts of labor that involve the intensely powerful and unrelenting eye of the computer. This new technology, Foucault points out, is a reinvention of an old form of control known as the panopticon, which was based on a 1787 architectural plan by Jeremy Bentham for containing convicts and paupers and was used ultimately in prisons, asylums, and factories. The design included a "twelve-sided polygon formed in iron and sheathed in glass in order to create the effect of . . . 'universal transparency'" (Zuboff 1988: 320). It is useful to quote Foucault at some length in order to appreciate the ways in which this architecture of control enacts a peculiar form of power, that which is "visible and unverifiable."

> All that is needed, then, is to place a supervisor in a central tower and to shut up in each cell a madman, a patient, a condemned man, a worker or a schoolboy. One can observe from the tower, standing out precisely against the light, the small captive shadows in the cells of the periphery. They are like so many cages, so many small theaters, in which each actor is alone, perfectly individualized and constantly visible. . . . Full lighting and the eye of a supervisor capture better than darkness, which ultimately protected. *Visibility is a trap. . . . Each individual, in his place, is securely confined to a cell from which he is seen from the front by the supervisor; but the side walls prevent him from coming*

into contact with his companions. He is seen but he does not see; he is the object of information, never a subject in communication. . . . And this invisibility is a guarantee of order. If the inmates are . . . workers, there are no disorders, no theft, no coalitions, none of those distractions that slow down the rate of work, make it less perfect or cause accidents. (1975:200; italics mine)

The atomized, individual nature of informatics work, in which keyers are physically divided from each other at cellular stations is achieved with a double layer of surveillance: the deep level of computer monitoring and the surface, and more quixotic layer of human supervision. Typically, a high degree of "security" is built into the physical plant as well (Soares 1991a). Electronically locked doors and security guards at the main entrances of data entry enterprises are installed to insure the protection of the computer equipment. Inside the windowless production areas, managers' and supervisors' glass-enclosed offices surround the data entry floor, allowing them to observe the overall hum of the shift while workers, susceptible to the supervisor's gaze, focus on the VDT screen. Even in its clean and "cool" appearance, the informatics open office is a haunting reinvention of Bentham's eighteenth-century panopticon. The individualized work stations appear to provide each operator with a personal, private space to which she returns day after day: her own desk, terminal, manuscript stand, and in some cases, calculator for processing insurance claims. But these stations are the very definition of anonymity and exposure. Indeed, these spaces feel "private" but they are visible to the supervisor. They are individual but they are also shared by workers on other shifts, and they become, in effect, depersonalized. Absent are the name plates and photographs of children and family, the plants, tissue holders, candy bowls, and decorative items that generally adorn the desks and work areas of office workers and make them "theirs."

Through the computer, the central tool of data processing and production, informatics lends itself to a level of worker control and surveillance far exceeding that found in other manufacturing industries and in traditional office settings. By monitoring workers' error rates, speed, quantity of items processed, lapses in keying, and length and frequency of breaks, these computer systems can calculate and compare worker productivity and discipline precisely and systematically. Donna described the lack of freedom inside the informatics workplace.

Every thing you do has to go on a time sheet. I personally call it slavery [she laughs]. Everything you do they keep track of. You call it the off-time sheet. It really burns me. Like when I come here to you, I'll probably go upstairs and start to work again, and then when the girl comes around I got to say, oh god, what time I went down and what time I got back up. I think it's to keep track of the time you spend on the computer but I really don't like it. Because sometime you might have a problem, suppose like the code that you might have is not there, or suppose you come to work and you get wet. [. . .] they have a code for sick leave and for staff meetings, personal off-time, but what are you going to say when your clothes get wet? You have to go and dry them but there's no code for that. So you got to put back in that time, so if you spent twenty minutes drying your clothes, maybe over lunch you will put back into the system, or you can let the girl know to deduct that twenty minutes from your check.

Claire made the same point more succinctly: "There ain't no freedom nowhere. Not in here."

In informatics, the electronic panopticon's power is ever-present and anonymous (Foucault 1975:202). The worker under its gaze knows that at any moment she may be observed, and thus she quickly learns to regulate herself, to watch herself. She does so when she is "on-line," or logged on to the computer, as well as when she is on break, going to the bathroom or making a telephone call. Self-regulation and surveillance take multiple forms on the open office floor. Women workers are profoundly aware that they are being observed both by the computers on which they work and by others across the work hierarchy. As such, their self-modulation involves giving acute care to the number of minutes they take for a bathroom break, as well as to the shade of nail polish or particular outfit to wear to work.

The open office is, at one and the same time, factorylike in its labor process and officelike in its muffled quiet ambience. A keyer produces a commodity (information) in much the same way as a garment worker assembles clothing for export. She adheres to strict codes of quality and her production is measured by the piece. But unlike on the traditional factory assembly line, where workers amuse themselves and break the monotony of their jobs by talking and joking with their fellow workers, on the data entry floor talking is minimally allowed (Yelvington 1990; Westwood, 1985). The talking and joking that helps to compensate for the tedium of assembly line work the world over is precluded by informatics' highly individualized work, where keyers are expected to ignore the other operators around them and focus closely on their particular screen. This demand for quiet is both a necessity and a burden from the workers' perspective. Some operators resent the restriction on talking, others comment that noise on the floor distracts them from their work and argue that their accuracy (and therefore incentive pay) suffers from "too much chat." Others say that talking reduces the monotony of their work. They feel that if they keep their voices low, their conversations should be tolerated. Many wear "Walkman" headphones and type to the sound of "oldies" or the latest dub music to entertain themselves and still keep within the bounds of closely monitored individual work that requires a high degree of concentration.[26] As Cherane put it, "Headphones are kind of a reprieve. [. . .] You get away from the talk and chat and you're in your own private world and you have the music and it helps." Lisa, another operator, added, "I don't like nothing 'bout this job. It's boring. Every day's the same. Just talking and listening to the radio make the time go faster."

The two forms of surveillance—human and electronic—denote, in effect, two forms of power within the industry. That of the computer is anonymous and depersonalized. A keyer performs her job at a particular rate of speed and accuracy, and her wage is figured accordingly. The power of the supervisor or manager, however, becomes embedded within relationships that may be formed out of personal rapport, or alternatively, personal animus. The supervisor, therefore, represents a mediating force between the anonymous surveillance and assessment of the computer and traditional management practices of local firms and plantations, based on a model of patronage and familiarity (shared village origins, family connections, affiliations through church, school, or political parties, etc.). Armed with the new techniques of TQM and PACS, the supervisor attempts to convey an air of impersonal moderation that is categorically new to the design of the Barbadian workplace. Certainly, other offshore companies, such as INTEL, have introduced highly rationalized labor processes and similar work hierarchies involving large numbers of production workers and small numbers of supervisors and managers trained by the foreign corporate staff. However, the peculiarly anonymous dimension of the computer as a form of manager is unprecedented in the experience of Barbadian workers. While most keyers complain of being chained or tied to their monitors through their computer's unrelenting gaze, an equally prevalent sentiment was that the computer is "fair." By measuring wages individually by productivity, it avoids the capriciousness and favoritism that supervisors are frequently charged with in other industries, such as garments, textiles, and electronics, and by overseers and managers on the plantation.

Some of the advantages of the more paternalistic model of local management, however, are not missed by workers even in this highly modern setting. By lobbying energetically, they have succeeded in forcing Data Air to "harmonize" to the local scene. The US$100,000 invested by Data Air for night-shift bus transportation is one such example. Strong pressure from female employees has also forced Data Air and other transnational corporations to dramatically rethink their standard worker profile and to abandon, for example, the use of pregnancy tests, which are commonplace recruitment requirements elsewhere on the global assembly line. As chapter 4 explores in detail, the shifting profile of the "ideal" worker between that of a young, single, childless "girl" and a "mature matriarch" and the manner in which these competing ideals are strategically invoked reflects not only the manipulation of management but also the realities, demands, and agency of these particular Afro-Caribbean women. In short, the experience of women workers in informatics typically involves the simultaneous dimensions of discipline and stress (through the dual forms of monitoring of their supervisors and their computers) as well as pleasure and pride. Women's agency in the open office takes many forms, from refining the companies' expectations of who constitutes an appropriate worker to temporarily masterminding the computer systems such that workers' substantially increased their pay. As chapter 6 will explore, they also enact their subjectivity and agency through complex expressions of "professionalism" as an ethic of appearance and demeanor that enhances their pleasure in their work and forges their own distinctive identities as workers. The modes of discipline within informatics extend beyond the surveillance of computers and supervisors in ways that bring us back to the issues of family and household introduced in chapter 4.

THE COMPANY AS A METAPHORICAL "FAMILY"

Household and family configurations and demands are frequently deployed in employers' rationales for particular strategies of labor recruitment and in the shifting prescriptions for who constitutes "ideal" workers in this new service industry. Women's reproductive roles and the expectation that women are the bearers and natural socializers and caretakers of children have historically been used to legitimate their "secondary" wage rates and their concentration in low-skilled, dead-end jobs. The notion of family is also used, however, in the context of the data entry operations themselves, in ways that contest and alternatively reinscribe both Barbadian and international corporate models of patriarchy. Family, therefore, becomes a central trope in two senses: in a rhetorical and ideological construct framed as "the corporate family," and in reference to women's real kin relations and obligations. In both notions of family there are disciplinary and concessionary dimensions, costs and benefits.

In its role of patron, the company enjoys positive public relations and a more contented work force. These predominantly female corporate "families" in a historically matrifocal society are headed by "patriarchs." As described above, at Multitext, this patriarchal management figure is the locus of controversy and disgruntlement. On several occasions at Data Air, in contrast, workers fondly mentioned experiences of going to talk with their general manager, emphasizing their use of his first name, and entrusting him with matters of their future. Maggie, in the prep department said, "The whole company sees him as someone to talk to and confide in. He's good friends with everyone." The reverence and familiarity embedded in their descriptions revealed a strong paternal relationship.

Family and household, as I note in chapter 3, are contested concepts across the Afro-Caribbean. The major difference between them is that members of a household share a common residence and may or may not be blood relatives, while family members are related but may not share a residence. Furthermore, the simultaneity of patriarchy and matrifocality and of the coexistence of widely held nuclear family ideals and a multitude of real family and household formations has been a difficult combination for many observers to absorb. As Joycelin Massiah put it, "In the Caribbean . . . matrifocality of the family is stressed but male authoritarianism is the ideal" (1982:8). Both forces are at work in the organization of Barbadian social relations. As such, when Data Air's motto pronounces "we are all one family" one must ask, what sort of family does this mean? Is the slogan imagining the idealized nuclear family with a male breadwinner / patriarch or a family in which a woman presides over her home piecing together a living by multiple means in order to support herself and her children? How are these multiple models played out in the work arena of informatics in the construct of the "company family"?

Rachel Grossman, in her early work about women workers in multinational factories, points out, "The factory becomes family-like for young women workers—with big brothers and a 'father' as compelling images of patriarchy in the plant" (cited in Young 1987:109). At Multitext and Data Air, where most of the supervisory staff are women and the few men in the companies are scattered across the work hierarchy and singularly occupy the ranks of top management, the patriarchal model of family is upheld. The "generational" squabbles and differences in manner and style between "older" workers who have been with the company for more than a few years and the "younger," recently hired school leavers resemble a sort of sibling rivalry. And, calling all workers "girls" regardless of their age and maternal status situates them in a single age-mate category beneath their management elders. At the most pragmatic level, workers are encouraged to believe that the company is concerned about them not only as individual workers but also as members of their own families and as members of the corporate family. Others writing about women workers in global factories cite similar rhetoric aimed at securing their commitment to company demands. Relatively unexplored in the literature, however, is the specific family form invoked by this transnational rhetoric of the "corporate family." Aihwa Ong (1995:173) notes that in Japanese-owned factories in Malaysia, one official company motto prescribes a patrilineal " 'family welfare' model, said to reflect the *keluarga* (kindred) emphasis on mutual obligation and loyalty." Its mission proclaimed the creation of "one big family, to train workers, to increase loyalty to the company, country and fellow workers." But the tensions surrounding foreign, non-Muslim managers led women workers to resent what they experienced as harassment and manipulation by their male supervisors and to resist the factory-sponsored ethic of competition, in favor of helping one another in the way siblings (*saudara saudari*) would. Unwittingly, they reproduce the goals of the "corporate family" ethic through their mutual dependence and resultant self-regulation.

In Barbados, where idealized notions of the nuclear family are widely contradicted by the multiple forms of people's realities, the corporate usage of this metaphor is left somewhat vague. At Data Air this rhetoric is more widely used than at Multitext, and the figurehead of the well-liked and admired general manager is, by implication, widely construed as the benevolent patriarch. The predominance of matrifocality in the region, and in these women's own lives, however, also carves out a logical space for the women who fill the majority of supervisory and floor-managerial positions.[27] In the informatics industry, unlike in many foreign-owned offshore plants on the global assembly line, women's roles and responsibilities as mothers and caretakers are favorably acknowledged in practices which allow them some flexibility in making up their time at work if family duties call them away early or keep them from arriving at work on time.[28]

Family values and the associated preservation of certain expressions of morality and feminine propriety are conveyed more subtly within the dictates of dress code and expectations of a "professional" demeanor. In brief, the concept of "professional" looks encodes an element of moral status that goes along with these feminine appearances, even while it heightens the illusory distinctions between white-collar and blue-collar work or between office and manufacturing work. The suit and briefcase adopted by many of the data entry operators create a look that is both fashionable and conservative. Admonitions against short skirts and flashy jewelry, or "dibby dibby" (sexually loose) styles are not merely prescriptions against casual or sloppy appearances; they codify a style prescription reflective of deeper social mores about femininity, respectability, and professionalism. These are asserted firmly by management, as well as among women workers themselves.

More abstractly, family is introduced as a metaphor for the close and unified ties and obligations within the company itself. The "company as family" metaphor is invoked often during times of stress, when demands for overtime work or some sort of reorganization requires greater understanding and generosity on the part of the workforce. However, both management and workers use the concept of "family" to achieve ulterior motives.[29] Operators are known to gain some flexibility in an otherwise tightly regimented shift schedule when their excuse for lateness or absence involves duty to family. For example, one data processor frequently took days off work to care for her asthmatic daughter without being penalized, and others noted that when they were simply fed up with working they would call in and say they had "family problems." In some instances the very stereotypes about women as matriarchs and the backbones of their families that form the basis for company expectations of loyalty and responsibility also enable workers to derive some dispensation from the stresses of production pressures. Where Lisa Rofel notes the use of similar claims for family and "female" reasons to take time off work by female factory workers in Southeast Asia, she argues that this pattern ultimately reproduces notions about women in the wider society as inherently less productive than men (cited in Ong 1991:299). For women in Barbados, interestingly, the wider effect is instead to entrench a belief that women are, indeed, invincible matriarchs, naturally capable of managing both demanding work schedules and the responsibilities of motherhood and running a household. The cost of maintaining this mythic image, however, is a refusal to acknowledge that women's capacity to juggle as many responsibilities as they do is less a choice than a simple and stressful necessity. Barbadian women are, in fact, resourceful and strong. However, these admired attributes are integrally tied to burdensome conditions they face in their efforts to support themselves and their children.[30] Further, corporate strategies of invoking the "family" nature of relations at work converge with their assumptions about women's real kinship roles and positions in the sense that both "dependent daughters" and "mature matriarchs" can be called on to perform particular duties in a responsible manner. The competing ideologies of femininity and family that women face in the rhetoric of the corporate family—that of the strong matriarch and that of the dependent daughter—must, therefore, be considered in relation to each other, as each has both beneficial and disciplinary implications for the gendered expectations of women as informatics workers.

Just as family (in the corporate, rhetorical sense and in women's real kinship relations) supports and benefits these women workers, so too does it represent an array of demands and obligations. In turn, the pink-collar informatics workers can be seen to comply with these family expectations and to elude or reconfigure them in ways that suit their own needs and desires. Their acts of accommodation and of resistance are played out in ways that are both subtle and clear, and with effects that simultaneously transform and reinscribe modes of discipline in a multitude of ways.

RESISTANCE AND TRICKERY ON THE OPEN OFFICE FLOOR

The extent to which data processors are inclined, almost in the same breath, to list the virtues of informatics and the drawbacks of their company or their job raises intriguing questions about the nature of agency. Indeed, in explicit comments, as well as in more subtle expressions and practices, women make clear their pride in association with their company, the offshore sector, or working with computers, as well as their resistance to the many pressures that confront them on the job. As a nuanced reading of power and resistance would predict, even for those women who extol the benefits of this industry, their jobs, and their overall experience as informatics workers, there are crevices of critique and dissent. Similarly, for those most critically conscious of workplace discipline and corporate manipulations for increasing productivity, there are simultaneous dimensions of pleasure. A burgeoning literature in anthropology, much of which draws on the work of Foucault, addresses the relationships between human agency, power, and the enactment of resistance in the course of everyday life (Ong 1987; Scott 1985; Kondo 1990; Abu-Lughod 1990; de Certeau 1984; Ortner 1995). The focus on everyday practices of resistance and the emphasis on agency and subaltern subjectivity has, in its extreme, led us to ask if "mere survival" for many people is not resistance. Indeed, the extent to which resistance implies a direct challenge to institutions of power, or reflects people's tenacious ability to preserve and even advance themselves in the face of power, appears to me to be a false opposition. What much of this literature reveals is that the work of resistance is not singular in form, nor is it typically practiced in isolation from compliance, accommodation, and even pleasure.[31] As Antonio Gramsci (1971), and later Raymond Williams (1977), demonstrate through the concept of hegemony, power is a process, incomplete, in need of renewal, recreation, and always challenged and resisted.

This constant process through which power is reinscribed and challenged both ideologically and materially is a relational one, always in tension. As Williams says, a lived hegemony is not to be confused for "passive dominance" or direct coercion but instead is "a whole body of practices and expectations over the whole of living, the shaping perceptions of ourselves and our world" (1977:110). The simultaneity of complicity and resistance, coercion, and challenge is expressed eloquently in the ethnographic exploration of Japanese workers by Dorinne Kondo: "That people inevitably participate in their own oppressions, buying into hegemonic ideologies even as they struggle against those oppressions and those ideologies—a familiar fact of life to women, people of color, colonized and formerly colonized peoples—is a poignant and paradoxical facet of human life" (1990:221). What forms these resistances take, and in what combinations, is, of course, culturally mediated and historically specific. Kondo's critique of James Scott (1985) makes a point that is indispensable for an analysis of informatics workers' simultaneous criticism of, resistance to, and pleasure in their work. She says that in order to see "the subtleties, ironic twists, and wrenching yet creative contradictions," we need to see power not merely as "repressive, a mechanism applied from above and outside, a substance some people possess and some people do not, which prevents the expression of authentic resistance" (Kondo 1990:221).

There continues to be an implicit sense more widely within workplace studies that organized union activity represents the ultimate expression of resistance, and the essential goal. For workers in most global industries, with their "footloose" capacity to skip across nations and avoid the constraints of unionization, such organization has been difficult to achieve, at best. Company-rigged elections, squashed union campaigns, mass firing of "dissident" workers, and militarization of free trade zones in places such as the Philippines, China, and Mexico have met attempts to organize. The more usual forms of resistance by these workers, therefore, have been clandestine, and individually as opposed to collectively enacted. Their significance, however, can be great. The "subaltern struggles" of the maquiladora shop floor, Peña points out, "are very difficult to control because, like fleeting ghosts, the protagonists move unpredictably through hidden networks" (1997:105). He distinguishes, however, between informal struggles that ultimately "mature" into direct confrontation with management, trade unions, and other official bodies—resistance that leads to "political recomposition"—and those acts that are limited to the shop floor and therefore remain "an ineffectual 'game,' because [they] cannot challenge or transform the formal and informal hierarchies that sustain the relations of domination at the point of production" (1997:123).[32] Although these movements from individual and small group struggles to grander political organizations are indeed remarkable, such privileging of direct confrontation over covert challenges ultimately brings us back to where we began—challenging the view of power and agency such that resistance is understood predominantly in the form of an organized strike. Such a view would lead us to see Barbadian informatics workers as highly accommodating and even actively complicit with the aims of corporate capital, missing not only the more subtle gestures of dissent but also, and this is perhaps most important, the complex interconnections between resistance and accommodation and between alienation and pleasure.

A number of studies specifically focusing on women's work experiences have noted numerous expressions of resistance exercised by women that fall both inside and outside the realms of organized labor, strikes, and protests. Kathryn Ward (1990a) and Lisa Rofel (1992), for example, point out that women's resistance may be explicit or covert and is frequently "intertwined with contradictory elements that reinforce their traditional roles as wives and mothers" (Ward 1990a). Sallie Westwood (1985) and Louise Lamphere (1985) both describe how maintaining feminine rituals of baby and bridal showers within the context of the factory challenges the separation between home and work; Aihwa Ong (1987) recounts the striking instance in which young Malaysian women employ the medium of a highly contagious spirit possession in response to extreme measures of disciplined production and effectively bring about a work stoppage.

Open resistance and confrontation in the context of many service jobs present distinctive kinds of risks for workers. The data processor, for example, may jeopardize her rapport with the supervisor who disburses work and provoke her to take her time in recognizing the operator's need for new pages to key, permission to go to the bathroom, or need for clarification of a typing code or procedure. Ignoring a data processor's gaze, or her wooden block placed atop her monitor signifying the need for more pages to key, is a subtle but powerful tool used by supervisors to discipline a particular operator without a direct verbal confrontation. Like the harried waitress who avoids the gaze of a boisterous or condescending customer, the supervisor who conveniently "doesn't see" the hand waving or insistent look of a worker on the floor exerts power and privilege over individuals in her group. If the operator should go above the supervisor's head to complain of being "unfaired" in this way, her supervisor can always claim not to have noticed her. Greta Paules, in her book about waitresses in a New Jersey restaurant (1991), describes power relations akin to probably every office place, open office, and factory floor. Again, just as there are many forms of power, so too are there multiple ways of resisting. She describes resistance in both explicit and veiled terms, depending upon the nature of the power relations between the individuals at hand; the greater the disparity in power, the greater the conceal-ment of resistance (198).

In both Data Air and Multitext, expressions of dissatisfaction and modes of resistance can be traced in a range of explicit and more subtle forms. Keyers, well aware of their expendability, tend to be reserved in their critical commentary while at work. Frank and biting assessments of individuals and the work process are more often reserved for private conversations over lunch breaks and in the context of women's homes on weekend gatherings. In contrast to the usual hushed tones of complaint in the workplace setting, there are, however, occa-sional outbursts and acts of refusal, like that which occurred at Multitext in a meeting with a new group of trainee typists and their nineteen-year-old super-visor, Jennifer. The keyers sat in a semicircle of chairs around their supervisor, and Jennifer began by reading aloud each typist's error rates for the week. Many heads bowed in public shame or shyness. During the pause that followed, a young woman named Melissa spoke up in a strong and self-assured voice, com-plaining about the bathroom policy that allows typists to use the bathroom only during shift and lunch breaks unless they get permission from a supervisor. The young trainee's point of contention was that to summon a supervisor and wait for permission rather than just going to the washroom when necessary wastes time. Her complaint reflected a much deeper frustration and humiliation over the restrictive nature of their work—as she put it, "feeling like I'm back in school"—and the mechanism of public shame to which they were currently sub-ject. Using the new language of the company, introduced by the British general manager and his penchant for management jargon, her criticism of the ineffi-cient "time maximization" was impossible for the young supervisor to defend, and she angrily changed the subject.

The dueling match continued when the supervisor complained about the group's "excessive" absences and reminded them that all absences must be ac-companied by a doctor's note. Again, Melissa challenged her with the indignant demand, "What if you get migraine headaches? On the money we make, we're supposed to go to a doctor every time to produce a note?" Defensive and irritated, the supervisor then asked if she had noted on her initial application that she got migraine headaches, implying that such a preexisting condition would have precluded her employment at the outset. When Melissa said that she had noted her headaches on her application, Jennifer floundered and replied that she had been speaking on general terms. Melissa "cut her eyes" and stiffened in her seat, saying, "Well, *I'm* not talking in general, I'm asking about *me, my* particular situation," in short, insisting that Multitext's corporate discipline be less impersonal and more human and address them not as generic "operators" or "production workers" or "girls" but as individual women. These sorts of direct and verbal challenges invariably focus on general company policies, such as shift hours and charges of inflexibility, and are almost always directed at the supervisors. In these expressions of contestation supervisors are often both the targets of complaint and the arbiters of discord, and those data processors who refuse opportunities for promotion to supervisor, as mentioned above, typically refer to these struggles as "hassles" they prefer to be spared.

The computer-generated discipline and stresses of informatics are most often borne silently, discussed quietly among the workers, or manifested in acts of "trickery." These acts typically begin as individual discoveries and eventually spread across the production floor. Two dramatic incidents of such computer-based "trickery" occurred during my fieldwork, one at Data Air and the other at Multitext. These covert forms of resistance—which ultimately were framed as theft and sabotage—revealed ingenuity and an unexpected mastery over a fragmented and apparently sealed system. Workers effectively "tricked" the system to lighten the load of their production quotas and increase their access to incentive bonuses. In each case, despite the close computer-generated surveillance, individual keyers figured out ways of "tricking the computer" either by copying disks or hitting particular keys in such a way as to achieve exceptional speed and accuracy reports and effectively doubling their paychecks in the process. In the most dramatic case, Data Air was faced with investing US$250,000 in new equipment, when management found itself unable to put an end to a computer-sabotage scheme with the existing system. Several keyers discovered that the key they type to indicate the completion of a ticket's data registers as a valid keystroke without effecting the data being processed. In short, by striking this key repeatedly they were able to increase their number of keystrokes per hour without interfering with the valid entry of airline ticket data. By simply arriving at the terminal early on a workday, or skipping the lunch break to sit mindlessly pressing this key, operators found that they were quickly and effortlessly able to supplement their usual paychecks. Because incentive pay is based on the number of keystrokes per hour they typed, some of these data processors more than doubled their bi-weekly wages. Indeed, the sudden phenomenon of low producers earning the same proficiency rates and incentive bonuses as those known to be the highest producers led these operators to quickly voice their concern that there was something wrong. Ruth Ann, one such high producer, recounted:

> The stats come out every day that show you how many batches you keyed and at the speed you keyed them. So, you can always find the good operator, someone who always pushing a higher volume of work. So, if you find that there are persons who just key six batches a day and they are still keying six batches and the person that is keying twelve batches still is not getting as much proficiency as they do [. . .] you say, "Hey, that is not right!" So, it was the other young ladies on the floor that first detect the [dummy] key. At first [management] said it was not possible, and we were still trying to say it is [. . .] that something was wrong. I felt bad knowing that I was one of the top keyers and I still could not key at 200 percent and there were persons keying lower than me that surpassed my speed and started keying at 200 percent. [. . .] You start wondering what's happening! We were always in the supervisor's office saying, "Hey, this body is not keying anything, how come their proficiency is so high?" and at first they could not understand what we were saying. You would complain and talk about it in meetings and it was only then when it started getting out of hand and [the company] did something.

Such schemes as "tricking the computer" into recording a doubled work production or reading copied or conferred-over work as perfect are detected only when complaints of poor quality work are made by Multitext's clients overseas. These incidents reveal a degree of ingenuity and understanding of the labor process and the technology that directly challenges the "closed-system" design of these jobs. Workers cleverly manipulate a tool that by design is meant to elude their understanding (the idea that workers do not need to know how the computer works, just how to use the software program in the way they are instructed), and a labor process that is predicated on the computer's imperviousness to such tampering. Both the use of the "dummy key" at Data Air and even more so, the system at Multitext of circumventing double keying by copying disks, are high-tech loopholes that, if even for a short time, enable operators to gain a sense of control over their labor and derive temporary profits.

The incident at Data Air had costly effects for both workers and the company management. Unable to solve the problem with computer consultants who attempted to reprogram the existing machines, Data Air ultimately replaced its entire system, at a cost of hundreds of thousands of dollars, with a new system the data processors found harder to use. Resentments were strong, particularly by highly productive operators who had not been involved in the computer trickery toward those who had exploited the former system, as it became increasingly difficult to achieve the standard production quotas and incentive bonuses. Interestingly, so many operators were assumed to be implicated in the scheme that no one was fired. Women refused to identify a single ringleader and because so many had profited across the range of high- and low-level producers, it was never clear where the boundaries between guilty and innocent parties could accurately be drawn. Together, then, all of the data processors shared the plight of having tighter production conditions and lower rates of pay than those they had come to expect.

Work in informatics is replete with instances and dimensions of discipline, as well as agency, from the independent decision to take a job in this new sector, and even more dramatically, the insistence by many to keep that job long beyond the international norm, to the expression of various demands, such as night transportation, time off for traditional cultural festivals, and certainly, the challenge to internationally prescribed gender ideologies for constituting the profile of an informatics worker. In many other ways, as well, women in this offshore sector make use of subtle strategies to exert themselves within and against high-tech modes of incorporation. Many of these modes of agency are themselves gendered practices. Women employ motherhood, for example, as a sacred and unchallengeable expression of Caribbean femininity to extract greater flexibility and even compassion from both local managers and foreign employers. Equally, they self-consciously make use of stereotypically feminine rituals to tailor corporate-sponsored productivity drives—such that a group meeting to discuss work-related problems and ideas for enhancing production turns into a baby shower or birthday party and whittles away an extra half hour of the work day.[33] Most striking of all are the complex ways in which expectations for a particular form of "professional" demeanor and appearance demand that women find innovative ways of fashioning themselves as pink-collar workers. These demands are, at one and the same time, forms of discipline and agency, repression and pleasure. They represent to a large extent what makes informatics distinct from other global manufacturing industries—what makes them simultaneously "electronic sweatshops" and comfortable "open offices."

Chapter 6

Fashioning Femininity and

"Professional" Identities:

Producing and Consuming Across

Formal and Informal Sectors

Discipline and worker control have been central to the incorporation of women workers along the global assembly line.
Their role in the management of the new "pink-collar" enclave is in some respects reminiscent of their role in other
industrial settings and in other respects their role is strikingly different. The
general expectation that offshore "office" workers conform to so-called traditional female stereotypes (i.e., that they be pleasant, loyal, courteous, well
groomed if not attractive, cheerful, etc.) adds both a hidden dimension of "emotional labor" (Hochschild 1993) and expense to the explicit labor process. The
discipline exerted in creating what virtually everyone in informatics refers to as a
"professional-looking" work force establishes as well the industry's most visible
marker.[1] Like the hidden but potent sign of the computer, the impressive appearance of the informatics worker is noted with a degree of wonder by virtually
every passerby. Together, the computer and the distinctly fashioned new pink-
collar worker are vital ingredients in a process through which the status and
position of this new sector and its employees are made strategically ambiguous.
The ambiguity between whether informatics constitutes white-collar office work
or blue-collar factory work and whether workers in the industry are assembly
line workers or clerical workers is manifested in the following comment by the
manager of one of the smaller local data entry operations:

> When you see a group of the young ladies, like the ones from Data Air, you
> can see that they're much better dressed than the ones from the assembly
> plant. That's my observation. They're probably not getting paid much better

but their work environment is a cleaner one, a purer one, and they in fact live out that environment. . . . The Data Air office is very plush, so the young ladies working in there perceive that they are working in an office and they dress like it and they live like it. It's a very interesting phenomenon—it only got started when the data entry business got started—this new breed of office-type workers. They equate themselves with . . . clerical staff in an office and they carry themselves in that way.

"Professionalism," Dress, and the Enactment of Conformity and Style

The enticing appeal of the clean, cool look of the open office, the carpeted and air-conditioned work environment (much of which is demanded by the computer technology itself) and the industry's reputation for a well-dressed work force distinguish informatics as a separate, new sector of the economy. "Professional" looks, when they cross work and nonwork, corporate family/real family boundaries, however, help to obfuscate the position and status of informatics and are integral to the idea of strategic ambiguity I mention above. Contradictions between informatics' factory wages and its new lexicon of specialized titles, such as "material controller" and "instructor specialist," add another dimension. While women generally denied that their work experience in the data processing industry had changed their image of themselves in any identifiable way, their clearly defined notions about how one should dress and behave at work in this new industry, with the constant refrain of "professional" demeanor and appearance, contrast with their descriptions of their previous work experience and, to some extent, of their class base. For example, some women acknowledged that they could be making more money even as domestic or agricultural workers. Their wages are comparable to or only slightly higher than those in a garment or electronics factory (and many have actually had these jobs). Significantly, however, all argued that they would rather be in informatics because of the job setting, the "cool" look of the place, and the promise represented by the computer.

Like the local manager quoted above, another corporate officer proudly proclaimed that the information processing industry offers a work environment on par with that of other offices and distinctly separate from manufacturing. "Women are expected to dress professionally here," he said. "This is not a production mentality like jeans and tee shirts." In fact, while a number of manufacturing industries are located next to these data entry facilities, many of the women themselves stated in frank and determined terms that "you can tell by the way she looks" whether a woman is on her way to work at one of the garment factories or in informatics. While they acknowledged little difference in the pay between the two, they clearly asserted that working in informatics is a step above working in the garment factories. Illustrating this point was the expression of disbelief and even indignation on the part of several data processors when they learned of a fellow worker who quit her job as a keyer and was now working at a piece rate in a neighboring cigar factory.

The manager's emphasis on women's "professional" presentation as bound up in a particular worker "mentality" implies that the way one looks both reflects and shapes one's work ethic and productive capacity. The importance of this notion is expressed and absorbed in numerous ways. This subtle additional job requirement, while positively striking to every onlooker, becomes invisible as a form of labor. In the arena of the open office, dress and fashion become powerful metaphors of corporate discipline, as well as a form of individual expression and pleasure. In fact, the importance of dress can be compared with its significance in the 1920s, when the hats worn by cotton-ginning women reflected their superior status (figures 6–7).

Rosie, a data processor at Multitext, in discussing the pros and cons of her job and the general atmosphere of this information enclave buzzing with computer keys and "plenty of gossip," emphasizes the importance of dress and appearance in maintaining the professional character of the workplace and touches on the misperception some workers have about the true nature of the industry.

> They had to talk to one or two people in there already about the way that they dress, but I never had to be spoken to like that. You should dress in a place like that not like if you're going to a party or a disco or going to town [. . . you should] dress as if you are working at an office [. . .] 'cause some people don't really look at it as being an office [. . .] but if they were working in an office they would dress a certain way, so I think that if you think that way about working at an office, think that way about working at Multitext and dress to suit the occasion.

A few quotations from Data Air's employee-produced newsletter further illustrate the grave importance attributed to dress and appearance and the complex way in which messages about dress are bound up in foreign corporate ideals as well as local cultural values. "What you wear is really who you are and how you feel about yourself. Clothing sends a message, a statement to others about you."

Figure 6. These well-dressed women carry out the delicate task of ginning cotton (ca. 1920). Their hats indicate their superior status. From Ann Watson Yates, *Bygone Barbados* (Christ Church, Barbados: Blackbird Studios, 1998), p. 148.

Figure 7. Data processors on the morning shift at Data Air. Photo by Michael Rowe.

"Clothing can whisper stability and high moral standards, or it can shout rebellion and discontent. It can serve as a form of identification." "Supervisors are concerned about the way you dress; for them it is more than an issue of personal taste. They want you to send the right message, one that projects you as a balanced, responsible person." And, finally, "Ladies, before you select what to wear, you must decide whether the clothing is suitable for work. Materials that are so revealing should be reserved for the bedroom. Stop and think about the impression you are giving to onlookers; and it matters *not* whether you are on the night or day shift. You are dressing for work!" Despite the fact that this service job is performed behind the scenes, in large, open production floors geographically remote and entirely removed from face-to-face contact with customers, data entry operators are expected to present themselves as though they are serving a client in a professional office, face-to-face.

Rachel, a data entry operator at Data Air, commented that the look, as well as the underlying pressure, in data entry makes it much different from other manufacturing industries. Having worked in a foreign-owned pharmaceutical company for about a year before coming to Data Air, she reflected on the two jobs:

> Here it's a lot more organized. Girls, they come in a certain dignified way [. . .] and you don't find that there's much gossiping [. . .] because they got to come and do the work. It's not like you're at a machine and sewing or unpacking and you could stop and talk or gossip. Here you got to be careful [. . .] you got to be studying what you're doing so I feel it is a bit more organized than in some other places.

Another data processor, Jane, added:

> Data Air is a good company in comparison to lots of other companies in Barbados. [. . .] The pay rate is better and I find that when you have a problem, at least they do try to cooperate. If you look at the environment [. . .] it's tidy, and you have a security guard to assist you. [. . .] The girls complained about the chairs and they fixed them. If you're not satisfied, you can go right to management.

The sense of order expressed by many of the informatics workers in their remarks about security and "tidiness" embody both positive and negative associations. While to greater and lesser degrees women readily acknowledged exploitative and highly pressured production quotas, labor practices, and what one called the "we say and you do" attitude, their pride associated with working in a "professional enterprise" helps to quell some of the frustrations. In the face of high female unemployment rates and few economic alternatives, this "professional" profile also contributes to the remarkably low attrition rates. For example, while excessive discipline is one of the most often mentioned complaints with their job (ranking with wage rates), it is also in a peculiar way a factor in what denotes the workplace professionalism so eagerly identified with the "office" environment. Janine put the contradiction well as she described on the one hand the company's obsessive concern for time and order—a half hour lunch, constant monitoring, and "rules and regulations on everything under the sun"— and on the other, complained:

> Many of the new girls don't understand the importance of a serious professional approach to their jobs. They talk when they should be working, and dress as though they're going out dancing or shopping in town, wearing short short skirts and off-the-shoulder tops or rolled-up pant legs and flat shoes.

Janine is well aware of and critical of the pressures of the job, the constraints of being "tied to the computer," and the strict discipline regarding lateness, absences, and demeanor on the production floor, but also she values the flip side of the excessive discipline—the professionalism—and so she is annoyed with her co-workers who do not. Informatics workers like Janine are both critical of and invested in modes of behavior that are simultaneously constraining and pleasurable. The tension between these dimensions of their work experience and identities are deeply ingrained within this concept of "professionalism."

The power of professionalism extends beyond the realm of workers' attempts to demarcate themselves through appearances from their counterparts in manufacturing. Indeed, expectations of professional commitment bring with them the demand for overtime and on some occasions Saturday work, often expressed in terms of "pitching in for the good of the corporate family," with the idea that "we're all in this together." The power of such slogans and management styles is evidenced by the fact that many women describe meeting such requests as part of their professional obligation. Rosemary Pringle notes a similar phenomenon among clerical workers who "earn little more than the lower clericals from whom they proudly distinguish themselves; but their long and irregular hours are perceived not as exploitation so much as a sign of their professional status" (1988:203).

Peer pressure in dress and demeanor plays into the hands of the corporate prescriptions; groups of workers may tease and harass a fellow worker for her "inappropriate" clothes or her "unmannerly" work habits. Women of all ranks refer to their enjoyment and expenditure in clothes, as well as to the "pressure to dress hard" and the rampant gossip and teasing when their hair styles, clothes, and accessories fail to conform. Margaret, who began as a supervisor for Data Air when the company opened and has since been promoted to shift manager, expressed her contradictory sense of the dress question in the following way:

> Our policy is governed by a dress code. . . . We are not a factory. We call ourselves an open office and if you were working in an office, you wouldn't go in a jeans skirt or jeans pants or short skirts. You would dress as if you were an executive. That's what we expect our persons to do. Now when we realize that our people are not dressing the way we think they should, we speak with them; we have even gone as far as to ask persons to go back home and change because their attire was not properly suited for the work atmosphere. And we instill that in our people, so by practice and counseling, we have reached the stage where people recognize us for the way we look. They usually say we work for a lot of money [she laughs]. It's not that, but you're governed by a particular code you have to adhere to—you are being watched. And not only that but, because there are so many young persons, they usually talk about you if you don't look good. They say, "How you could come in here looking like that?" and they want to keep the image up, and certainly as a manager, I wouldn't like to think that my people are coming in here and looking better than me [she laughs again]. So you want to dress a certain way to be in line with them, because they do speak about you.

She describes how, even as a manager, she is the object of surveillance—in her position she is watched not only from above but also from below, as she receives scrutiny and criticism from younger, fashion-conscious women on the production floor. Jean, a keyer, expressed the peer pressure and expectations for respectability in more general cultural terms when she compared Barbados to the United States.

> There [in the United States], nobody bothers about what you do and you could put on anything and sit anywhere [. . .] just like the tourists that come here [. . .] but here we are so reserved, saying, "Look what she is wearing" and "She didn't put on a petticoat" or "She didn't comb her hair."

Janine articulated in even more detail the sort of standards of propriety in dress that Jean mentions.

If I were to go into town, if I didn't have on pants, I would put on just a little short skirt like what you have on there [motioning to my white cotton skirt]. Some girls here [at work] would wear to work what you have on there [she grimaces with downcast eyes of disapproval]. Some of them come in pants rolled up at the bottom and tee shirts and whatnot [. . .] just like they're going to town or going down the road to buy something. [. . .] I feel you should leave tee shirts and pants unless it's a dress pant, leave a tee shirt and pants, say if you come in [to work] on a Saturday. But, I feel during the week you shouldn't come in anything like that.

And, acknowledging the effort and thought it takes to maintain this professional appearance, she says, "While I'm on my way home on evenings, I'll be studying what I['m] gonna wear to work the next morning." This sense of fashion pressure entered into my own fieldwork when I quickly realized that the casual cotton wardrobe and open sandals I had brought to Barbados did not conform to the expected levels of both style and formality. This was additionally made clear to me when one of the data entry workers I got to know gave me a tailored suit that she had made and outgrown with the birth of her first child. According to the description of appropriate attire for work, for church, for shopping in town, and other occasions as defined for me by Janine and several other women, my own clothes fit more into the "casual town shopping" category. It seemed both ironic and fitting that fashion and dress played such an important role in carrying out my fieldwork—ironic because fashion is hardly what anthropologists in the field are known for, and fitting because it plays such a central role in the lives of the subjects of my work. Unexpectedly, "skirt suits" and heels (though I wore simpler, less highly styled suits and lower heels than those that most of the data entry operators wore) became part of my everyday experience, and self-conscious awareness of my own appearance and "appropriateness" in dress became a heightened preoccupation.

Recently, and independently, work groups at both Data Air and Multitext have designed and commissioned needleworkers to make them uniforms of brightly colored skirt suits and dresses with distinctive scarves and pocket handkerchiefs to match. While in some workplaces, one might read the imposition of a uniform as suppressing individuality and personal choice, in this instance women derive a sense of pride and shared identification from the uniform they have fashioned themselves. To them, the uniform is a symbol of professional status just as it is for airline workers and bank tellers (who also wear uniform suits or dresses in Barbados) and presents an economical way of adhering to the style protocol.

For the traditional uniformed technician or service worker, the uniform, Paules (1991:103) says "helps create an image or 'package' of sameness common to other technicians within the company . . . [and] fosters a brand image to help assure a purchaser the service will be essentially similar each time he uses it." However, the data entry operator's service is not provided to a visible public. The overseas clients she serves will never see or speak to her. Even more remote than the airline reservation worker or telephone operator, she is a "back office" service worker who is both invisible and voiceless to her customer.[2] Independently fashioning uniforms for work, therefore, reflects a distinct phenomenon for the pink-collar worker offshore. It goes beyond the companies' prescription of professional attire (modest skirt suits and high heels) and reflects the operators' desire to distinguish themselves both apart from blue-collar (traditional factory) workers, and with their employers and the "office"-based work they perform.

Labor analysts might easily assume that uniforms reflect a deliberate company strategy of homogenizing its work force and enforcing allegiance to the company through dress, but how should one interpret the actual instigation and fashioning of work uniforms by the workers themselves? Some might be inclined to interpret these acts as an expression of workers' false consciousness.[3] It is true that capital expands itself through these forms of "professionalism" in that women's investment in the concept helps to insure their compliance with the demands of production. However, the gains made by women in multiple forms of capital (both economic and symbolic) and the clarity with which they express the contradictory dimensions of their work as a labor process and as a source of identity lead me to argue that more is going on than corporate hegemony through the vehicle of fashion. The informatics workers consent to the demands of professionalism in ways that are additionally "self-disciplining" and at the same time redefine the meanings and boundaries of professionalism itself.

The concern about appearance and the desire to "look professional," as so many women described their work dress and comportment, has as much (or more) to do with demarcating informatics operators from factory workers as it does with identifying with their foreign employers and their corporate ethics. The public dispute between Christine and her angry former boyfriend Paul in chapter 2 pointed explicitly to the power of such efforts to distinguish themselves from the "factory girls" around them. "Professional" dress has everything to do with the public persona they wish to cultivate in their own communities. While no one but fellow workers and staff may come in contact with the data entry operator in the course of the workday, many will see her at the bus stand on her way to work, on her lunch break, or on her way home.

The association between professional looks and professional remuneration, however, is fraught with contradiction. As Margaret, the shift manager above, and the earlier bus stand incident reveal, the assumption "that we work for a lot of money" is both enjoyed and resented by the informatics workers, bringing a sense of pride as well as burden to those whose family members and boyfriends "feel they should get some." Whereas Deborah Heath (1992:19) notes for urban elites in Senegal, "dressing well forges a link between having and being, displaying both wealth and social identity,"[4] in Barbados among the data entry operators, dress embodies social identities but not wealth, per se. Within this gap between image and material reality tensions emerge. Women in this new sector go to great lengths to project a particular office-worker image, which in itself demands additional economic strategies.

The focus on appearances as part of "professional service" by the informatics employer is reminiscent of retail and "front office" campaigns. From as early as the recruitment process, subjective assessment of "presentation" and dress come into play. After interviewing a candidate for employment, for example, a member of personnel at Data Air commented to me that while the young woman's typing test was okay, her appearance was sloppy. Her fingernails were painted and chipped and her demeanor "awkward," giving the personnel officer reservations about employing her. The implication was that a woman who was perceived as careless or sloppy in her own appearance could not be counted on to produce in an environment that demands precision and high quality.

Management is able to create a professional-looking working environment through decor and office ergonomics and can expect, in return, professional-looking workers who behave as professionals, putting in overtime on demand, for example. Corporate imperatives such as meeting deadlines, accommodating rush orders, or processing heavy batches of tickets by month-end demand a great deal of overtime and flexible scheduling on the part of the work force, and one way of encouraging a willingness to "go the extra mile" is to make employees feel that in meeting these goals, their own interests are served as well (i.e., "as part of the corporate family"). Dress becomes one component of the worker's professional persona. Unlike the "maid-like" uniform of the restaurant waitress, which diminishes her status, the executive uniform of the "professional" woman, who is admonished to "dress for success," enhances her status.[5]

Tensions surrounding dress on the two shifts of Data Air were expressed by numerous supervisors intent on preserving the same rigor and discipline on the evening shift as that of the mornings. The pattern among most data processors is to "dress down" or more informally on the evening shift. In the Dominican Republic, a noticeable difference in appearance between day and evening shifts reflected cultural differences in patterns of adornment between the Spanish-speaking Caribbean and Barbados, with its strong Anglophone tradition. Whereas in Barbados, data entry operators on the second shift dress in a markedly more casual fashion than do their morning counterparts, the exact opposite is true among the operators in Data Air's Santo Domingo plant. The fact that people are out socializing and on the streets at night in the Dominican Republic means that workers feel they are more visible to the public when they travel to work in the evening. In the morning, by contrast, the sense is that few will take notice of them and therefore more casual clothes are perfectly appropriate. Their dress on the second shift, therefore, reflects this sense of public display, and higher heels and more formal office wear replace the jeans, short skirts, and flat shoes of the morning shift.

Among the Bajan data processors, the care and the attention to detail in dress and appearance is evident immediately in the degree to which outfits are matched and cared for (pressed meticulously and varied in wear so that the same suit is not worn more than once or twice in a week). Innovations are introduced in small details such as unusual buttons, a striking belt, or matching trim on sleeve cuffs and skirt pockets. Joyce, a new, eighteen-year-old claims approver at Data Air, said, "I'm very fashion-conscious. I think Barbadian women, on the whole, love to dress. You find when the fashions coming through [. . .] like on TV or in the magazines, you know, *the girls tend to grab them*. It's nice, 'cause you know, you don' expect people to come to work in jeans and short skirts." Barbara, a member of the Data Air "old guard," talks of women's sense of "professionalism" with pride. "You want to present a certain image. From day one it was like that and of course as you work and have your own money you would improve. I was never able to dress like this before [she laughs] and as you go on, you improve and you catch up as you go. Lots of us have improved. So, it's been a constant self-upliftment, I would call it."

While Cherane, another young keyer from Data Air, who works overtime without fail each day, bemoaned the fact that she has to get up at 5:30 every morning but expressed no regret over leaving a more flexible (and profitable) arrangement where she worked part-time at the University Law Library and as a seamstress at home. "I like it here," she said. "It's strict but it's professional." Women's appreciation for the "professional" appearance of their jobs by no means implies categorically, as Linda Lim (1985) claims, that employment within these foreign offshore high-tech companies liberates women from the constraints of local patriarchal traditions, or in itself promotes greater economic autonomy for them. Rather, like multinationals in other parts of the world (Ong 1987), these high-tech enterprises have shrewdly tapped into a strong Barbadian concern with appearance and have turned this set of cultural values to the advantage of international capital by encouraging workers to identify with a well-defined corporate image.

Barbadian women's well-known sense of pride in appearance was historically marked by the practice of changing out of work clothes and into more respectable garb for their walk from the cane fields to their village homes. As James Anthony Froude commented in 1887 about Barbados:

> The women struck me especially. They were smartly dressed in white calico, scrupulously clean, and tricked out with ribands and feathers; but their figures were so good, and they carried themselves so gracefully, that although they might make themselves absurd, they could not look vulgar. Like the Greek and Etruscan women, they are trained from childhood to carry weights on their heads. They are thus perfectly upright, and plant their feet firmly and naturally on the ground. They might well serve for sculptors' models, and are well aware of it. (In Thomas 1889:71)

Writing in the 1930s in the island's newspaper, George Bernard, a teacher, said of "our girls":

> Bimshire can be pardonably proud of its girls, and the most seasoned globe-trotter who witnesses such a show as the fete, the annual exhibition or a big dance would be constrained to look twice at the sylphs of our seagirt, sun-kissed isle. What a lavish wealth of colour would greet his eye at every turn. White faces, black faces and an infinite variety of shades between those two. . . . A blaze of bright dresses too, would dazzle our globetrotter's eyes. A never-ending variety of modes. The latest creations of Paris. Dresses cut in fashions which make their wearers' old grannies shake their head in shocked disapproval and despair, and go off into sermons on the hopelessness of the "young generation." None but the bravest artist would attempt to imprison on canvas the medley of tints which run riot with such bewitching abandon. ([1934] 1985:19)

A general openness to innovation and the expression of individualism itself have been argued to be rooted in the most dehumanizing assault on selfhood imaginable, the legacy of Caribbean slavery.

> Early on, then, the slaves were elaborating upon the ways in which they could be individuals—a particular sense of humor, a certain skill or type of knowledge, even a distinctive way of walking or talking, or some sartorial detail, like the cock of a hat or the use of a cane. (Mintz and Price 1992:50–51)

Indeed, a tradition of adornment and distinction is so well known that many of the informatics workers (as well as local university students and professors) responded to my questions about dress by arguing that there is nothing remarkable about the strong emphasis on fashionable dress in this arena of work. As many put it, simply, "All Bajan [or Caribbean] women like to dress up!"[6]

According to a report in the Barbados press, the "fashion explosion" began hitting this small island economy in the early 1980s, marking the expansion of mass tourism (and Barbadians traveling abroad in greater numbers), the intensification of the Cropover festival, and the influence of U.S. popular culture (*Weekend Nation*, March 1, 1991). This fashion frenzy is represented in the vast continuum encompassing informal imports as well as small, home-based independent needleworkers who make everything from school uniforms to corporate-looking suits, extensive production operations for garment subcontractors, and fashion designers who sell and exhibit in local boutiques and international shows. A majority of the informatics workers are members of households in which they contribute to the household economy but are not sole wage earners and thus are able to spend a significant portion of their earnings on "personal" items and clothes. Networks of family and friends abroad, as well as global media, provide important sources of style and material goods. Young women's and young men's desire for brand-name clothes and shoes and the latest "exotic hairdos" and "dance hall fashions" is often satisfied through "barrels" sent by parents and relatives overseas (Leo-Rhynie 1998:250). The escalating preoccupation with fashion was even noted in a recent sermon of a Pentecostal preacher who bemoaned the trend for young people today to come to the house of God merely "to check a style." Local needleworkers confirm that they go just about anywhere for new fashion ideas. A great deal of criticism is levied against Barbadian women for their engagement of these forms of reputation. They are attacked in radio call-in programs and popular music and from many a church pulpit for being "materialistic" and having "obsessive" concerns with fashion.[7] For the informatics workers, however, the desire to "dress hard" and sport the latest styles is also integrally bound up with their pink-collar identities as "professional" employees in this new high-tech sector. Their adornment cannot be read solely as an expression of frivolous consumerism, or as a matter of individual taste and choice. The fashion statement they make through their "professional" appearance is a mode of distinction as much proclaiming who they *are not* as proclaiming who they *are*.[8]

The issue here, then, is to explore the relationship between a well acknowledged local concern with appearance and its role in establishing a category of worker (and of womanhood) who not only dresses appropriately but acts in a particular manner. How does the "professional" dress of the Bajan pink-collar worker express both international corporate and local cultures? June Nash (1983:28) used the notion of transculturation from structural anthropology to describe the dialectical relationship between local culture and multinational capital. In this formulation she argues that while multinational corporations dictate the flow and control over technology, labor organization, and conditions of production, these management practices and labor relations are in turn shaped by cultural features of the host country. This relationship, sometimes referred to as "harmonization" in the multinational arena, "refers to the process of adjusting the priorities of a powerful productive unit to the particular practices of the environment in which it becomes adapted" (Nash 1983:29). Nash focuses her discussion on formal production relations, the negotiations that take place between labor unions and foreign management, and the less formal relations between management and the work force. Others have emphasized the ways in which workers resist and renegotiate these control mechanisms in the course of their workday (Peña 1987:148). As Aihwa Ong (1987:155) points out, labor becomes subjugated to capital in highly specific ways according to the "discourse/ practices" of the cultural context and, one might add, its historical moment.

In the Barbadian context, this process of renegotiating multinational expectations with respect to the conditions and values of the local context is practiced in both explicit and subtle ways. Examples of explicit expressions are the bargains struck by workers and their bosses that have led to the greater longevity of informatics workers than in other industries and geographical locales and the perks that women have fought for and won, such as night transportation on private buses hired by the companies. Among the more subtle expressions is the official dress code, a manifestation of multinational corporate discipline that becomes interwoven with the pervasive Barbadian ethic that places great emphasis on both style and display as well as grooming and deportment. But in this mix, women do not merely conform to proper decorum through dress, but also create new styles and new meanings out of appearances.

The tension between dress as an expression of proper (modest, conservative) etiquette and dress as a mode of creative, distinctive display brings us back to the Caribbean paradigm of reputation and respectability. Peter Wilson (1969) and others (e.g., Miller 1990, 1994; Wilk 1990) have argued that an emphasis on clothes, and in particular, on style (buying new clothes and dressing up) is associated with the realm of reputation. For Miller (1994), discussing the case of Trinidad, style expresses competition, individualism, and reputation, or, in his formulation of the dualism, transience.[9] Style is about originality and sartorial achievement in which the individual creates for himself or herself a personalized statement by putting together elements of clothing in a unique way, at the forefront of fashion and not in its wake. "Style is often based upon competitive display among a few peers and it is originality and expressive ability with respect to this small group that is paramount" (1994:223).[10] The originality sought is accomplished either by having items handmade by seamstresses, altering ready-made items with new buttons or accessories, or importing "designer" or "imitation designer" things from abroad, activities we turn to in more detail later in the chapter.

In contrast, respectable, or what Miller refers to as transcendent patterns of dress express social conformity and are manifested in "layering" in the form of stockings, flounces, and slips, and (at the time of Miller's fieldwork) a code of shiny materials for special occasions and matte finishes for ordinary wear. Of course, like most analysts of fashion, Miller is careful to note that an original style may soon find itself reproduced as fashion among many, and when it does, it moves from an expression of distinction (transience) to one of conformity (transcendence). The gendered permutations of these concepts are slippery at best. In Miller's account, women and men are both engaged in the pursuit and expression of style. Whether in fashion shows, at fetes, or in the context of the workplace, he cites this quest for originality, innovation, and individuality across gender lines. On the other hand, the conservative realm of transcendent dress, in its layered, modest, and conventional form, is left as an unmarked but intuitively feminine arena. Where the flamboyant "saga boy," known for flashy clothes and promiscuous sex, is paralleled with the well-adorned prostitute, Miller's account has no masculine figure comparable to that of the respectable churchgoing woman garbed in a flounced dress and petticoat, brimmed hat, stockings, and closed shoes, all in the sweltering tropical heat. The perception that adherence to proper conventions of appearance remains a female preoccupation has become a pervasive legacy of the reputation/respectability paradigm.

Also problematic is the notion that conformity and innovation are necessarily opposed. Among the Barbadian informatics workers, the central role played by dress as both a mark of propriety and of innovation bears a distinctively creole (local) flavor even as it answers the explicit (foreign) corporate dress code. In effect, women's manner of fashioning "professional dress" allows them to express, simultaneously, dimensions of respectability and reputation and of conformity and distinction. Georg Simmel describes the coexistence of impulses toward reputation and respectability, or, as he names them, the drive toward conspicuousness and toward imitation, in a particularly apt manner.

> Those in a weak position find protection only in the typical form of life, which prevents the strong person from exercising his exceptional powers. But resting on the firm foundation of custom, of the average, of the general level, women strive strongly for all the relative individualization and general conspicuousness that thus remains possible. Fashion offers them this very combination to the most favourable extent, for we have here, on the one hand, a sphere of general imitation, the individual floating in the broadest social current, relieved of responsibility for their tastes and their actions, and yet, on the other hand, we have a certain conspicuousness, an individual emphasis, an individual ornamentation of the personality. . . . *Thus it seems as though fashion were the valve, as it were, through which women's need for some measure of conspicuousness and individual prominence finds vent, when its satisfaction is more often denied in other spheres.* ([1904] 1997:196; italics mine)

For Simmel, where men have occupations through which to distinguish themselves and gain social recognition, women have fashion and appearances. The role these processes of adornment and distinction play within the work setting adds yet another dimension to the simultaneous impulses toward convention and innovation.

Writing about women workers in Silicon Valley and the simultaneous processes of both gendering and ethnically inscribing workers in the electronics industry, Karen Hossfeld (1990:158–59) describes ways in which managers encourage those forms of work culture that enhance traditional forms of femininity. She says that while factory work and wage earning have long been a part of working-class women's experience, the ideology remains that such work is "unfeminine." Consequently, such expensive and time-consuming feminine rituals as manicures and hair stylings were important parts of their weekly routine to compensate for the unfeminine nature of their manufacturing work. In the data entry operations, on the other hand, participating in the feminine rituals of adornment are an expression of compliance with the prescriptions of the workplace itself. In both cases, however, emphasis on fashion and feminine adornment become vital to the women workers. For the factory worker, a manicure may help her counter the gender inconsistency between manual labor and femininity; for the informatics operator, the skirt suit emphasizes the "clerical" nature of her otherwise repetitive factorylike production. As Hossfeld aptly adds, "femininity in its various permutations is not something all-bad and all-disempowering: women find strength, pride, and creativity in some of its forms" (1990:162).

The Bajan women's experimentation with clothes reveals an aesthetic inventiveness that can be interpreted alternately as conformity (to international corporate consumer culture and to local conventions of proper attire) or as exploration of alternative subjectivities. The information-centered nature of their employment adds to this ambiguity in the sense that the nature of their service-production is itself betwixt and between. In a sense, the product they are most conscious of producing is *themselves*—"professional"-like, clerical-like pink-collar workers.

Gender and Re-classifying the Pink-Collar Worker

If the production of new feminine "selves" is integral to the occupation of offshore informatics workers in Barbados, and the practice of distinction is central to these new selves, what implications do these women workers pose for our understandings of class and the relationship between class and gender? As I argue in chapter 2, the feminine arena of the offshore industry of informatics introduces a number of wrinkles to traditional ways of interpreting class. The nature of the labor process and the symbolic power of computer-based open offices introduce a blurry boundary between what we once described as mental, white-collar work and manual, blue-collar work. The very name "pink collar" is an explicit acknowledgment of the gendered, and in particular, feminine construction of this new sector. The importance of dress and of the notion of "professionalism" in defining these new workers draws our attention to the role of status (in the Weberian sense) and its relation to the demarcation of social classes. Industrialists and academics speculating about the informatics industry in the late 1980s suspected that the demand for higher skill and educational prerequisites (three O-level certificates and typing skills), and the more professional-looking environment of these enterprises might manifest themselves in a workforce drawn from a higher sector of the working class than that of traditional factory workers. A local company owner observed, "When data entry started here, it started a whole new category of work; it was not your typical factory floor job assembling electronic components. It was a lot cleaner and it created a new strata of workers." What he meant by a new "strata" of workers relates precisely to this complex of a distinctly clean, cool, office-like environment where women workers gain status and prestige through the association with computer technology and the "look" of both the workplace and themselves.

Data entry operators know that the wages they make and the material conditions of their lives are virtually the same as those of their sisters and friends in traditional factory jobs. They come, almost without exception, from working-class homes with various constellations of kin who are employed in agriculture, trades, or service. But there is no doubt that the data processors' jobs in the information industry are considered a step up from women's traditional wage work on the factory assembly line, in agricultural labor, or in domestic service where women in the Barbadian economy have been heavily concentrated. While women unanimously considered the prestige and status of teaching, nursing, or other predominantly female (professional) arenas to be greater than that of a data processor, many also perceived their job on par with that of other clerical workers and superior to that of hotel workers, domestics, and agricultural laborers, in status if not in pay.

Disaggregating boundaries of class is particularly complex for women in the clerical sector. Because of the perception of clerical jobs as more closely linked to management and the sense that they represent "head" work as opposed to manual labor, these workers have often fallen between the cracks of class analyses. Additionally, because this is a distinctly gendered arena, we are faced with the question, to what extent does a woman's partner/husband/family or, in the case of the data entry worker, her "matriarchal" or "dependent girl" status determine her class identity, and what characteristics or conditions are necessary for class mobility? From a Marxist perspective, there is certainly no confusion: the relation that these information workers have to the means of production and the frequent piece-rate sale of their labor power places them clearly within the working class. However, the meanings of their particular class fraction and its emergent cultural habitus cannot be inferred from this structural position alone.[11]

Reflecting on their own life circumstances, many data entry operators remarked about the better standard of living they enjoy compared with that of their mothers in their youth, but rather than seeing it as an indication of upward mobility, their sense is that these improvements relate to generalized modernization of the country. They perceive their own life circumstances, as shaped by their data entry jobs as little different from that of their sisters, cousins, or friends who work in manufacturing jobs. In essence they seem to express that working as a data processor offers a status that exceeds that of ordinary factory work (through one's appearance, the office-like work environment, and the involvement with computers), though not the basis for "real" class mobility as a professional educational track or occupation might.[12] They differentiate between the unquestionably superior appearance of their job and that of traditional manufacturing work, and like the industrial development officers, they sustain a degree of ambiguity about the exact relationship between this difference and its broader (economic) meanings.

It has been noted that women employed in multinational factories around the world tend to be part of the working classes, and not to be among the very poor. So, where do data entry operators in Barbados fit in terms of local configurations and definitions of the working classes? We must begin with the acknowledgment that class is not fixed or static, nor is class experienced in some universal set of ways. So, even if we agree, in the crudest terms, that the working class constitutes those whose livelihood depends entirely on the sale of their labor power, that the bourgeoisie represent those who own or control the means of production, and the middle classes are situated in various places between these two groups, there are still dimensions left unclear about the class identity and consciousness of these offshore information workers. Rosemary Pringle cautions that in analyzing class we must avoid definitive, bounded categories or classifications and look instead at people's actual experiences, the ways in which their lives and consciousness are shaped by their "social origins, their families, lifestyle, [and] culture." She adds, "The meaning of terms like working and middle class changes constantly and they have meant different things for women than for men" (1988:199). Or, put another way, classes are "relationally constituted. . . . They define themselves always in implicit reference to the other[s]" (Ortner 1991:172).

Using examples of working-class life from numerous ethnographic studies, Sherry Ortner observes that within working- or lower-class culture itself, there is a split that echoes the broader societal split between middle and working classes. This "subcultural typology of 'styles' " that Ortner describes is generally reminiscent of Peter Wilson's (1969) reputation/respectability paradigm. Within the working class, women are said to be more closely "aligned, from both the male point of view and, apparently, their own, with the 'respectable,' 'middle class' side of [the] oppositions and choices" (Ortner 1991:173). This conception of women as aspiring toward and adopting more of the values and practices of the middle class than men emerges from both workplace and domestic arenas.[13] Rather than use this frequent observation as the basis for an essential duality, however, I take this to indicate the inextricable relationship between gender and class and to reassert the fact that people experience class as gendered subjects. In turn, we experience our gender as members of class groups, unfixed as these may be.[14]

What emerges from the informatics workers' testimonies is that those nonmaterial aspects of working in the open offices that make these jobs preferable and the source of status and pride, together with the somewhat ambiguous combination of mental/manual labor and centrality of computer technology, contribute to the creation of a new stratum of a feminine proletariat. The fact that these symbolic and cultural forms of capital play such an integral role in situating (or blurring the position of) the pink-collar workers is particularly interesting and illuminating as an expression of gender, and in particular, femininity.

The compensatory nature of fashion, according to Simmel ([1904] 1997:196) is particularly important to women. In effect, Simmel argues that given women's structurally weak status, they must strive for individuality through fashion. Interestingly, in the Afro-Caribbean, the compensatory role of fashion is often noted as central to masculine patterns of conspicuous consumption and adornment. Sondra, a Data Air keyer, complained, "The guys in Barbados, to me, now [. . .] they're just concerned about looks and the way they dress—when you go out you got to look good and if you don't look good, no girl gon' look at you! So you got to dress good, you got to know what to wear, some brand names, well the girls do that too, but not as much!" Her sentiment is echoed by Katherine: "I mean, when I think of the money men spend on clothes, like a new disco outfit [. . .] and I think they could say, 'Let me put this money aside, like if my girl gets pregnant that she could keep the baby' or something like that. [. . .] But some of the guys just don't think that way." These are precisely the kinds of criticisms of displays of "reputation" that are often hurled at women. The fact that the same expressions of condemnation are leveled at men and at women for not fulfilling their proper gendered roles and priorities is indicative of the reality that for most Afro-Caribbean men and women reputation and respectability are not separable realms of practice and belief.

Elsie LeFranc (1989), in her work about petty traders and higglers in Jamaica, notes the frequent postwar Caribbean literary and social science references to the "worthless and/or idle black male and the strong, hard working black women, . . . the economically marginalized and frustrated black male and the coping black female." In a similar vein, she says, has been a black male preponderance for useless "posture on the basis of little substance, . . . for example, the ubiquitous but empty briefcase, or the well-dressed young man on his way to nowhere" (LeFranc 1989:112). Status through appearance becomes a replacement for economic prosperity in a ritualized process whereby structural constraints such as race and class prevent individuals from reaching those goals and values held most highly by the society. She argues that this split between economic appearance (through dress and material display) and real economic means has been supported by the dominant classes as a mechanism for maintaining their own economic control. In contrast, so bound up in their role as primary provider, women, she says, are seen to be much less vulnerable to this strategy and better equipped to "manipulate the economic system and the split referred to" (LeFranc 1989:112). Echoing Simmel in his discussion on women ([1904] 1957), in effect, Peter Wilson (1973) and Diane Austin (1983) argue that such displays and values of reputation help to *compensate men* for their economic marginality. However, as Peter Pyde (1990) and Kevin Yelvington (1993) assert, working-class men, compared with working-class women, still retain relative power and access to wage labor and other sources of income and thus can afford to be more invested in forms of symbolic capital than women. The fact that these practices are so vividly enacted by the informatics workers implies that the simultaneity of distinction and conformity is not singularly gendered, or "compensatory" in exactly the same ways for men and for women.[15]

The relationship between these powerful forms of symbolic capital and a discussion of class takes its central importance not as an exercise in pigeon-holing these women's "real" or "essential" class position but in exploring their sense of class consciousness. Several others writing about the experience of women workers in multinational factories around the globe have noted the absence of class consciousness as a result of the imperative to hold on to even a low-paying factory job (Gallin 1990:190). Others (Safa 1993; Yelvington 1995) have argued that older or younger women, respectively, are more likely to exhibit signs of class consciousness and to take action as a result of this consciousness. Class consciousness in these cases, however, seems to be equated exclusively with organized protest and explicit forms of resistance to the exploitative nature of work.

Ong (1991) has suggested that expressions of worker (class) consciousness and the multiple ways in which subjects are constituted demand analyses that are multifaceted and not static and universalized. In Gayatri Spivak's words, "the arena of the subaltern's consciousness is situational and uneven, and the subaltern's subjectivity is locally shaped and delimited" (Ong 1991:296). Workers in multinational factories rarely organize or express their resistance in terms of industrywide or globalized terms, and as Ong points out, while women have certainly demonstrated and closed factories down in Central America and Asia, these protests have tended to take the form of individual wildcat strikes. Safa (in Gallin 1990:180) defines class consciousness as "a cumulative process by which women recognize they are exploited, . . . recognize the source of their exploitation, . . . and are willing and able to organize and mobilize in their own interests." But here again we are confronted with what appears to be a singular sense of "organizing and mobilizing" interests. If we see class resistance only in the form of collective strikes and protests, and class consciousness as reflected in these acts, we miss a host of complex ways in which women have found it possible, and perhaps most effective, to register their awareness of exploitation and their opposition to it and to deliberately blur boundaries of class that they experience as constraints. The adoption of professionalism as one such murky set of practices encompasses women's agency in ways that work against the rigid corporate discipline they otherwise are bound by, and in a manner that strategically distances them from other working-class factory women in an effort to imagine themselves otherwise.

Through these practices of distinction, and these inclinations toward individualism, propriety, and the ideals of middle-class nuclear family life, Barbadian pink-collar workers express a new, gendered class consciousness in ways that straddle elements of both respectability and reputation. They counter Wilson's original assertion that "a person is either respectable or not respectable, high class or low class, or middle class. But no matter what, the individual is a prisoner of such judgments" (Wilson 1973:228). In the realm of informatics, we see both processes of conformity and distinction at work. Furthermore, the models held up as "respectable" are changing and they do so not, as Wilson might have presumed, as a mere attempt to imitate the models of Euro-American culture but out of local economic and cultural conditions. According to the informatics workers, to be a respectable woman does not necessitate a domesticated married life but can include "professional" work (including informatics work). In the skirt suit alone we can trace elements of conformity ("proper" length of hem and sleeves, high heels, stockings, slip) and distinction (bold buttons or a newly imported style of belt, a designer bag and shoes to match). Indeed, as Kathleen's story in chapter 4 demonstrates, informatics work may actually facilitate home ownership and "settling down" in a respectable manner. And, as the refashioning of "professionalism" implies, the same individual may clearly exhibit respectability and perform acts of reputation, at one and the same time, as well as at different stages of life. Her class consciousness, then, is articulated less by association than by distinction. She fashions herself as other than a traditional factory worker and, as such, she is part of an emergent class fraction.

Many social critics have debated the issue of fashion (e.g., Mills 1956; Peiss 1986; Simmel [1904] 1957; Veblen [1899] 1953) and its relationship to gender and to class. Is fashionable dress a form of female oppression or compensation, self-expression or co-optation? "Is it part of empty consumerism, or is it a site of struggle symbolized in dress codes? Does it muffle the self, or create it?" (Wilson 1990:231). For the informatics workers, dress becomes an arena in which women both contest and consent to local, class-based, and international corporate values, themselves imbued with contradiction. As Elizabeth Wilson convincingly states, the puritanical position that construes consumer culture as an opiate, "duping the masses into a state of false consciousness" fails to do justice to the complexities involved in women's decision making and the social and psychological pressures and pleasures derived from fashion and styles of dress. Similarly, the counter extreme, which posits fashion as a liberatory device transporting women out of the shackles of domesticity or other forms of patriarchal authority, runs the risk of simplification. This study aims not to solve the debate, but to complicate its terms outside the confines of morality (consumption is "good" or "bad") and to demonstrate consumption's integral and dynamic place as a form of production itself. As such, it is not only possible but also necessary to see that women's pursuit of and compliance with a particular workplace fashion in the arena of data entry acts both to distinguish them from one sector of workers (manual, factory workers) and to imitate or integrate themselves symbolically into another group to whom they aspire (office workers and professional women).

Describing women, dress, and work in North America, Grant McCracken (1988:100) observes, "Imitation . . . is not the simple pursuit of prestige nor the work of some generalized force; it is a culturally purposeful activity motivated by an appreciation of the symbolic liabilities of one style of dress, and the symbolic advantages implicit in another." Stylized consumer goods first became available to working-class people on a mass scale in the United States in the late nineteenth century as garment industries began to produce inexpensive fashions imitative of upper-class styles (Ewen 1988:75). Intimately connected to one's class, clothing quickly became associated with the possibility of social mobility and the accumulation of material goods marking improved standards of living. In 1902, Jane Addams (cited in Ewen 1988:73) noted the importance of dress among young women working in the new industrial cities of America, in a way that resonates with that of the Barbadian data entry operators, and perhaps working-class women more widely as well:

> The working girl, whose family lives in a tenement, . . . who has little social standing and has to make her own place, knows full well how much habit and style of dress has to do with her position. Her income goes into her clothing, out of all proportion to the amount which she spends upon other things. But if social advancement is her aim, it is the most sensible thing she can do. She is judged largely by her clothes. Her house furnishing, with its pitiful little decorations, her scanty supply of books, are never seen by the people whose social opinions she most values. Her clothes are her background, and from them she is largely judged.

While social advancement in any real sense may be improbable in the data entry operators' experience of "dressing for success," I found that pure pleasure in creating and putting together distinctive combinations of colors, materials, and styles was also a central aspect of the concern for dress and fashion. Additionally, while these women know that they are not truly professional workers, they enjoy looking like them, and when they look like them, they come to feel themselves to be different. Quoting Georg Lukács, Ewen (1988:77) says:

In a world where scrutiny by unknown others had become the norm, style provided people with an attractive otherness, a "phantom objectivity" . . . to publicly define oneself, to be weighed in the eye's mind. A central appeal of style was its ability to create an illusory transcendence of class or background. While hierarchy and inequities of wealth and power were—in many ways— increasing, the free and open market in style offered a symbolic ability to name oneself.

This is not to imply, then, that people are actually duped into thinking that they and the material realities of their lives have been transformed simply by donning a smart suit or a designer-styled dress but to suggest that the feeling derived through appearance is indeed one that boosts one's self-image as well as one's public persona. This feeling may account for the fact that in their interviews women were very clear about their belief that data entry work is a job and not a profession. For example, while they might have hoped when first employed that they would learn about computers and move up to more highly skilled work somewhere else, they quickly realize that opportunities for mobility are limited. But seeming to contradict this level of awareness was the persistent distinction drawn between data entry and other sorts of production work (traditional factory jobs), which invariably led to associations between "office" environments, computer technology, and a vague sense of superiority. Indeed a profound awareness of historic class boundaries constitutes a powerfully motivating (if subconscious) force behind women's degree of investment in "professional" dress itself. Again, with startling prescience, Simmel noted almost a century ago that fashion, in effect, compensates women for their "lack of position in a class based on a calling or profession" ([1904] 1957:551). And taking this further, appearances, even when apparently illusory, can come to have real meaning. If the nature of women's work in informatics and its aura of "professionalism" helps to blur the boundaries of class identification and to diminish the women's sense of class consciousness (in terms of identifying with other industrial workers), their involvement in other activities outside the parameters of the informatics sector facilitate and complicate this ambiguity even further.

A question that has yet to be explored is, as one bystander posed it, "How in the world do these girls dress so?" How do these women achieve these fashionable appearances on the wages they actually earn? Underlying women's new practices of consumption is another realm of informatics life that has little to do directly with the input of information or the discipline of computer-monitored work. I refer here to the vibrant arena of informal trade and services within and just outside the realm of these "open offices." As Ruth Ann, a data processor, remarked: "You can just about live inside Data Air; anything you want you can get in here." As in many other industrial workplaces in the offshore sector, the informatics industry's vast employment of women workers presents a captive market to vendors of all kinds of merchandise. Early in the morning, at lunch-time and between shifts, one can witness a parade of minivan entrepreneurs in front of the informatics industrial park. On any given day they may be selling an array of goods that includes fresh farm produce, perfume, shoes, "fashion jewelry," and underwear of all cuts and styles. Others, with their vans adorned with Kung-Fu action photos, romantic dramas, and X-rated posters, rent the latest pirated videos.

In addition to the mobile marketers who drive their minivan-convenience stores through the countryside and around the industrial enclaves in town, the data processors themselves carry on an active informal trade in goods and services. On the shop floor before the workday begins and on breaks in-between, trays of produce and bags of goods of all kinds emerge from under desktops for sale to fellow workers and staff. Some women sell on commission for bigger "wholesalers" while others bring eggs or vegetables from home, or take orders for goods to be bought on a trip abroad. Another group offers services they provide from home in their "off-time" from their data entry jobs. Some prepare pudding and souse or traditional black cake for special occasions or, given a set of measurements and material, fashion a new skirt suit for work, a ruffled church dress, or lace curtains for the home.[16] Others cut, weave, and braid hair in the latest styles. As Ruth Ann says, women can get "just about anything" when they go to work.

Recent research and theoretical treatments of the global economy have gener-ated increasing attention to the proliferation of the "informal sector" and its relation to the formal economy (Beneria and Roldan 1987; Castells and Portes 1989; Portes and Walton 1981; Sen and Grown 1987; Ward 1990b).[17] Further-more, a number of analyses of women workers in multinational factories around the world have emphasized the fact that in the face of insufficient wages women have participated actively in informal networks of trade and services on top of their formal employment. At a time when the traditional areas of employment, such as agriculture and manufacturing, decline in Barbados, changing config-urations of the global assembly line have had additionally dramatic effects on vast numbers of women workers who are often pushed into the "triple shifts" of formal employment, informal sector work, and housework.[18]

In conjunction with a growing body of literature about the proliferation of the informal sector throughout the developing world and its particular implications in women's lives and the well-being of households Beneria and Roldan 1987; Bolles 1983; Espinal and Grasmuck 1993; Portes and Sassen-Koob 1987; Schmink 1986; Sen and Grown 1987; Ward 1990a), I now turn to the integral relationship between Barbadian women's experiences and identities as formal informatics workers and their participation in a variety of informal marketing, trade, and service activities. In doing so, it becomes clear that these women engage in extra income-generating activities that not only supplement their formal wage but also further their formal-sector feminine styles so integral to their pink-collar identities. While part of a long historical tradition of marketers (i.e., "hawkers" or "higglers"), and certainly not unique in their involvement in new forms of informal economic activity, the Barbadian data processors illustrate that formal and informal sector work are intimately connected in ways that go beyond merely economic survival and "getting by." Their multiple roles as formal and informal workers together enmesh them within the international division of labor, as well as within an increasing globalization of tastes in consumer goods and fashions.

In the following discussion, therefore, I examine first the long history of women's participation in the informal sector and competing theoretical approaches to its role with respect to the formal economy. I then turn to the relationships between these sectors in the lives of Barbadian women.

Caribbean Women and the Informal Sector

Caribbean women have long been known for their hard work and creative ingenuity in finding "sources of livelihood" (Massiah 1986). As an old West Indian saying goes, "Woman is a donkey, she work at work and then she go home and work again" (cited in Senior 1991:116). Their involvement in informal economic activities dates to the days of slavery, when women became the informal growers and sellers of agricultural goods; they were the original marketers. Marketing was crucial for the improvement of slaves' nutrition and as a mechanism that allowed them to possess property and travel about under otherwise harsh and restrictive conditions. But more important, it represented their tenacious independent spirit bound up in everyday expressions of resistance to the degradation of slavery (Beckles 1989a: 73; Harrison 1988). As early as 1657, Ligon observed, "On Sunday they rest, and have the whole day at their pleasure; and the most of them use it as a day of rest and pleasure; but some of them who ill make benefit of the dayes liberty, go where the Mangrove trees grow, and gather the bark, of which they make ropes, which they tuck away for other Commodities, as Shirts and Drawers" ([1657] 1976:48). Along with agricultural and domestic work, needleworking historically has been one of the primary arenas of income-generating activity for women.[19] In more recent history, in addition to Caribbean women's traditional agricultural trade, their informal economic pursuits have again included home-based needleworking, as well as independent or subcontracted assembly work and food preparation and the purchase and marketing of imported consumer goods. This last development has undoubtedly taken traditional higglering to new bounds.

Since the mid 1970s women have faced increasing pressures to find employment and manage the simultaneous trends of climbing inflation rates and increasing economic demands within their families. Their movement into "informal commercial importing," as one newly burgeoning area of the informal economy has been officially called in Jamaica, generally involves flying to neighboring countries (most often Puerto Rico, Venezuela, Panama, Curaçao, or the United States) to buy wholesale and later resell consumer items (often those that have been officially restricted by limited foreign exchange reserves).

Although little substantive work has yet explored these new expansions of traditional marketing practices, a few recent studies of higglering in the region make clear the importance of "suitcase traders" as one expression of a changing economic picture within individual women's lives and in Caribbean national economies more generally (St. Cyr 1990; Taylor 1988; Quiñones 1997). Whereas some women may receive start-up loans from banks, family members, or informal credit unions, as Joaquin St. Cyr (1990:8) points out, the economic basis or "seed money" for women's entry into informal trade often comes from their employment in one of the export processing industries. The link between their involvement in the informal marketing of nonfood items and the formal economy varies from case to case and from country to country, however the predominance of clothing, shoes, accessories, and electronics cuts across them all. As has always been true, women are heavily represented in these new arenas of higglering, petty commodity production, and the informal exchange of services. Not surprisingly, the most prevalent items and services of trade cater to a female market (e.g., the importation and home-based fashioning of clothes as well as household appliances and accessories). In the context of the data entry industry, women's involvement in this sort of trade and distribution of goods, as well as other forms of informal work, helps to subsidize women's formal wage from an economic standpoint and contributes as well to the maintenance of the professional office-worker image that forms the core of their pink-collar identity.

With economic fluctuations and structural adjustment measures testing Caribbean women's well-known ability to "cut and contrive," the informal sector has ballooned dramatically (Harrison 1988, Taylor 1988; Ward 1990b).[20] Its scale alone has forced theoretical analyses to abandon the dualistic models popular in the late 1970s that construed the informal sector as economically marginal. While there are several competing theories addressing the significance and basis for the informal economy, it has become clear that this arena formally referred to as the "underground economy" is far from hidden and cannot be ignored. Neomarxist analyses of the informal sector stress the inherently exploitative relationships between formal sector capitalists and informal workers. Structuralist perspectives, however, view the expansion of this sector as based on an overabundant supply of labor that the formal sector simply cannot absorb. Close links and interrelationships between formal and informal economies are widely acknowledged by the internationalization-of-capital approach, which emphasizes the subsidizing role played by informal industry and subcontractors in the broader scheme of multinational corporations (Beneria and Roldan 1987; Ward 1990b).

Only recently considered a drain on the official economy and the underbelly of legitimate industry, actors in the informal sector today are called "microentrepreneurs." They are praised for their ingenuity and recognized as integral to the total economic picture, both locally and internationally. On one hand, their involvement in trade and distribution of illegally imported goods has been strongly condemned by government and local industry who resent the duties avoided and business taken away by, for example, the proliferating "suitcase trade." On the other hand, in the face of high unemployment and economic uncertainty, the rise of small home-based businesses has been highlighted as an important contribution toward stabilizing the national economy. Joan Smith and Immanuel Wallerstein (1992) have described the growing inability of wage workers to survive solely on their formal wages, and the frequent combination of both formal and informal means of income generation by individuals and the households to which they contribute. Increasingly, development agencies and national governments are recommending that loans be offered to support these enterprises, and some politicians hail them as the hidden backbone of the economy. Despite the enthusiasm from some corners, the state and private sectors also reveal some ambivalence toward this burgeoning informal arena.[21] In Barbados in 1991, with the support of local clothing manufacturers and retailers, the minister of trade called for patriotic Barbadians to boycott illegal suitcase traders, whose vibrant business was contributing to their own business woes (*Barbados Advocate*, August 16, 1991). His public outcry was joined by others calling for stiffer controls to be placed in the airport customs area, with the intention of catching Barbadians traveling back and forth to the United States to buy and sell large quantities of clothes and goods. Indeed, on any given day, one can witness women leaving Barbados for San Juan, Caracas, Miami, New York, and other cities. Their large empty bags are unmistakable signifiers of their foreign shopping missions. Travel agencies and airlines frequently advertise special weekend packages designed explicitly as shopping excursions and arrange transportation between inexpensive motels and shopping malls to facilitate buying expeditions.

The goods purchased on these weekend shopping trips are for both personal and household consumption and for trade and range from electronics, "software" (tennis sneakers), clothing, and shoes, to hardware and tools that are either unavailable or expensive at home. Before Christmas and during the Easter holidays, group trips from the informatics firms are popular among rank-and-file keyers and management alike as sources of pleasure (with outings to night clubs and restaurants) and opportunities to further their personal consumption and their profit-making trade. Shopping tours are popular among Bajans nationwide. However, what links these shopping journeys even more explicitly to the formal sector identities of the data processors is that for those working at Data Air, the trips are made possible through company "thank-you cards." In effect, their formal job makes possible these informal economic ventures. Those who sew buy material and notions for their informal needleworking business, and others purchase household items, jewelry, clothes, hair products, and toiletries, all for resale. Others arrange for a relative living in North American cities to send goods regularly and in small quantities or varied styles to avoid duties and the suspicions of customs officers.

One of the advantages for the women workers as consumers of these services and goods is a customary extension of credit and installment payment. The recent popularity of sewing and design classes and home needlework, as well as this expansion of casual retailing and suitcase trade, take on increasing importance for clothing manufacturers, distributors, and the national economy as a whole, as well as for the culture in fashioning popular tastes and styles. By exploring the experience of women who engage informally in making and selling clothes, we may highlight their new forms of consumption as well as their role in shaping and responding to contemporary fashions and styles across transnational circuits.

The Informal Sector and the Open Office

Workers, and specifically women workers, have long been known to juggle income-earning activities across the boundaries of formal and informal arenas. The case of pink-collar workers in these new high-tech enterprises provides a particularly powerful illustration of the complex interconnections between local and international economic forces and ideologies about gender and work. To explore the relationship between gender ideology and the processes of production, reproduction, and consumption across formal and informal sectors, it is essential to go beyond purely economistic models.[22] In the case of the Barbadian informatics workers it is important to get a sense of how much money is earned through informal work and how that income is used and distributed within the household as a first step in the analysis. However, to fully appreciate the relationship between these two sectors, the symbolic cultural value of new forms of consumption is also vital. In other words, the informal sector is not just an arena for generating income supplementary to an insufficient wage; it also plays directly into the contours of the formal wage-earning informatics job itself. Three phenomena together constitute the context for informal-formal sector interrelationships for the Data Air workers: the company dress codes and the intense pressure to dress in a particular professional office-worker style, the women's extensive involvement in trade and fashioning of clothes and accessories, and the fact that airline travel is provided as a production incentive that facilitates overseas purchasing for the informal trade in apparel and consumer goods.

Of the data entry operators I surveyed, 70 percent are involved in some form of informal economic activity. Of those women, 26 percent are involved in two or more different informal activities. As the cash economy becomes increasingly the order of the day, exchanges and obligations that at one time might have been made in-kind have largely become financial transactions (Barrow 1986:134). It is yet to be seen whether periods of economic flux and the imposition of structural adjustment measures will create a shift in this cash-centered economy, but the expansion of informal services and trade and the predominant role in this arena by women is already apparent.[23] Interestingly, the informal sector is expanding at the same moment that there appears to be a contraction of reliance on extended kin networks. Taken together, these trends seem to imply that the emphasis on market transactions for both goods and services is likely to continue to expand within both formal and informal sectors.[24]

In a recent article Kathyrn Ward (1990a:15) argues that men and women tend to become active in the informal sector with different agendas, women for survival and men for mobility. These young Barbadian women have busy lives that often have them running from data factory to sewing machine to housework and child care, or making trips overseas carrying bags laden with the latest in household goods and work and casual wear. Yet there is a clear sense that economic benefit is only one element of their employment in the offshore information industry and of their supplementary needleworking and clothing trade. While not undermining the central importance of making a living, women also express other motivating factors behind their commitment even to what may seem to be monotonous and dead-end work in the data entry industry. Their enjoyment of the "cool" high-tech environment, carefully designed ergonomics, and office-like context of work are also integral to their experience.[25] Dressing up to go to work embodies a sense of pride associated with the new data processing industry as well as the status that comes from being a full-time wage earner. In the light of the importance played by "professional"-looking dress in the workplace, as described above, it is worth noting some of the costs behind these officelike wardrobes.

Half of the data entry operators I interviewed said they own between ten and fifteen suits or outfits for work; 24 percent have between five and ten work outfits, and 16 percent have more than fifteen such dresses and suits. As for where these clothes come from, more than half (57 percent) have their clothes made locally (9 percent make their own and 48 percent pay a needle-worker); roughly 40 percent say their clothes are bought abroad (by themselves, a relative, or a suitcase trader); and only very few (3 percent) purchase their clothes from local stores and boutiques. Expenditure on clothes for work ranges typically between $300 and $500 (US$150–$250) a year. More than half of the women (51 percent) described spending somewhere in this range; 27 percent spend more than $500 a year (between $500 and 1000; US$250–$500) and 22 percent spend less than $300 (US$150). Given the median wage of the data entry operators at $728 a month (US$364), their work clothes represent roughly 6 percent of their annual earnings. While not insignificant, this figure is substantially less than what it would cost to purchase these clothes in the formal arena of retail shops. Typically, for example, a needleworker charges $40–$50 (US$20–$25) to sew a skirt suit for work. The material would cost between $20 and $40 (US$10–$20), bringing the finished outfit to about $55–$60 (US$28–$30). Store-bought clothes of a similar sort can cost two times or more the needleworker's price. We see, therefore, the importance of these informal workers as providers of less expensive services that subsidize the data entry operator's budget and the companies, whose dress code demands such apparel.

Feminine Narratives

In the context of this broad set of economic and ideological relationships, brief portraits of three of those women who combine work in the data entry industry with an active needleworking and suitcase trade illustrate the importance of these "extra" jobs as expressions of women's economic inventiveness and the interaction between international capital and local culture. These women are of interest for the energy and ingenuity they display in combining varied economic roles, representing to greater and lesser degrees a triple shift of formal, informal, and domestic work. Their status as daughters, mothers, partners, and wives also demonstrates some of the diversity of household composition and the impossibility of characterizing them as either "docile dependent girls" or "strong and independent matriarchs." Their producer and consumer practices are embedded across local and transnational spaces and, as such, they come to embody points of articulation between corporate international enterprises and local Barbadian culture in the fashioning of new feminine identities.

JANINE

Janine is twenty-six. She and her nine-year-old daughter live at home with her parents and her two sisters and three brothers. Her mother was a home-based seamstress and taught Janine and her sisters to sew when they were young girls. Janine is now taking over her mother's business because her mother intends to "wind down and retire." Janine's dream is to become a fashion designer. When she left school, she first got a job in a supermarket and then in a video store. She now works at Multitext and at her home sewing machine in her off-time. Janine describes the advantages of combining wage work in data entry with her home-based needlework largely in terms of a guaranteed income. While she expressed frustration with the low wages she receives (between US$2.20 and $3.00 an hour, or about US$400 per month), in the end she said that, since taking this job:

> I can have a lot of things that I couldn't afford at one time. [. . .] Now I can see I can get my bills paid and know I getting money every month. When I do my own work [sewing] I ain't sure when I gonna get money—cause I ain't sure when people gonna bring the money, when people want something made and whatnot. So with this job, well I know I will have a certain amount of money every month and I can plan what I gonna do with it when I get it. Since I got this job I've been more aware of how I spend my money. Before I use to just get my money and spend it, but I am more aware now how to budget. Getting paid by the month you have to be able to keep that money to last you for a month and if it run out—you would really be in trouble.

Beyond Janine's monthly take-home pay from her data entry job, her boyfriend gives her $400 (US$200), and she averages an additional $400 (US$200) each month from her sewing (more during heavy months of holidays and weddings). While she has been combining formal and informal jobs for a number of years, her employment in the data entry operation is significantly more structured and more demanding of her time than her job in the video store was. Janine is a single mother. By living "at home" she admits, however, that she has few household or child care responsibilities. Her mother takes a great deal of the responsibility for her daughter, and Janine said that if she had another child the same would be true. Like her sisters and brothers, she makes a monthly contribution (US$50 or more) to the household economy, largely to pay for utility bills and groceries. She is now paying in installments for her bedroom furniture and otherwise saving her money for a trip to Puerto Rico or Venezuela to go shopping and eventually sell clothes and accessories when she returns.

CAROL ANN

Carol Ann lives at home with her mother, sister, and two brothers. Her mother works at a garment factory, and her sister works as a keyer at Data Air next to Multitext where Carol Ann works. She is twenty-seven and is planning to get married next year to her thirty-eight-year-old boyfriend, who is a primary school teacher. He is already the father of two. They have a piece of land and a house in the process of being built. Before her current job, at Multitext, Carol Ann worked at Data Air on the graveyard shift but was eventually laid off. She did two years of secretarial studies at the Polytechnic and had hoped to get a job as a secretary, but, she said, Multitext "is okay for now." Carol Ann was awarded "most improved employee of the year" at Multitext and received a trophy and a casserole dish from the company in honor of her high productivity and attendance. Following the award ceremony, she went "straight to a [photography] studio to have a picture taken" in her new work uniform and holding her trophy. She puts in an average of forty hours of overtime every month, and in addition to her monthly pay of about $800 (U.S. $400), including her incentive, she often earns an extra $80–$120 (U.S.$40–$60) braiding hair on the weekends, and more when she sews clothes for people. Her boyfriend bought her a sewing machine and she sews mostly for herself, her sister, and her friends at work. Carol Ann commutes one hour by bus to work each day because she lives on the east coast of the island, an area so remote that Bajans are known to refer to it as "behind God's back." She described her days as follows:

> When I working nights I find time during the day to wash and cook and clean the house. I am responsible for cleaning the house; we all do our own chores [clothes and cooking] but I clean the house on weekends and during the day when I work nights. On a morning shift, I get up at quarter to five or five o'clock and I have to rush in the bath and rush back out and hurry to get ready because my bus comes at quarter to six and you really have to rush to get ready for that bus. Then I go to work from seven thirty to three thirty and then now that I'm doing the course [cosmetology] on Mondays, Wednesdays, and Thursdays, sometimes I work overtime till five o'clock and then go up to class. Class finish about eight but sometimes it goes over to about nine or ten. A long day for me. Then I go home at night by bus. Sometimes I get home after ten. Then I have to set my hair in curlers, prepare something to eat—sometimes I make tea and prepare a few sandwiches and go to sleep—sometimes, like last night I go to sleep—minutes to two to get up to get in to work this morning [she laughs]. I guess it don't show, but I feel it. Especially when I sit down on that bus and take that long ride home; I just fall asleep—I can't help myself. Saturday I find myself doing a lot of washing; sometimes I wash my hair and then I cook. Every Saturday I do cou cou and something that we call stew food (sweet potatoes and pumpkin and English potatoes [. . .] stuff like that). My boyfriend comes by me on Saturdays and I cook for him. We might relax and watch television. Sometimes I find myself working and working—I don't have time to sleep. I do sewing on weekends—some weekends all I do is sew and some Saturdays and Sundays I have to put time to braid hair. I braid

hair on weekends; especially when you're getting to a time when there are bank holidays and stuff, I get a lot of people want their hair braid. I used to do three people in a day, but I find I can't do that now; there's too much to do.

JUNE

June is married and has a six-year-old daughter. Her husband is a police sergeant of fifteen years and operates a food cart at weekend fetes, cricket matches, and horse races. He built the cart himself, and on occasion hires others to run it for him. On a good day he earns as much as BDS$2,000 (US$1,000) selling hot dogs, cotton candy, popcorn, and drinks. He and June also keep chickens and turkeys in their small yard, selling eggs regularly and turkeys at Christmastime. June worked at Multitext for three years and recently quit her job. Prior to her data processing job, she was an office clerk and then spent a year at home occasionally making and selling coconut breads to police officers, government employees, and friends.

The combination wood and wall house they live in is owned by her father-in-law, and June says that her husband pays for all of the major household expenses. While she worked at Multitext, he would give her $200 (US$100) a month in addition to her $850 (US$425) monthly paycheck. She spent her money on clothes and fabric for herself and her daughter, as well as a number of other household "extras" such as ceramic ornaments and shelving units for the living room. June began to sew several years ago when a needleworking friend from her village taught her to cut and put together simple patterns. During the years she spent at Multitext, she increased her sewing commission enormously. She made herself four skirt suits for work during one vacation and began to sew regularly for several of her fellow data processors. Weekends and off-time would find June leaning over her machine, squeezed into a corner of her crowded bedroom. Like the other needleworkers, she cuts all her material free hand and can make a simple suit in a matter of an hour or two. After her three years at Multitext, June realized a life's dream. She has opened a small shop from home, cooking food and selling goods to people in the surrounding village. She is licensed to sell alcoholic beverages, and as the "proprietress" she hires part-time help. Her shop has a bar, a television, and a small dining area and well-stocked shelves of "basic necessities," such as local rum, imported face cream, soap powder, and bubble gum. Like Janine, she continues to make regular higglering trips to San Juan with friends from her days in informatics to buy clothes, accessories, and household goods for her family and for sale.

These three cases highlight themes central to women's experience as members of the new high-tech service sector and of families and household groups, such as their saving and budgeting strategies and their means of exercising personal autonomy and creative ingenuity through income-generating activities. The stories demonstrate the fact that the ways in which women juggle work within and outside their homes relates to several factors: their specific household constellation, the employment or income-generating patterns and contributions of its members, and the availability of other kin to assist with child care and domestic responsibilities. Women's particular life-cycle stages, in conjunction with their household and family formations, also represent an important factor in the balance they strike between formal, informal, and domestic activities. The permutations implied by motherhood, for example, are easily masked by the profile of the young, single, childless woman assumed to encompass offshore workers across the developing world.

Female heads of households and poor women generally are more likely than other single and married women to work within the informal sector (Ward 1990b). Over 40 percent of Barbadian households are female headed and St. Cyr (1990) found that 90 percent of the traders he surveyed in the Caribbean region were supporting dependent children. In light of these patterns, it is perhaps not surprising that of the three, the woman with the greatest autonomy is probably Janine. By piecing together sources of livelihood from her formal employment (data entry), informal work (sewing), and contributions from her boyfriend, she is able to save money for the home she and her boyfriend plan to buy and to reinvest in her informal retail enterprise through travel. Because her mother bears the bulk of the responsibility for her child, she has even greater freedom than does June, who is married. All of the women interviewed emphasized the importance of informal "fashioning" for supplementing their formal wage and increasing their purchasing power, as well as for providing enjoyment and satisfaction. Along with their ready acknowledgment of the necessity and desire they feel to dress well and keep up with the styles was a clear sense that their informal work enhanced their pleasure in fashion both within and outside their formal working lives.

The role played by the informal needleworker and suitcase trader is significant because they provide a cheaper alternative to the machine-made clothes in the boutiques mushrooming around the island and clearly enable fashion to play a large role in the lives of these working-class women. But more than that, they appear to be bound up in a growing globalization of consumption and style.

These Bajan women remind us that a model of the international division of labor that depicts third world women as the producers of goods to be consumed by first world "housewives" (Mies 1986) is both partial and distorted. Their formal employment as data processors together with their informal economic activities place them firmly within an international sphere where they are simultaneously producers and consumers of services, commodities, and styles.

Barbadian women have for centuries consumed imported goods, fashions, and aesthetics. What is remarkable in this particular moment of globalization, however, is the manner in which they are bound up in these transnational flows. Not only are women traveling to the metropole and selecting particular goods and elements of style themselves but also they are going to other parts of the Caribbean where their notion of fashion and "modern" femininity is further embellished and creolized. As such, their engagement in transnational higglering has embedded them further in circuits of trade between the traditional colonial trading partners of Britain, Canada, and the United States but has also reconfigured their sense of the Caribbean region to include their Hispanic neighbors. Not long ago, travel for a Barbadian would invariably have meant a trip to Britain, Canada, or the United States, in that order of priority. So strong have these patterns of migration and cultural connection been that of those informatics workers who had been away from Barbados prior to their employment in this sector, more had been to England or Toronto or New York than to Jamaica or Trinidad (let alone across the former colonial/linguistic divides to Puerto Rico, the Dominican Republic, Martinique, or Guadeloupe).[26] The "thank-you card" journeys, then, are significant because they facilitate women's participation in trade, fashion-hunting, and travel while also exposing them to dimensions of Caribbean-ness that have historically been narrowly defined.[27] Their ability to negotiate both shopping and leisure activities within a Spanish-speaking context, and their exposure to new foods, new music, and new people becomes a novel dimension of these transnational higglering trips. Kathleen, a lead operator in the insurance claims area of Data Air, described her trip to Caracas with pride and a sense of accomplishment. "I brought *a lot* of clothes. It was four days, and every day all we did was shop shop shop. I went with my mother and a friend. [. . .] I carried a Spanish book with me and told them what I wanted. Some people spoke English and we had a tour guide so it wasn't difficult."

For these women, the travel itself is a mark of modernity and prestige. By traveling abroad and coming back with stories of adventure, as well as material "rewards" in the form of new clothes, new gadgets, and new styles, these women enact what are well-known practices of reputation by Caribbean migrants on their return "home." Again, in his original formulation of the respectability/reputation paradigm, Wilson emphasizes that labor migration and travel in general is a significant vehicle for enhancing men's reputation. Sexual exploits, and their accompanying stories, as well as the sporting of stylish imported clothes are important forms of currency in displays of reputation. Citing R. T. Smith's ethnography (1956:137) as evidence, Wilson (1964:74) adds: "In British Guiana the young men of the village leave to work in the bauxite mines and when they return, their smart clothes, their swagger, their generosity are not only attractions to the girls, they are also assertions of a man's own accomplishments and his reputation."

Here again, the informatics workers demonstrate their simultaneous engagement in "classic" activities of reputation in part to enhance their economic position and their style and at the same time to conform to the demands of "professional" identity. The fashions designed and produced by women in their homes as well as those brought in from overseas in the suitcase trade mark a new juncture between their formal and informal sector subjectivities. Women's highly styled "professional" wear subsidizes the corporate image that forms such a potent element of their identity as offshore office workers. The ambiguity expressed by many women about where the concern for "professional dress" originates (whether integrally part of Barbadian pride in appearance or part of the foreign corporate prescription) exemplifies the wider contradictions concerning their informal economic activities. Managers often referred to women's involvement in the informal sector as a rationale for their low wages. By noting that Caribbean women are involved in complex exchange and informal economic relations within their communities, employers rationalize that they can "get by on less." Further underlying their rationalizations are a number of familiar stereotypes about "traditional femininity" and about the "matriarchal" Barbadian family structure that neatly complement other assumptions about why women make the "ideal" operators in this new informatics industry. These comments explicitly acknowledge that through these informal activities women subsidize their formal wage, and thus the industry at large.

In effect, then, the economic strategies exercised by women such as "meeting turns" and trade in goods and services at more reduced rates than in the formal economy remove the responsibility of the state and the employer to bear the expense of both social services (e.g., child care) and higher rates of pay.[28] In addition to revealing the persistence of contradictory gendered stereotypes, the point here is to emphasize that as women confront greater economic stress and respond with resilience and ingenuity in expanding their sources of livelihood, the state and the corporation are subsequently let off the hook. Workers in the formal sector not only subsidize their formal wage through their informal labor but also absorb greater unpaid reproductive costs and, to top it all off, sustain the mirage of "professional" prosperity for women that the Barbadian government and the private sector so anxiously assert.

The "pink collar," therefore, represents a feminine, professional "disguise" as well as an enactment of women's sense of distinction. The data entry operator essentially performs "blue-collar" work, but in place of the dust and fumes of garment and electronics houses, she is situated within a cleaner, cooler "white-collar" setting, and as part of the trade, she is expected (and expects herself) to appear distinctly feminine and "professional." Prescriptions for appropriate dress and admonition for "slackness" as described above play a large role in the sorts of informal income-generating activities these women perform. In this regard the importance of dress and appearance become an arena of pleasure and creativity, as well as a form of hidden labor behind the informatics operators' formal work.

The contemporary Barbadian needleworker and the suitcase trader who personally selects her styles from overseas straddle local and international aesthetics with creativity and style. Women workers don their smart "professional" look that bears both an international corporate emblem and a distinctively Caribbean flair, using bright combinations of tropical colors and prints with custom-designed accessories and adaptations of mass-produced patterns to embellish the contours of a matching, skirted suit. Fashion and dress, defined by both local aesthetics and corporate prescriptions, are symbolic of the more general dialectical relationships that reinforce and challenge women's subjectivities and gender ideologies in these new high-tech offshore arenas. Furthermore, in this complex interaction between formal, informal, and household realms, the home needleworker and the suitcase trader mark a historical tradition of female entrepreneurship and creative strategies for piecing together a living at the same time that they occupy a new space where local and international culture and capital meet and where production as well as consumption are both globalized and deeply interconnected. "Professional" fashion for the informatics worker becomes the "vent" through which women are able to express themselves creatively and distinctively and a realm of practice through which they also come to feel themselves, and in a certain sense to be, distinct.

Chapter 7

Epilogue

Since the early 1990s when I concluded this research, some changes and startling additions have been made to the informatics arena that signal the fulfillment of some of the goals laid out in the Barbados Development Report for the period, as well as some ironic twists. "High-tech" calls for rapid change and the informatics sector is no exception. The International Development Corporation now counts thirty-six information services companies operating in Barbados, six of which employ over one hundred people. The range of activities these firms perform continues to span low-level data entry and higher-skilled work from insurance adjudication to software production. Data Air continues to be the largest and longest established facility on the island. Multitext has been taken over by a parent company based in California that has other such operations in Mexico, Grenada, and China. The low-level data entry work has been moved from Barbados to the lower-wage sites, especially China. There, double and sometimes triple keying (by three typists) insures high quality work at still lower rates than in Barbados or the United States. Mark-up, however, the skilled work of entering typesetting codes for multimedia printing is performed in Barbados.[1]

Barbados rests its greatest hopes in informatics on the high end (skills and value added) of the industry. This ideal is, in a sense, best represented in a recent joint venture between the United States and India in software production. For the investors, Barbados is an idyllic "near-shore" location, a term they use to distinguish it from "on-shore" in the United States or faraway "offshore" locations such as India or China. The company is inspired by the Indian software production industry and by the premise that imported computer engineers could be offered higher salaries than they would earn at home (though less than in metropolitan cities in the United States), luxurious lifestyles, and idyllic working conditions and still insure substantial corporate profits (Hopkins 1998).[2] The company already employs over three hundred computer engineers. Interestingly, again, many of them are young, single, and female. These are highly skilled jobs, and the conditions of work are not just comfortable, they are perfectly enviable. Unlike the data processing operations, and the garment and electronics factories that preceded them, however, most of the employees are not Barbadian. Although the Barbados government hopes that this new venture will spawn the employment of its own Barbadian and other Caribbean programmers, most are currently imported from other countries. Indeed, by entreating Asian programmers to move to Barbados to work for a joint U.S.-Indian venture, these new firms have brought the global assembly line full circle. A popular news report describes "young, single Indian women reinventing their lives in this place [Barbados] half a world away, where freedom and possibility make them giddy" (Hopkins 1998). The particular construction of an "ideal" profile for these skilled global engineers is as yet unclear, and the gendered dimensions of such a profile will be of particular interest. Here we have another new kind of work, office, identity, and lifestyle provided through the dynamics of global capital and global labor and once again taking root in specific ways in the Bajan locale. What this will mean for the newest, imported, transnational work force involved and how their experience will relate to that of the pink-collar workers nearby is yet to be seen. In a sense, the young Indian women computer engineers embody a dream held by many of the Barbadian informatics workers performing lower skilled jobs at Data Air and Multitext. The processes through which labor, identity formation, production, and consumption are intertwined in their lives and inspire such dreams constitutes the center of my analysis and, hence, my conclusions.

This account centers on the interstices of several potent dualisms that have received increasing attention in recent times: local/global, production/consumption, and discipline/pleasure. These take shape in distinct ways across particular cultural contexts and within particular theoretical traditions. Each is permeated with a tension between "ideal" formulations and "real" practices. In Barbados, these take the form of the "ideal" global female worker and the complex realities and meanings of work in local Barbadian women's lives; the "ideal" of white-collar office jobs and the reality of highly regimented pink-collar open offices; the "ideal" panopticon of corporate control and the real forms of practice through which agency and discipline become both melded and contested; the "ideal" boundaries that neatly divide classes according to relations of production and forge class consciousness accordingly, and the modes of consumption that blur these distinctions; the "ideal" of feminine respectability and the realities of gender in which conformity and distinction, tradition and innovation coexist. My intent has been to make the broad issues of labor, economic development, and globalization meaningful in specific grounded ways through the experiences of one group of people actively involved in their making—Afro-Barbadian women workers in the offshore informatics industry. It becomes clear that much more is being produced inside the realm of these new offshore open offices than data for foreign publishers or airlines and foreign exchange for the local economy. New pink-collar identities have become as integral to these production zones as the computers and satellite technologies on which they depend. After all, informatics is not an "ordinary" factory, and its workers, as it turns out, are determined that they not be mistaken for "ordinary" factory workers. The powerful tension between ideal projections and real practices pervades their experiences and shapes their identities as informatics workers. Indeed, this tension permeates all levels and dimensions of this study, for it also informs the ideas and actions of a range of people across perspectives and positions, from the Barbados national development plan's conceptualization of growth and modernity to the negotiations between local and transnational actors in determining the direction and meanings of high-tech production in modern Caribbean life.

The Barbados Development Plan that coincided with the period of this research (1988–93) is symbolically illustrated by a simple line drawing, a graphic portrait of the country's prospects as of 1988. A climbing graph depicting a hopeful growth curve sits above the heads of four individuals. They represent an idealized family (a father, mother, and two children) and, according to the preface, "the matrix of our society." The figures are looking upward toward a bright yellow sphere—the sun, "the symbol of hope and continuing life" as well as, of course, the chief symbol in the island's tourism brochures. As the preface says, "the design depicts . . . the fact that there has been growth in the economy in recent years and that this growth is projected through the years of the Plan period" (Government of Barbados n.d.:i). Informatics is envisioned as a key to this development, as the "fastest growing and most dynamic of the sectors . . . in Barbados."

The growth motif of the graph represents an idealized projection for what in fact was a period of recession for the Barbadian economy. The nuclear family icon emphasized an even more idealized norm, since 40 percent of Barbadian households are headed by single females. The importance of these images and ideals underscores the power of metaphors in constructing cultural meanings both locally and globally. The nuclear family does not represent the lived reality of family life for the majority of Barbadians, but its symbolic potency is unquestionable. As an ideal or a form against which other configurations of family are defined, it remains powerful even (or especially) for those who do not experience it directly. Similarly, the "ideal" global informatics worker in her original internationally prescribed form (young, childless, single, etc.) remains a powerful image even when she is countered by the equally potent "ideal" of the powerful Barbadian matriarch. What seem at first glance to be merely rhetorical images and symbols (the "ideal" nuclear family, the "ideal" expression of global femininity, the "professional" informatics worker) have very real meanings and effects. Just as the explanatory ingredients are multiple and range from physiological and temperamental dispositions to household and family responsibilities and individual life stages, so too are the effects of these rationales. The informatics workers at Data Air and Multitext demonstrate in a rich and complex manner that it is in the crevices between the "real" and the "ideal" that people live their lives and define themselves. These crevices represent at one and the same time opportunities for self-expression, individuality, and distinction and spaces in which cultural, social, and economic forces structure and constrain these very opportunities.

The ambiguity of informatics as "factory" or "office" and of informatics workers as white- or blue-collar workers provides an aperture for precisely this convergence between discipline and distinction, and for the gendered practices of reputation and respectability. What makes the blurriness particularly powerful is the degree to which all of the actors involved—the women, the local and foreign managers and owners, and the state—are invested in its creation and maintenance. For the local and foreign industry representatives, "professionalism" brings the benefits of a loyal and flexible labor force, willing to work overtime on demand, to meet production quotas, and to insure their profits. For them, the costs of "professionalism" include a variety of worker perks such as night bus transportation, holiday parties, and a degree of flexibility in accommodating their family responsibilities. The most dramatic expression of this flexibility takes shape in what has emerged as two "generations" of data processors. In this sense, "professionalism" has come to encompass competing ideals of femininity that are also tied to a wide range of household and family constellations. These "generations" demonstrate that there is no monolithic "ideal" female worker. Transnational corporations cannot count on establishing homogeneous operations and prescriptions from one point on the globe to another. They are constantly negotiating difference, and they do so along with local actors and to different ends. In Barbados, the very profile of who can be an informatics worker has been redrawn by the women operators, and in turn, reinterpreted and redeployed by their corporate employers. For the informatics workers, "professionalism" and the "pink collar" represent the point of articulation between corporate discipline and individual creative invention, between the supposedly static "ideal" worker and the multiple realities and dimensions that mark their lives, and between the conforming and innovating practices of respectability and reputation. Through the medium of "professionalism," prescribed and enacted in a multitude of ways, Barbadian women and their foreign employers are engaged in creating a labor process and a workplace ethic that is, on one hand, highly regimented. They must meet the requisite quotas and demands for quality under the constant gaze of their computer, supervisor, and managers. They are simultaneously involved in the production of a new form of femininity as expressed through the controlled and regimented labor process and through their demeanor and appearance. The latter—the focus on appearance and fashion—turns out to be not "epi-phenomenal" but fundamental to the very definition of these workers. Appearance and demeanor become central to their work ethic and to their sense of themselves outside the mirrored walls of the informatics companies, as workers and as women. What may look like mere "facade" or masquerade instead speaks to processes in which women are in fact defining themselves (as much against other women workers of the laboring classes as with some other group) and ultimately forging a new class consciousness.

As such, the centrality of appearances to an analysis of labor highlights the importance of culture in the realm of economy and the power of gender in the realm of class. The convergence of all of these sources of identity around the "professional" informatics worker's boldly fashioned skirt suit demands as well that our understanding of labor and production take seriously the realm of consumption. Thorstein Veblen, in his classic treatise on leisure and consumption ([1899] 1953), described a century ago the powerful meanings of items of style and adornment in the crafting of selves and identities. He countered the notion that value can only be interpreted in purely economic terms, and apposite to the informatics workers at hand: "The commercial value . . . for clothing in any modern community is made up to a much larger extent of the fashionableness, the reputability of the goods than of the mechanical service which they render in clothing the person of the wearer. *The need of dress is eminently a 'higher' or 'spiritual need.'* " (119; italics mine).

The "higher" or "spiritual need" embodied in dress, some have argued, is particularly important to women and to other marginal groups as a means of compensating for their lack of power and status. But we need to go beyond consumption as a compensatory practice and eschew the moral stance of consumption as either victimizing or liberating in and of itself. For the informatics workers, the connection between new modes of consumption and new forms of production gives rise to new ways of seeing themselves as modern Barbadian working women. Like any cultural practice—that of religion, of cuisine, of kinship, and of work—the construction of one's identity through consuming new styles and producing "a look" becomes as well a part of how one feels, how one relates to the world, and who one is. This enactment is circumscribed by material conditions and resources and entails acknowledgments of certain conventions, as well as opportunities for expressing individuality. As such, it represents a dramatic convergence between the Caribbean values of reputation and respectability.

For the Barbadian informatics workers, "professionalism" and in particular, "professional appearance" becomes both a metaphor and a literal enactment of the simultaneously pleasurable and disciplining dimensions of the industry at large. They are subject to the gaze and control of a panopticon far and above what Bentham envisioned and what Foucault decried. However, at precisely the point Foucault argued that the panopticon has its greatest effects—in its internalization—Barbadian women give surveillance an ambiguous effect. It is at once self-policing and personalized, disciplined and distinctive, ever-present but suddenly not homogeneous. By internalizing the discipline of every level of the panopticon—the gaze of computer, the gaze of supervisor, the manager, the fellow production worker, and finally the internal gaze of the self—they make it personal and distinctive as opposed to anonymous and homogeneous. In the process of being observed, observing one another and themselves, the informatics workers become simultaneously an arm of discipline and its mediator. They conform to its dictates but also enhance, personalize, and individualize them. In the process they also affect the ideologies and practices of management by insisting, for example, on their own definitions of family (corporate or not) and the reciprocal obligations these entail. Through the "matriarch" ideal, they manage to personalize some of the measures of surveillance as well, just as they figure out how to trick the computer. In numerous ways, from holding birthday parties in work group meetings to honing the fashionable look of the operations through new styles of dress, they work against the anonymity of the open office and in so doing, they further entrench both the discipline and the pleasures of "professionalism."

At the same time, they raise the stakes of the panopticon to a dizzying extreme when one considers the multiple forms of labor they must perform in order to foster these distinctions and pleasures. To do so typically requires that they engage in yet other realms of labor outside the boundaries of informatics. In short, to be a "professional" woman in this new high-tech sector women find themselves performing extra income-generating activities that tie them to age-old practices of higglering and home-based production in the informal sector of the economy. As such, their formal transnational production is also increasingly tied to informal local and transnational production and consumption, whether as suitcase traders shopping in malls in Miami or as needleworkers fashioning skirt suits modeled on stylish American soap opera characters.

The fact that women complicate and in some ways challenge the host of "ideals" that permeate their incorporation into informatics has effects that are simultaneously beneficial and costly. For both the "powerful matriarchs" and the younger "girls" who juggle their informatics jobs with informal work and domestic responsibilities the pleasures of consumption are also integrally tied to new production demands—they require more money. Consumption and its role in the creation of "professionalism," then, becomes a pleasure and a burden at one and the same time. We might, perhaps, compare these pleasures and burdens to those of the working classes in late eighteenth-century Britain whose consumption of sugar on a grand scale, Sidney Mintz says, bestowed upon them a new sense of status.

> This is not to claim that ordinary working people in late eighteenth-century Britain became totally different sorts of human beings simply by becoming consumers of such substances. Nonetheless, consuming exotic products purchased with their own labor—which allowed them to see themselves as *being* different because they were able to choose to consume differently—surely helped to *make* them different. . . . In the new scheme of things, what one consumed became a changing measure of what [and of who] one was. *Status did not so much define what one could consume; what one consumed helped to de-*

fine one's status. The individual—a producer—came to be redefined as a consumer; her desires were continuously remodeled. (1996b:78; italics mine)

The informatics workers demonstrate at every turn that globalization is not enacted in a uniform manner, nor is it simply homogenizing in its effects. Modernity in the Caribbean has a long history and its expression in the lives of these women bears marks of both tradition and innovation. They are in the midst of defining themselves in ways that resemble centuries-old practices through which Afro-Caribbean women have pieced together their livelihoods and aspired to local ideals of femininity, and at the same time they embody the shift in late-twentieth-century society in which identities are increasingly permeated by consumer-based practices and markers that span local and transnational spaces. Through the notion of "professionalism" they forge a new expression of femininity that intertwines respectability with reputation, production (formal and informal) with consumption, and class with gender.

By consuming goods and styles from abroad and acquiring symbolic capital at home, they enhance their status, and this has symbolic and potentially material implications. While their informatics jobs and their newly fashioned femininity do not signal their becoming middle class, they are gaining status and in so doing redefining a segment of the working classes. By dissociating themselves from other factory workers, they express a disinclination toward industrial unionization, and in turn forge a new consciousness—that of new pink-collar workers. As such, these third world women workers are configured by local and global, cultural and economic forces and in turn define themselves across these same terrains. Their modes of distinction bear emblems of imported modern styles and are at the same time unmistakably Caribbean. They are fashioned amid modes of discipline that rely on new transnational practices of management and draw on local "plantation-style" paternalism. Their pink-collar "professionalism" gives their work and travels, their sense of feminine identity new expressions and new meanings that are subject to multiple forces of control (state, corporate, patriarchal, and self), and creative, pleasurable ingenuity.

These distinctions and new identities are forged in significant but partial ways. These women, though they speak fluently in the language of "professionalism" and adorn themselves proudly in its clothing, are not "tricked" into thinking that they are actually "professional" women. Their pink-collar consciousness is not "false" or imaginary. They are as clear about, for example, the education and capital, status and class that separated my life from theirs as they are about the material and symbolic distinctions between themselves and the accountants, fashion designers, and boutique owners they aspire to be. On the other hand, for some, the desire to make more of their link to computers, "office" work, and foreign travel leads them to dare to imagine themselves otherwise and even to pursue new opportunities that might one day make such transformations possible.

The Barbadian pink-collar workers remind us that the global is always imbued with local meaning and that local actors reconfigure the very form that global processes take. They do so in ways that highlight the dialectics of gender and class, production and consumption, formal and informal labor, and the enactment of reputation and respectability. These relationships illuminate an understanding of discipline, not as a total or closed system of power by which these Barbadian women workers are controlled, but as a set of practices and ideologies that they in turn give expression to, and as such, change. They speak to the ways in which local actors in specific cultural contexts confront, experience, and give shape to the forms of globalization. Offshore informatics on this small tropical island is a site in which local and transnational processes of production and consumption not only converge but reshape each other. In short, informatics becomes a locus for the crafting of identities, where prescriptions for particular kinds of feminine workers are imposed, challenged, and reformulated and where women enact their lives in ways that draw on Caribbean cultural traditions and change their very form within new conditions of the global cultural economy.

Notes

1 Introduction

1 "Bajan" is a common expression for "Barbadian."

2 I use pseudonyms for the women and men described in these workplaces, and for the two operations I analyze in this study. I am unable to conceal the identities of these operations fully, however by disguising the kind of work they perform (as Westwood [1985] and others have done) because the relationship between the workers and the work is integral to my analysis. I agreed not to name specific clients of the off-shore enterprises. Direct quotes are kept in the original form in which they were spoken, in Barbadian dialect as well as in more standardized English.

3 Louise Kapp Howe in her study (1977) of the changing shape of women's work in the United States, uses "pink collar" to denote realms of service work that have been feminized. Probert and Wilson (1993) also use this term in the title of their book *Pink Collar Blues*, which focuses on the role of technology and changing notions of "skill" associated with women's work.

4 In this context, "creolized" refers to the result of the creolization process, which is described by the Barbadian poet and historian, Edward Brathwaite, as "a sociological description and explanation of the way the four main culture carriers of the region—Amerindian, European, African, and East Indian—interacted with each other and with their environment to create new societies of the New World" (1974:29–30).

5 The work of Sidney Mintz (1985, 1989, 1996b) and M. R. Trouillot (1992) is indispensable in mapping the processes through which the Caribbean is, and has been from its very inception, quintessentially modern and transnational.

6 Export production in the Dominican Republic has had a recent boom as a result of tariff incentives set up by the U.S. to support off-shore assembly, as well as a reduction in foreign exchange earned by traditional agricultural exports, devaluation, economic crisis, and an accompanying reduction in labor costs there. Dominican wages dropped from U.S. $1.33/hour in 1984 to U.S. $0.56/hour in 1990 (Safa 1995:101).

7 I say "persuaded" here because these women rarely went to the beach, even on weekends. The expression "The sea ain't got no back door" was a constant refrain because few could swim. "But it too hot!" they would say when I suggested a dip on our way home from work, or at Christmastime they had the reverse fears that "the sea too cold." Clearly swimming was not a favored recreation. A few of the women I came to know best had gained so much weight in their late twenties because of pregnancy or marriage that they were self-conscious about donning swimsuits. As children they may have gone for the occasional "sea bath"—dunking and playing in the water on a calm beach—or picnicked on a shady part of a beach, but swimming in the sea, as a tourist imagines the Caribbean, was not a part of their ordinary recreation.

8 I use "friend" cautiously here, not to imply that the boundaries and power dimensions of class, race, and culture that separated me from my informants were surmounted, but more to denote a degree of familiarity and ease that enabled these differences to be acknowledged and thus fostered a sense of understanding that, I believe, is truly a dimension of friendship.

2 Pink-Collar Bajans

1 See Williams 1991 for a rich ethnographic exploration of the ways in which even the smallest acts, objects, and ideas both contain and enact representations of politics and economic difference. Williams (1991:30) quotes Michael Gilsenan, who says, "English furniture? Well, yes. Furniture, ways of sitting, mores of dress, politeness, photography, table manners and gestures overturn societies, too. Such conventions, techniques, and ways of acting in and on the world are as important as any religion, and changes in them may be as dislocating as changes in belief."

2 The acknowledgment that globalization and technological transformations of work have differential effects not only on women but in particular on women of color is made by Beneria and Roldan (1987), Colclough and Tolbert (1992), and Glenn and Tolbert (1987), who note that minority clerical workers in the United States face greater risks of job losses, while more skilled white workers confront restrictions on mobility out of low-paying jobs.

3 As such, Barriteau argues, black Barbadians "experience little racial discrimination in the areas of health services, education, transportation, housing and public sector employment" (1995:151). The corporate elite are still critiqued for maintaining a tradition of patronage and nepotism, evidenced by the publication of Beckles's book (1989b) on the history of the Barbados Mutual Life Assurance Society, and a series of "race debates" that flared along these lines during the period of my fieldwork.

4 For example, expressions such as "dark" or "clear skinned" for light or "brown skin" or "that girl with fine hair" for straight hair emerged in jokes and casual conversation or in identifying individuals to me. These were similar to other explicit physical descriptors used to call attention to particular people in their graphic directness (e.g.,

"Mary? Oh she that fat, fat girl") or comments made to me, such as "Carla, you just dipped in bleach!" when I returned to Barbados after a year, or "You looking more and more like a chicken every day . . . what man will have you now?" when I had lost some weight.

5 These terms are more widely used in Barbados than elsewhere in the Caribbean, though they differ from "black" and "white" in the United States. Furthermore, the "black" ownership of some of these local firms is not limited to "brown-skin" elites, as is more likely in other Caribbean countries and as might have been at an earlier time in Barbados as well.

6 Though Jamaica is historically a Caribbean nation in which the color/class hierarchy is marked, Pearson (1993) notes that the informatics industry there is notable in the fact that local ownership of new firms "come neither from the traditional land-owning oligarchy nor the capital-owning elite of Jamaican society. They are the up-wardly mobile products of the post-independence expansion of technical and profes-sional education amongst the black middle classes who have been mainly educated at the University of the West Indies" (290).

7 Some recent discussions that theorize in different ways the forces behind and man-ifestations of the contemporary global and transnational culture and economy are: Appadurai 1996; Bash et al. 1994; Bird et al. 1993; Cvetkovich and Kellner 1997; Featherstone 1990; Friedman 1994; Giddens 1990; Gilroy 1993; Guarnizo and Smith 1998; Hannerz 1996; Harvey 1989; King 1991; Lash and Ury 1987; Ong and Nonini 1997; Robertson 1992; Swedenberg and Lavie 1996; Wilson and Dissaya-nake 1996. Where some have attempted to distinguish between these terms (limit-ing "transnationalism" to those movements explicitly anchored in one or more na-tional territories, and reserving "globalization" to flows that are truly boundaryless), I employ them more broadly here. In either case, the specificity of the producing and consuming cultures is vital to understanding the meanings of these processes.

8 Appadurai (1996) has made this argument of "post-nationalism" whereas Gertler (1997) argues that the nation-state continues to be a key regulatory force, econom-ically and otherwise.

9 "Flexibility" can refer to a number of aspects of production and marketing: "fi-nancial flexibility (wages), numerical flexibility (hours, workloads, or numbers of workers) and functional flexibility (multiskilling and broadbanding)" (Henry and Franzway 1993:133).

10 Fröbel, Heinrichs, and Kreye (1980) are credited with coining the expression "new international division of labor."

11 The paradigm described by "dependency" theorists set the stage for Fröbel's interna-tional division of labor (IDL) framework, as they had long identified globalized capi-tal accumulation (through colonialism) as the basis for underdevelopment in the third world (Frank 1967; Amin 1974). Like some proponents of the dependency school, Fröbel, Heinrichs, and Kreye saw that, contrary to persistent dualisms of

neoclassical economic frameworks that presented core and periphery as linked, though quintessentially separate in their roles in the IDL, losses of decision-making power and labor restructuring occur within both spheres.

Other approaches, most notably those adopted by international development agencies, have taken a more neoclassical economic view of world market industrialization. Their premise is that the free flow of capital internationally will gradually lead to a leveling of inequalities in exchange, thereby creating an economic equilibrium. In other words, investment in industry should ultimately help to equalize wages and prices worldwide. Sharing many of these premises is another model that describes a "vertical integration" of global production. Here, first and third world countries are hierarchically organized in an international division of labor where the latter, on the bottom, provide manual labor, and as we move up the production ladder "nationality becomes increasingly European in the command centers of research, knowledge and management" (Nash 1983:3). Like the neoclassical models, the vertical integration perspective presents relations between "core" and "periphery" as an essential and timeless feature of the global market and lacks any historical discussion of the bases for the hierarchy that now defines them.

12 These industries are "labor intensive" both in the amount of labor required to produce a good and in the quality of the labor process entailed.

13 As part of these new economic geographies we also see the emergence of "global cities" in highly industrialized nations (Cox 1997; Sassen 1991).

14 For a fascinating historical exploration of commodification and consumption that avoids the simplicity Gupta and Ferguson warn of, see Burke 1996.

15 Notably, Miller (1994) makes a similar argument in his treatment of modernity and mass consumption in Trinidad. He asserts that mass consumption of imported goods, far from wiping out distinctive culture, actually enhances and sharpens notions of "Trinidadian-ness." Mintz (1977) and Trouillot (1989) have eloquently discussed anthropology's view of the Caribbean, long ignored and even repudiated for its lack of "purity" of culture and a truly indigenous population of natives. Interestingly for precisely these reasons, the Caribbean now appears to be gaining anthropological currency.

16 Expressions of resistance to globalization often adopt a sense of an "invented primordial" culture defined against these flows/dependencies.

17 Important recent exceptions include Ong and Nonini 1997 and Lowe and Lloyd 1997. See also Bell and Valentine 1997; Breckenridge 1995; Burke 1996; de Guy et al. 1997; Howes 1996; Miller 1995a, 1995b; Mintz 1996b; Watson 1997.

18 See Goddard (1998) for a useful explanation of the decline of the Barbadian sugar industry.

19 It is worth noting here that this legislation did not apply to sugar manufacturing, and, similarly, the national income accounts of Barbados consider sugar milling a separate economic category. These phenomena relate closely to sugar's association with slavery and the conceptualization of agriculture as a separate (different) entity

altogether from "modern" industry. The irony is that investment in sugar factory machinery and technology has been substantial, but it is not eligible for the tax incentives and exemptions given to other export industries.

20   As Safa (1995:8) points out, the U.S. apparel industry is estimated to have lost roughly three hundred thousand jobs, with half moving to Mexico, Central America, and the Caribbean. The passage of NAFTA between Canada, the United States, and Mexico has intensified these movements, and has posed detrimental effects to non-member Caribbean nations. Already, Jamaica has experienced significant job losses as garment industries have fled to Mexico for preferential trade relations.

21   These descriptions are developed in greater detail in chapter 3. Briefly, the emphasis on order and politeness take shape in numerous cultural stereotypes by and about Bajans as conservative, cautious, and polite. The chairman of the Central Bank during my fieldwork was quoted in a speech as saying, "Bajans aren't necessarily warm like Jamaicans and Trinidadians, but they can be counted on for politeness." Grounded in Barbados's history as a stable parliamentary democracy, these cultural stereotypes are strategically employed as promotional tools by economic development representatives and state bureaucrats in tourism and industry alike.

22   This point requires greater elaboration and is explored in greater depth in later chapters. On one hand, cultural imperialism is of great concern to social critics within the West Indies. Rex Nettleford, among other local intellectuals, has decried forces of British and U.S. cultural imperialism for the past twenty-five years, in relation to such issues as western (white) ideals of beauty depicted in advertising and beauty pageants (Barnes 1997). Others, such as the former senator Carmeta Fraser, have tied these issues to economic concerns in asserting local production (of food, clothing, and other imports). On the other hand, the belief that many "imported" cultural forms have now become "Bajan" or "Caribbean," such as fashion shows, beauty pageants, pop radio, and the association of red apples with Christmas (Miller 1994) is also a widely argued point.

23   Fuentes and Ehrenreich (1983:15) asserted, "The factory system relies upon and reinforces the power of men in the traditional patriarchal family to control women." Quoting Cynthia Enloe, they add, "Even recruitment is a family process. Women don't just go out independently to find jobs; it's a matter of fathers, brothers and husbands making women available after getting reassurances from the companies. Discipline becomes a family matter since, in most cases, women turn their paychecks over to their parents. Factory life is, in general, constrained and defined by the family life cycle."

24   In a fascinating recent work on the British common law practice of coverture in the late eighteenth and early nineteenth centuries, Margot Finn (1996) explores the powerful role consumption practices played in married women's ability to evade these strictures, purchase goods on their husbands' credit, and gain some degree of independence from unsuccessful unions. See also de Grazia 1996 for an exceptional collection of historical essays on gender and consumption.

25   See, for example, Abraham-Van der Mark 1983; Beneria and Roldan 1987; Bolles 1983; Elson and Pearson 1981a, 1981b; Fernandez-Kelly 1983; Kelly 1987; Lim 1985; Mies 1986; Nash and Fernandez-Kelly 1983; Ong 1987; Safa 1981, 1995; Ward 1990a; Warren and Bourque 1991; Wolf 1992.

26   Notable exceptions include Bolles on Jamaica (1983, 1996); Kelly on St. Lucia (1987); and, though not about a foreign-owned, export-oriented factory, Yelvington's 1995 study of a Trinidadian small-appliance factory is a relevant addition to this literature.

27   The observation that, despite the hopes of economic planners, free trade zones and export production have not decreased unemployment rates has been related to this point. In short, the argument has been that women had not been counted as part of the labor force, never having worked for wages previously. Therefore, in the light of the recruitment of female labor and the high rates of turnover in these industries, they have both marginalized male labor, and ironically, contributed to rising unemployment figures (Fernandez-Kelly 1983). Tiano (1990) presents a different argument, countering the presumption that female maquila employment is directly tied to male unemployment, by asserting that these women are not largely drawn from families with unemployed male heads of households. Male joblessness is not what led most of these women into taking these jobs, nor is male unemployment necessarily related at all to female selection within these industries. Instead, she argues that women take these jobs either because there is no male supporting the household or because the contributions made by the male of the household are insufficient to support the entire family. These factors, according to Tiano, are related more generally to the broad state of the Mexican economy than to the specific recruitment and employment practices of the maquiladora sector.

28   Peña (1997:16) has also pointed out that women have long been wage workers in Mexico, indicating that the rhetoric of women as "first-time" workers in the free trade zones is contradicted by history. The power of this assumption is great, however, and as the above accounts reveal, it fuels the general feminine stereotype of the Mexican woman as naturally domestic, passive, inexperienced and therefore in need of protection, and so on.

29   This point is made as well in Ong and Nonini 1997 with regard to Chinese capitalism and tradition.

30   Speculating an answer to this question, some say that the more dire economic conditions in the Dominican Republic account for men's employment in this sector. Interestingly, the conception of these jobs as "computer jobs" seems, as well, to be emphasized as a way of compensating men for what otherwise might be construed as "feminine" work (i.e., typing).

31   Diane Wolf (1992:258) also presents evidence from her study of women factory workers in Java to challenge the presumption that women work as part of family-articulated, household strategies for survival. In her study, she says, "These young Javanese women initially seek factory employment to gain new experience and some

cash for themselves—not for the family's economic good. Family benefits accrue only later, over time."

32 Intel, which operated a microcomputer chip assembly plant in Barbados prior to the opening of the informatics industry, had attempted to impose a pregnancy test on prospective workers. After a short but strong bout of resistance to this practice, the proposal was dropped. Interestingly, women in the informatics industry reported this to me with horror—asserting that their employer would never have attempted such a repressive policy.

33 This relationship between work and fertility rates is not so for Indo-Caribbean women agricultural workers (Aisha Khan, personal communication, 1997). Richard Stoffle's study (1977) of the impact of industrialization on mating patterns asserts that individuals typically pass through several predictable union stages (visiting, common-law, and legally recognized marriage) and that women's entry into industrial work actually accelerates their progression in the mating process.

34 The most selective industries (traditionally, electronics, in contrast to garments or textiles) are known to take extreme measures in much of the world, requiring, for example, pregnancy tests or sterilization certificates to ensure that their workforce remains childless and therefore available.

35 See Benson 1984; Crompton 1986; Fernandez-Kelly 1983; Hochschild 1983; Murphree 1984; Nash and Fernandez-Kelly 1983; Paules 1991; and Pyle 1990 for useful discussions of the gendering of work in various female-centered arenas, from clerical work to that of flight attendant, waitress, and assembly-line producer.

36 It is important to note that deskilling occurs unevenly even within the same industry. For example, workers may be laid off by machines, generating a demand for other skilled workers to maintain and repair these machines (Block 1990).

37 For a nuanced ethnography of culture and computerization, see Hakken and Andrews 1993.

38 See Boris and Daniels 1989; Christensen 1988; Hartmann, Kraut, and Tilly 1986–87; and Webster 1996 for both historical and contemporary analyses of home-based and other related restructuring arrangements as they relate to gender and changing technology.

39 See Appelbaum 1987; Carter 1987; 9 to 5, 1990; Posthuma 1987; and Samper 1987 for excellent discussions of these processes of technological transformations and the gendering of labor.

40 A good illustration of the appeal of these jobs is the response by two thousand applicants to the announcement of thirty positions in an operation that opened in 1993.

41 The idea that these jobs are stepping stones for the Dominican men is, I should emphasize, their expressed hope, just as many Bajan women hope that their jobs will lead to something better. The fact that in the Dominican Republic, however, workers stay in the jobs for an average of two years does set them dramatically apart

from their Barbadian counterparts. How successful the Dominicans are in achieving their upwardly mobile goal, I do not know. The trajectory of workers who leave these zones is still to be explored.

42   See Skeggs 1998 for a recent critique of these rejections of the significance of class.

43   This is so, with the exception of some women's ownership of sewing machines with which they create garments and household accessories for sale on the informal market. With respect to their capacity as wage workers in informatics, they occupy the position of proletariat from the point of view of Marx's classical model of class structure. It is important to note, as well however, that, historically, women of the bourgeoisie have also lacked such capital and rights. Assigning women to one or another class position, again, relies on a view not only of their labor/occupation or that of their husbands/fathers but also, depending on the particular cultural and historical context, an understanding of all of these factors and their relation to and reliance on multiple forms of capital.

44   For insightful analyses of Bourdieu along these lines, see Jenkins 1992; Knauft 1996; and Skeggs 1998.

45   Interestingly, in his comparative chapter based on ethnography in Zambian mines Burawoy resists arguing that culture plays a significant role in the production process, because he sets out to counter arguments of African "primordialisms" (e.g., the myth of the indolent worker). To disprove the "ideological" arguments, he emphasizes structure—specifically the role played by colonial structures that enact cultural idioms (prejudices surrounding racial and ethnic categories) "in which to couch production relations" (1979:215). In fact, he goes so far as to conclude, "Activities of Zambian workers on the shop floor, in the mines and in the office were determined within the narrow limits by the relations in production. . . . ethnic and racial categories are usually important only when reproduced by the labor process itself" (1979:215). In the end, economic structure supersedes ideological superstructure.

46   See also Olin Wright 1997 for a reformulation of the Marxist concept of social class and a discussion of the ambiguities of class identity.

47   According to Fernandez-Kelly and Sassen 1995, 75 percent of all global assembly workers are reported to be women. See also Cagatay and Ozler 1995; Standing 1989.

48   A good example of this process is the convincing set of ideologies that persuaded thousands of American wives and homemakers during the Second World War that patriotism and factory labor were not antithetical to femininity, and then reversed its tune with a new cult of domesticity when men were available to return to the labor force.

49   The University of the West Indies campuses now offer training in gender and development studies. For recent works by both Caribbean and non-Caribbean scholars on gender ideologies, women's studies, and local feminisms, see Barriteau 1995; Barrow 1997; Bolles 1997; Douglass 1993; Lopez-Springfield 1997; McClaurin 1996; Mohammed 1994; Momsen, 1993; Reddock 1994, 1998; Yelvington 1995.

50 Yelvington notes in his ethnography about a factory in Trinidad (1995) that sexuality is often the medium through which workers articulate ideas about gender. For an excellent examination of the relationships between gender, kinship, and sexuality, see Yanigasako and Delaney 1995.

51 See, for example, Bennholdt-Thomsen 1988; Mies 1986; Ward and Pyle 1995; Werlhof 1988.

52 Acevedo 1995; Beneria and Roldan 1987; Fernandez-Kelly 1983; and Safa 1990 have each explored the significance of life-cycle stage for the particular meanings of women's wage earning.

53 Cuales (1988:121) attributes this tentative engagement between analyses/politics of class and gender in the Caribbean to "the relative weakness of the left and of class struggle in the region" and to a tendency to take up class or gender as the major locus of struggle. Although she points to the need for greater appreciation of family structures and patterns in developing our understanding of class and gender consciousness, and in particular the implications of "visiting" relationships for class and gender equality, her own discussion does not integrate these theoretical frames with regard to the historical or contemporary contexts of Caribbean societies. Rosina Wiltshire-Brodber (1988:142) argues that because race and class mutually reinforce each other in the Caribbean, with whites predominantly at the top and blacks predominantly at the bottom of the social order, race and class have superseded gender as the "principal organizing forces for resistance and change."

54 While, surely, women's notions of modernity transcend the realm of computers and informatics (e.g., through the media, the tourism sector, the intensity of imported commodity goods) the importance of the computer here is emphasized because this tool is a special modernist icon. It feeds into a long tradition privileging education as the source of upward mobility and heightens this ethic with the hyperbolic sense of technological change—the emergence of a computer fast-track from which passive or unsuspecting nations might find themselves marginalized. For these women, then, the computer is a sign—a symbol laden with meaning and its meaning is the Future—distinct from agriculture and from factories. It is linked to finance, to accounting (the career goal most often cited among the women I interviewed) and to white-collar, professional work in general. Correspondence courses in computer fields (from programming to various sorts of "literacy" courses) are very popular, as are evening and part-time courses at the Community College and Polytechnic.

55 See also Hochschild 1983 for a discussion of the increasing importance of "emotional labor" within services, especially those performed by women workers.

56 In this same passage, Mills continues by noting that the difference (in dress between the wage worker and the white-collar worker or the salaried worker) is "revealed by the clothing budgets of wage workers and white collar people, especially of girls and women. After later adolescence, women working as clerks, compared with wage-working women of similar income, spend a good deal more on clothes; and the same

is true for men, although to a lesser extent" (1956:241). See also Susan Porter Benson's (1986) historical discussion of dress, femininity, and class among department store saleswomen and their customers; and Kathy Peiss's (1986) analysis of the importance of dress among working-class immigrant women in early-twentieth-century New York.

3 Localizing Informatics: Situating Women and Women and Work in Barbados

1 Gordon Lewis (1968:227) mentions the same joke about Barbados, adding that though "apocryphal—for Trollope repeated the joke, in a different context, as going back to the period of the Napoleonic Wars—it nonetheless testifies to a temper of glorious self-congratulation most outsiders find amusing, sometimes intolerable."

2 Williams (1970:142) adds that exports from Barbados constituted 4 percent of Britain's total external trade. For a fuller discussion see Dunn 1969.

3 The "triangular trade" on which Caribbean colonies were established involved the shipping of metropolitan goods to the coast of West Africa, where they were exchanged for slaves. Slaves were brought across to the West Indies in what is called the "middle passage" where they worked on the sugar plantations, and, completing the triangle, sugar, rum, and other Caribbean products were shipped to the metropole in exchange for slaves (Williams 1970:141).

4 Women have been pivotal also as consumers in this integrated realm of transnational trade, a point that I elaborate in greater detail in chapters 6 and 7.

5 Beckles 1990:31, citing Philip Curtin's census of the African slave trade.

6 A small number of Amerindians, however, were brought to Barbados from South America, and though they perished early, their legacy is evident in the list of plants they introduced that became integral to the island's economy or diet: cotton, tobacco, maize, cassava, pineapple, potatoes (Gmelch and Gmelch 1997:19).

7 Williams (1970:97) notes as well, "In 1640 two hundred young Frenchmen were kidnapped, concealed and sold in Barbados for nine hundred pounds of cotton each, for terms varying from five to seven years." Williams (1970:198) estimates that between 1654 and 1685, ten thousand indentured servants sailed from Bristol alone for all the British colonies. See also Sheppard 1977.

8 Until 1780, when living conditions improved, slave owners expected roughly one-third of their slaves to die within their first three years in Barbados. By the end of the eighteenth century, the vast majority of slaves were creoles—island born—and only 5 percent of slaves were African born (Watson 1979).

9 In his classic *Capitalism and Slavery* Eric Williams ([1944] 1994) advances the thesis that the capital accumulation required to launch the Industrial Revolution derived in large part from the profits of the West India sugar trade.

10 Only in the early nineteenth century were slaves allowed to offer testimony in court against whites. The slave codes stipulated the basic provisions slaves were to be given (food and clothing) and gave planters license to punish and even kill slaves if their properties or lives were threatened (Gmelch and Gmelch 1997:33–34).

11 As many have pointed out (Osirim 1997; Senior 1991), motherhood in the Afro-Caribbean includes not only biological maternity but also a well-established system of surrogacy ("child sharing") whereby most women take on the responsibility for children in their extended families, villages, or communities.

12 Beckles (1995:137) distinguishes between these two important groups of Caribbean women by calling the former leaders "rebel women" ("nanny," "Queen Mother," and "Priestess"), and the more numerous "typical woman in the fields," "natural rebels."

13 During the brief period of vast male migration between 1891 and 1921, women's numbers significantly outpaced those of men. Gross overstatements about the disproportionate number of women in Barbados were frequently made to me by a diverse array of individuals, from male corporate managers to female workers. Some presented this as a rationale for why women are overrepresented in low-level factory/offshore jobs ("There are simply more women out there who need a job") and, more generally, to justify the tendency for men to have more than one woman ("They've got to have an outside woman, since there are just not enough men to go around"). The 1990 population statistics reported the total number of adult females to be 98,000 and of males, 85,000.

14 In fact, the sex ratio of women to men in the white population of Barbados paralleled that of the slave population, and between 1673 when the first census recorded a white population of 21,309 (60.4 percent males and 39.6 percent females) and 1715, white women outnumbered men by about 1 percent (Beckles 1989a:14–15). This female predominance was true for "blacks, whites, and free coloureds" (7).

15 During the early sugar years documented by Ligon ([1657] 1976), 1647–50, white indentured female servants labored in the field gangs with enslaved black women. The division of labor at that time was not divided along racial lines, and planters did not believe servants were entitled to different treatment than that of slaves. By 1660, however, slavery constituted the predominant form of labor on the plantations, and "whatever their social background or the reasons for their servitude, white women were no longer to be employed as field hands." White and "coloured" labor, both bonded and free, was removed from the fields and tended to be moved into more skilled artisanal and supervisory areas (Beckles 1989a:29).

16 The belief that women were preferred over men because they were assumed to be less threatening and more docile is debated. Beckles (1989a:153) cites this argument but contests it by saying that "slave owners were as fearful, suspicious and distrustful of women's potential activities as antislavery agents as they were of men's." In insurrections by women, for example, slave masters did not spare the brutal punishments meted out to men, except for women in the late stages of pregnancy, when, Beckles argues, the masters may have been more concerned to protect the capital investment in the unborn child than the body of the rebellious slave woman.

17 Senior (1991:108) emphasizes that this was particularly true in Jamaica where the emergence of a peasantry was more significant.

18 The 1993–2000 Development Report of the Barbados Government (n.d.) states that the government has implemented a policy of equal pay for equal work in the public sector.

19 Bourque and Warren (1987) argue that the demand for higher levels of education for girls and young women by manufacturing industries is not an adequate indication of greater progress and opportunity for them. The fact that most of these jobs are low skilled and low paid relegates women, despite their increased education, to the bottom of the employment hierarchy.

20 Significantly, however, apart from the heavy male-migration years 1891–1921, Barbadian women's relative overrepresentation has never been expressed in their proportion of the employed labor force (Massiah 1986).

21 Patricia Zavella's work on Chicano cannery workers (1987) demonstrates a similar point made by Safa. Chicana women gained a degree of leverage in their homes when they became employed. However, while gendered ideologies about work changed within their households, and while women did benefit from more help, the fundamental divisions of labor did not change.

22 One weakness in Beckford's discussion of the sociocultural legacy of plantation society is that it presents no way of describing the complexities of ethnic and cultural life brought about by the particular histories of large East Indian communities of Guyana and Trinidad.

23 For example, television, transport and public works, a national bank, an insurance company, an agricultural development corporation, an agricultural marketing corporation, the port authority, and an equity interest in the telephone company—many of which have recently been or are now in the process of being privatized.

24 On occasion this could be an ad hoc response to a sudden problem, as when in 1975 the Barbados government assessed a special levy on sugar exports to cover the unexpected costs of energy imports during the oil crisis following the Yom Kippur war. The US$15 million thus raised went a long way toward stabilizing the country's foreign exchange position while steps to reduce energy consumption were implemented.

25 These proceeds from the 1940s and 1950s, pooled in what was called the price stabilization fund, were later tapped by government to fund the building of the largest public hospital, the deep-water harbor, and a labor college.

26 Ironically, considering the potency of the link between sugar and slavery, the Barbados government recently invested in an unsuccessful attempt at agricultural diversification by planting cotton rather than sugar.

27 Interestingly, this speech, delivered in 1967 at King George V Park, was made in the same year that sugar reached its all-time peak production level and income generation for the country.

28 The earliest International Business Company Act was passed in 1965 for those companies in operation "which do not derive income or profit from the sale of services to residents of Barbados."

29　See Worrel 1982 for further discussion, and in particular, Edsil Phillips's essay on the tourist industry.

30　CBERA (Caribbean Basin Economic Recovery Act) refers to the legislation creating CBI, and the two acronyms are often used interchangeably.

31　"Labor force," as a percentage of total adult population, includes both those working and those unemployed.

32　Many corporate managers described an initial sense of anxiety over sending their office work (often large volumes of paper documents) overseas. These feelings were particularly pronounced among those who had experimented with or considered Asian countries as possible locations for similar work, and found language and distance to be insurmountable obstacles (psychologically as much as practically). Short travel distance by plane and shared time zones for telephone and fax calls, therefore, were significant advantages particularly in the eyes of managers of East Coast U.S. companies.

33　In 1992 a travel advisory was posted by the U.S. government against Barbados in response to its escalating crime rate. The recent surge in crime has, according to an IDC spokesman, been a visible deterrent to foreign investment in this industry.

34　Two foreign-owned data entry operations in Barbados are rumored to simultaneously run such "sweatshops" in North America, where the nonunion operations are filled with highly vulnerable, and therefore easily exploited, immigrant labor. On the other hand, the Barbadian manager of Data Air remarked that a budget of over $US100,000 had been allocated for employee benefits, such as evening transportation, a staff Christmas party, participation in the IDC games, and that no such funds are spent for similar "perks" for employees of the same parent company based in the United States.

35　The only official minimum wage exists for domestic workers and shop assistants, who are paid a minimum rate of BDS$30 (US$15) per day.

36　According to the convention, "The payment of wages must be in legal tender and no conditions may be imposed in any contract that effectively influences the manner in which earned wages are to be spent." Additionally, no deductions in wages may be made to repay advances made to employees or for penalties imposed on them (IDC n.d.). Night work (between 6 P.M. and 7 A.M.) is prohibited for young people between the ages of fifteen and eighteen, and children under the age of fifteen are barred from working in any industrial setting. Night work for adults can only be required if permission is granted by the chief labor officer, and if provisions are made for meals, rest intervals, and adequate transportation. All workers are entitled to a paid holiday of three weeks a year after one year of employment (taken in one or two periods), and four weeks a year after the fifth year of employment. Maternity leave for a period of twelve weeks is also guaranteed after at least twelve months of employment, and the worker's job must be retained during this time. An employee is not entitled to receive maternity leave more than three times from any one employer. Finally, all employers (and employees) are required to support the Barbados

National Insurance and Social Security schemes, which cover worker compensation benefits for sickness, hospitalization, maternity, funeral expenses, old age pensions, survivor's benefits, and unemployment, as well as work-related illness or injury. Employers contribute 8.25 percent of the gross salary/wage of every employee and the employees contribute 9.75 percent in turn. Self-employed persons between the ages of sixteen and sixty-five are obligated to contribute to the National Insurance and Social Security scheme as well.

37 Typically these cosmopolitan scholars have been educated abroad and live and teach between the Caribbean, the United States, Canada, and Britain.

38 Warren and Bourque (1991) make a similar argument in comparing women's labor in multinational factories in a variety of locales, including Hong Kong and Mexico.

4 Myths of Docile Girls and Matriarchs

1 A popular style of wide skirtlike pants usually worn with a matching top or jacket.

2 Africa is a notable exception to this global characterization of sources of ideal women workers for multinational corporate investments.

3 Interestingly, low wages are not the fundamental attraction of Barbados for firms engaging in offshore informatics. Although relative wage differentials certainly contribute to the profits that can be made by moving there, other factors are even more central, such as the island's technological infrastructure, educated labor force, tax structure for offshore investment, political stability, and support of this industry. Indeed, Barbados has relatively high wages in relation to its Caribbean neighbors (and competitors in the industry) and is therefore aiming for the high end of informatics work over rudimentary and lower-skilled data entry.

4 Jean Pyle's excellent work (1990) on state policies and female employment in Ireland reveals the culturally and historically specific nature of women's incorporation into new export industries. In contrast to well-documented cases of Singapore, Malaysia, the Philippines, and Mexico, where women constitute the vast majority of offshore industrial labor forces, women's (and in particular, married women's) incorporation into the Irish wage economy has been severely curtailed by state legislation surrounding family and reproductive rights as well as high fertility rates and patriarchal household relations that militate against women's independent decision making.

5 This is an intriguing fact, given the well-entrenched pattern of gender segregation in traditional multinational factories in the Dominican Republic (e.g., garments, electronics, food processing). Managers and workers in the Dominican Data Air speculated that the draw of the computer technology along with increasing unemployment and underemployment rates accounted for the presence of young men in this special case of free zone work. They also asserted that a high proportion of these young men are students in technical or university programs who perceive these jobs as a temporary vehicle for getting experience with computers and earning money to help pay for school books and supplies. Additionally, the implementation of labor

laws protecting pregnant women, in the 1990s, may account for employers' preference for male workers in what had been considered feminine occupations.

6   There are recent indications of the gender profile of transnational workers shifting in other industries and other countries. In maquiladora industries on the Mexican border, where employers offer greater benefits to attract labor, more men have begun to be employed in traditionally female industries (Catanzarite and Strober 1993; Sklair 1993), and in Taiwan and South Korea, the governments are deliberately shifting the shape of export production toward higher technology, automation, heavier industries, and, thus, male workers (Ward and Pyle 1995:46).

7   Adonijah is addressing other calypsonians, here, who tend to objectify women in their songs, presenting them in sexual terms, as seductresses, and in generally unflattering ways.

8   Moses (1977) has asserted that gender ideologies learned by men and women in the Afro-Caribbean are both inherently contradictory and nearly impossible to fulfill. European ideals of male strength and providership and feminine domesticity and economic dependence create a recipe that condemns most men to failure through limited economic opportunity and leaves girls only somewhat better prepared for the lives that await them. Interestingly, she argues that girls, taught to be submissive to men, but managers of the domestic arena and the source of emotional support for the family, are able to achieve some of the goals set by the ideals of "proper" femininity—parenting and resourceful homemaking. As such, they experience less "gender failure" than men, and put their so-called feminine skills to productive use. Girls, "because they have more achievable goals, are actually better equipped to survive" (Senior 1991:41).

9   As Skeggs argues, this legacy is profound for poor English women as well and points to the centrality of class in the yardstick of feminine domesticity.

10 Certainly for Trinidad and Guyana in particular, and other islands as well, India represents a significant cultural source from which notions of West Indian-ness are derived. For the Barbadian case, however, the cultural polarities are drawn exclusively to Europe (Britain) and Africa, and perhaps for this reason, these dualisms have been particularly resilient as both "emic" and "etic" modes of description and explanation.

11 There is a certain irony in the extent to which this has become such a central paradigm for Caribbean studies. When Wilson (1969:70) first articulated his thesis, he said, "It is not my aim . . . to attempt weighty conclusions and profound insights. I wish merely to call attention to certain neglected possibilities that might lead to further research and increase our understanding of Caribbean social organization." One can scarcely encounter a discussion about gender in the Caribbean without reference to Wilson's dualism.

12 There are several problems with Wilson's elaboration of these values as constitutive of Caribbean life. He fails to address any external elements, political or other institutional structures that contribute to the shaping of social realities, and he overstates

the purely feminine nature of "respectability." See Besson 1993; Miller 1994; Moses 1977; Pyde 1990; Sutton 1974; Yelvington 1995 for various critiques, commentary, and reformulations of Wilson's respectability and reputation paradigm.

13   This formulation resonates with the *casa/calle* dualism of gendered space in Spanish and Mediterranean culture.

14   Critiques by both Sutton (1974) and Besson (1993) demonstrate many ways in which Caribbean women, too, engage in acts of reputation, and they challenge the portrayal of women as uncritical imitators and disproportionate beneficiaries of colonial culture. In contrast, Besson (1993:19) says, the "male value system of reputation which Wilson advances as a model for development, is partially based on unequal and exploitative gender relations." The very idea of Caribbean/African American creolization, wonderfully and succinctly explored by Mintz and Price (1992), would in and of itself challenge the stark division between European- and African-derived value systems as they are somewhat crudely expressed in Wilson's original model.

15   Christine Barrow clarifies the notions of independence and autonomy for Afro-Caribbean women by saying that while the tenuous nature of employment for most men and women means that they frequently have to rely upon economic support from others, most women establish strong networks of kin and friends with whom they engage in relationships of reciprocity. This implies that while they cannot claim "independence" in the strict sense of the term, they nonetheless maintain autonomy by "being able to choose from several options, making decisions freely for oneself and having control over one's life, to the extent of being able to refuse support and the strings attached" (Barrow 1986a:8).

16   In a recent article about gender ideologies in contemporary romance novels produced for Caribbean audiences, Jane Bryce (1998:323) emphasizes, as well, the fact that it is the tension rather than resolution between ideal/real gender that is most "real" in the Caribbean.

17   Miller (1994) uses the formulation of "transience" and "transcendence" for Wilson's reputation and respectability and similarly emphasizes the relational ways in which these define cultural practices along the lines of gender, ethnicity, and class in Trinidad.

18   The coexistence of an illusory sense of a past in which women are seen to have complied with certain feminine ideals and an experience of the present in which women's defiance of these norms poses a problem for the "natural" order of things are themes that emerged in many popular forums during this fieldwork. A public forum was held entitled "Are Caribbean Males in Crisis?" in which much of the discussion focused on "dealing" with the "changes" brought about by women's increasing independence, "latchkey children," and the "decline of the extended family."

19   Interestingly, in these invocations of the strong matriarch image, the emphasis is on strength as it is tied to responsibility rather than power. One might argue that a matriarch derives power in part through the labor over which she controls, for example, her children. It is possible that this dimension of the figure of the "matriarch" is

less well developed in the context of informatics largely because these women are, with few exceptions, mothers of still very young children.

20 Again, this is also the prevailing ideology of femininity within multinational industries across the globe. Interestingly, Olwig (1993b:163) describes that for Nevisian women who migrate to Britain, ironically, it is only by leaving home (migrating) that they are able to fulfill the ideals of femininity and domesticity prescribed by respectability, such as a nuclear family or a "proper home."

21 As Safa (1990:94), Stolke (1984:286), and others have pointed out, the portrayal of the family as the primary locus of female domination and inequality becomes particularly problematic in the Caribbean context, where the family may as well be viewed as a locus of support, nurturance, and primary identification even for women who also work for wages. For example, Safa (1990:94) found that women workers in the Dominican Republic and Puerto Rico considered their paid employment as part of their domestic identity since they saw their work as contributing to the survival of their families as opposed to their own autonomy or self-esteem. Family, for Caribbean women, then, must be viewed both as a significant locus of social identity and a potential site of patriarchal subordination. What is sometimes overlooked in all of this discussion is the fact that while wages from work may be vital to the survival of a woman's household (whether or not she is head of the household), women work for reasons other than just to support their families.

22 Seven ordinary, or O-level certificates and two advanced, or A-level certificates is an impressive academic achievement and would probably satisfy the minimum requirements for attending university.

23 Peña (1987:132) also notes this observation and practice on the part of managers in maquiladoras in Mexico.

24 As noted earlier, there has been a historical trend of wage differentials between typically male and typically female arenas of work in Barbados. For example, between jobs of comparable skill, a machine attendant and a "light" industry assembly operator, the former performed by men receives a median wage of US$119 a week and the latter, by women, US$75 a week.

25 Continuing along these lines, one manager said he had heard (and counted on the fact) that Barbadian women would make good workers because they bear the bulk of responsibility for their children alone, and therefore must be responsible to their employees. However, he argued instead that the matriarchal and extended family seems to provide young people with a guaranteed safety net, thereby obviating precisely the autonomy and sense of responsibility he had hoped to find. Free Trade Zone employers in the Dominican Republic are cited as similarly expressing shifting ideas about ideal labor recruitment. Safa notes (1995:105) for example, that some prefer women with children because of their greater job commitment (dependency) while others engage in a wide variety of measures to circumvent the burden of maternity leave, ranging from distributing birth control pills free of charge to requiring pregnancy tests or requiring a sterilization certificate before a worker is hired.

26 The argument that women far outnumber men in Barbados has at some moments in history had greater truth than at others and depends on labor migration trends as noted in chapter 3.

27 In fact, it is commonly believed that the threat of unemployed women poses a greater social problem than the threat of unemployed men. One point of view often expressed in the popular press holds that unemployed women are somehow more dangerous to society than unemployed men. According to Victoria Durant-Gonzalez (1982:4), whereas unemployed men are known to "lime" or "hang out" at rum shops and on the streets, women are believed to be more likely to turn to prostitution and destroy the moral fabric of the society. On the other hand, employed women tend to make greater economic contributions to the support of their children and families, whereas men are more likely to "spend their income among more than one household and in the rum shops" (4). For this reason, and contradicting the former argument, one frequently hears that women's employment not only preserves the moral fabric of society but also insures that wages are "better" (or more altruistically) spent.

28 Massiah (1984b:102) notes that, of the 42.9 percent of households headed by women in Barbados, the median age for female heads is 54.9, well above the age bracket of the data entry operators described here.

29 Interestingly, in Kelly's survey (1987) of female electronics workers in St. Lucia, 70 percent were mothers. The lower figure in my sample may reflect a combination of shifting recruitment and retention policies, as well as Barbados's well-entrenched and highly successful family planning program.

30 As noted earlier, the argument about a disproportional number of women was used frequently by Barbadian men to account for their "need to have more than one woman at a time."

31 Brackette Williams (1991:55) grounds the desire on the part of young men to work in contexts that allow them physical freedom and the capacity to socialize in the history of nineteenth-century plantation life in Guyana. As she puts it, the emphasis on independence among Afro-Guyanese men is one in which "controlling the amount of time one must spend working rather than socializing and, when working, the constraints imposed by job-related obligations and regulations" is central (64). The distinction between "making a living" and "making life" emphasizes the necessary balance between individual industry and one's embeddedness in social activity and exchange.

32 The "others" include fathers (18 percent), husbands or boyfriends (18 percent), mothers (8 percent), and siblings (9 percent). These figures correspond closely with those of Massiah (1989:216) describing the results of the 1986 Women in the Caribbean Project (WICP) research. She emphasizes that women's union status, and the economic activity of their partners is significant in this regard, implying that those with an employed partner were most likely to describe their partner's contribution as primary to the household economy. While Euro-centered traditions of male

household headship and authority are more closely adhered to among Barbadian black and white middle and upper classes, this pattern is also idealized among working-class women and men, even if not part of their actual experience. Senior (1991) notes that women cohabiting with a male partner (husband or boyfriend) are likely to refer to him as household head, regardless of his economic contribution or participation in the household.

33 Interestingly, the confusion or contradictory notions about women heading their own households is not confined to corporate managers with capitalist agendas at stake. In a recent newspaper article, the director of the Barbados Bureau of Women's Affairs was quoted as saying that women who head households are "often more successful than married women who are under strict control of their husbands." She added that "men who control their homes might be retarding women's progress." Her argument was vigorously contested by a prominent Barbadian woman who is a member of the UN panel monitoring the status of women internationally. This university law lecturer argued that there is no empirical evidence to support the claim (Best 1992). Once again, it should be noted that female-headed households continue to be among the poorest in the nation, and that the women's bureau director's admitted choice to head her own family may give her freedom and flexibility but must be understood in the context of her particular class base.

34 This is not so for the sister plant of Data Air in Santo Domingo. There, workers tend to stay with their jobs for two years on average, and the general manager of this plant cited two years as the optimum life span for a data operator. She remarked that productivity levels begin to decline after the second year of employment. Safa (1990:78–79) notes that attrition rates are high in multinational factories in general in the Dominican Republic because of labor practices that include rapid hiring and firing, as well as other factors related to the labor force recruited. While young women express a desire to resume employment after marriage or motherhood young single women work a few years until they marry or have a child. By contrast, in Safa's study of Puerto Rico (1990), higher job stability, denoted by long-term employees of twenty to thirty years of experience, is attributed to higher rates of unionization across the export sector.

35 I use the term *generations* largely because several women workers and managers employed this formulation for describing these two categories of workers. There is not a clear demarcation for how long it takes a worker to move from one generation to the other, since life events play a significant role in the transformation. A young woman only two years out of secondary school may be as likely to adopt the ethics of the "old guard" when she gives birth to her first child as an "older" woman working at Data Air or Multitext for five years but living at home with her parents and able to spend her time off and her wages more freely.

36 This view of women workers, whose "supplemental" wage goes toward the frivolous whims of feminine desire, seems to have long historical roots. Fernandez-Kelly and Sassen (1995:115) quote a 1909 textbook of economics that echoes this view exactly:

"A man in industry requires a wage sufficient to maintain himself and his family, whereas many women living at home, with little or nothing to do, are willing to go into industry in order to secure spending money or enough money to guarantee the little necessities and luxuries of life that a young woman naturally desires."

37 Studies of women workers in multinational factories elsewhere frequently echo this preference for young girls without prior work experience on the basis that they are less likely to have been exposed to trade unions and thus likely to be less politicized (Fernandez-Kelly 1983:220; Tiano 1987:84).

38 Motherhood, too, would enter this formula and imply that only in conjunction with a woman's socialization into the corporate culture and workplace discipline do these factors imply an advantageous workforce.

39 Susan Joekes is cited in Safa (1990:78) as noting that employers in export manufacturing in the Dominican Republic have also been known to express a preference for women with children, whose economic necessity ensured greater job commitment, though it is not made clear whether this reflected an inclination to retain women after they became mothers, or a deliberate shift in hiring practices. Safa (1995) has also observed that garment workers in Puerto Rico have contradicted the model of the global assembly line by tending to be married with children, and increasingly to be heads of households, as well. Linda Lim (1985:59) mentions this notion that multinational industries themselves exhibit "life cycles" and argues that the longer they have been established in a country, the more likely it is that they will harmonize with local political and economic interests (e.g., unionization, higher wages, a higher degree of capital intensive production) and exhibit lower attrition rates.

40 The fact that women are found to defy the pattern of corporate hiring and firing on short-term bases and to keep their jobs over longer time spans is now being noted in several other parts of the world. This occurred first in less competitive industries such as garments and textiles (Fernandez-Kelly 1983). In a later discussion of the electronics industry in Asia, Vivian Lin asserts that contrary to earlier reports, it seems that more women in both Singapore and Malaysia are staying in the electronics industry after marriage, and even after childbirth (Lin 1987:118–19). Their feelings about this increased longevity differ, however, in ways that reflect different cultural expectations surrounding womanhood and femininity at the current moment. Malaysian women say that if not for economic necessity, they would prefer to stay home, but the Singaporeans, more fully enmeshed in a capitalist self-vision, see themselves as integrally tied to the labor force. Like Safa, Lin notes that women's role within their families has changed through their employment, and asserts that their ability to negotiate and bargain for certain privileges otherwise restricted by patriarchal conventions increased when they became wage earners. For the Malaysians, this meant being an independent consumer, "being able to buy anything I want," whereas for Singporean workers, choosing their own marriage partners and providing advice on family finances were expressed as the major advances (Lin 1987:127).

41   Several historical factors introduced in chapter 3 have constituted the predominance of matrifocal households in the Caribbean (e.g., the fact that during slavery, a woman's children became the property of her slave master, giving greater "legitimacy to the centrality of the mother's role, a notion that was firmly entrenched in the kin systems of the West African tribes transported to the New World" (Massiah 1982:62). Several factors associated with contemporary economic development policies implemented in the region have as well been correlated with rising numbers of female-headed households. Much has been written about the structural marginality of the Afro-West Indian male (Rodman 1971; Mathurin 1977; Errol Miller 1986), and the relative social and economic independence of the Afro-West Indian female (Barrow 1986a). Without advancing a more detailed analysis of these historical themes here, it is worth noting their persistence in ongoing debates about matrifocality and male marginality (Besson 1998) as they continue to be resurrected in attempts to explain the varied shape of household forms in Barbados in general and these different profiles of feminine workers in particular.

42   Her ideal contrasts with the average family size of 5.4 cited for Barbados by the WICP survey in 1986. Olivia Harris (1981) notes that in many social and historical contexts, despite what are often powerful domestic ideologies, few units in practice actually conform to the "ideal."

43   There is a great deal of speculation as to why this "breakdown" may be occurring—from women's continuation of work (formal and/or informal) such that they are less available to care for grandchildren and other kin; the suburbanization process in which families are increasingly living further apart from their natal kin; the influence of foreign media and its cultural valuation of female independence and de-emphasis on the extended family. Apart from these conjectures, however, there is little concrete data to fully document and explain how these changes are taking place. This is clearly an important set of questions that need to be empirically studied.

44   Wage work, furthermore, is integral to women's identities in ways that go beyond economic survival, as I show in more detail in chapters 5 and 6.

45   Multinational factories routinely terminate their workers after designated periods of service to avoid paying seniority and other benefits that may be required by the host government. Aihwa Ong (1987:148) says that in Malaysia, for example, workers with less than three years of employment are prohibited from participating in unions, and pregnancy is cited in world market factories in general as a frequent cause for dismissal. Ill health as well as the precarious nature of market forces are also causes of women's short-term employment in export processing industries. Women are literally "used up" after excessive overtime and closely focused microscope work in environments frequently polluted with toxic fumes and dust and working conditions that lead to exhaustion and chronic fatigue (Elson and Pearson 1981a).

46   Susan Tiano (1990) discusses the dual nature of Mexican maquila women's work as "por gusto" (for personal satisfaction) and "por necesidad" (for economic need) (201)

and demonstrates the contradictions between ideology and practice when women, on one hand, echo the traditional gender expectations by saying that "women generally should not work outside the home" and, on the other, intend themselves to remain in the labor force even if their wage is not "needed" to support the household (220).

47 Leslie Sklair (1993:172), too, offers a similar argument about the role of gender in configuring idealized global workers: "In the last resort it does not matter to capital whether it is employing men or women—capital is not sexist (nor racist, for that matter), though it does use sexism (and racism) to suit its purposes, which are the production of profits and the accumulation of private wealth."

5   Inside Multitext and Data Air

1 Significantly, the telephone rates for high-speed data transmission have been a contentious issue within this industry widely, and pressure on Cable and Wireless to reduce its rates has become a political issue.

2 This $11 million annual amount refers to the total expenditure of the Data Air operation in Barbados—largely employee salaries and operating expenses including telecommunications and utilities. To give some indication of the significance of this one company's contribution to the Barbadian economy, in the same year, sugar earned BDS$50 million (US$25 million) in foreign exchange.

3 Circulation of the two daily newspapers together total between sixty thousand and seventy thousand copies. Considering the fact that newspapers are regularly shared among several people, one could safely estimate that over 60 percent of the adult population read newspapers daily.

4 This response rate is not unique to the data entry industry. When a new shopping mall opened in late 1989, over five hundred people (a majority of whom were women) lined up in the hot sun to apply for seventy-five jobs (*Barbados Advocate* October 12, 1989).

5 Following the British educational system, O-level certificates are subject areas in which students have passed standardized tests at the secondary school level.

6 Following Millicent's success, three other deaf students from the Barbados School for the Deaf and Blind were trained and given jobs at Multitext.

7 I do not have data on whether this trajectory is, in fact, realized. However, even the expressed expectation that such job mobility and advancement is possible was more prevalent among the Dominican workers than among their Barbadian counterparts.

8 Again, this strategy relates to the widespread concern about poaching of trained workers across the industry.

9 Interestingly, unlike supervisors who feel some resentment about the fact that high-incentive earners on the production floor can make more money than they do, those in mark-up feel themselves to be a step above data processors in the work they perform, and they express relief at making a set and predictable salary.

10 Another advantage of mark-up is that it is performed only on the morning shift, and so its workers never have to juggle their schedules to accommodate night work.

11 An exception is newspaper journalists, professional white-collar workers who work under tight deadlines and have experienced similarly high levels of repetitive stress injuries and VDT-related illnesses.

12 In fact, an organization based in Philadelphia has made its sole focus the evaluation of workplaces for the incidence or likelihood of carpal tunnel syndrome. The rationale and popularity of their services is clearly a preventative measure against expensive law suits for work related illness.

13 Total quality management refers to an increasingly popular approach to management that emphasizes quality as the basis for higher levels of productivity and competitiveness. The concept is credited to W. Edwards Deming, who introduced the quality revolution in Japan's automotive industry in the 1950s, and who long criticized top management of U.S. industry as responsible for sluggishness and uncompetitiveness. In the 1980s businesses in the United States began to embrace Deming's model of total quality and seminars and consulting agencies specializing in TQM now abound internationally (Garvin and March 1986).

14 Sexual harassment is noted by Peña as a fundamental aspect of control on production floors in the Mexican maquiladoras (in Ruiz and Tiano 1987:141). Yelvington, writing about a locally owned small appliance factory in Trinidad also discusses the prevalence of "flirtation" and sexual harassment on the shop floor, as well as women's creative "interventions" and resistance of these forces (1995:190).

15 Micaela di Leonardo's essay "The Female World of Cards and Holidays" (1987) makes explicit the gendered dimensions of what she calls the "work of kinship" and the need to integrate rather than oppose our analyses of labor with those of kinship and the domestic arena. I am grateful to Amy Lang for emphasizing the symbolic potency of Data Air's naming these productivity incentive vouchers "thank-you cards."

16 Kadooment is part of an annual festival known as Cropover that is celebrated in Barbados in August. Although a celebration to end the sugar crop is noted in colonial texts as early as the eighteenth century, the contemporary Cropover celebration is an invention of the tourism industry and was initiated as an attempt to bolster the slow summer months of tourism. Interestingly, this has become an important festival not only for local Barbadians and tourists but also for "gone away Bajans," or those who have migrated to North America or Britain. The latter groups take advantage of reasonable summer airfares and flock "home" in large numbers to participate in this annual national festival.

17 Grenier 1988 provides an excellent critique of the use of such participatory management tactics in American industry.

18 As a form of struggle over gender ideologies, both Lamphere (1985) and Hossfeld (1990) have argued that these tactics can pose powerful implications, such as mini-

mizing differences between workers along the lines of race and ethnicity and therefore ultimately creating greater possibilities for organized class struggle. Writing about factory regimes in China and the construction of "maiden workers," Chin Kwan Lee (1997:124–26) explores the contested meanings workers and managers invested in this concept. For managers, an emphasis on young women's "single status, immaturity, imminent marriage, short-term commitment to factory work in Shenzhen, low job aspirations, and low motivation to learn skills" forged a pact between kin and management control over factory discipline and the retention of women in the low-ranked positions. The women, in turn, subscribed to the notion of "maiden worker" to other ends. For them, withstanding the discipline of the factory embedded in their "maiden" identity allowed them, as well, to enjoy the freedom derived from income earning and the possibility of romantic relationships, mate choice, and opportunities to transcend factory employment by learning other skills in their free time (typing, computers, English). See also Lisa Rofel's (1992) discussion of women workers' self-conscious use of portrayals of themselves as "slow" and "dullwitted" country bumpkins to subvert a gendered regime of discipline that restricted their movements within a Chinese silk factory.

19 Both venues are popular among tourists and locals alike, for the food, entertainment, and dancing.

20 In 1995, however, under a new government, there were some attempts by the BWU to unionize the workers in the informatics industry, following particular incidents such as the closure of one operation and attempt to rehire operators at lower rates of pay (*Barbados Advocate*, August 14, 1995). As yet, however, there has been no successful mobilization of the informatics workers into the union.

21 This criticism of the unions referred to what many believed to be a mishandling of a sugar factory workers' strike held shortly before my final round of interviews. The BWU, historically very strong, and long and actively representing agricultural workers, halted the sugar crop by shutting down the factories at a time when the sugar industry was facing impending decline. Their insistence on pay increases for the factory workers came also at a time when all government workers had just been forced to accept an 8 percent wage cut and was not supported vigorously even by the sugar workers themselves. Two of the three BWU leaders who demanded wage hikes for the sugar factory workers also voted for the mandatory cut in civil servants' pay.

22 One of the BWU leaders who had served as a member of Parliament for the DLP government later called for the administration of the Barbados Labour Party, in power at the time, to intervene in efforts to unionize two of the offshore companies (*Barbados Advocate*, October 14, 1997).

23 In the early days of Data Air, the company hired many of the former employees of the INTEL plant that had recently left the island. These women, according to the general manager, had been employed for a couple of years and had often pursued various continuing education courses after they lost their jobs. "They had greater skills and more maturity," he said. Again, here the general manager articulates the

"mature matriarch" model for the ideal informatics worker, despite the fact that the company continued to recruit the "international profile" of the younger school leaver, who by virtue of age alone was more likely to be a first-time wageworker.

24   See Foucault 1975 and Ong's (1987) use of Foucault.

25   This sort of monitoring is widespread across the data processing industry and has been the focus of great concern by clerical labor activists in North America. In Barbados most operations either use this system or employ a paper version, keeping track of productivity until they get the electronic monitoring in place. One manager made a point of saying that with the manual version, on paper, operators were able to "fudge" their productivity, and he was anxious for the computer system to be put in place as soon as possible.

26   See du Gay et al. 1997 for a fascinating study of the Sony Walkman from the unusual perspectives of both production and consumption.

27   Senior quotes a Caribbean psychiatrist who speculates a connection between this notion of Afro-Caribbean women as moral authority and their maligned/resented status by men: "The traumatic socialization practices, the absent father . . . and the dual image of the mother (as satisfier and as depriver) constitute a situation which could call forth from males in such a confrontation only responses like hostility, withdrawal, status envy, rejection and schizophrenic fear of the female" (1992:180). She goes on to say that women's economic vulnerability also fosters this dual sense— that they are providers but also deprivers because of their own sense of independence/dependence.

28   Unlike the offshore industries in some other countries, where multinationals are known to blatantly discriminate against married women applicants and mothers (Fernandez-Kelly 1983; Ong 1987), the operations in Barbados know that motherhood, if not marriage, is a basic reality for many women of the age bracket they recruit, and they must make some, even if minimal, concessions to their familial roles. As noted in chapter 4, both Data Air and Multitext secure workers' jobs when they take maternity leave and have found that with few exceptions, women come back to work after the birth of a child.

29   Interestingly, Yelvington (1995:190) notes that this formulation of "company as family" so common elsewhere in industrial settings is absent in the Trinidadian factory he studied.

30   Yelvington similarly describes such practices as turning "necessity" into "virtue," or of women "using the very cultural forms that ensure their subordination in order to resist" (1995:190).

31   See also di Leonardo (1985), Lamphere (1985), Costello (1985), and Zavella (1985) for excellent examples of the coexistence of resistance and compliance in women's work culture.

32   Karen Hossfeld's conclusion (1990) is similar, in the sense that the tactics by which women workers in Silicon Valley "use the logic" of sexism and racism against their employers to gain small compensations in the course of the workday are ultimately

measured against the larger aims of collective action. She does emphasize, however, that while the instances she describes are not enough in themselves to subvert the mechanisms of inequality between workers and their bosses, "they do demonstrate to managers that gender logic cannot always be counted on to legitimate inequality between male and female workers. *And dissolving divisions between workers is a threat to management hegemony*" (173; italics mine).

33　The effects of such instances are double edged: they create a welcome respite in the midst of the working day, but they reduce the amount of potential incentive pay operators might earn by being "on the system."

6　Fashioning Femininity and "Professional" Identities

1　Prasad and Prasad (1994) describe the "ideology of professionalism" as a powerful strategy through which the computerization of a health maintenance organization was facilitated and a "climate of acceptance" was achieved. Casey (1996) notes the power and contradictory nature of the notion of "professionalism" among clerical workers in Puerto Rico as well. Indeed, the ambiguity of clerical work as white-/pink-collar labor and its close proximity (though structural subservience) to professional work (particularly for the personal secretary) invites this tension. The "industrial" label associated formally with informatics, however, highlights the particular irony and potency of this "professionalism" concept.

2　An interesting example of a similar emphasis on appearance despite the invisibility of the actor to her or his audience/customer is expressed by David Brinkley in his memoir (1995). He says that in the 1960s, in the early days of his career at NBC, the network required its radio announcers to wear tuxedos. Despite their obvious invisibility, they believed this gave announcers an air of respectability.

3　I am inclined to agree with Paules's somewhat cynical remark that "often the truth or falseness of a people's consciousness is determined by the degree to which it coincides with the ideology of the observer. Apparent contentment with conditions the observer defines as exploitative is a sure sign that one suffers from false consciousness, while revolt against these conditions reflects enlightenment or 'true' consciousness" (1991:186). The clear degree to which the informatics workers are simultaneously critical of dimensions of their employment and certain about its pleasures leads me to reject the idea that their pleasure in "professional" appearance is reducible to their "false" or misguided consciousness.

4　This observation echoes Simmel's (1950:344) discussion of adornment (which is translated from the original as "jewels" or "jewelry").

5　Interestingly, self-fashioning and requests for a uniform by the informatics workers is not unique to Barbados. The workers in Multitext's Dominica operation were the first to introduce uniforms in this company and the concern about appearance and the desire for uniforms has been noted elsewhere in the region as well.

6　Pamela Franco's (1998) historical discussion, titled "Dressing up and Looking Good," about female maskers in Trinidadian Carnival describes the carnival cos-

tume of the "Bajan Cook," which by 1911 was a well-established and popular masquerade costume. An ironic twist on the realities of a domestic's occupational routine, the "Bajan Cook" costume consisted of a "pristine white dress . . . made of sheer
material like organza or organdy. A white head tie, white shoes and stockings" (66).
In the early twentieth century, she notes, domestic occupations such as cook, laun-
dress, and butler provided opportunities for "Afro-Creole women to gain a measure
of financial independence . . . [and] allowed them to *create a feeling of identity that was
in direct opposition to the less sophisticated female agricultural workers*" (66; italics
mine). Here again, we see the use of dress as a mark of distinction between one
group of women workers and another.

7 Often underlying these criticisms is the allusion to sexual impropriety and the assumption that material goods are being exchanged for sex. As Leo-Rhynie recently
notes, "Sex is . . . increasingly seen as a commodity to be exchanged for a variety of
material goods. . . . Much of this consumerism, . . . as well as the payment of school
fees, purchase of school books and educational supplies, is supported by 'payment
in kind' for sexual favours" (1998:250).

8 Mary Douglass (1997:30) argues, along these lines, that "the shopper is not expect-
ing to develop a personal identity by choice of commodities; that would be too difficult. Shopping is agonistic, a struggle to define not what one is, but what one is not."

9 Miller's (1994) dualism transience/transcendence is his reworking of Wilson's original reputation/respectability paradigm. For Miller, the former is best illustrated by
Trinidadian carnival, in all of its "live for the moment" excesses, display, and innovation. The latter, transcendence, refers to cultural practices and values that reflect
tradition, continuity, and many of the constituents of respectability, such as proper
decorum and morality. These are, for Miller, best demonstrated in the rituals associated with Trinidadian's celebration of Christmas, much of which revolves around
continuity and repetition of traditions and takes place in the interior realm of the
domestic sphere.

10 Miller (1994) continues his discussion about style and competition by arguing that
"to the extent that women lack an institutional equivalent to liming in which they
subsume their individuality, this may account for the evidence that it is they rather
than men who take the project of transience to its greatest extreme." The kinds of
small and intimate social groups formed in the informatics sector among women co-
workers, however, would seem to defy this description and indeed resemble more
closely the "crews" and liming groups that both Wilson and Miller describe as the
focal point of male engagement in reputation. The small groups of informatics
workers who as friends and co-workers take shopping trips abroad, or travel for one
another to buy clothes and other consumer goods, are engaged in precisely the kind
of "liming institution" he argues women lack. "Women" he says, "are associated
with an environment of more unremitting competition and friendships which while
briefly intense have a sense of fragility based around the prospect of a cuss-out or
equally intense disagreement" (1994:229).

11 For Bourdieu (1984), *habitus* denotes the unconscious understandings, dispositions, classificatory systems, and preferences that inform an individual's everyday
knowledge and experience. These, in turn, differ between social classes and express
themselves in the form of distinct tastes and habits or lifestyles.

12 Writing about class mobility in Barbados, Beckles (1990:207) points out that the
"expansion of white controlled and owned local corporate sector . . . and growth of
foreign multinational companies in tourism, manufacturing, banking and finance,
stimulated the development of a black professional middle class which constitutes
perhaps the most noticeable social feature of the post-independence era." He adds
that this led to the "cult of professional elitism" and then began to bridge the gulf
between black and white classes. Education was the driving force behind expanding class mobility and, as evidenced by the vast majority of the state and professional elite who have come from working or lower middle classes, "working class
families were able to produce individuals who could be found within all social
groups."

13 Similar discussions about the relationship between gender and class and, in particular, arguments that women exhibit a tendency to use more "prestige" linguistic
forms than men from similar social backgrounds have emerged in linguistic analyses (see Labov 1966, 1972; for a discussion of the literature more generally, see
Graddol and Swan 1989).

14 E. O. Wright's *Class Counts* begins to explore this two-way relationship (1997) and
hints at an area of research that would greatly benefit from closer ethnographically
detailed study.

15 Interestingly, Sobo (1993:192) argues that women who are higglers are "more directly in control of their lives and often richer than housewives," yet they are less
"respected" because of their engagement in "noisy debates," their agility in negotiating verbal abuse in the marketplace, and their general contact with "lower class
people."

16 Pudding and souse is a traditional Bajan dish. The pudding is a dark sausage in
which pig intestine is stuffed with seasoned sweet potato and the souse is pig's head,
feet, and flesh cooked and pickled with lime juice and spices. Traditional black cake
is a fruit cake soaked in rum and served at Christmastime and on other special
occasions.

17 First used by British anthropologist Keith Hart (1973) to describe the diverse activities of poor city dwellers in Ghana, the notion of the "informal sector" has been
debated as a concept and used to encompass a wide variety of income-earning activities outside of but clearly and integrally related to the "formal" economy. I use the
term "informal sector" to describe those small-scale production and service activities that generate income outside contractual and legally regulated employment.
(See Portes and Walton 1981 for an early explication of the concept; Peattie 1987 for a
discussion of its varied uses; and Portes and Schauffler 1993 for a useful review of its
application in the Latin American context.)

18 Ward (1990) uses this notion of the "triple shift" to refer to women's involvement in formal, informal, and household work and to expand the now familiar concept of the "double day."

19 Between 1891 and 1921 female labor force participation represented 61 percent, and, as Massiah (1986) notes, was concentrated in these three areas.

20 Official regional unemployment figures during the years of this fieldwork (1989–92) ranged between 15 and 25 percent and were surpassed by rates of underemployment.

21 Illustrating the ambivalence felt by the state and private sectors toward the informal economy has been a battle in the tourism sector surrounding the ubiquitous beach vendors who ply hotel strips for trade. Jet ski operators, hair braiders, and salesmen with briefcases of "native" (often Taiwanese) jewelry and bottled aloes and coconut oil are now being encouraged by hoteliers concerned with increased reports of beach harassment to join an organized beach vender association and display aprons or badges to identify them as legitimate. By organizing them in this fashion, it has been the hope of government to "formalize" the vendors in the sense of accounting for their imports and income, in addition to weeding out the few whose aggressive or illicit behavior has played a part in periods of decline in the tourism industry.

22 I am drawing on the feminist argument made by Michele Barrett that ideology is not simply the reflection or expression of "economic contradictions at the mental level" (1988:85).

23 Bolles (1983) describes an expansion of women's informal strategies and exchanges in the face of job losses from export manufacturing industries and general economic decline in Jamaica in the 1980s.

24 As noted in chapter 4, the increased reliance on child care by paid baby-sitters or day care centers demonstrates this shift toward services paid in cash.

25 Grantley, the nineteen-year-old prep worker mentioned in chapter 4, is also engaged in both formal sector work as an employee of Data Air and informal sector work for his self-employed grandfather. His grandmother is a seamstress and his grandfather a small farmer who grows vegetables, keeps fifteen cows, and, according to Grantley, "produces the largest amount of christophene in the island. He sells to super-markets and other vegetables he buys and retails them again." "To tell the truth, my grandfather feel that if I stay at home and work closer with him, we could make more money [than what he earns at Data Air], but for myself, I know it's true [. . .] but I like to get out and mix with other people, work with other people. As such, Grantley tries to juggle his shifts at Data Air and helping his grandfather in his off hours. His decision to keep his Data Air job reflects his desire for some of the forms of cultural capital enjoyed by the women workers in informatics, and, like them, he is able to enhance his formal wages with income derived from informal sector work.

26 The destinations are, in large part, determined by the nature of the "thank-you cards" themselves. A trip to Puerto Rico, for example, can be earned with two "thank-you cards" and New York and Canada require three.

27 Joan French (1989:35) describes the importance of travel among Guyanese higglers,

even when their profits from their trade were small. "It was a way to get out of the home. The level of 'homification' in Guyana, I think, is at a higher level than it is here [Jamaica] and these women just loved to get out and loved to be out there and liked the whole excitement and adventure of the trips. Making money was important but really if they didn't make any this trip, too bad. Next trip you would try and make up for it, because it was nice to be out there." Describing a Guyanese woman traveling to Haiti, she remarked, "Not only was she a good business expert but she was really enjoying being a business expert, and enjoying the fact that she had been to all these places and could tell you about the different cultures and had had a lot of exposure."

28 A "meeting," "meeting turn," or "sou sou" is a widespread practice in the Caribbean and Africa and refers to informal savings clubs through which women (predominantly) make weekly or biweekly contributions to a common pool, and on a rotating basis each individual claims the total amount. Meeting turns have long been used as an alternative to traditional credit and lending institutions. These Barbadian women typically contribute US$5 or US$10 a week, for a return of US$50 or US$100 at the end of the four-week cycle.

Epilogue

1 Scientific and technical publications requiring complex typesetting formulae have become a special niche for Multitext in Barbados. One of their chief competitors for this work is located in the Scottish Western Isles (Bibby 1997:3).

2 The employment of recent Indian immigrants in the southeastern United States at lower salaries than typically demanded in northern metropolitan areas is also a growing phenomenon. So too is the emergence of "virtual immigration" or "global telecommuting" where the programmers stay at home and export their programs electronically (Allen R. Myerson, *New York Times*, January 18, 1998, Week in Review, 4).

Bibliography

Abraham-Van der Mark, Eva. 1983. "The Impact of Industrialization on Women: A Caribbean Case." In June Nash and Maria Patricia Fernandez-Kelly, eds., *Women, Men, and the International Division of Labor.* Albany: State University of New York Press.

Abrahams, Roger D. 1979. "Reputation vs. Respectability: A Review of Peter J. Wilson's Concept." *Revista/Review Interamericana* 9, no. 3:374–53.

Abu-Lughod, Lila. 1990. "The Romance of Resistance: Tracing Transformations of Power through Bedouin Women." *American Ethnologist* 17, no. 1:41–55.

——. 1993. "Finding a Place for Islam: Egyptian Television Serials and the National Interest." *Public Culture* 5, no. 3:493–513.

——. 1995. "The Objects of Soap Opera: Egyptian Television and the Cultural Politics of Modernity." In Daniel Miller, ed., *Worlds Apart: Modernity Through the Prism of the Local.* London: Routledge.

Acevedo, Luz del Alba. 1995. "Feminist Inroads in the Study of Women's Work and Development." In Christine E. Bose and Edna Acosta-Belen, eds., *Women in the Latin American Development Process.* Philadelphia: Temple University Press.

Acker, Joan. 1990. "Hierarchies and Jobs: Notes for a Theory of Gendered Organizations." Unpublished paper.

Agnew, Jean Christophe. 1993. "Coming Up for Air: Consumer Culture in Historical Perspective." In John Brewer and Roy Porter, eds., *Consumption and the World of Goods.* London: Routledge.

Alexander, G. 1986. "The Calypso Blues: Why the Caribbean Basin Initiative Isn't Working." *Policy Review* 38 (fall):55–59.

Ambursley, Fitzroy, and Robin Cohen, eds. 1983. *Crisis in the Caribbean.* New York: Monthly Review Press.

Amin, Samir. 1974. *Accumulation on a World Scale: A Critique of the Theory of Underdevelopment.* New York: Monthly Review Press.

Anderson, Patricia. 1984. "Introduction: Women, Work and Development in the Caribbean." In Margaret Gill and Joycelin Massiah, eds., *Women, Work, and Development.* Women in the Caribbean Project, vol. 6. Cave Hill, Barbados: Institute of Social and Economic Research, University of the West Indies.

———. 1986. "Conclusion: Women in the Caribbean." *Social and Economic Studies* 35, no. 2:291–324.

Antrobus, Peggy. 1988. "Women in Development Programmes: The Caribbean Experience (1975–1985)." in Patricia Mohammed and Catherine Shepherd, eds., *Gender in Caribbean Development.* Mona, Jamaica: Women and Development Studies Project, University of the West Indies.

Appadurai, Arjun, ed. 1986. *The Social Life of Things: Commodities in Cultural Perspective.* Cambridge: Cambridge University Press.

———. 1990. "Disjuncture and Difference in the Global Cultural Economy." *Public Culture* 2, no. 3:1–24.

———. 1991. "Global Ethnoscapes: Notes and Queries for a Transnational Anthropology." In Richard Fox, ed., *Recapturing Anthropology: Working in the Present.* Santa Fe: School of American Research.

———. 1993. "Consumption, Duration, and History." *Stanford Literature Review* 10, no. 1–2:11–34.

———. 1996. *Modernity at Large: Cultural Dimensions of Globalization.* Minneapolis: University of Minnesota Press.

Appelbaum, Eileen. 1987. "Restructuring Work: Temporary, Part-Time, and At-Home Employment." In Heidi Hartmann, Robert E. Kraut, and Louise A. Tilly, eds., *Computer Chips and Paper Clips: Technology and Women's Employment,* vol. 2. Washington, D.C.: National Academy Press.

———. 1987. "Technology and the Redesign of Work in the Insurance Industry." In Barbara D. Wright, ed., *Women, Work, and Technology: Transformations.* Ann Arbor: University of Michigan Press.

Apple, Michael. 1984. "Teaching and 'Women's Work': A Comparative Historical and Ideological Analysis." In E. Gumbert, ed., *Expressions of Power in Education: Studies of Class, Gender, and Race.* Atlanta: Center for Cross Cultural Education.

Ash, Juliette, and Elizabeth Wilson, eds. 1993. *Chic Thrills: A Fashion Reader.* Berkeley and Los Angeles: University of California Press.

Auslander, Leora. 1996. "The Gendering of Consumer Practices in Nineteenth-Century France." In V. de Grazia, ed., *The Sex of Things: Gender and Consumption in Historical Perspective.* Berkeley and Los Angeles: University of California Press.

Austin, Diane J. 1983. "Culture and Idology in the English-Speaking Caribbean: A View from Jamaica." *American Ethnologist* 10, no. 2:232–40.

Baran, Barbara. 1987. "The Technological Transformation of White-Collar Work: A Case Study of the Insurance Industry." In Heidi Hartmann, Robert E. Kraut, and Louise A. Tilly, eds., *Computer Chips and Paper Clips: Technology and Women's Employment,* vol. 2. Washington, D.C.: National Academy Press.

Baran, Barbara, and Suzanne Teegarden. 1987. "Women's Labor in the Office of the Future: A Case Study of the Insurance Industry." In Lourdes Beneria and Catherine Stimpson, eds., *Women, Households, and the Economy*. New Brunswick, N.J.: Rutgers University Press.

Barbados Advocate. 1989. "500 Turn Up for Jobs at New Mall," October 31, 28.

Barbados Statistical Service. 1991. *Labor Force Survey.* Government of Barbados.

Barker, Jane, and Hazel Downing. 1980. "Word Processing and the Transformation of the Patriarchal Relations of Control in the Office." *Capital and Class* 10:64–99.

Barnes, Natasha B. 1997. "Face of the Nation: Race, Nationalisms, and Identities in Jamaican Beauty Pageants." In Consuelo Lopez-Springfield, ed., *Daughters of Caliban: Caribbean Women in the Twentieth Century*. Bloomington: Indiana University Press.

Barrett, Michele. 1988. *Women's Oppression Today: Problems in Marxist Feminist Analysis*. London: Verso.

Barrett, Michele, and Mary McIntosh. 1991. 2d ed. *The Anti-Social Family*. London: Verso.

Barriteau, Eudine. 1995. "Postmodernist Feminist Theorizing and Development Policy and Practice in the Anglophone Caribbean: The Barbados Case." In Marianne H. Marchand and Jane L. Parpart, eds., *Feminism/Postmodernism/Development*. New York: Routledge.

———. 1998. "Liberal Ideology and Contradictions in Caribbean Gender Systems." In Christine Barrow, ed., *Caribbean Portraits: Essays on Gender Ideologies and Identities*. Kingston: Ian Randle Publishers.

Barrow, Christine. 1986a. "Autonomy, Equality, and Women in Barbados." Paper presented at the 11th annual meeting of the Caribbean Studies Association, Caracas, Venezuela, May.

———. 1986b. "Finding the Support: Strategies for Survival." *Social and Economic Studies* 35, no. 2:131–76.

———. 1986c. "Male Images of Women in Barbados." *Social and Economic Studies* 35, no. 3:51–64.

———. 1988. "Anthropology, the Family, and Women in the Caribbean." In Patricia Mohammed and Catherine Shepherd, eds., *Gender in Caribbean Development*. Mona, Jamaica: Women and Development Studies Project, University of the West Indies.

———, ed. 1998. *Caribbean Portraits: Essays on Gender Ideologies and Identities*. Kingston: Ian Randle Publishers.

Basch, Linda, Nina Glick-Schiller, and Cristina Szanton-Blanc. 1994. *Nations Unbound: Transnational Projects, Post-colonial Predicaments, and Deterritorialized Nation-States*. Langhorn, Pa.: Gordon and Breach.

Beckford, George L. 1972. *Persistent Poverty: Underdevelopment in Plantation Economies in the Third World*. Oxford: Oxford University Press.

———, ed. 1975. *Caribbean Economy: Dependence and Backwardness*. Mona, Jamaica: Institute of Social and Economic Research, University of the West Indies.

Beckles, Hilary McD. 1989a. *Corporate Power in Barbados: The Mutual Affair: Economic Injustice in a Political Democracy*. Bridgetown, Barbados: Caribbean Graphics.

——. 1989b. *Natural Rebels: A Social History of Enslaved Black Women in Barbados*. London: Zed Books.

——. 1990. *A History of Barbados: From Amerindian Settlement to Nation-State*. Cambridge: Cambridge University Press.

——. 1995. "Sex and Gender in the Historiography of Caribbean Slavery." In Verena Shepherd, Bridget Brereton, and Barbara Bailey, eds., *Engendering History: Caribbean Women in Historical Perspective*. Kingston: Ian Randle Publishers.

Beechey, Veronica. 1987. *Unequal Work*. London: Verso.

Bell, Daniel, and Gill Valentine. 1997. *Consuming Geographies: We Are Where We Eat*. London: Routledge.

Bell, Quentin. 1976. *On Human Finery*. New York: Schocken Books.

Beneria, Lourdes, and Martha Roldan. 1987. *The Crossroads of Class and Gender*. Chicago: University of Chicago Press.

Beneria, Lourdes, and Gita Sen. 1986. "Accumulation, Reproduction, and Women's Role in Economic Development: Boserup Revisited." In Eleanor Leacock and Helen Safa, eds., *Women's Work: Development and the Division of Labor By Gender*. South Hadley, Mass.: Bergin and Garvey Publishers.

Benn, Denis. 1987. *Ideology and Political Development: The Growth and Development of Political Ideas in the Caribbean, 1774–1983*. Mona, Jamaica: Institute of Social and Economic Research, University of the West Indies.

Bennett, Karl. 1987. "The Caribbean Basin Initiative and Its Implications for CARICOM Exports." *Social and Economic Studies* 36, no. 2:21–40.

Bennett, Tony. 1995. *The Birth of the Museum: History, Theory, Politics*. London: Routledge.

Bennholdt-Thomsen, Veronika. 1988. " 'Investment in the Poor': An Analysis of World Bank Policy." In Maria Mies, Veronika Bennholdt-Thomsen, and Claudia von Werlhof, eds., *Women: The Last Colony*. London: Zed Books.

Benson, Susan Porter. 1984. "Women in Retail Sales Work: The Continuing Dilemma of Service." In Karen Sacks and Dorothy Remy, eds., *My Troubles Are Going to Have Trouble with Me: Everyday Trials and Triumphs of Women Workers*. New Brunswick, N.J.: Rutgers University Press.

——. 1986. *Counter Cultures: Saleswomen, Managers, and Customers in American Department Stores, 1890–1940*. Urbana: University of Illinois Press.

Berleant-Schiller, Riva. 1977. "Production and Division of Labor in a West Indian Peasant Community." *American Ethnologist* 4:253–72.

Bernard, George. [1934] 1985. *Wayside Sketches: Pen Pictures of Barbadian Life*. Bridgetown, Barbados: Nation Publishing Company.

Besson, Jean. 1993. "Reputation and Respectability Reconsidered: A New Perspective on Afro-Caribbean Peasant Women." In Janet Momsen, ed., *Women and Change in the Caribbean*. Bloomington: Indiana University Press.

——. 1998. "Changing Perceptions of Gender in the Caribbean Region: The Case of the Jamaican Peasantry." In Christine Barrow, ed., *Caribbean Portraits: Essays on Gender Ideologies and Identities*. Kingston: Ian Randle Publishers.

Best, Lloyd. 1968. "The Mechanism of Plantation-Type Economies: Outlines of a Model of Pure Plantation Economy." *Social and Economic Studies* 17, no. 3:283–326.

———. 1971. "Independent Thought and Caribbean Freedom." In Norman Girvan and Owen Jefferson, eds., *Readings in the Political Economy of the Caribbean*. Kingston: New World Group.

Best, Tony. 1992. "Bajan Women Do Better without Men." *Sunday Sun*, February 2.

Bhabha, Homi. 1994. *The Location of Culture*. London: Routledge.

Bibby, Andrew. 1997. "Offshore Information Processing in Barbados." Internet report (*http://www.eclipse.co.uk.pens/bibby/telework.html*).

Billette, A., and J. Piche. 1987. "Health Problems of Data-Entry Clerks and Related Job Stressors." *Journal of Occupational Medicine* 29, no. 12:942–48.

Bird, John, Barry Curtis, Tim Putnam, George Robertson, and Lisa Tickner. 1993. *Mapping the Futures: Local Cultures, Global Change*. London: Routledge.

Block, Fred. 1990. *Postindustrial Possibilities: A Critique of Economic Discourse*. Berkeley and Los Angeles: University of California Press.

Blomstrom, Magnus, and Bjorn Hettne. 1984. *Development Theory in Transition: The Dependency Debate and Beyond: Third World Responses*. London: Zed Books.

Bluestone, Barry, and Bennett Harrison. 1982. *The Deindustrialization of America*. New York: Basic Books.

Bobcock, Robert. 1993. *Consumption*. London: Routledge.

Bohmah, D. O. 1985. "Wage Formation Employment and Output in Barbados." *Social and Economic Studies* 34:199–217.

Bolles, A. Lynn. 1983. "Kitchens Hit by Priorities: Employed Working Class Jamaican Women Confront the IMF." In June Nash and Maria Patricia Fernandez-Kelly, eds., *Women, Men, and the International Division of Labor*. Albany: State University of New York Press.

———. 1986. "Economic Crisis and Female-Headed Households in Urban Jamaica." In June Nash and Helen Safa, eds., *Women and Change in Latin America*. South Hadley, Mass.: Bergin and Garvey.

———. 1987. "My Mother Who Fathered Me and Others: Gender and Kinship in the Caribbean." Paper presented at the Annual Meetings of the American Anthropological Association, Chicago, November.

———. 1988. "Theories of Women in Development in the Caribbean: The Ongoing Debate." In Patricia Mohammed and Catherine Shepherd, eds., *Gender in Caribbean Development*. Mona, Jamaica: Women and Development Studies Project, University of the West Indies.

———. 1996. *Sister Jamaica: A Study of Women, Work, and Households in Kingston*. Lanham, Md.: University Press of America.

Bolles, A. Lynn, and Deborah D'Amico-Samuels. 1989. "Anthropological Scholarship on Gender in the English-Speaking Caribbean." In Sandra Morgen, ed., *Gender and Anthropology: Critical Reviews for Research and Training*. Washington, D.C.: American Anthropological Association.

Boris, Eileen, and Cynthia R. Daniels, eds., 1989. *Homework: Historical and Contemporary Perspectives on Paid Labor at Home.* Urbana: University of Illinois Press.

Borrell, Jerry. 1990. "Is Your Computer Killing You? Industrial-Age Problems Give Way to Information-Age Problems." *Macworld,* July, 23–26.

Boserup, Esther. 1970. *Women's Role in Economic Development.* London: George Allen and Unwin.

Bourdieu, Pierre. 1977. *Outline of a Theory of Practice.* Cambridge: Cambridge University Press.

——. 1983. "The Forms of Capital." In John Richardson, ed., *Handbook of Theory and Research for the Sociology of Education.* New York: Greenwood Press.

——. 1984. *Distinction: A Social Critique of the Judgment of Taste.* Cambridge, Mass.: Harvard University Press.

——. 1987. "What Makes a Social Class?" *Berkeley Journal of Sociology* 22:1–18.

Bourque, Susan C., and Kay B. Warren. 1987. "Technology, Gender, and Development." *Daedalus,* fall, 173–93.

Brana-Shute, Gary. 1979. *On the Corner: Male Social Life in a Paramaribo Creole Neighborhood.* Prospect Heights, Ill.: Waveland Press.

Brathwaite, Edward. 1974. "Timehri." In Orde Coombs, ed., *Is Massa Day Dead?* New York: Doubleday, Anchor Press.

Braverman, Harry. 1974. *Labor and Monopoly Capitalism.* New York: Monthly Review Press.

Breckenridge, Carol A., ed. 1995. *Consuming Modernity: Public Culture in a South Asian World.* Minneapolis: University of Minnesota Press.

Brewer, Anthony. 1980. *Marxist Theories of Imperialism: A Critical Survey.* London: Routledge.

Brinkley, David. 1995. *A Memoir.* New York: Alfred A. Knopf.

Brodber, Erna. 1982. *Perceptions of Caribbean Women.* Women in the Caribbean Project, vol. 4. Cave Hill, Barbados: Institute of Social and Economic Research, University of the West Indies.

——. 1986. "Afro-Jamaican Women at the Turn of the Century." *Social and Economic Studies* 35, no. 3:23–50.

Brodeur, Paul. 1990. "The Magnetic-Field Menace." *Macworld,* July, 136–45.

Bryce, Jane. 1998. " 'Young T'ing is the Name of the Game': Sexual Dynamics in a Caribbean Romantic Fiction Series." In Christine Barrow, ed., *Caribbean Portraits: Essays on Gender Ideologies and Identities.* Kingston: Ian Randle Publishers.

Burawoy, Michael. 1979. *Manufacturing Consent: Changes in the Labor Process under Monopoly Capitalism.* Chicago: University of Chicago Press.

——. 1985. *The Politics of Production: Factory Regimes under Capitalism and Socialism.* London: Verso.

Burke, Timothy. 1996. *Lifebouy Men, Lux Women: Commodification, Consumption, and Cleanliness in Modern Zimbabwe.* Durham: Duke University Press.

Bush, Barbara. 1990. *Slave Women in Caribbean Society, 1650–1838.* Bloomington: Indiana University Press.

Cagatay, Nilufer, and Sule Ozler. 1995. "Feminization of the Labor Force: The Effects of Long Term Development and Structural Adjustment." *World Development* 23, no. 11:1883–94.

Campbell, Colin. 1990. "Character and Consumption: An Historical Action Theory Approach to the Understanding of Consumer Behavior." *Culture and History* 7:37–48.

Campbell, P. F. 1973. *An Outline of Barbados History.* Bridgetown, Barbados: Caribbean Graphics.

Carnoy, Martin, Manuel Castells, Stephen Cohen, and Fernando Henrique Cardoso, eds. 1993. *The New Global Economy in the Information Age.* University Park: Pennsylvania State University Press.

Carter, Kenneth L. 1997. *Why Workers Won't Work: The Worker in a Developing Economy: A Case Study of Jamaica.* London: Macmillan.

Carter, Valerie J. 1987. "Office Technology and Relations of Control in Clerical Work Organizations." In Barbara D. Wright, ed., *Women, Work, and Technology: Transformations.* Ann Arbor: University of Michigan Press.

Casey, Geraldine. 1996. "New Tappings on the Keys: Changes in Work and Gender Roles for Women Clerical Workers in Puerto Rico." In Altagracia Ortiz, ed., *Puerto Rican Women and Work: Bridges in Transnational Labor.* Philadelphia: Temple University Press.

Castells, Manuel. 1993. "The Informational Economy and the New International Division of Labor." In Martin Carnoy et al., eds., *The New Global Economy in the Information Age.* University Park: Pennsylvania State University Press.

Castells, Manuel, and Alejandro Portes. 1989. "World Underneath: The Origins, Dynamics, and Effects of the Informal Economy." In Alejandro Portes, Manuel Castells, and Lauren Benton, eds., *The Informal Economy: Studies in Advanced and Less Developed Countries.* Baltimore: Johns Hopkins University Press.

Catanzarite, Lisa and Myra Strober. 1993. "Gender Recomposition of the Maquiladora Workforce." *Industrial Relations* 32:133–47.

Cavendish, Ruth. 1982. *Women on the Line.* London: Routledge and Kegan Paul.

Chaney, Elsa, and Marianne Schmink. 1980. "Women and Modernization: Access to Tools." In June Nash and Helen Safa, eds., *Sex and Class in Latin America.* Brooklyn, N.Y.: J. F. Bergin Publishers.

Christensen, Kathleen, ed. 1988. *The New Era of Home-Based Work: Directions and Policies.* London: Westview Press.

——. 1989. "Home-Based Clerical Work: No Simple Truth, No Single Reality." In Eileen Boris and Cynthia R. Daniels, eds., *Homework: Historical and Contemporary Perspectives on Paid Labor at Home.* Urbana: University of Illinois Press.

Cockburn, Cynthia. 1986. "The Relations of Technology: What Implications for Theories of Sex and Class?" In Rosemary Crompton and Michael Mann, eds., *Gender and Stratification.* Cambridge, Mass.: Polity Press.

Colclough, Glenna, and Charles M. Tolbert II. 1992. *Work in the Fast Lane: Flexibility, Divisions of Labor.* Albany: State University of New York Press.

Collins, Patricia Hill. 1991. *Black Feminist Thought: Knowledge, Consciousness, and the Politics of Empowerment.* New York: Routledge, Chapman and Hall.

Coppin, Addington. 1995. "Women, Men, and Work in the Barbados Labor Market." *Social and Economic Studies* 44, no. 2–3:103–25.

Cossy, Marva. 1991. "UNDP Puts Barbados at Top of Developing World." *Daily Nation,* May 22.

Costello, Cynthia B. 1985. " 'WEA're Worth It': Work Culture and Conflict at the Wisconsin Education Association Insurance Trust." *Feminist Studies* 11, no. 3:497–518.

Council on Scientific Affairs. 1987. "Health Effects of Video Display Terminals." *Journal of the American Medical Association* 257, no. 11:1508–12.

Cox, Kevin, ed. 1997. *Spaces of Globalization: Reasserting the Power of the Local.* New York: Guilford Press.

Cox, Winston. 1982. "The Manufacturing Sector in the Economy of Barbados, 1946–1980." In Delisle Worrell, ed., *The Economy of Barbados, 1946–1980.* Bridgetown, Barbados: Central Bank of Barbados.

Craik, Jennifer. 1994. *The Face of Fashion: Cultural Studies in Fashion.* New York: Routledge.

Crompton, Rosemary. 1986. "Women and the 'Service Class.' " In Rosemary Crompton and Michael Mann, eds., *Gender and Stratification.* Cambridge, Mass.: Polity Press.

——. 1993. *Class and Stratification: An Introduction to Current Debates.* Cambridge, Mass.: Polity Press.

Crompton, Rosemary, and Michael Mann, eds. 1986. *Gender and Stratification.* Cambridge, Mass.: Polity Press.

Cuales, Sonia. 1988. "Theoretical Considerations on Class and Gender Consciousness." In Patricia Mohammed and Catherine Shepherd, eds., *Gender in Caribbean Development.* Mona, Jamaica: Women and Development Project, University of the West Indies.

Cvetkovich, Ann, and Douglas Kellner, eds. 1997. *Articulating the Global and the Local: Globalization and Cultural Studies.* Boulder, Colo.: Westview Press, 1997.

Dann, Graham. 1984. *The Quality of Life in Barbados.* London: Macmillan.

Davies, Margery W. 1982. *Woman's Place Is at the Typewriter: Office Work and Office Workers, 1870–1930.* Philadelphia: Temple University Press.

——. 1988. "Women Clerical Workers and the Typewriter: The Writing Machine." in Cheris Kramarae, ed., *Technology and Women's Voices: Keeping in Touch.* New York: Routledge and Kegan Paul.

de Certeau, Michel. 1984. *The Practice of Everyday Life.* Translated by Steven Rendall. Berkeley and Los Angeles: University of California Press.

Deere, Carmen Diana. 1986. "Rural Women and Agrarian Reform in Peru, Chile, and Cuba." In June Nash and Helen Safa, eds., *Women and Change in Latin America.* New York: Bergin and Garvey.

——. 1989. "Alternative U.S. Policies Toward the Caribbean." Paper presented at the 15th annual congress of the Latin American Studies Association, San Juan, Puerto Rico.

——. 1990. "A CBI Report Card." *Hemisphere* 3, no. 1:29.

Deere, Carmen Diana, and Edwin Melendez. N.d. "U.S. Trade Policy and Caribbean Economic Recovery: Sorting Out the Contradictions." Unpublished paper.

Deere, Carmen Diana, Peggy Antrobus, Lynn Bolles, Edwin Melendez, Peter Phillips, Marcia Rivera, Helen Safa, eds. 1990. *In the Shadows of the Sun: Caribbean Development Alternatives and U.S. Policy*. Boulder, Colo.: Westview Press.

de Grazia, Victoria, ed. 1996. *The Sex of Things: Gender and Consumption in Historical Perspective*. Berkeley and Los Angeles: University of California Press.

Delphy, Christine, and Diana Leonard. 1992. *Familiar Exploitation: A New Analysis of Marriage in Contemporary Western Societies*. Cambridge, Mass.: Polity Press.

Deyo, Frederic C. 1980. "The Single Female Factory Worker and Her Peer Group." *Human Organization* 39, no. 1:80–84.

di Leonardo, Micaela. 1985. "Women's Work, Work Culture, and Consciousness: An Introduction." *Feminist Studies* 11, no. 3:491–96.

——. 1987. "The Female World of Cards and Holidays: Women, Families, and the Work of Kinship." *Signs* 12, no. 3:440–53.

——, ed. 1991. *Gender at the Crossroads of Knowledge: Feminist Anthropology in the Postmodern Era*. Berkeley and Los Angeles: University of California Press.

Douglass, Lisa. 1992. *The Power of Sentiment: Love, Hierarchy, and the Jamaican Family Elite*. Boulder, Colo.: Westview Press.

——. 1993. "Jamaican Gender Ideology, Sexuality, and the 'Cult of Masculinity.'" Paper presented at the annual meeting of the American Anthropological Association, Washington, D.C., November.

Douglass, Mary. 1997. "In Defense of Shopping." In Pasi Falk and Colin Campbell, eds., *The Shopping Experience*. London: Sage.

Duarte, Isis. 1989. "Household Workers in the Dominican Republic: A Question for the Feminist Movement." In Elsa M. Chaney and Mary Garcia Castro, eds., *Muchachas No More: Household Workers in Latin American and the Caribbean*. Philadelphia: Temple University Press.

DuBois, W. E. B. 1961. *The Souls of Black Folk*. New York: Premier Books.

du Guy, Paul, Stuart Hall, Linda Janes, Hugh Mackay, and Keith Negus. 1997. *Doing Cultural Studies: The Story of the Sony Walkman*. London: Sage.

Dunn, Richard. 1969. "The Barbados Census of 1680: Profile of the Richest Colony in English America." *Barbados Museum of Historical Society Journal* 33, no. 2:57–75.

Durant-Gonzalez, Victoria. 1982. "The Realm of Female Familial Responsibility." In Joycelin Massiah, ed., *Women and the Family*. Women in the Caribbean Project, vol. 2. Cave Hill, Barbados: Institute of Social and Economic Research, University of the West Indies.

Dwyer, Daisy, and Judith Bruce. 1988. *A Home Divided: Women and Income in the Third World*. Stanford: Stanford University Press.

Dy, Fe Josefina F. 1985. *Visual Display Units: Job Content and Stress in Office Work*. Geneva: International Labour Office.

Edgell, Zee. 1982. *Beka Lamb*. Caribbean Writers. London: Heinemann.

Ehlers, Tracy Bachrach. 1990. *Silent Looms: Women and Production in a Guatamalan Town*. Boulder, Colo.: Westview Press.

Elson, Diane, and Ruth Pearson. 1981a. "Nimble Fingers Make Cheap Workers: An Analysis of Women's Employment in Third World Export Manufacturing." *Feminist Review*, spring, 87–107.

——. 1981b. "The Subordination of Women and the Internationalisation of Factory Production." In Kate Young, Carol Wolkowitz, and Roslyn McCullagh, eds., *Of Marriage and the Market: Women's Subordination Internationally and Its Lessons*. London: Routledge and Kegan Paul.

Enloe, Cynthia. 1990. *Bananas, Beaches, and Bases: Making Feminist Sense out of International Politics*. Berkeley and Los Angeles: University of California Press.

——. 1994. "Feminists Try On the Post-Cold War Sneaker." Paper presented at the Women's Studies 10th Anniversary Conference, Duke University, Durham, N.C.

Espinal, Rosario, and Sherri Grasmuck. 1993. "Gender, Households, and Informal Entrepreneurship in the Dominican Republic." Paper presented at the 18th annual convention of the Caribbean Studies Association, Kingston and Ocho Rios, Jamaica.

Etienne, Mona, and Eleanor Leacock, eds. 1980. *Women and Colonization: Anthropological Perspectives*. New York: Praeger.

Ewen, Stuart. 1988. *All Consuming Images: The Politics of Style in Contemporary Culture*. New York: Basic Books.

Faulkner, Wendy, and Erik Arnold, eds. 1985. *Smothered by Invention: Technology in Women's Lives*. London: Pluto Press.

Featherstone, Mike, ed. 1990. *Global Culture, Nationalism, Globalization and Modernity*. London: Sage.

Fernandez-Kelly, Maria Patricia. 1983. *For We Are Sold, I and My People: Women and Industry in Mexico's Frontier*. Albany: State University of New York Press.

——. 1985. "Contemporary Production and the New International Division of Labor." In Steven Sanderson, ed., *The Americas in the New International Division of Labor*. New York: Holmes and Meier.

——. 1989. "Broadening of Purview: Gender and International Economic Development." Paper presented at the International Conference on Women and Development, State University of New York at Albany, March.

Fernandez-Kelly, Maria Patricia, and Saskia Sassen. 1995. "Recasting Women in the Global Economy: Internationalization and Changing Definitions of Gender." In Christine E. Bose and Edna Acosta-Belen, eds., *Women in the Latin American Development Process*. Philadelphia: Temple University Press.

Fine, Ben, and Ellen Leopold, eds. 1993. *The World of Consumption*. New York: Routledge.

Finkelstein, Joanne. 1991. *The Fashioned Self*. Philadelphia: Temple University Press.

Finn, Margot. 1996. "Women, Consumption and Coverture in England, c. 1760–1860." *Historical Journal* 39, no. 3:703–22.

———. 1998. "Working-Class Women and the Contest For Consumer Control in Victorian County Courts." *Past and Present: A Journal of Historical Studies* 161:116–54.

Fisher, Lawrence E. 1985. *Colonial Madness: Mental Health in the Barbadian Social Order.* New Brunswick, N.J.: Rutgers University Press.

Forde, Norma M. N.d. *Where Are We Now? An Assessment of the Status of Women in Barbados.* Barbados: Bureau of Women's Affairs, Ministry of Labour and Community Development.

Foster, Robert J. 1991. "Making National Cultures in the Global Ecumene." *Annual Review of Anthropology,* 20:235–60.

Foucault, Michel. 1979. *Discipline and Punish: The Birth of the Prison.* New York: Vintage Books.

Franco, Jean. 1986. "The Incorporation of Women: A Comparison of North American and Mexican Popular Narrative." In Tania Modlesky, ed., *Studies in Entertainment: Critical Approaches to Mass Culture.* Bloomington: Indiana University Press.

Franco, Pamela. 1998. " 'Dressing Up and Looking Good': Afro-Creole Female Maskers in Trinidad Carnival." *African Arts* 31, no. 2 (spring):62–67.

Frank, Andre G. 1967. *Capitalism and Underdevelopment in Latin America.* New York: Monthly Review Press.

Freeman, Carla. 1993. "Designing Women: Corporate Discipline and Barbados' Off-Shore Pink Collar Sector." *Cultural Anthropology* 8, no. 2:169–86.

———. 1997. "Reinventing Higglering in Transnational Zones: Barbadian Women Juggle the Triple Shift." In Consuelo Lopez-Springfield, ed., *Daughters of Caliban: Caribbean Women in the Twentieth Century.* Bloomington: Indiana University Press.

———. 1998. "Femininity and Flexible Labor: Fashioning Class through Gender on the Global Assembly Line." *Critique of Anthropology* 18, no. 3:245–62.

French, Joan. 1989. "It's Nice." In Michael Witter, ed., "Higglering/Sidewalk Vending/ Informal Commercial Trading in the Jamaican Economy." Proceedings of a symposium, Department of Economics, University of the West Indies, Mona, Jamaica.

Friedman, Jonathan. 1990a. "Being in the World: Globalization and Localization." In Mike Featherstone, ed., *Global Culture: Nationalism, Globalization, and Modernity.* London: Sage.

———. 1990b. "The Political Economy of Elegance: An African Cult of Beauty." *Culture and History* 7:101–25.

———, ed. 1994a. *Consumption and Identity.* New York: Harewood.

———. 1994b. *Cultural Identity and Global Process.* London: Sage.

Frisby, David, and Mike Featherstone, eds. 1997. *Simmel on Culture.* London: Sage.

Fröbel, Folker, Jürgen Heinrichs, and Otto Kreye. 1980. *The New International Division of Labour.* Cambridge: Cambridge University Press.

From Bonding Wires to Banding Women. 1988. Proceedings of the International Consultation on Micro-Chips Technology, Manila, Philippines, 1986. Quezon City: Center for Women's Resources.

Froude, James Anthony. 1888. *The English in the West Indies, or, The Bow of Ulysses*. New York: Scribner, 1888.

Fuentes, Annette, and Barbara Ehrenreich. 1985. *Women in the Global Factory*. Boston: South End Press.

Gailey, Christine. 1985. "The State of the State in Anthropology." *Dialectical Anthropology* 9, no. 1–2:65–89.

Gallin, Rita. 1990. "Women and the Export Industry in Taiwan: The Muting of Class Consciousness." In Kathryn Ward, ed., *Women Workers and Global Restructuring*. Ithaca, N.Y.: ILR Press.

Garvin, David A., and Artemis March. 1986. "A Note on Quality: The Views of Deming, Juran, and Crosby." *Harvard Business Review*, Special Collection, 9-687-011.

Gertler, Meric S. 1997. "Between the Global and the Local: The Spatial Limits to Productive Capital." In Kevin Cox, ed., *Spaces of Globalization: Reassessing the Power of the Local*. New York: Guilford.

Giddens, Anthony. 1990. *The Consequences of Modernity*. Cambridge, Mass.: Polity Press.
———. 1991. *Modernity and Self Identity*. Cambridge, Mass.: Polity Press.

Gill, Margaret, and Joycelin Massiah, eds. 1984. *Women, Work, and Development*. Women in the Caribbean Project, vol. 6. Cave Hill, Barbados: Institute of Social and Economic Research, University of the West Indies.

Gilroy, Paul. 1993. *The Black Atlantic: Modernity and Double Consciousness*. Cambridge, Mass.: Harvard University Press.

Girvan, Norman. 1967. *The Caribbean Bauxite Industry*. Kingston: Institute for Social and Economic Research, University of the West Indies.

Girvan, Norman, and Owen Jefferson, eds. 1971. *Readings in the Political Economy of the Caribbean*. Kingston: New World Group.

Glenn, Evelyn, and Roslyn Feldberg. 1977. "Degraded and Deskilled: The Proletarianization of Clerical Work." *Social Problems* 25:52–64.

Glenn, Evelyn Nakano, and Charles M. Tolbert II. 1987. "Technology and Emerging Patterns of Stratification for Women of Color: Race and Gender Segregation in Computer Occupations." In Barbara D. Wright, ed., *Women, Work, and Technology: Transformations*. Ann Arbor: University of Michigan Press.

Glick-Schiller, Nina, Linda Basch, and Cristina Szanton-Blanc, eds. 1992. *Towards a Transnational Perspective on Migration: Race, Class, Ethnicity, and Nationalism Reconsidered*. Annals of the Academy of Sciences, vol. 645. New York: Academy of Sciences.

Gmelch, George, and Sharon Gmelch. 1997. *The Parish Behind God's Back: The Changing Culture of Rural Barbados*. Ann Arbor: University of Michigan Press.

Goddard, Robert. 1998. "The Decline and Fall of the Barbadian Planter Class: An Interpretation of the 1980s Crisis in the Barbados Sugar Industry." Unpublished manuscript.

Goldthorpe, John. 1987. *Social Mobility and Class Structure in Modern Britain*. 2d ed. Oxford: Clarendon Press.

Government of Barbados. N.d. *Development Plan, 1988–1993*. Bridgetown, Barbados: Government Printing Department.

Government of Barbados. N.d. *Development Plan, 1993–2000*. Bridgetown, Barbados: Government Printing Department.

Graddol, David, and Joan Swan. 1989. *Gender Voices*. New York: Blackwell.

Gramsci, Antonio. 1971. *Selections from the Prison Notebooks*. Edited and translated by Quinten Hoare and Geoffrey Nowell Smith. London: Wishart.

Grasmuck, Sherri, and Patricia Pessar. 1991. *Between Two Islands: Dominican International Migration*. Berkeley and Los Angeles: University of California Press.

Greenfield, Sidney M. 1966. *English Rustics in Black Skin: A Study of Modern Family Forms in a Pre-industrialized Society*. New Haven: College and University Press.

Grenier, Guillermo J. 1988. *Inhuman Relations: Quality Circles and Anti-unionism in American Industry*. Philadelphia: Temple University Press.

Griffith, Winston H. 1989. "Lewis and Caribbean Industrialization: Policy, Theory, and the New Technology." *Journal of Developing Areas* 25:207–30.

Grossman, Rachael. 1979. "Women's Place in the Integrated Circuit." *Southeast Asia Chronicle* 66 (January–February).

Guarnizo, Luis Eduardo, and Michael Peter Smith, eds. 1998. *Transnationalism From Below*. New Brunswick, N.J.: Transaction Publishers.

Gunder Frank, André, and Barry K. Gills, eds. 1993. *The World System: Five Hundred Years of Five Thousand?* New York: Routledge.

Gupta, Akhil. 1992. "The Song of the Nonaligned World: Transnational Identities and the Reinscription of Space in Late Capitalism." *Cultural Anthropology* 7, no. 1:63–79.

Gupta, Akhil, and James Ferguson. 1992. "Beyond 'Culture': Space, Identity, and the Politics of Difference." *Cultural Anthropology* 7, no. 1–6–23.

Gussler, Judith D. 1980. "Adoptive Strategies and Social Networks of Women in St. Kitts." In E. Bourguignon, ed., *A World of Women: Anthropological Studies of Women in the Societies of the World*. New York: Praeger.

Gutman, Matthew. 1996. *The Meanings of Macho: Being a Man in Mexico City*. Berkeley and Los Angeles: University of California Press.

Haddad, Carol J. 1987. "Technology, Industrialization, and the Economic Status of Women." In Barbara D. Wright, ed., *Women, Work, and Technology: Transformations*. Ann Arbor: University of Michigan Press.

Hakken, David, with Barbara Andrews. 1993. *Computing Myths, Class Realities: An Ethnography of Technology and Working People in Sheffield, England*. Boulder, Colo.: Westview Press.

Hall, Stuart. 1977. "Pluralism, Race, and Class in Caribbean Society." In *Race and Class in Post-Colonial Society: A Study of Ethnic Group Relations in the English-Speaking Caribbean, Bolivia, Chile, and Mexico*. Paris: UNESCO.

———. 1991. "The Local and the Global: Globalization and Ethnicity." In Anthony King, ed., *Culture, Globalization, and the World System*. Binghamton: Department of Art and Art History, State University of New York.

Hannerz, Ulf. 1987. "The World in Creolization." *Africa* 57:546–59.

——. 1990. "Cosmopolitans and Locals in World Culture." In Mike Featherstone, ed., *Global Culture: Nationalism, Globalization, and Modernity*. London: Sage.

——. 1991. "The State in Creolization." Paper presented at the Annual Meeting of the American Anthropological Association, Chicago, November.

——. 1992. *Cultural Complexity*. New York: Columbia University Press.

——. 1996. *Transnational Connections: Culture, People, Places*. London: Routledge.

Hannerz, Ulf, and Orvar Lofgren. 1994. "The Nation in the Global Village." *Cultural Studies* 8, no. 2:198–207.

Harris, Olivia. 1984."Households as Natural Units." In Kate Young, Carol Wolkowitz, and Roslyn McCullagh, eds., *Of Marriage and the Market: Women's Subordination Internationally and Its Lessons*. London: Routledge and Kegan Paul.

Harrison, Faye V. 1988. "Women in Jamaica's Urban Informal Economy: Insights from a Kingston Slum." *Nieuwe West-Indische Gids* 62, no. 3–4:103–28.

Hart, Keith. 1973. "Informal Income Opportunities and Urban Government in Ghana." *Journal of Modern African Studies* 11:61–89.

Hartmann, Heidi. 1976. "The Historical Roots of Occupational Segregation: Capitalism, Patriarchy, and Job Segregation by Sex." In Martha Blaxall and Barbara Reagan, eds., *Women and the Workplace*. Chicago: University of Chicago Press.

——. 1981. "The Unhappy Marriage of Marxism and Feminism: Towards a More Progressive Union." In Lydia Sargent, ed., *Women and Revolution: The Unhappy Marriage of Marxism and Feminism*. London: Pluto Press.

Hartmann, Heidi I., Robert E. Kraut, and Louise A. Tilly, eds. 1986–87. *Computer Chips and Paper Clips: Technology and Women's Employment*. 2 vols. Washington, D.C.: National Academy Press.

Harvey, David. 1989. *The Conditions of Postmodernity*. Oxford: Blackwell.

Hayes, Dennis. 1989. *Behind the Silicon Curtain: The Seductions of Work in a Lonely Era*. Boston: South End Press.

Haynes, Cleviston. 1982. "Sugar and the Barbadian Economy, 1946–1980." In Delisle Worrell, ed., *The Economy of Barbados, 1946–1980*. Bridgetown, Barbados: Central Bank of Barbados.

Heath, Deborah. 1992. "Fashion, Anti-Fashion, and Heteroglossia in Urban Senegal." *American Ethnologist* 19, no. 1:19–33.

Heinze, Andrew R. 1990. *Adapting to Abundance: Jewish Immigrants, Mass Consumption, and the Search for American Identity*. New York: Columbia University Press.

Henderson, Jeffrey, and Manuel Castells, eds. 1987. *Global Restructuring and Territorial Development*. London: Sage

Hendrickson, Hildi, ed. 1996. *Clothing and Difference: Embodied Identities in Colonial and Post-Colonial Africa*. Durham: Duke University Press.

Henry, Miriam, and Suzanne Franzway. 1993. "Gender, Unions, and the New Workplace: Realizing the Promise?" In Belinda Probert and Bruce W. Wilson, eds., *Pink Collar Blues: Work Gender, and Technology*. Melbourne: Melbourne University Press.

Henry, Ralph. 1988. "Jobs, Gender, and Development Strategy in the Commonwealth

Caribbean." In Patricia Mohammed and Catherine Shepherd, eds., *Gender in Caribbean Development*. Mona, Jamaica: Women and Development Studies Project, University of the West Indies.

Herod, Andrew. 1997. "Labor as an Agent of Globalization and as a Global Agent." In Kevin Cox, ed., *Spaces of Globalization: Reasserting the Power of the Local*. New York: Guilford Press.

Heyzer, Noeleen. 1989. "Asian Women Wage Earners." *World Development* 17:1109–24.

Higman, Barry. 1984. *Slave Populations of the British Caribbean, 1807–1834*. Baltimore: Johns Hopkins University Press.

Hochschild, Arlie R. 1983. *The Managed Heart: Commercialization of Human Feeling*. Berkeley and Los Angeles: University of California Press.

Hodge, Merle. 1974. "The Shadow of the Whip." In Orde Coombs, ed., *Is Massa Day Dead? Black Moods in the Caribbean*. New York: Anchor Books.

———. 1982. "Introduction." Erna Prodber, *Perceptions of Caribbean Women: Towards a Documentation of Stereotypes*. Cave Hill, Barbados: Institute of Social and Economic Research, University of the West Indies.

Hopkins, Michael. 1998. "The Antihero's Guide to the New Economy." *Inc.* 20, no. 1:36–48.

Hossfeld, Karen. 1990. " 'Their Logic Against Them': Contradictions in Sex, Race, and Class in Silicon Valley." In Kathryn Ward, ed., *Women Workers and Global Restructuring*. Ithaca, N.Y.: ILR Press.

Howard, Michael. 1989. *Dependence and Development in Barbados, 1945–1985*. Bridgetown, Barbados: Carib Research and Publications.

Howe, Louise Kapp. 1977. *Pink Collar Workers: Inside the World of Women's Work*. New York: G. P. Putnam's Sons.

Howes, David, ed. 1996. *Cross-Cultural Consumption: Global Markets, Local Realities*. London: Routledge.

Hurston, Zora Neale. [1938] 1990. *Tell My Horse: Voodoo and Life in Haiti and Jamaica*. New York: Harper and Row.

Huws, Ursula. 1984a. *The New Homeworkers: New Technology and the Changing Location of White Collar Work*. London: Low Pay Unit.

———. 1984b. "New Technology Homeworkers." *Employment Gazette*, January.

Industrial Development Corporation (IDC). N.d. "Doing Business in Barbados." Promotional brochure.

International Labour Office. 1986. "Employment Effects of Multinational Enterprises in Export Processing Zones in the Caribbean." A joint ILO/UNCTC research project by Frank Long. Working paper no. 42. Geneva: International Labour Office.

Jackson, Peter. 1993. "A Cultural Politics of Consumption." In John Bird, Barry Curtis, Tim Putnam, George Robertson, and Lisa Tickner, eds., *Mapping the Futures: Local Cultures, Global Change*. London: Routledge.

James, C. L. R. 1980. *Spheres of Existence*. Westport, Conn.: Lawrence Hill.

Jameson, Frederic. 1991. *Postmodernism, or, The Cultural Logic of Late Capitalism*. Durham: Duke University Press.

Jayawardena, Chandra. 1963. *Conflict and Solidarity in a Guianese Plantation.* London: Athlone Press, University of London.

Jenkins, Richard. 1992. *Pierre Bourdieu.* London: Routledge.

Joekes, Susan, and Roxana Moayedi. 1987. *Women and Export Manufacturing: A Review of the Issues and AID Policy.* Washington, D.C.: International Center for Research on Women.

Kahn, Joel S., and Josep R. Llobera, eds. 1981. *The Anthropology of Pre-capitalist Societies.* London: Macmillan.

Katzin, Mary Fisher. 1959. "The Jamaican Country Higgler." *Social and Economic Studies.* 8:421–40.

Kelly, Deirdre. 1987. *Hard Work, Hard Choices: A Survey of Women in St. Lucia's Export-Oriented Electronics Factories.* Occasional paper no. 20, Institute of Social and Economic Research. Cave Hill, Barbados: University of the West Indies.

King, Anthony, ed. 1991. *Culture, Globalization, and the World System.* Current Debates in Art History, 3. Binghamton: Department of Art and Art History, State University of New York.

Klak, Thomas. 1993. "Recent Caribbean Industrial Trends and Their Impacts on Household Well-Being." Paper presented at the annual meeting of the Caribbean Studies Association, Jamaica, May.

Klein, Misha. 1988a. "Panoptic Watchtower: The VDT as Disciplinary Tool." Unpublished paper, Department of Anthropology, University of California, Berkeley.

——. 1988b. "Punch It In Is All We Do: Stress Illnesses of VDT Workers." Unpublished paper, Department of Anthropology, University of California, Berkeley.

Knauft, Bruce M. 1996. *Genealogies for the Present in Cultural Anthropology.* New York: Routledge.

Knight, Franklin W. 1978. *The Caribbean: The Genesis of a Fragmented Nationalism.* New York: Oxford University Press.

Kondo, Dorinne K. 1990. *Crafting Selves: Power, Gender, and Discourses of Identity in a Japanese Workplace.* Chicago: University of Chicago Press.

Koptiuch, Kristin. 1991. "Third-Worlding at Home." *Social Text* 28:87–99.

Kramarae, Cheris, ed. 1988. *Technology and Women's Voices: Keeping in Touch.* New York: Routledge and Kegan Paul.

Labov, William. 1966. *The Social Stratification of English in New York City.* Washington, D.C.: Center for Applied Linguistics.

——. 1972. *Sociolinguistic Patterns.* Philadelphia: University of Pennsylvania Press.

Laclau, Ernesto, and Chantal Mouffe. 1982. "Recasting Marxism: Hegemony and New Political Movements." *Socialist Review* 12, no. 6 (November–December).

LaGuerre, Michel S. 1983. *Urban Life in the Caribbean.* New York: Shankman.

Lamming, George. 1953. *In the Castle of My Skin.* London: McGraw Hill.

Lamphere, Louise. 1985. "Bringing the Family to Work: Women's Culture on the Shop Floor." *Feminist Studies* 11, no. 3:519–40.

Lamphere, Louise, and Guillermo J. Grenier. 1988. "Women, Union, and 'Participative Management': Organizing in the Sunbelt." In Ann Bookman and Sandra Morgen, eds., *Women and the Politics of Empowerment*. Philadelphia: Temple University Press.

Lancaster, Roger. 1992. *Life Is Hard: Machismo, Danger, and the Intimacy of Power in Nicaragua*. Berkeley and Los Angeles: University of California Press.

Lash, Scott, and Jonathan Friedman, eds. 1992. *Modernity and Identity*. Oxford: Blackwell.

Lash, Scott, and John Urry. 1987. *The End of Organized Capitalism*. Cambridge, Mass.: Polity Press.

Leach, William R. 1984. "Transformations in a Culture of Consumption: Women and Department Stores, 1890–1925." *Journal of American History* 71, no. 2:319–342.

Leacock, Eleanor, and Helen Safa. 1986. *Women's Work*. South Hadley, Mass.: Bergin and Garvey.

Lee, Chin Kwan. 1997. "Factory Regimes of Chinese Capitalism: Different Cultural Logics in Labor Control." In Aihwa Ong and Donald Nonini, eds., *Underground Empires: The Cultural Politics of Modern Chinese Transnationalism*. New York: Routledge.

Lee, Martyn J. 1993. *Consumer Culture Reborn: The Cultural Politics of Consumption*. New York: Routledge.

LeFranc, Elsie. 1989. "Petty Trading and Labour Mobility: Higglers in the Kingston Metropolitan Area." In Keith Hart, ed., *Women and the Sexual Division of Labour in the Caribbean*. Kingston: Consortium Graduate School of Social Sciences.

Leidner, Robin. 1993. *Fast Food, Fast Talk: Service Work and the Routinization of Everyday Life*. Berkeley and Los Angeles: University of California Press.

Leo-Rhynie, Elsa. 1998. "Socialisation and the Development of Gender Identity: Theoretical Formulations and Caribbean Research." In Christine Barrow, ed., *Caribbean Portraits: Essays on Gender Ideologies and Identities*. Kingston: Ian Randle Publishers.

Levitt, Kari, and Lloyd Best. 1975. "Character of Caribbean Economy." In George L. Beckford, ed., *Caribbean Economy: Dependence and Backwardness*. Mona, Jamaica: Institute of Social and Economic Research, University of the West Indies.

Levy, Claude. 1980. *Emancipation, Sugar, and Federalism: Barbados and the West Indies*. Gainesville: University of Florida Press.

Levy, Diane, and Patricia Lerch. 1991. "Tourism as a Factor in Development: Implications for Gender and Work in Barbados." *Gender and Society* 5, no. 1:67–85.

Lewis, Gordon K. 1968. *The Growth of the Modern West Indies*. New York: Monthly Review Press.

———. 1983. *Main Currents in Caribbean Thought*. Baltimore: Johns Hopkins University Press.

Lewis, W. Arthur. 1954. "Economic Development with Unlimited Supplies of Labour." *Manchester School of Economic and Social Studies* 22 (May).

Liff, Sonia. 1987. "Gender Relations in the Construction of Jobs." In Maureen McNeil, ed., *Gender and Expertise*. London: Free Association Books.

Ligon, Richard. [1657] 1976. *A True and Exact History of the Island of Barbados*. London: Frank Cass.

Lim, Linda. 1983. "Capitalism, Imperialism, and Patriarchy: The Dilemmas of Third World Women Workers in Multinational Factories." In June Nash and Maria Patricia Fernandez-Kelly, eds., *Women, Men, and the International Division of Labor.* Albany: State University of New York Press.

———. 1985. *Women Workers in Multinational Enterprises in Developing Countries.* Geneva: International Labour Office.

Lin, Vivian. 1987. "Women Electronics Workers in Southeast Asia: The Emergence of a Working Class." In Jeffrey Henderson and Manuel Castells, eds., *Global Restructuring and Territorial Development.* London: Sage.

LiPuma, Edward, and Sarah Keene Meltzoff. 1989. "Toward a Theory of Culture and Class: An Iberian Example." *American Ethnologist* 16, no. 2:313–34.

Lohr, Steve. 1988. "The Growth of the 'Global Office.'" *New York Times,* October 18.

Long, Frank. 1989. "Manufacturing Exports in the Caribbean and the New International Division of Labour." *Social and Economic Studies* 38, no. 1:115–31.

Lopez-Springfield, Consuelo, ed., 1997. *Daughters of Caliban: Caribbean Women in the Twentieth Century.* Bloomington: Indiana University Press.

Lovibond, Sabina. 1989. "Feminism and Postmodernism." *New Left Review,* no. 178 (November–December):5–28.

Lowe, Lisa, and David Lloyd, eds. 1997. *The Politics of Culture in the Shadow of Capital.* Durham: Duke University Press.

Lutz, Catherine A., and Jane L. Collins. 1993. *Reading National Geographic.* Chicago: University of Chicago Press.

Mandle, Jay R. 1982. *Patterns of Caribbean Development.* New York: Gordon and Breach.

Martella, Maureen. 1992. "The Rhetoric and Realities of Contingent Work: The Case of Women in Clerical Temporary Work." Ph.D. dissertation, Temple University.

Massiah, Joycelin, ed., 1982. *Women and the Family.* Women in the Caribbean Project, vol. 2. Cave Hill, Barbados: Institute of Social and Economic Research, University of the West Indies.

———. 1983. *Women as Heads of Households in the Caribbean: Family Structure and Feminine Status.* Paris: UNESCO.

———. 1984a. "Employed Women in Barbados: A Demographic Profile, 1946–1970." Occasional paper no. 8, Institute of Social and Economic Research, University of the West Indies.

———. 1984b. "Indicators of Women in Development: A Preliminary Framework for the Caribbean." In Margaret Gill and Joycelin Massiah, eds., *Women, Work, and Development.* Women in the Caribbean Project, vol. 6. Cave Hill, Barbados: Institute of Social and Economic Research, University of the West Indies.

———. 1986. "Work in the Lives of Caribbean Women." *Social and Economic Studies* 35, no. 2:177–240.

———. 1989. "Women's Lives and Livelihoods: A View from the Commonwealth Caribbean." *World Development* 17, no. 7.

Mathurin, Lucille Mair. 1975. *The Rebel Woman in the British West Indies during Slavery.* Kingston: African-Caribbean Publications.

———. 1987. *Women in the Rebel Tradition: The English Speaking Caribbean.* N.p.: Women's International Resource Exchange.

Maurer, Bill. 1997. *Recharting the Caribbean: Land, Law, and Citizenship in the British Virgin Islands.* Ann Arbor: University of Michigan Press.

McClaurin, Irma. 1996. *Women of Belize: Gender and Change in Central America.* New Brunswick, N.J.: Rutgers University Press.

McCracken, Grant. 1988. *Culture and Consumption: New Approaches to the Symbolic Character of Consumer Goods and Activities.* Bloomington: Indiana University Press.

McKenzie, Hermione. 1982. "Introduction: Women and the Family in Caribbean Society." In Joycelin Massiah, ed., *Women and the Family.* Women in the Caribbean Project, vol. 2. Cave Hill, Barbados: Institute of Social and Economic Research, University of the West Indies.

McNeil, Maureen. 1987. *Gender and Expertise.* London: Free Association Books.

Mies, Maria. 1986. *Patriarchy and Accumulation on a World Scale: Women in the International Division of Labor.* London: Zed Books.

Miller, Daniel. 1990. "Fashion and Ontology in Trinidad." *Culture and History* 7:49–77.

———. 1994. *Modernity: An Ethnographic Approach: Dualism and Mass Consumption in Trinidad.* Oxford: Berg.

———, ed. 1995a. *Acknowledging Consumption: A Review of New Studies.* London: Routledge.

———, ed. 1995b. *Worlds Apart: Modernity through the Prism of the Local.* London: Routledge.

Miller, Daniel, Peter Jackson, Nigel Thrift, Beverly Holbrook, and Michael Rowlands. 1998. *Shopping, Place, and Identity.* London: Routledge.

Miller, Errol. 1986. *Marginalization of the Black Male: Insights from the Development of the Teaching Profession.* Kingston: Institute of Social and Economic Research, University of the West Indies.

———. 1991. *Men at Risk.* Kingston: Jamaica Publishing House.

Mills, C. Wright. 1956. *White Collar: The American Middle Classes.* New York: Oxford University Press.

Ministry of Labour, Consumer Affairs, and the Environment, Barbados. 1991. *Labor Market Information Newsletter* 9, no. 4 (October–December).

Mintz, Sidney W. 1955. "The Jamaican Internal Marketing Pattern: Some Notes and Hypotheses." *Social and Economic Studies* 14, no. 1:95–105.

———. 1971. "Men, Women, and Trade." *Comparative Studies in Society and History* 13, no. 3:247–69.

———. 1974. "The Caribbean Region." *Daedalus* 103, no. 2:45–71.

———. 1977. "The So-Called World System: Local Initiative and Local Response." *Dialectical Anthropology* 2, no. 4:253–70.

———. 1985. *Sweetness and Power: The Place of Sugar in Modern History.* New York: Viking, Penguin.

———. 1989. *Caribbean Transformations*. New York: Columbia University Press.

———. 1993. "Goodbye, Columbus: Second Thoughts on the Caribbean Region at Mid-Millenium." Walter Rodney Memorial Lecture, Centre for Caribbean Studies, University of Warwick.

———. 1996a. "Enduring Substances, Trying Theories: The Caribbean Region as Oikoumene." *Journal of the Royal Anthropological Institute* 2:1–23.

———. 1996b. *Tasting Food, Tasting Freedom: Excursions into Eating, Culture, and the Past*. Boston: Beacon Press.

Mintz, Sidney W., and Richard Price. 1992. *The Birth of African American Culture: An Anthropological Perspective*. Boston: Beacon Press.

Mintz, Sidney W., and Sally Price, eds. 1985. *Caribbean Contours*. Baltimore: Johns Hopkins University Press.

Mitter, Swasti. 1986. *Common Fate, Common Bond: Women and the Global Economy*. London: Pluto Press.

Mohammed, Patricia. 1988. "The Caribbean Family Revisited," in Patricia Mohammed and Catherine Shepherd, eds., *Gender in Caribbean Development*. Mona, Jamaica: Women and Development Studies Project, University of the West Indies.

———. 1994. "Nuancing the Feminist Discourse in the Caribbean." *Social and Economic Studies* 43, no. 3:135–67.

Mohanty, Chandra Talpade. 1997. "Women Workers and Capitalist Scripts: Ideologies of Domination, Common Interests, and the Politics of Solidarity." In M. Jacqui Alexander and Chandra Talpade Mohanty, eds., *Feminist Genealogies, Colonial Legacies, Democratic Futures*. London: Routledge.

Moi, Toril. 1991. "Appropriating Bourdieu: Feminist Theory and Pierre Bourdieu's Sociology of Culture." *New Literary History* 22:1017–49.

Morrissey, Marietta. 1976. "Intellectual Imperialism, Imperial Designs: A Sociology of Knowledge Study of British and American Dominance in the Development of Caribbean Social Science." *Latin American Perspectives* 3, no. 4.

Moses, Yolanda. 1977. "Female Status, the Family, and Male Dominance in a West Indian Community." *Signs* 3, no. 1:142–53.

Murphree, Mary C. 1984. "Brave New Office: The Changing Role of the Legal Secretary." In Karen Sacks and Dorothy Remy, eds., *My Troubles Are Going to Have Trouble with Me: Everyday Trials and Triumphs of Women Workers*. New Brunswick, N.J.: Rutgers University Press.

———. 1987. "New Technology and Office Tradition: The Not-So-Changing World of the Secretary." In Heidi I. Hartmann, Robert E. Kraut, and Louise A. Tilly, eds., *Computer Chips and Paper Clips: Technology and Women's Employment*, vol. 2. Washington, D.C.: National Academy Press.

Nash, June. 1983. "The Impact of the Changing International Division of Labor on Different Sectors of the Labor Force." In Nash and Maria Patricia Fernandez-Kelly, eds., *Women, Men, and the International Division of Labor*. Albany: State University of New York Press.

———. 1989. *From Tank Town to High Tech: The Clash of Community and Industrial Cycles.* Albany: State University of New York Press.

Nash, June, and Maria Patricia Fernandez-Kelly, eds. 1983. *Women, Men, and the International Division of Labor.* Albany: State University of New York Press.

Nash, June, and Helen Safa, eds. 1986. *Women and Change in Latin America.* New York: Bergin and Garvey.

Nichols, David. 1985. *Haiti in Caribbean Context: Ethnicity, Economy, and Revolt.* New York: St. Martin's Press.

9 to 5. 1989. *White Collar Displacement: Job Erosion in the Service Sector.* Cleveland: 9 to 5, National Association of Working Women.

———. 1990. *Stories of Mistrust and Manipulation: The Electronic Monitoring of the American Workforce.* Cleveland: 9 to 5, Working Women Education Fund.

———. 1992. *High Performance Office Work: Improving Jobs and Productivity.* Cleveland: 9 to 5, Working Women Education Fund.

O'Conner, David C. 1987. "Women Workers and the Changing International Division of Labor in Microelectronics." In Lourdes Beneria and Catherine Stimpson, eds., *Women, Households, and the Economy.* New Brunswick, N.J.: Rutgers University Press.

Offe, Claus. 1985. *Disorganized Capitalism: Contemporary Transformations of Work and Politics.* Cambridge, Mass.: MIT Press.

Office of Technology Assessment. 1985. *Automation of America's Offices.* Washington, D.C.: U.S. Government Printing Office.

Olin Wright, Erik. 1985. *Classes.* London: Verso.

———. 1997. *Class Counts: Comparative Studies in Class Analysis.* Cambridge: Cambridge University Press.

Olwig, Karen Fogg. 1993a. *Global Culture, Island Identity: Continuity and Change in the Afro-Caribbean Community of Nevis.* Chur, Switzerland: Harwood Academic Publishers.

———. 1993b. "The Migration Experience: Nevisian Women at Home and Abroad." In Janet Momsen, ed., *Women and Change in the Caribbean.* Bloomington: Indiana University Press.

———. 1999. "Follow the People: Movement, Lives, Family." Paper presented at conference, "Migration and Transnational Theory Re-examined," Santo Domingo, Dominican Republic, April.

Ong, Aihwa. 1987. *Spirits of Resistance and Capitalist Discipline: Factory Women in Malaysia.* Albany: State University of New York Press.

———. 1988. "Colonialism and Modernity: Feminist Representations of Women in Non-Western Societies." *Inscriptions,* no. 3–4.

———. 1991. "The Gender and Labor Politics of Postmodernity." *Annual Review of Anthropology* 20:279–309.

———. 1995. "State versus Islam: Malay Families, Women's Bodies, and the Body Politic in Malaysia." In Ong and Michael Peletz, eds., *Bewitching Women, Pious Men: Gender and Body Politics in Southeast Asia.* Berkeley and Los Angeles: University of California Press.

———. 1999. *Flexible Citizenship: The Cultural Logics of Transnationality.* Durham: Duke University Press.

Ong, Aihwa, and Donald Nonini, eds. 1997. *Underground Empires: The Cultural Politics of Modern Chinese Transnationalism.* New York: Routledge.

Ortiz, Altagracia, ed. 1996. *Puerto Rican Women and Work: Bridges in Transnational Labor.* Philadelphia: Temple University Press.

Ortner, Sherry B. 1991. "Reading America: Preliminary Notes on Class and Culture." In R. G. Fox, ed., *Recapturing Anthropology: Working in the Present.* Santa Fe: School of American Research Press.

———. 1995. "Resistance and the Problem of Ethnographic Refusal." *Comparative Study of Society and History* 37, no. 1:173–93.

Osirim, Mary Johnson. 1997. "We Toil All the Livelong Day: Women in the English-Speaking Caribbean." In Consuelo Lopez-Springfield, ed., *Daughters of Caliban: Caribbean Women in the Twentieth Century.* Bloomington: Indiana University Press.

Padavic, Irene. 1992. "White-Collar Work Values and Women's Interest in Blue-Collar Jobs." *Gender and Society* 6, no. 2:215–30.

Parkin, Frank. 1972. *Class Inequality and Political Order.* London: Paladin.

———. 1979. *Marxism and Class Theory: A Bourgeois Critique.* London: Tavistock.

Patterson, Orlando. 1967. *The Sociology of Slavery: An Analysis of the Origins, Development, and Structure of Negro Slave Society in Jamaica.* London: London University Press.

Paules, Greta Foff. 1991. *Dishing It Out: Power and Resistance Among Waitresses in a New Jersey Restaurant.* Philadelphia: Temple University Press.

Payne, Anthony, and Paul Sutton, eds. 1984. *Dependency under Challenge: The Political Economy of the Commonwealth Caribbean.* Manchester: Manchester University Press.

Pearson, Ruth. 1986. "The Greening of Women's Labour: Multinational Companies and Their Female Work Force in the Third and in the First World." In Kate Purcell, ed., *The Changing Experience of Employment.* London: Macmillan.

———. 1993. "Gender and New Technology in the Caribbean: New Work for Women?" In Janet Momsen, ed., *Women and Change in the Caribbean.* Bloomington: Indiana University Press.

Peattie, Lisa. 1987. "An Idea in Good Currency and How It Grew: The Informal Sector." *World Development* 15, no. 7:851–60.

Peiss, Kathy. 1986. *Cheap Amusements: Working Women and Leisure in Turn-of-the-Century New York.* Philadelphia: Temple University Press.

Peña, Devon. 1987. "Tortuosidad: Shop Floor Struggles of Female Maquiladora Workers." In Vicki L. Ruiz and Susan Tiano, eds., *Women on the U.S.-Mexico Border: Responses to Change.* Winchester, England: Allen and Unwin.

———. 1997. *The Terror of the Machine: Technology, Work, Gender, and Ecology on the U.S.-Mexico Border.* Austin: University of Texas, CMAS Books.

Personick, Valerie A. 1987. "Projections 2000: Industry Output and Employment through the End of the Century." *Monthly Labor Review* 110, no. 9:30–45.

Phillips, Edsil. 1982. "The Development of the Tourist Industry in Barbados, 1956–

1980." In Delisle Worrell, ed., *The Economy of Barbados, 1946–1980.* Bridgetown, Barbados: Central Bank of Barbados.

Popular Memory Group. 1982. "Popular Memory: Theory, Politics, and Method." In Richard Johnson, ed., *Making Histories: Studies in History Writing and Politics.* Minneapolis: University of Minnesota Press.

Portelli, Allesandro. 1986. "The Peculiarities of Oral History." *History Workshop* 12:96–107.

Portes, Alejandro, and Saskia Sassen-Koob. 1987. "Making It Underground: Comparative Material on the Informal Sector in Western Market Economies." *American Journal of Sociology* 93, no. 1:30–61.

Portes, Alejandro, and Richard Schauffler. 1993. "Competing Perspectives on the Latin American Informal Sector." *Population and Development Review* 19, 1:33–60.

Portes, Alejandro, and John Walton. 1981. *Labor, Class, and the International System.* New York: Academic Press.

Posthuma, Annie. 1987. "The Internationalisation of Clerical Work: A Study of Offshore Office Services in the Caribbean." SPRU Occasional Paper Series no. 24. University of Sussex.

Powell, Dorian L. 1976. "Female Labour Force Participation and Fertility: An Exploratory Study of Jamaican Women." *Social and Economic Studies* 25, no. 3:234–58.

Prandy, Ken. 1986. "Similarities of Life-Style and the Occupations of Women." In Rosemary Crompton and Michael Mann, eds., *Gender and Stratification.* Cambridge, Mass.: Polity Press.

Prasad, Pushkala, and Anshumann Prasad. 1994. "The Ideology of Professionalism and Work Computerization: An Institutionalist Study of Technological Change." *Human Relations* 47, no. 12:1433–58.

Pred, Allan, and Michael John Watts. 1992. *Reworking Modernity: Capitalisms and Symbolic Discontent.* New Brunswick, N.J.: Rutgers University Press.

Pringle, Rosemary. 1988. *Secretaries Talk: Sexuality, Power, and Work.* London: Verso.

Prior, Marshal. 1997. "Matrifocality, Power, and Gender Relations in Jamaica." In Caroline B. Brettell and Carolyn Seargent, eds., *Gender in Cross Cultural Perspective.* Upper Saddle River, N.J.: Prentice Hall.

Probert, Belinda, and Bruce W. Wilson. 1993. *Pink Collar Blues: Work, Gender, and Technology.* Melbourne: Melbourne University Press.

Puckrein, Gary A. 1984. *Little England: Plantation Society and Anglo-Barbadian Politics, 1627–1700.* New York: New York University Press.

Pyde, Peter. 1990. "Gender and Crab Antics in Tobago: Using Wilson's Reputation and Respectability." Paper presented to the American Anthropological Association Conference, New Orleans, November.

Pyle, Jean Larson. 1990. *The State and Women in the Economy: Lessons from Sex Discrimination in the Republic of Ireland.* Albany: State University of New York Press.

Quiñones, Maria. 1997. "Looking Smart: Consumption, Cultural History, and Identity among Barbadian 'Suitcase Traders.'" *Research in Economic Anthropology* 18:167–82.

Rakow, Lana F. 1988. "Women and the Telephone: The Gendering of a Communications Technology." In Cheris Kramarae, ed., *Technology and Women's Voices: Keeping in Touch*. New York: Routledge and Kegan Paul.

Redclift, Nanneke. 1985. "The Contested Domain: Gender, Accumulation, and the Labour Process." In Nanneke Redclift and Enzo Mingione, eds., *Beyond Employment: Household, Gender and Subsistence*. London: Basil Blackwell.

Reddock, Rhoda E. 1985. "Women and Slavery in the Caribbean." *Latin American Perspectives* 12, issue 44, no. 1.

——. 1998. "Contestations over National Culture in Trinidad and Togbago: Considerations of Ethnicity, Class and Gender." In Christine Barrow, ed., *Caribbean Portraits: Essays on Gender Ideologies and Identities*. Kingston: Ian Randle Publishers.

——. 1994. *Women, Labour, and Politics in Trinidad and Tobago: A History*. London: Zed Books.

Reiter, Rayna R., ed. 1975. *Toward an Anthropology of Women*. New York: Monthly Review Press.

Robertson, Roland. 1992. *Globalization: Social Theory and Global Culture*. London: Sage.

Rodman, Hyman. 1971. *Lower-Class Families: The Culture of Poverty in Negro Trinidad*. Oxford: Oxford University Press.

Rofel, Lisa. 1992. "Rethinking Modernity: Space and Factory Discipline in China." *Cultural Anthropology* 7, no. 1:93–114.

Rosaldo, Michelle Z., and Louise Lamphere, eds. 1974. *Women, Culture, and Society*. Stanford: Stanford University Press.

Rosen, Ellen. 1987. *Bitter Choices: Blue Collar Women In and Out of Work*. Chicago: University of Chicago Press.

Rouse, Roger. 1991. "Mexican Migration and the Social Space of Postmodernism." *Diaspora*, spring.

Rubin, Gayle. 1975. "The Traffic in Women: Notes on the Political Economy of Sex." In Rayna R. Reiter, ed., *Toward an Anthropology of Women*. New York: Monthly Review Press.

Ruiz, Vicki L., and Susan Tiano, eds. 1987. *Women on the U.S.-Mexico Border: Responses to Change*. Winchester, England: Allen and Unwin.

Rutz, Henry J., and Benjamin S. Orlove. 1989. *The Social Economy of Consumption: Monographs in Economic Anthropology*. Lanham, Md.: University Press of America.

Sacks, Karen. 1974. "Engels Revisited: Women, the Organization of Production, and Private Property." In Michelle Z. Rosaldo and Louise Lamphere, eds., *Woman, Culture, and Society*. Stanford: Stanford University Press.

Safa, Helen I. 1981. "Runaway Shops and Female Employment: The Search for Cheap Labor." *Signs* 7, no. 2:418–33.

——. 1983. "Women, Production, and Reproduction in Industrial Capitalism: A Comparison of Brazilian and U.S. Factory Workers." In June Nash and Maria Patricia Fernandez-Kelly, eds., *Women, Men, and the International Division of Labor*. Albany: State University of New York Press.

——. 1986a. "Economic Autonomy and Sexual Equality in Caribbean Society." *Social and Economic Studies* 35, no. 3:1–22.

——. 1986b. "Female Employment in the Puerto Rican Working Class." In June Nash and Helen Safa, eds., *Women and Change in Latin America*. South Hadley, Mass.: Bergin and Garvey Publishers.

——. 1990. "Women and Industrialization in the Caribbean." In Sharon Stichter and Jane L. Parpart, eds., *Women, Employment, and the Family in the International Division of Labour*. Philadelphia: Temple University Press.

——. 1995. *The Myth of the Male Breadwinner: Women and Industrialization in the Caribbean*. Boulder, Colo.: Westview Press.

Samper, Maria Luz Daza. 1987. "A Comparative Survey of Responses to Office Technology in the United States and Western Europe." In Barbara D. Wright, ed., *Women, Work, and Technology: Transformations*. Ann Arbor: University of Michigan Press.

——. 1993. "Ownership of Quality and Labor Management Cooperation in the Global Workplace: A Challenge for Labor Relations in the Caribbean." Paper presented at the annual conference of the Caribbean Studies Association, Kingston and Ocho Rios, Jamaica.

Sanderson, Steven, ed. 1985. *The Americas in the New International Division of Labor*. New York: Holmes and Meier.

Santiago Carlos E. 1991. "The Labor Market Implications of Structural Adjustment in the Caribbean." Discussion paper no. 91-02, Department of Economics, State University of New York at Albany.

Sassen, Saskia. 1988. *The Mobility of Labor and Capital: A Study of International Investment and Labor Flow*. Cambridge: Cambridge University Press.

——. 1991. *The Global City: New York, London, Tokyo*. Princeton: Princeton University Press.

——. 1998. *Globalization and Its Discontents: Essays on the New Mobility of People and Money*. New York: New Press, 1998.

Schmink, Marianne. 1986. "Women and Urban Industrial Development in Brazil." In June Nash and Helen Safa, eds., *Women and Change in Latin America*. South Hadley, Mass.: Bergin and Garvey.

Schnorr, Teresa M., et al. 1991. "Video Display Terminals and the Risk of Spontaneous Abortion." *New England Journal of Medicine* 324, no. 11:727–33.

Scott, James. 1985. *Weapons of the Weak: Everyday Forms of Peasant Resistance*. New Haven: Yale University Press.

——. 1990. *Domination and the Arts of Resistance: Hidden Transcripts*. New Haven: Yale University Press.

Scott, Joan. 1988. *Gender and the Politics of History*. New York: Cambridge University Press.

Sen, Gita, and Caren Grown. 1987. *Development, Crises, and Alternative Visions: Third World Women's Perspectives*. New York: Monthly Review Press.

Sen, Krishna, and Maila Stivens, eds. 1998. *Gender and Power in Affluent Asia*. London: Routledge.

Senior, Olive. 1991. *Working Miracles: Women's Lives in the English-Speaking Caribbean.* Bloomington: Indiana University Press.

Sheppard, Jill. 1977. *The "Redlegs" of Barbados: Their Origins and History.* Millwood, N.Y.: KTO Press.

Simmel, Georg. 1950. *The Sociology of Georg Simmel.* Translated and edited by K. H. Wolff. New York: The Free Press.

——. [1904] 1957. "Fashion." *American Journal of Sociology* 62, no. 6:541–88.

——. [1911] 1984. *Georg Simmel: On Women, Sexuality, and Love.* Translated by Guy Oakes. New Haven: Yale University Press.

Skeggs, Beverly. 1997. *Formations of Class and Gender.* London: Sage.

Sklair, Leslie. 1991. *Sociology of the Global System.* Baltimore: Johns Hopkins University Press.

——. 1993. *Assembling for Development: The Maquila Industry in Mexico and the United States.* San Diego: Center for U.S.-Mexican Studies, University of California.

Slater, Don. 1997. *Consumer Culture and Modernity.* Cambridge, Mass.: Polity Press.

Smith, Joan, and Immanuel Wallerstein, eds. 1992. *Creating and Transforming Households: The Constraints of the World Economy.* Cambridge: Cambridge University Press.

Smith, M. G. 1962. *West Indian Family Structure.* Seattle: University of Seattle Press.

——. 1965. *The Plural Society in the West Indies.* Berkeley and Los Angeles: University of California Press.

——. 1984. *Culture, Race, and Class in the Commonwealth Caribbean.* Mona, Jamaica: Extra-Mural Unit, University of the West Indies.

Smith, R. T. 1956. *The Negro Family in British Guiana.* London: Routledge and Kegan Paul.

——. 1971. "Culture and Social Structure in the Caribbean: Some Recent Work on Family and Kinship Studies." In Michael Horowitz, ed., *Peoples and Cultures of the Caribbean.* Garden City, N.Y.: Natural History Press.

——. 1978. "The Family and the Modern World System: Some Observations from the Caribbean." *Journal of Family History* 3, no. 2:337–60.

——. 1987. "Hierarchy and the Dual Marriage System in West Indian Society." In Jane Collier and Syl Yanagisako, eds., *Gender and Kinship: Essays Toward a Unified Analysis.* Stanford: Stanford University Press.

Soares, Anjelo. 1991a. "The Hard Life of the Unskilled Workers in New Technologies: Data Entry Clerks in Brazil—A Case Study." In H.-J. Bullinger, ed., *Human Aspects in Computing: Design and Use of Interactive Systems and Information Management.* Amsterdam: Elsevier Science Publishing.

——. 1991b. "Work Organization in Brazilian Data Processing Centres: Consent and Resistance." *Labour, Capital and Society* 24, no. 2:154–83.

——. 1992. "Telework and Communication in Data Processing Centres in Brazil." In U. E. Gattiker, ed., *Technology-Mediated Communication.* New York: Walter de Gruyter.

Sobo, Elisa. 1993. *One Blood: The Jamaican Body.* Albany: State University of New York Press.

Softley, E. (1985). "Word Processing: New Opportunities for Women Office Workers?" In

Wendy Faulkner and Erik Arnold, eds., *Smothered by Invention: Technology in Women's Lives*. London: Pluto Press.

Sokoloff, Natalie. 1980. *Between Money and Love*. New York: Praeger.

Standing, Guy. 1989. "Global Feminization through Flexible Labor." *World Development* 17, no. 7:1077–95.

St. Cyr, Joaquin. 1990. "Participation of Women in Caribbean Development: Inter-Island Trading and Export Processing Zones." Report prepared for the Economic Commission for Latin America and the Caribbean, Caribbean Development and Co-operation Committee, Kingston.

Stewart, John O. 1989. *Drinkers, Drummers, and Decent Folk: Ethnographic Narratives of Village Trinidad*. Albany: State University of New York Press.

Stoffle, Richard W. 1977. Industrial Impact on Family Formation in Barbados, West Indies." *Ethnology* 16, no. 3:253–67.

Stolcke, Verena. 1984. "The Exploitation of Family Morality: Labor Systems and Family Structure on Sao Paulo Coffee Plantations, 1850–1979." In R. T. Smith, ed., *Kinship, Ideology, and Practice in Latin America*. Chapel Hill: University of North Carolina Press.

Sunshine, Cathy. 1985. *The Caribbean: Survival, Struggle, and Sovereignty*. Boston: South End Press.

Sutton, Constance. 1974. "Cultural Duality in the Caribbean." *Caribbean Studies* 14, no. 2:96–101.

———. 1987. "The Caribbeanization of New York City and the Emergence of a Transnational Socio-Cultural System." In Sutton and E. M. Chaney, eds., *Caribbean Life in New York City: Sociocultural Dimensions*. New York: Center for Migration Studies.

Sutton, Constance, and Susan Makiesky-Barrow. 1977. "Social Inequality and Sexual Status in Barbados." In Alice Schlegel, ed., *Sexual Stratification: A Cross-Cultural View*. New York: Columbia University Press.

Sutton, Paul, ed. 1986. *Dual Legacies in the Contemporary Caribbean: Continuing Aspects of British and French Domination*. London: Frank Cass.

Swedenburg, Ted, and Smadar Lavie, eds. 1996. *Displacement, Diaspora, and Geographies of Identity*. Durham: Duke University Press.

Tardanico, Richard, ed. 1987. *Crises in the Caribbean Basin*. New York: Sage.

Taylor, Alicia. 1988. "Women Traders in Jamaica: The Informal Commercial Importers." Report prepared for the Economic Commission for Latin America and the Caribbean, Caribbean Development and Co-operation Committee, Kingston.

Taylor, F. W. 1903. *Shop Management*. New York: Harper and Brothers.

———. 1911. *The Principles of Scientific Management*. New York: Harper and Brothers.

Thomas, Clive Y. 1988. *The Poor and the Powerless: Economic Policy and Change in the Caribbean*. New York: Monthly Review Press.

Thomas, J. J. 1889. *Froudacity: West Indian Fables Explained*. London: Unwin.

Thompson, E. P. 1968. *The Making of the English Working Class*. Hammondsworth, England: Penguin.

Tiano, Susan. 1986. "Labor Composition and Gender Stereotypes in the Maquilas." *Journal of Borderlands Studies* 5, no. 1:20–24.

———. 1987. "Maquiladoras in Mexicali: Integration or Exploitation?" In Vicki L. Ruiz and Susan Tiano, eds., *Women on the U.S.-Mexico Border: Responses to Change*. Winchester, England: Allen and Unwin.

———. 1990. "Maquiladora Women: A New Category of Workers?" In Kathryn Ward, ed., *Women Workers and Global Restructuring*. Ithaca: ILR Press.

Tilly, Louise A., and Joan W. Scott. 1978. *Women, Work, and Family*. New York: Holt, Rinehart and Winston.

Tomlinson, Alan, ed. 1990. *Consumption, Identity and Style: Marketing, Meanings, and the Packaging of Pleasure*. London: Routledge.

Tomlinson, John. 1991. *Cultural Imperialism*. Baltimore: Johns Hopkins University Press.

Trollope, Anthony. 1860. *The West Indies and the Spanish Main*. New York: Harper and Brothers, 1860.

Trouillot, Michel Rolph. 1992. "The Caribbean Region: An Open Frontier in Anthropological Theory." *Annual Review of Anthropology* 21:19–42.

Veblen, Thorstein. 1953. *The Theory of the Leisure Class*. 1899. Reprint, New York: NAL Penguin.

Visweswaran, Kamala. 1997. "Histories of Feminist Ethnography." *Annual Review of Anthropology* 26:591–621.

Wagley, Charles. 1960. "Plantation America: A Culture Sphere." In Vera Rubin, ed., *Caribbean Studies: A Symposium*. 2d ed. Seattle: University of Washington Press.

Wakefield, E. G. 1968. *The Collected Works of Edward Gibbon Wakefield*. Edited by M. F. L. Prichard. Glasgow: Collins.

Walby, Sylvia. 1986. *Patriarchy at Work*. Minneapolis: University of Minnesota Press.

Wallerstein, Immanuel. 1974. *The Modern World System*. New York: Academic Press.

———. 1993. "World System versus World-Systems." In André Gunder Frank and Barry K. Gills, eds., *The World System: Five Hundred Years of Five Thousand?* New York: Routledge.

Ward, Kathryn. 1990a. "Gender, Work, and Development." *Annual Review of Sociology*. September.

———, ed. 1990b. *Women Workers and Global Restructuring*. Ithaca, N.Y.: ILR Press.

Ward, Kathryn B., and Jean Larson Pyle. 1995. "Gender, Industrialization, Transnational Corporations and Development: An Overview of the Trends." In Christine E. Bose and Edna Acosta-Belen, eds., *Women in the Latin American Development Process*. Philadelphia: Temple University Press.

Warren, Kay B., and Susan C. Bourque. 1991. "Women, Technology, and International Development Ideologies: Analyzing Feminist Voices." In Micaela di Leonardo, ed., *Gender at the Crossroads of Knowledge: Feminist Anthropology in the Postmodern Era*. Berkeley and Los Angeles: University of California Press.

Waters, Malcolm. 1995. *Globalization*. London: Routledge.

Watson, James, ed. 1997. *Golden Arches East: McDonald's in East Asia*. Stanford: Stanford University Press.

Watson, Karl. 1979. *The Civilized Island: Barbados*. Bridgetown, Barbados: Caribbean Graphics.

Watts, Michael John. 1992. "Capitalisms, Crises, and Cultures I: Notes Toward a Totality of Fragments." In Allen Pred and Michael John Watts, eds., *Reworking Modernity: Capitalisms and Symbolic Discontent*. New Brunswick, N.J.: Rutgers University Press.

Weber, Max. 1938. *The Protestant Ethic and the Spirit of Capitalism*. London: Unwin.

——. [1947] 1964. *The Theory of Social and Economic Organization*. Edited by Talcott Parsons. New York: Free Press.

Webster, Juliet. 1996. *Shaping Women's Work: Gender, Employment, and Information Technology*. London: Longman.

Werlhof, Claudia von. 1988. "Women's Work: The Blind Spot in the Critique of Political Economy." In Maria Mies, Veronika Bennholdt-Thomsen, and Claudia von Werlhof, eds., *Women: The Last Colony*. London: Zed Books.

Westwood, Sallie. 1985. *All Day, Every Day: Factory and Family in the Making of Women's Lives*. Urbana: University of Illinois Press.

Wilk, Richard. 1990. "Consumer Goods as Dialogue about Development." *Culture and History* 7:79–100.

Williams, Brackette. 1991. *Stains on My Name, Blood in My Veins: Guyana and the Politics of Cultural Struggle*. Durham: Duke University Press.

Williams, Eric. 1970. *From Columbus to Castro: The History of the Caribbean, 1492–1969*. New York: Harper and Row.

——. [1944] 1994. *Capitalism and Slavery*. Chapel Hill: University of North Carolina Press.

Williams, Raymond. 1977. *Marxism and Literature*. London: Oxford University Press.

Willis, Paul. 1977. *Learning to Labour*. Westmead, England: Saxon House.

Willis, Susan. 1991. *A Primer for Daily Life*. New York: Routledge.

Wilson, Elizabeth. 1985. *Adorned in Dreams: Fashion and Modernity*. Berkeley and Los Angeles: University of California Press.

——. 1990. "The Postmodern Chameleon." *New Left Review* 180 (March–April).

Wilson, Fiona. 1991. *Sweaters: Gender, Class and Workshop-Based Industry in Mexico*. New York: St. Martin's Press.

Wilson, Peter H. 1969. "Reputation and Respectability: A Suggestion for Caribbean Ethnography." *Man* 4, no. 1:70–84.

——. 1973. *Crab Antics: The Social Anthropology of English-Speaking Negro Societies of the Caribbean*. New Haven: Yale University Press.

Wilson, Rob, and Wimal Dissanayake, eds. 1996. *Global/Local: Cultural Production and the Transnational Imaginary*. Durham: Duke University Press.

Wiltshire-Brodber, Rosina. 1988. "Gender, Race, and Class in the Caribbean." In Patricia Mohammed and Catherine Shepherd, eds., *Gender in Caribbean Development*. Mona, Jamaica. Women and Development Studies, University of the West Indies.

Witter, Michael, ed. 1989. "Higglering/Sidewalk Vending/Informal Commercial Trading in the Jamaican Economy." Proceedings of a symposium, Department of Economics, University of the West Indies, Mona, Jamaica.

Wolf, Diane L. 1990. "Linking Women's Labor with the Global Economy: Factory Workers and Their Families in Rural Java." In Kathryn Ward, ed., *Women Workers and Global Restructuring*. Ithaca, N.Y.: ILR Press.

———. 1992. *Factory Daughters: Gender, Household Dynamics, and Rural Industrialization in Java*. Berkeley and Los Angeles: University of California Press.

World Bank. 1989. "Offshore Information Industry Potentials in Barbados." Unpublished report.

Worrell, Delisle, ed. 1982. *The Economy of Barbados, 1946–1980*. Bridgetown, Barbados: Central Bank of Barbados.

Wright, Barbara Drygulski, ed. 1987. *Women, Work, and Technology: Transformations*. Ann Arbor: University of Michigan Press.

Wright, Erik Olin. 1979. *Class Structure and Income Determination*. New York: Academic Press.

———. 1985. *Classes*. London: Verso.

———. 1997. *Class Counts: Comparative Studies in Class Analysis*. Cambridge: Cambridge University Press.

Yanigasako, Sylvia, and Carol Delaney, eds., 1995. *Naturalizing Power: Essays in Feminist Cultural Analysis*. New York: Routledge.

Yelvington, Kevin. 1989. "The Support Networks of Female Factory Workers in Trinidad: Some Preliminary Considerations." Paper presented at the 15th Annual Congress of the Latin American Studies Association, Miami, Florida.

———. 1995. *Producing Power: Ethnicity, Gender, and Class in a Caribbean Workplace*. Philadelphia: Temple University Press.

Young, Gay. 1987. "Gender Identification and Working Class Solidarity among Maquila Workers in Cuidad Juarez: Stereotypes and Realities." In Vicki L. Ruiz and Susan Tiano, eds., *Women on the U.S.-Mexico Border: Responses to Change*. Winchester, England: Allen and Unwin.

Young, Kate, Carol Wolkowitz, and Roslyn McCullagh, eds. 1981. *Of Marriage and the Market: Women's Subordination Internationally and Its Lessons*. London: CSE.

Young, Virginia Heyer. 1993. *Becoming West Indian: Culture, Self, and Nation in St. Vincent*. Washington, D.C.: Smithsonian Institution Press.

Zavella, Patricia. 1985. "'Abnormal Intimacy': The Varying Work Networks of Chicana Cannery Workers." *Feminist Studies* 11, no. 3:541–57.

———. 1987. *Women's Work and Chicano Families: Cannery Workers of the Santa Clara Valley*. Ithaca, N.Y.: Cornell University Press.

Zinn, Maxine Baca. 1987. "Structural Transformation and Minority Families." In Lourdes Beneria and Catherine Stimpson, eds., *Women, Households, and the Economy*. New Brunswick, N.J.: Rutgers University Press.

Zuboff, Shoshana. 1988. *In the Age of the Smart Machine: The Future of Work and Power*. New York: Basic Books.

Index

Age. *See* Women: age and work; Informatics: and workers' age

Agency, women's: in Barbados, 40; and capitalism, 28, 29, 38–39, 40; and consumption, 36; and discipline, modes of, 212; and gender ideologies, 138, 212; and professionalism, 202, 212, 234; and women, 36, 202, 212, 255

Anthropology, 3; in the Caribbean, 266 n.15; and globalization, 29; and transnationalism, 20, 29

Appadurai, Arjun, 30

Apple, Michael, 54, 55, 152

Barbados: agency (women's) in, 40; child care in, 128–129; class in, 290 n.12; conservatism in, 84, 165, 267 n.21; Cropover, 285 n.16; cultural imperialism in, 267 n.22; Data Air in, 1, 40–41, 101, 140, 141, 143–146, 148, 149, 165, 188, 223, 253, 275 n.34, 284 n.2; divisions of labor in, 48, 73, 76; dress in, 219, 223–225, 228; economic development in, 5, 8, 30, 31, 66, 67, 68, 76, 77, 78, 83, 84–85, 86–91, 92–93, 94, 97, 99, 274 n.28; education in, 93; employee benefits in, 47, 97, 275 n.34; employment in, 77–78, 91–92, 280 n.26, 284 n.4, 291 n.19; and England, 8; and export industrialization, 67, 90–92; family in, 19, 129, 130, 133–4, 204, 255–256, 283n; fashion in, 232; femininity in, 73, 108, 110, 111–112, 136; and foreign-owned industry, 93; and foreign travel, 32; gender ideologies in, 58, 73, 76, 107, 108, 110, 115, 116, 118, 138; history of, 7–8, 30, 32, 66–71, 75, 83, 86–91; households in, 126–128, 280 nn.28 and 32; 283 n.41; informal sector in, 239, 242; and informatics, 9, 31, 93–97, 106, 140, 141, 152, 163, 165, 166, 179, 185, 187, 188, 193, 194, 195, 202, 224, 225, 253, 254, 275 n.32, 276 n.3, 284 n.7, 287 n.28; INTEL in, 269 n.32; labor in, 58, 73; localization in, 226; map of, 7; manufacturing in, 30–31, 86–89, 90–92, 94; marriage in, 109–110, 128–129; masculinity in, 232; "meeting turn," 292 n.28; men in, 232, 273 n.13, 280 n.26; and migration, 32, 76; motherhood in, 128–130, 134; Multitext in, 140, 141, 142, 143, 145, 147, 150, 151, 152, 165, 253, 284 n.6; and the North American Free Trade Agreement (NAFTA), 88;

Barbados (*cont.*)

people and society in, 68–69, 70–71; post-Emancipation labor conditions in, 75; race in, 24, 264 n.4; recruitment of labor in, 145–147; reputation and respectability in, 22, 23, 34, 108–110, 111, 112, 234; slavery in, 68–69, 70–71, 73, 74, 272 n.8; and sugar, 67–68, 69, 70, 83–84, 85, 86, 90–91, 266 n.19, 274 n.24, 286 n.20; tourism in, 5, 30–31, 86, 89; trade unions in, 5, 62, 96, 97, 193, 194, 195; urbanity in, 19; wages in, 97, 98 (table), 101, 116, 152, 153, 156, 157, 158, 166, 276 n.3, 279 n.24; women in, 1, 5, 32–33, 47, 59, 62, 71–78, 91, 107, 108, 111–115, 116, 117, 128–129, 134–136, 225, 230, 231, 239, 242, 250, 253, 254, 256, 257, 273 n.13, 278 n.19, 279 n.25, 280 n.26, 283 n.41; women, work, and family in, 41–42, 58, 71, 72–74, 76, 78–79, 86, 97, 107, 111, 112–115, 116, 117, 120, 126, 127–136, 139, 202, 205, 206, 279 n.25, 280n; working conditions in, 144, 145

Barbados Workers' Union: and informatics, 96, 193, 194, 195; and sugar, 286 n.20. *See also* Trade Unions

Barrow, Christine, 110, 278 n.15

Beckford, George, 82, 274 n.22

Beckles, Hilary, 273 n.16, 290 n.12

Boserup, Esther, 62

Bourdieu, Pierre: on class, 50, 51–52; on *habitus*, 290 n.11; on localization, 63

Braverman, Harry: on labor forces, 105; on work and technology, 53, 56

Burawoy, Michael, 50–51, 270 n.45; on culture and production, 270 n.45

Capitalism: and agency (women's), 28, 29, 38–39, 40; and class, 49; and gender, 35, 40, 59; and globalization and trans-

nationalism, 25, 28, 137; and power, 28; and resistance (women's), 40; and work, 53, 59

Caribbean, the: and anthropology, 266 n.15; consumption in, 7, 31; cultural imperialism in, 267 n.22; decentralization and, 46; divisions of labor in, 42; economic development in, 5–6, 30–31, 80–82, 86, 89–90, 92–93, 97, 99; and export industrialization, 30–31; family in, 31–32, 127, 128, 203; femininity in, 10, 11, 42, 107, 108, 111, 212, 277 n.8; and foreign-owned industry, 93; gender ideologies in, 3, 5, 10, 11, 108, 110–112, 277 n.8, 287 n.27; gender relations in, 38; history of, 272 n.7; households in, 78–79, 127, 203; informal sector in, 239–243; and informatics, 46–47, 152; and labor migrations, 32; map of, 8; masculinity in, 90, 232, 233, 277 n.8; men in, 192, 232, 233, 251; motherhood in, 128; and the New World group, 81; production in, 6, 31; race in, 24; reputation and respectability in, 10, 108–109, 227, 277 n.12; sex segregation in, 192; slavery in, 38, 108, 272 n.3, 273 n.15; sugar plantations in, 6, 70; tourism in/from, 32; transnationalism in, 5, 6, 31–32; and the United States, 31; women in, 107, 108, 111, 117, 132–133, 156, 192, 239–243, 260, 273 n.12, 278 n.15; women, work, and family in, 5, 10–11, 33, 37, 41, 42, 71–72, 107, 128, 132–133

Caribbean Basin Initiative (CBI), 90, 91, 275 n.30; in Barbados, 128–129, 130

Carpal Tunnel Syndrome. *See* Repetitive Stress Injury

Child care: in Barbados, 128–129; and hiring, 147

Child sharing, 273 n.11

China: Multitext in, 253

Class: in Barbados, 290 n.12; class consciousness, 65, 234, 260, 261; and consumption, 36, 61, 63, 260; and dress, 4, 21–22, 33, 63, 64, 65, 213, 214, 221, 222, 235–237, 257, 271 n.56; and femininity, 229; and gender, 3, 53, 57, 59, 230, 232, 257; and identity, 60–62, 237; and informatics, 61, 213, 229, 230–237, 260; and labor, 49; Karl Marx on, 49; and pink-collar workers, 22, 213, 229; and professionalism, 221, 222, 235, 237; and resistance, 234; theories of, 48–53; Max Weber on, 49; and women, 60–62, 229–232, 234, 235, 236, 237, 255, 257, 260, 261, 270 n.43; and work, 234

Clerical sector: decentralization of, 45; feminization of, 45, 54; fragmentation of, 45; moving offshore of, 46; in the United States, 43; workers' expectations of, 44–45

Clothing. *See* Dress

Computers: as panopticons, 198; as symbols of modernity, 147, 148, 270 n.54

Consumption, 3; and agency (women's), 36; and class, 36, 61, 63, 260; in the developing world, 35; and dress, 249, 250; and gender, 35, 36, 267 n.24; and identity (women's), 23, 34, 60, 65, 135, 258; and the informal sector, 243; and informatics, 5, 34, 238, 243; and the international division of labor, 35, 36, 250; paradigms of, 3, 34–35; and production, 29, 235, 257, 258, 259, 260; and professionalism, 259; and sex, 289 n.7; shifting patterns of, 27; and tourism, 33, 187; and transnationalism, 35, 249, 250, 259; and women, 238, 242, 243, 249, 250, 255, 258, 259, 260

Creole/creolization, 263 n.4; in Barbados, 70, 71; in the Caribbean, 6, 110; and

gender, 110; and reputation/respectability, 110; and transnationalism, 25

Cuales, Sonia, 271 n.53

Cultural capital: and women's class identities, 61

Cultural imperialism: in Barbados, 267 n.22; in the Caribbean, 267 n.22

Culture, 3; and class, 51; and production, 51

Data Air, 1, 12, 13, 14, 33, 47; attrition rates, 120–21; in Barbados, 1, 40–41, 101, 140, 141, 143–146, 148, 149, 165, 188, 223, 253, 275 n.34, 284 n.2; "corporate family" at, 203, 204; discipline, modes of, 196; in the Dominican Republic, 40–41, 47, 94, 101, 106, 149, 223, 276 n.5, 281 n.34; and dress, 123, 215, 223; and health workers, 177–178; hierarchy in, 164; hiring preferences, 124; hiring process, 146; and incentives, 153, 154, 156; and informal sector, 238; labor process of, 169–170; and localization, 187, 188; and management, 179, 188–190; and men, 276 n.5; Participatory Action Circles (PACS), 188, 189, 195; and professionalism, 123, 215, 220; promotion in, 164; and public relations, 185, 188; and quality monitoring, 170; recruitment, 145, 146; and resistance, 210–212; and rewards, 33, 186, 188; schedules in, 166; supervisors at, 156; wages, 152, 153, 154, 156; and women workers, 117, 286 n.23; and workers' ages, 121–126; workers' expectations of, 47. *See also* Informatics

Davies, Margery, 56

Decentralization: of information-based services, 45; and workers, 46

Democratic Labour Party (DLP), 96, 193; and the Barbados Workers' Union, 195

Dependency theory, 28, 82, 97, 99; and development planning, 92–93; and the international division of labor, 265 n.11; and the New World Group, 81–83

Dickson, William, 71

Discipline, modes of, 1, 2; and agency, 212; within capitalism, 38–39; computers as panopticons, 198, 199, 200, 258; corporate, 197; at Data Air, 196; and dress, 215, 217, 218, 219, 258; and family, 202; Michel Foucault on, 198; in informatics, 151, 195, 196–202, 210, 212, 213, 217, 218, 219, 257; at Multitext, 151; panopticon as, 198, 199, 200, 258; and pink-collar workers, 254; and power, 198; and professionalism, 212, 213, 215, 217, 218, 257, 258, 260; and resistance, 208, 209, 210, 259; surveillance as, 198, 199, 201, 258, 259; and women, 255, 257, 258, 259

Distinction, 64; and dress, 252, 289 n.6; and identity, 252; and women, 234–235, 252, 260, 289 n.6

Domesticity, 46

Dominica: Multitext in, 143, 288 n.5

Dominican Republic: Data Air's workforce in, 40–41, 47, 94, 101, 106, 149, 223, 276 n.5, 281 n.34; dress in, 223; export in, 263 n.6; informatics in, 1, 165, 171, 268 n.30, 269 n.41, 281 n.34, 282 n.39, 284 n.7; men in, 268 n.30, 276 n.5; and mothers as workers in, 279 n.25; research in, 15; wages in, 101, 263 n.6; workers' expectations in, 101, 269 n.41, 248 n.7

Double day, 132–133, 139, 291 n.18

Dress: and appearance, 4, 22, 33, 233; in Barbados, 219, 223–225, 228; and class, 4, 21–22, 33, 63, 64, 65, 213, 214, 221, 222, 235–237, 257, 271 n.56; and conformity, 227, 228; costs of, 244, 245;

and discipline, 215, 217, 218, 219, 258; and display, 192; and distinction, 252, 289 n.6; in the Dominican Republic, 223; and femininity, 34, 65, 229; and identity, 4, 21–22, 33, 63, 221, 222, 229, 235, 236, 237, 251, 252, 257; and individuality, 227, 228, 232; and the informal sector, 4, 238, 244, 245, 249, 251, 252; in informatics, 22, 34, 49, 63, 123, 214–229, 235, 237, 244, 251, 252, 257, 288 n.5; and localization, 228; and men, 232; and pink-collar workers, 4, 22, 34, 64, 213, 229; and power, 258; and professionalism, 4, 63, 64, 123, 213, 214–224, 226–229, 235, 237, 244, 245, 251, 252, 257, 258; and reputation and respectability, 227, 228; and "suitcase trading," 249; uniforms, 220–221, 288 n.5; and women, 225, 232, 236, 238, 244, 245, 249, 250, 251, 252, 253, 257, 258, 289 n.6. *See also* Fashion; Style

Duarte, Iris, 132

Economic development: in Barbados, 5, 8, 30, 31, 66, 67, 68, 76, 77, 78, 83, 84–85, 86–91, 92–93, 94, 97, 99, 274 n.28; in the Caribbean, 5–6, 30–31, 80–82, 86, 89–90, 92–93, 97, 99; women and, 37

Electronics industry: and women workers, 104

Emancipation: in Barbados, 75

False consciousness, 48, 221, 235, 288 n.3

Family, 126–128; in Barbados, 19, 129, 130, 133–4, 204, 255–256, 283 n.43; breakdown of, 283 n.43; in the Caribbean, 30–31, 127, 128, 203, 278 n.18, 279 n.21; "corporate," 202–205; as discipline, 202; and factory workers, 267 n.23; and the informal sector, 244; and transnationalism, 31–32; and women

Globalization (*cont.*)
and tourism, 28; and women, 35–36, 99, 261, 264 n.2

Hall, Stuart, 137
Harvey, David: on nation-states and trans-nationalism, 93; on the "new world capitalist order," 27; on postmodernity, 25; on women and development in the Caribbean, 95–96
Health: in informatics, 175–178
Higglers, 74, 290 n.15. *See also* Informal Sector
High heels, 4. *See also* Dress
Hossfeld, Karen, 228
Households, 126–128; in Barbados, 126–128, 280 n.28, n.32, 283 n.41; in the Caribbean, 78–79, 127, 203, 279 n.21; and class identity, 60; women as members of, 60, 78, 79, 126–128, 133, 249, 279 n.21, 280 n.32, 283 n.41; and women's work, 249, 279 n.21. *See also* Family
Howard, Michael, 92–93, 96
Hurston, Zora Neale, 74

Identity, women's: Bajan, 2, 4, 11, 22, 65; and class, 60–62, 237; and consumption, 23, 34, 60, 65, 135, 258; and cultural capital, 61; and distinction, 252; and dress, 4, 21–22, 33, 63, 221, 222, 229, 235, 236, 237, 251, 252, 257; and gender and class, 53, 61; and informatics, 32–33, 65, 115, 251, 252, 255, 261; pink-collar, 4, 22, 61, 135, 139, 252, 255; and professionalism, 23, 214, 221, 222, 229, 237, 251, 252, 257, 260; and reputation and respectability, 260; and rewards, 187; and tourism, 33, 187; and wages, 283 n.45; and work, 3, 34
Incentives: in informatics, 153–159; and stress, 178

Industrial Development Corporation (IDC), 94, 95; and wages, 152; worker training, 149, 150, 152
Informal sector, 290 n.17; in Barbados, 239, 242; in the Caribbean, 239–243; and dress, 4, 238, 244, 245, 249, 251, 252; and family, 244; and informatics, 238, 241, 242, 243, 251; and micro-entrepreneurs, 241, 242; and professionalism, 241, 244, 245, 251, 252, 259; and "suitcase trading," 240, 241, 242, 244, 245, 292 n.27; theories of, 241; and tourism, 242, 250, 291 n.21; and transnationalism, 250; and triple shifts, 239; and wages, 251, 252; and women, 48, 238–252, 259, 270 n.43
Informatics, 2, 3, 12, 23, 26; and attrition rates, 281 n.34; and Barbados, 9, 31, 93–97, 106, 140, 141, 152, 163, 165, 166, 179, 185, 187, 188, 193, 194, 195, 202, 224, 225, 253, 254, 275 n.32, 276 n.3, 284 n.7, 287 n.28; and the Barbados Workers' Union, 96, 193, 194, 195; and the Caribbean, 46–47, 152; and class, 61, 213, 229, 230–237, 260; and consumption, 5, 34, 238, 243; and the "corporate family," 203–206; in the Dominican Republic, 165, 171, 268 n.20, 269 n.41, 281 n.34, 282 n.39, 284 n.7; and dress, 22, 34, 49, 63, 123, 214–229, 235, 237, 244, 251, 252, 257, 288 n.5; and femininity, 61, 115, 164, 190, 213, 229; and gender, 155, 158, 159, 161, 164, 170; and gender ideologies, 103, 115–119, 121–126, 134, 135, 137, 139, 213; and health, 175–178; hierarchical conflicts in, 158, 159; hierarchy in, 140; hiring preferences in, 124; hiring process in, 146, 147; historical shifts in, 4–5; and identity (women's), 32–33, 65, 115, 251, 252, 255, 261; and incentives, 153, 155,

156, 159; in Jamaica, 160, 161, 265 n.6; labor process, 166–169, 172–175; localization in, 187, 226; management in, 179–185, 188–192, 195, 201, 202, 218; men in, 155, 164, 165, 170, 268 n.27, 269 n.41, 291 n.25; and modernity, 179; and mothers as workers, 126, 132, 139, 147, 279 n.25, 282 nn.38–39, 287 n.28; and the open office, 141, 142, 200; the panopticon in, 198, 199, 200; and Participatory Action Circles (PACS), 188, 189, 195, 196; paternalism in, 203; professionalism, 4, 23, 34, 63, 123, 196, 213, 214–224, 226–229, 235, 237, 245, 251, 252, 256, 257, 288 n.1; promotion in, 157–165; and quality monitoring, 43, 168–172, 195, 196, 199, 287 n.25; race in, 24; recruitment in, 145–147; and reputation and respectability, 164, 235, 251; and resistance, 190, 191, 206, 208–212; rewards in, 185, 186, 187, 188, 291 n.26; schedules in, 165, 166; as a service industry, 43; sexual harassment, 182–183; shifts in, 152; stress in, 175, 178, 202; supervisors in, 158, 159, 160, 162; surveillance, 198, 199, 201; as symbolic capital, 48; and trade unions, 96, 190, 193, 194, 195, 286 n.20; training in, 149–152; in the United States, 12; wages in, 101, 152–159, 166, 214, 251, 252, 275 n.3, 284 n.9; women workers in, 4, 5, 33, 34, 65, 100, 103, 115, 116–127, 133, 135, 138, 148, 149, 154, 158, 159, 160, 161, 162–165, 171–172, 174–183, 190–192, 194–197, 199–206, 208–212, 214–239, 241–248, 250–252, 254–261, 269 n.40, 279 n.25, 282 n.40, 286 n.23, 291 n.19; and work environment, 197; and workers' ages, 117, 121, 132, 134, 196, 203, 282 n.37; workers' perceptions/expectations of, 47, 48, 147–

149, 154, 269 n.41, 284 n.7. *See also* Data Air; Multitext

Information industries. *See* Informatics; Service industries

Information technology, 44–45

INTEL: in Barbados, 93, 101, 269 n.32

International Division of Labor: and consumption, 35, 36, 250; and dependency theory, 265; and the global assembly line, 27, 37; history of, 27; the "new," 35, 37; and race, 23; and vertical integration, 266 n.11; and wages, 101; and women workers, 104

Ireland: informatics in, 1, 94, 106; women's labor in, 276 n.4

Jamaica: informatics in, 160, 161, 265 n.6; work ethics in, 197

Jameson, Fredric, 27

Kin networks. *See* Family

Kondo, Dorinne, 207

Labor: in Barbados, 58, 73; and class, 49; feminization of, 44, 54–55, 58, 61, 100; fragmentation of, 45, 53; and gender ideologies, 10; in informatics, 44, 45; rationalization of, 2, 45; women's, 58, 73. *See also* Labor migration; Labor process; Work

Labor migrations, 32, 76, 273 n.13

Labor process: at Data Air, 169–170; in informatics, 166–169, 172–175; at Multitext, 167, 168, 170

Labor unions. *See* Trade unions

LeFranc, Elsie, 233

Lewis, Arthur, 81, 86

Life cycle, women's: in Barbados, 136; and class identities, 59; and work, 41, 134

Lin, Vivian, 282 n.40

LiPuma, Edward, and Sarah Keene Meltzoff, 51, 52

Localization: in Barbados, 226; in culture and identity, 63; at Data Air, 187, 188; and dress, 228; and globalization, 3, 28, 261; in informatics, 187, 226; and professionalism, 228

Management: at Data Air, 179, 188–190; in informatics, 179–185, 188–192, 195, 201, 202, 218; at Multitext, 180, 183, 184, 185, 191, 192; and Participatory Action Circles (PACS), 188, 189

Manufacturing, 2; in Barbados, 30–31, 86–89, 90–92, 94; in the Caribbean, 90

Marriage: in Barbados, 109–110, 128–129. *See also* Union status

Marx, Karl: on class, 49

Masculinity: in Barbados, 232; in the Caribbean, 90, 232, 233, 277 n.8; and fashion, 232, 233; and reputation and respectability, 108–109, 155, 233, 251

Mass production: history of, 26

McNeil, Maureen, 55

"Meeting turns," 292 n.28

Men: in Barbados, 232, 273 n.13, 280 n.26; in the Caribbean, 192, 232, 233, 251, 273 n.13; and class, 233; in the Dominican Republic, 268 n.30, 276 n.5; and dress, 232, 233; in industry, 277 n.6; in informatics, 155, 164, 165, 170, 268 n.27, 269 n.41, 276 n.5; and promotion, 165; and reputation/respectability, 108–109, 155, 233, 251; and unemployment, 268 n.27

Microentrepreneurs, 241, 242

Mies, Maria, 35

Miller, Daniel: on consumption, 266 n.15; on reputation and respectability, 227; on style, 227; on transience/transcendence, 278 n.17, 289 n.9

Mills, C. Wright, 64; on dress and class, 271 n.56

Mintz, Sidney: on Caribbean culture, 84; on consumption, 259–260; on industrialization and modernity in the Caribbean, 6, 67, 69–70

Modernity, 56; in Barbados, 22, 67; in the Caribbean, 6, 23; concept of, 23; and informatics, 179; and pink-collar "classification," 22; and tradition, 6, 22, 32–33, 39

Mohanty, Chandra T., 36

Motherhood: in Barbados, 128–130, 134; and work, 116, 126, 129, 132, 139, 147, 269 n.34, 282 nn.38 and 39

Multinational corporations, 3, 40; and decentralization, 45, 46; fragmentation of, 45; and localized labor forces, 38, 39, 40

Multitext, 12–16; attrition rates, 20; in Barbados, 140–150, 151, 152, 165, 253, 284 n.6; in China, 253; corporate family, 203, 204; in Dominica, 143, 288 n.5; and dress, 215; and health, 176–177; hiring process, 147; incentives, 153–154, 156–157; labor process, 167, 168, 170; management, 180, 183, 184, 185, 191, 193; and Participatory Action Circles (PACS), 180–185, 191–192; and professionalism, 215, 220; and public relations, 185; quality monitoring, 170, 171, 184; recruitment of labor, 145; schedules in, 166; supervisors, 156–157; training at, 150, 151, 152; wages, 153, 156–157; and workers' resistance, 209, 210, 211

Nash, June, 226

New World Group, 81–82, 83

North American Free Trade Agreement (NAFTA), 27, 88, 93, 267 n.20

Ong, Aihwa: on class, 234; on the "corporate family," 204; "open office," 20, 140, 141, 142

Padavic, Irene, 48; on women and work in Malaysia, 38, 39
Panopticon, 198, 199, 200, 258
Participatory Action Circles (PACS), 188, 189, 195
Patriarchy, 35, 40, 59
Paules, Greta F., 159–160, 288 n.3; on resistance, 209
Pearson, Ruth, 160, 161, 265 n.6
Pena, Devon, 162; and discipline, 254; on resistance, 207; on women and work in Mexico, 268 n.27
"Pink collar," 3, 5, 263 n.3; and class, 22, 213, 229; and dress, 4, 22, 34, 64, 213, 229; and femininity, 4, 5, 34, 229; and the global assembly line, 23; and identity, 4, 22, 61, 135, 139, 252, 255; and professionalism, 64, 213, 229, 252; and service industries, 43; and women workers, 114
Postindustrialism, 42
Power: and discipline, 198; and dress, 258; and resistance, 206, 207, 208
Pringle, Rosemary: and class, 231; on femininity and clerical work, 56
Production, 3; and consumption, 29, 235, 257, 258, 259, 260; ideology in, 270 n.45; and the international division of labor, 36; paradigms of, 3, 34–35; shifting patterns of, 27; and women, 255
Professionalism: and agency (women's), 202, 212, 234; and class, 221, 222, 235, 237; and consumption, 259; and Data Air, 123, 215, 220; and dress, 4, 63, 64, 123, 213, 214–224, 226–229, 235, 237, 244, 245, 251, 252, 257, 258; and discipline, 212, 213, 215, 217, 218, 257, 258,

260; and femininity, 204, 205, 229, 256, 257, 260; and identity, 23, 214, 221, 222, 229, 237, 251, 252, 257, 260; and the informal sector, 241, 244, 245, 251, 252, 259; and informatics, 2, 4, 23, 34, 63, 123, 196, 213, 214–224, 226–229, 235, 237, 245, 251, 252, 256, 257, 288 n.1; and localization, 228; and Multitext, 215, 220; and perceptions of work, 63; and reputation and respectability, 135, 228, 235, 260; and resistance, 234; and uniforms, 220–221; and women, 212, 235, 241, 244, 245, 251, 252, 257, 259, 260

Quality monitoring, 45–46; at Data Air, 43, 168–172, 195, 196, 199; in informatics, 43, 168–172, 195, 196, 199, 287 n.25; at Multitext, 170, 171, 184; and workers' stress, 46

Race: in Barbados, 24, 264 n.4; as a factor in research, 17; in informatics, 23–24
Recruitment of labor: in Barbados, 145–147; and Data Air, 145, 146; and the hiring process, 147; in informatics, 145–147; and local cultural and economic conditions, 47; and Multitext, 145
Repetitive Stress Injury (RSI), 176–177, 285
Reputation/respectability: in Barbados, 22, 23, 34, 108–110, 111, 112, 234; in the Caribbean, 10, 108–109, 227, 277 n.12; critiques of, 108–110, 277 n.12; and dress, 227, 228; and femininity, 110, 155; and identity, 260; in informatics, 164, 235, 251; and masculinity, 108–109, 155; and men, 233, 251; and professionalism, 135, 228, 235, 260; and tourism, 251; Peter Wilson on, 108–109, 234, 235, 251, 277 n.11; and women, 233, 234, 235, 251
Research methodology, 12–19

Resistance, Women's: and capitalism, 40; and class, 234; and discipline, 208, 209, 210, 259; and globalization, 266 n.16; in informatics, 190, 191, 206, 208–212; and power, 206, 207, 208; and professionalism, 234; and trade unions, 207; and woman-centered events, 190; and women, 190, 191, 206, 208–212, 234, 259, 287 n.32

Rewards: at Data Air, 33, 186, 188; in informatics, 185, 186, 187, 188, 291 n.26; and tourism, 291 n.26

Safa, Helen: on class consciousness, 234; on industrialization and women's lives, 78–79; on women and family, 279 n.21, 282 n.40; on women and patriarchy, 65

Service industries: decentralization in, 45; fragmentation, 45; gender ideologies in, 43; and postindustrialism, 42; in the United States, 12, 42; and women workers, 43

Sexual harassment, 182–183, 285 n.14

Slavery: in Barbados, 68–69, 70–71, 73, 74, 272 n.3; in the Caribbean, 38, 108, 272 n.3, 273 n.15

Status, 162. See also Women: and status

Stoffle, Richard W.: on industry and family in Barbados, 78

Stone, Carl, 197–198

Stress: and incentives, 178; in informatics, 175, 178, 202. See also Repetitive Stress Injury

Style, 227. See also Dress; Fashion

Sugar, 5, 30–31, 70; in Barbados, 67–68, 69, 70, 83–84, 85, 86, 90–91, 266 n.19, 274 n.24; and the Barbados Workers' Union, 286 n.20; plantations and industrialization, 6, 69–70

Suitcase trading, 240, 241, 244, 245, 292 n.27. See also Informal sector

Surveillance: as discipline, 198, 199, 201, 258, 259; in informatics, 198, 199, 201

Technology. See Information technology

Temporary work, 11

Textile industry: in Barbados, 91; employment in, 91

"Thank-you cards." See Rewards

Tiano, Susan, 283 n.46

Total Quality Management (TQM), 285 n.13

Tourism: Bajan women's, 33, 186, 187, 250, 251; in Barbados, 5, 30–31, 86, 89; and globalization, 28; and the informal sector, 242, 250, 291 n.21, 292 n.27; and rewards, 291 n.26

Trade unions: in Barbados, 5, 62, 96, 97, 193, 194, 195, 286 n.20; and informatics, 96, 190, 193, 194, 195, 286 n.20; and resistance, 207. See also Barbados Workers' Union

Tradition: and modernity, 6, 22, 32–33, 39

Training: in informatics, 147–152

Transnational corporations. See Multinational corporations

Transnationalism, 2, 3, 24–25, 265 n.7; and anthropology, 20, 29; and capitalism, 25; in the Caribbean, 5, 6, 31–32; and consumption, 35, 250, 259; and indigenization, 25; and the informal sector, 250; and pink-collar "classification," 22; and political networks, 32; and power and identity, 30; theories of, 29–30; and tourism, 32; and women workers, 38–39, 99

Triple shifts, 33, 132, 239, 245–246, 247, 248, 291 n.18

Uniforms, 220–221, 288 n.5

Union status: and household status, 280n and women workers, 78, 269 n.33. See also Family; Marriage

United States: and the Caribbean, 31; de-industrialization in, 12; femininity in, 270 n.48; and information technology, 43; postindustrialism in, 42

Veblen, Thorstein, 257

Wages: in Barbados, 97, 98 (table), 101, 116, 152, 153, 156, 157, 158, 166, 276 n.3; in the Dominican Republic, 101, 263 n.6; and identity, 283 n.45; and incentives, 153–159; and the informal sector, 251, 252; in informatics, 101, 152–159, 166, 214, 251, 252, 276 n.3, 284 n.9; supervisors', 156, 157, 158; and women, 251, 252
Weber, Max, 49
West Indian culture: and femininity, 107; and traditions of work, 48; and women's economic independence, 109
Williams, Brackette, 264 n.1, 280 n.31
Williams, Eric: on Barbados, 66; on Caribbean modernity, 22–23; on industrialization in the Caribbean, 6; on sugar and capitalism, 272 n.9
Wilson, Peter, 108–109, 110, 277 n.11. *See also* Reputation/Respectability
Wiltshire-Brodber, Rosina, 38; on race and class, 271 n.53
Wolf, Diane, 135, 268 n.31
Women: age and work, 134, 196, 203, 282 n.37; and agency, 36, 202, 212, 255; in Barbados, 1, 5, 32–33, 47, 59, 62, 71–78, 91, 107, 108, 111–115, 116, 117, 128–129, 134–136, 225, 230, 231, 239, 242, 250, 253, 254, 256, 257, 273 n.13, 279 n.25, 280 n.26, 283 n.41; in the Caribbean, 107, 108, 111, 117, 132–133, 156, 192, 239–243, 260, 273 n.12, 278 n.15; as cheap labor, 105–106, 116, 117, 118–119; and choices of work, 48; and class, 60–62, 65, 229–232, 234, 235, 236, 237, 255, 257, 260, 261, 270 n.43; and class consciousness, 65, 234, 260, 261; in the clerical sector, 160; and consumption, 238, 242, 243, 249, 250, 255, 258, 259, 260; and the devaluation of labor, 54–55, 160, 161; and discipline, 255, 257, 258, 259; and distinction, 234–235, 252, 260, 289 n.6; and dress, 225, 232, 236, 238, 244, 245, 249, 250, 251, 252, 253, 257, 258, 289 n.6; and education, 274 n.19; and fertility, 269 n.33; and flexible labor, 57; and friendships at work, 165, 289 n.10; on the global assembly line, 9–10, 37, 270 n.47; and globalization, 35–36, 99, 261, 264 n.2; and health in the workplace, 175–178; as ideal workers, 43, 58, 102–106, 115, 128, 136, 137, 138, 256; and identity (*see* Identity, women's); and independence, 278 n.15; Indian, 254, 292 n.2; in industry, 99–100, 105–106, 281 n.36, 283 n.45; and the informal sector, 48, 238–252, 259, 270 n.41; in informatics, 4, 5, 33, 34, 65, 100, 103, 115, 116–127, 133, 135, 138, 148, 149, 154, 158, 159, 160, 161, 162–165, 171–172, 174–183, 190–192, 194–197, 199–206, 208–212, 214–239, 241–248, 250–252, 254–261, 268 n.30, 269 n.40, 279 n.25, 282 n.40, 286 n.23; and marriage, 109; as matriarchs, 120, 278 n.19; as members of households, 60, 78, 79, 126–128, 133, 249, 279 n.21, 280 n.32, 283 n.41; and money, 155–156; and patriarchy, 60; and production, 255; and professionalism, 212, 235, 241, 244, 245, 251, 252, 257, 259, 260; and promotion, 158–165; and reputation and respectability, 233, 234, 235, 251; as reserve armies of labor, 105; and resistance, 40, 190, 191, 206, 208–212,

Women (*cont.*)

234, 259, 287 n.32; as secondary wage earners, 46, 100, 117, 118–119, 138, 281 n.36; and social stigmas around factory work, 100; and status, 162; and stress (work-related), 175; and tourism, 250, 251; and triple shifts, 239, 245–246, 247, 248, 249, 291 n.18; and wages, 251, 252; and work, 100, 234, 239, 264 n.2, 274 n.19, 282 n.39, 287 n.31, 291 n.19; and work and family, 41–42, 58, 71, 72–74, 76, 78–79, 86, 97, 107, 111, 112–115, 116, 117, 120, 126, 127–136, 139, 202, 205, 206, 287 n.28; and work preferences, 214, 215. *See also* Barbados: women; Caribbean: women

Work, 3; and class, 49–50; culture of, 51; and dress, 4; feminization of, 3, 54–55, 58; and fertility, 269 n.34; and gender ideologies, 38, 39, 286 n.18; meaning in, 47; and union status, 269 n.33; and women, 234, 239, 264 n.2, 274 n.19, 282 n.40, 287 n.32, 291 n.19; women's choices of, 48

Yelvington, Kevin, 52

Carla Freeman is Assistant Professor, Department of
Anthropology and Institute of Women's Studies, Emory
University.

Library of Congress Cataloging-in-Publication Data
Freeman, Carla.
High tech and high heels in the global economy : women, work, and
pink-collar identities in the Caribbean / Carla Freeman.
    p.   cm.
Includes bibliographical references and index.
ISBN 0-8223-2403-2 (cl. : alk. paper). —
ISBN 0-8223-2439-3 (pa. alk. paper)
1. Women electronic data processing personnel—Barbados.
2. Women offshore assembly industry workers—Barbados.
I. Title.
HD6073.D372B354   1999
331.4'81004'0972981—dc21   99-25937   CIP

DATE DUE			

HIGHSMITH #45230

Printed
in USA